P9-DCL-272

STAGES OF FAITH

Stages of Faith

The Psychology of Human Development
and the Quest for Meaning

JAMES W. FOWLER

HarperSanFrancisco

A Division of HarperCollins*Publishers*

Grateful acknowledgment is made to the following: Viking Press for permission to quote selections from *Ordinary People,* by Judith Guest. Copyright © 1976 by Judith Guest. Alfred A. Knopf, Inc., for permission to reproduce the table found on p. 111, from Daniel J. Levinson et al., *The Seasons of a Man's Life,* p. 20. Copyright © 1978 by Daniel J. Levinson.

STAGES OF FAITH: *The Psychology of Human Development and the Quest for Meaning.* Copyright © 1981 by James W. Fowler. All rights reserved. Printed in the United States of America. No part of this book may be used or reproduced in any manner whatsoever without written permission except in the case of brief quotations embodied in critical articles and reviews. For information address HarperCollins Publishers, 10 East 53rd Street, New York, NY 10022.

Designed by Jim Mennick

FIRST HARPERCOLLINS PAPERBACK EDITION PUBLISHED IN 1995

An Earlier Edition of This Book Was Cataloged As Follows:

Fowler, James W.
  Stages of Faith.
  Includes index.
  ISBN 0–06–062840–5 (cloth)
  ISBN 0–06–062866–9 (pbk.)
  1. Faith. 2. Developmental Psychology. 3. Meaning (Philosophy) I. Title.
BV4637.F664 1981
234'.2 80-7757

03 02 01   RRD 20 19 18 17 16 15

For Lurline, Covenant Partner

Contents

Acknowledgments

I take great pleasure in expressing gratitude to the many persons whose contributions add to the richness of this book and whose work inspired, encouraged and corrected me at many points. I especially want to thank the men and women—former and present graduate students and others —who were on my research staffs at Harvard Divinity School, Boston College and Emory University from 1972 to the present. These include Dr. Romney M. Moseley, Dr. Ronald Marstin, Dr. Robert G. Kegan, Dr. Clark Power, Mrs. Vasiliki Eckley, Dr. John Chirban, Mrs. Norene Carter, Ms. Lisa Cross, Mr. Lawrence Cunningham, Dr. Hank Greenspan, Dr. Michael Basseches, Ms. Glenna Mingledorf, Mr. Melvin Kawakami, Dr. Sharon Parks, Mr. Roger Ard, Mr. David Galloway, Mr. Richard Osmer, Mr. Jake Kincaid, and Mr. Jeffrey Pulis. Sister Anne Lonergan, though never on the payroll, made extraordinary contributions to interviewing and editing during her year in Cambridge.

Colleagues who have encouraged or collaborated with me in parts of this work deserve my warm gratitude. These include Professor Gary Chamberlain, Professor Leroy Howe, Dr. Richard Shulik, Professor Charles Gerkin, Professor Edmond Sullivan, Professor Margaret Gorman, R.S.C.J., Dr. Lyle Linder, and Dr. Eugene Mischey. To my friend Lawrence Kohlberg I am especially indebted for sponsorship and for exceptional encouragement at many crucial points.

A grant to the Research Project on Moral and Faith Development from the Joseph P. Kennedy, Jr., Foundation (1973–1979) provided funding for research assistants and for transcription of interviews. The confidence expressed in this tangible way by the trustees of the Foundation, especially Mrs. Eunice Kennedy Shriver, made this book, and much of the research that undergirds it, possible. I consider this present writing to be a final report on our work to the Foundation and hereby express my lasting thanks for its generous help.

I must also express gratitude to my students in the research courses I have given at Harvard Divinity School, Boston College and Emory.

Many of the interviews I report on in Part IV were conducted by these students. Their interviews and analyses, laboriously typed and prepared, gave our data a richness and depth impossible but for their enthusiasm and commitment.

Finally, very special thanks go to the men and women, girls and boys, who consented to be interviewed and to share richly with us from their lives and faith. Though promises of confidentiality prevent me from mentioning any of them by name, they have given us the most precious of gifts—the opportunity to look deeply into their lives so as to gain knowledge that may help us all.

Dean Jim L. Waits of the Candler School of Theology generously made possible a semester's leave of absence in the academic year 1979–1980, during which major parts of this manuscript were prepared. To him, and to Candler's gracious policy of providing for the typing of faculty manuscripts, I am deeply indebted. Due to Candler's generosity I have had the expert and willing assistance of two wonderful persons, Mrs. Marilyn Wilborn and Mrs. Mary Lou McCrary, in the preparation of this manuscript.

To my editor at Harper & Row, Mr. John Loudon, I want to express warm thanks. John initiated this project and has been particularly supportive throughout its development. At a number of points his astute suggestions have improved the book and encouraged its author.

This book is dedicated to my wife, Lurline. She and I, joined by the other two members of our four-career family, Joan and Margaret, celebrate its completion and offer it to you with gladness.

Introduction

Four A.M., in the darkness of a cold winter morning, suddenly I am fully and frighteningly awake. I see it clearly: I am going to die. *I* am going to die. This body, this mind, this lived and living myth, this husband, father, teacher, son, friend, will cease to be. The tide of life that propels me with such force will cease and I—this *I* taken so much for granted by *me*—will no longer walk this earth. A strange feeling of remoteness creeps over me. My wife, beside me in bed, seems completely out of reach. My daughters, asleep in other parts of the house, seem in this moment like vague memories of people I had once known. My work, my professional associates, my ambitions, my dreams and absorbing projects feel like fiction. "Real life" suddenly feels like a transient dream. In the strange aloneness of this moment, defined by the certainty of death, I awake to the true facts of life.

In that moment of unprecedented aloneness experienced in my thirty-third year, I found myself staring into the abyss of mystery that surrounds our lives. As never before, I found myself asking, "When all these persons and relations and projects that shape and fill my life are removed, who or what is left? When this biological embodiment of me ceases to function, is there—will there be—any *I*? When the *I* that is *me* steps into the velvet darkness, will there be this center of consciousness, this *I am*, or not? And if so, by whom will *I* be met? What continuities will there be between these full, fleeting days and years I now taste and savor and any enlargement of time *I* may experience?"

Had you met me on the day before this happened you would have come to know one who understood himself—and was understood by others—as a man of faith. A Christian, a minister, a teacher of theology, a counselor, yes, even a *witness* for his faith. But in the distancing of that strange awakening my faith, like my wife and children, seemed remote and detached from me. I looked at it as one might look at an overcoat hanging on the far side of a room. During those moments I was not *in* my faith. I seemed to stand completely naked—a soul without body, raiment, relationships or roles. A soul alone with—with what? With whom?

Faith is a coat against this nakedness. For most of us, most of the time, faith functions so as to screen off the abyss of mystery that surrounds us. But we all at certain times call upon faith to provide nerve to stand in the presence of the abyss—naked, stripped of life supports, trusting only in the being, the mercy and the power of the Other in the darkness. Faith helps us form a dependable "life space," an ultimate environment. At a deeper level, faith undergirds us when our life space is punctured and collapses, when the felt reality of our ultimate environment proves to be less than ultimate.

This book is about faith. I want to invite you to look with me at some of the many facets of this complex, mysterious phenomenon. It will have to be a personal book—personal for me as writer, personal for you as reader. I will try to tell you some of what seems true in the research I and my associates have conducted on faith, its origins and growth. I will share experiences of my own and of others that give us windows into the nature and workings of faith. You will be invited, as partner in this communication experience, to reflect on your own life and experiences. You will be addressed in ways which call you to look deeply into the patterns of trust and commitment that shape and sustain your life. You will be invited to relive your own pilgrimage in faith.

To say that this will be a personal book does not mean that it is purely subjective, a mere sharing of anecdotes and fantasies, or a self-indulgent "confessional" filled with solipsistic universals. As I hope will become obvious, I am committed to rigorous examination and clarification of the meanings we share. This intends to be a book of responsible scholarship and research. But to communicate and to bring its truths to expression we will have to write and read in personal ways.

You may find yourself saying now, "I know nothing of faith. I'm not religious. I'm not sure there's anything I really believe. Why should I involve myself in a conversation about faith?" If so, I hope you will read further. As I try to clarify the dynamics of faith as the ways we go about making and maintaining meaning in life, I hope you will find that your way of moving into life has been included and addressed.

Or you may be thinking, "I've got this matter of faith settled. By virtue of my conversion experience (or through more gradual growth I've experienced in a religious community) my faith is clear and firm and tested. Why should I risk potential confusion by opening myself to look at faith as a human universal? Why should I take seriously the faith experiences of people from religions other than my own? Or even stranger, why should I consider the faith patterns of people who don't even claim to be religious? What have they to do with faith?" To you I want to affirm the largeness and mystery of faith. So *fundamental* that none of us can live well for very long without it, so *universal* that when we move beneath the symbols, rituals and ethical patterns that express it, faith is recognizably the same phenomenon in Christians, Marxists, Hindus and Dinka, yet it is so *infinitely varied* that each person's faith is unique. Faith is inexhaustibly mysterious. Liveliness and continuing growth in faith require self-examination and readiness for encounter with the faith perspectives of others. Any of us can be illumined in our efforts to relate to the holy by the integrity we find in the faith stances of others, whether they are religious or nonreligious.

I believe faith is a human universal. We are endowed at birth with nascent capacities for faith. How these capacities are activated and grow depends to a large extent on how we are welcomed into the world and what kinds of environments we grow in. Faith is interactive and social; it requires community, language, ritual and nurture. Faith is also shaped by initiatives from beyond us and other people, initiatives of spirit or grace. How these latter initiatives are recognized and imaged, or unperceived and ignored, powerfully affects the shape of faith in our lives.

In these pages I am offering a theory of growth in faith. At the heart of the book you will find an account of a theory of seven stagelike, developmentally related styles of faith that we have identified. A theory means an elaborate, dynamic model of very complex patterns in our lives. Theories can be exciting and powerful, giving us names for our experiences and ways to understand and express what we have lived. They can also become blinders, limiting our ability to see to only those features of phenomena that we can name and account for. Erik Erikson, himself a great theory maker, once said, "We must take our theories with a serious playfulness and a playful seriousness."[1] In that gentle warning there is a kind of double faith—faith that we can in some measure grasp, clarify and work effectively with the most vital processes of our lives, but also faith that the reality of any such complex process will not be exhaustively contained in our theoretical frameworks.

I have taken care to make each part of this book accessible to interested nonspecialist readers. The best way to read it, of course, is from beginning to end. But for those who want to go directly to the heart of what the book has to teach about developmental stages of faith, it is possible to read Parts I and IV, and Sections 23 and 24 of Part V, without undue loss of continuity. A thorough understanding of stages of faith, however, depends upon familiarity with the materials treated in Parts II and III and Section 22 as well.

For setting out a theory of faith, playful seriousness and serious playfulness seem exquisitely descriptive of our approach and goal. Join me in the serious play of looking at the human life of faith, its movements and transformations, its breaking downs and coming togethers, its unique features and its predictable stages.

JAMES W. FOWLER

Emory University
Epiphany 1981

Part I

Human Faith

1. Human Faith

‖‖

Once, about ten years ago, I started out from Interpreters' House, where I worked, toward Asheville, North Carolina, where I was leading a workshop on faith. Driving along, I reflected on my plans for the workshop. I rehearsed a set of questions I planned for the opening session, a set of questions designed to open up some honest talk about faith in our lives. I thought about what I would ask:

- What are you spending and being spent for? What commands and receives your best time, your best energy?
- What causes, dreams, goals or institutions are you pouring out your life for?
- As you live your life, what power or powers do you fear or dread? What power or powers do you rely on and trust?
- To what or whom are you committed in life? In death?
- With whom or what group do you share your most sacred and private hopes for your life and for the lives of those you love?
- What *are* those most sacred hopes, those most compelling goals and purposes in your life?

Not an easy set of questions. No simple game of value clarification. I congratulated myself on my cleverness in coming up with such a useful, probing workshop opener. Then it hit me. How would *I* answer my own questions? My sense of cleverness passed as I embraced the impact of the questions. I had to pull my car over to the shoulder and stop. For the next forty minutes, almost making myself late for the workshop, I examined the structure of values, the patterns of love and action, the shape of fear and dread and the directions of hope and friendship in my own life.

These are questions of faith. They aim to help us get in touch with the dynamic, patterned process by which we find life meaningful. They aim to help us reflect on the centers of value and power that sustain our lives. The persons, causes and institutions we really love and trust, the images of good and evil, of possibility and probability to which we are committed—these form the pattern of our faith.

Faith is not always religious in its content or context. To ask these questions seriously of oneself or others does not necessarily mean to elicit answers about religious commitment or belief. Faith is a person's or group's way of moving into the force field of life. It is our way of finding coherence in and giving meaning to the multiple forces and relations that make up our lives. Faith is a person's way of seeing him- or herself in relation to others against a background of shared meaning and purpose.

Even our nearest relatives in the animal world are endowed with far more set and specific instinctive guidance systems than are we. Matters such as mating, building dens or lairs, searching for food and knowing how to care for their young are far more programmed even in the chimpanzee than they are in us. But as far as we know none of these other creatures bears the glory and burden we carry of asking what life is about. They do not struggle under the self-consciousness of shaping their lives through the commitments they make or of searching for images of meaning by which to give sense to things. *Homo poeta* Ernest Becker calls us, man the meaning maker.[2] We do not live by bread alone, sex alone, success alone, and certainly not by instinct alone. We require meaning. We need purpose and priorities; we must have some grasp on the big picture.

In the 1950s Paul Tillich published a small book that became a classic. *Dynamics of Faith*[3] struck a fresh note of honesty about the ways we order our lives and the hungers we have. Pushing aside a too easy identification of faith with religion or belief, Tillich challenges his readers to ask themselves what values have centering power in their lives. The "god values" in our lives are those things that concern us ultimately. Our real worship, our true devotion directs itself toward the objects of our ultimate concern. That ultimate concern may center finally in our own ego or its extensions—work, prestige and recognition, power and influence, wealth. One's ultimate concern may be invested in family, university, nation, or church. Love, sex and a loved partner might be the passionate center of one's ultimate concern. Ultimate concern is a much more powerful matter than claimed belief in a creed or a set of doctrinal propositions. Faith as a state of being ultimately concerned may or may not find its expression in institutional or cultic religious forms. Faith so understood is very serious business. It involves how we make our life wagers. It shapes the ways we invest our deepest loves and our most costly loyalties.

About the same time Tillich was writing, another theologian, H. Richard Niebuhr, worked out a similar approach to faith. In an unpublished manuscript (I suspect because publishers in 1957 really found that portion of the book too far ahead of its time) Niebuhr carries out a searching description of what I want to call human faith.[4] He sees faith taking form in our earliest relationships with those who provide care for us in infancy. He sees faith growing through our experience of trust and fidelity—and of mistrust and betrayal—with those closest to us. He sees faith in the shared visions and values that hold human groups together. And he sees faith, at all these levels, in the search for an overarching, integrating and grounding trust in a center of value and power sufficiently worthy to give our lives unity and meaning.

Faith, so Niebuhr and Tillich tell us, is a universal human concern. Prior to our being religious or irreligious, before we come to think of ourselves as Catholics, Protestants, Jews or Muslims, we are already engaged with issues of faith. Whether we become nonbelievers, agnostics or atheists, we are concerned with how to put our lives together and with what will make life worth living. Moreover, we look for something to love that loves us, something to value that gives us value, something to honor and respect that has the power to sustain our being.

In her sensitive first novel, which became a best-seller and is now a movie, Judith Guest tells a moving story of faith in crisis. *Ordinary People*[5] begins by taking us inside the lead character, a seventeen-year-old youth named Conrad Jarrett. The previous summer Conrad and his brother, older by one year, were sailing in the large lake near their summer home. A savage freak storm capsized the boat, throwing both boys into the dark, turbulent water. For nearly an hour they managed to cling to the overturned boat. Then, despite Conrad's desperate efforts to prevent it, his brother lost his grasp and was torn away by the waves. The brother drowned; Conrad survived. In the grief-stricken days and weeks that followed, Conrad carried a double burden. He felt intense guilt for being the survivor. His brother was the stronger swimmer and the natural leader of the two. Buck had been an outgoing boy, his mother's favorite. Conrad felt that he should have died and his brother should have lived. Now, having survived, Conrad felt saddled with the

impossible burden of trying to fulfill the hopes and expectations the
parents had held for both the boys. Somehow, Conrad felt, he must
make up for the family's loss of his brother. The grief, guilt and strain
proved too heavy for him. In the fall he made a serious attempt to end
his own life. Found before the self-inflicted wounds could finish what
he had intended, Conrad was hospitalized. He spent the next four
months in a psychiatric hospital. As Guest opens the story, Conrad has
been home from the hospital about a month. Desperately he tries to
re-enter the world of everyday life and purpose.

To have a reason to get up in the morning, it is necessary to possess a
guiding principle. A belief of some kind. A bumper sticker, if you will. People
in cars on busy freeways call to each other *Boycott Grapes,* comfort each other
Honk if You Love Jesus, joke with each other *Be Kind to Animals—Kiss a
Beaver.* They identify, they summarize, they antagonize with statements of
faith: *I have a Dream, Too—Law and Order; Jesus Saves at Chicago Fed; Rod
McKuen for President.*

Lying on his back he gazes around the walls of his room, musing about what
has happened to his collection of statements. They had been discreetly
mounted on cardboard, and fastened up with push pins so as not to deface
the walls. Gone now. Probably tossed out with the rest of the junk—all those
eight by ten colorprints of the Cubs, White Sox, and Bears, junior high
mementos. Too bad. It would be comforting to have something to look up
to. Instead, the walls are bare. They have been freshly painted. Pale blue. An
anxious color. Anxiety is blue; failure gray. He knows these shades. He told
Crawford [his doctor] they would be back to sit on the end of his bed,
paralyzing him, shaming him, but Crawford was not impressed. *Lay off. Quit
riding yourself. Less pressure more humor go with the stuff that makes you
laugh.*

Right, of course. Right again. Always right: the thing that is missing here
is a Sense of Humor. *Life Is a Goddamn Serious Big Deal*—he should have
that printed up to put on his bumper—if he had a bumper, which he doesn't,
not Conrad Jarrett the Anxious Failure dress this guy in blue and gray. A
thousand-word book report due Wednesday in English Lit. The book has not
been read. A test over the first six chapters in U.S. history. A surprise quiz
in trig, long overdue.

He rolls onto his stomach, pulling the pillow tight around his head, blocking
out the sharp arrows of sun that pierce through the window. Morning is not
a good time for him. Too many details crowd his mind. Brush his teeth first?
Wash his face? What pants should he wear? What shirt? The small seed of
despair cracks open and sends experimental tendrils upward to the fragile skin
of calm holding him together. *Are You on the Right Road?*

.   .   .

His father calls to him from the other end of the house. He thrashes to a sitting position, connected at once to sanity and order, calling back: "Yeah, I'm up!" and, miraculously, he *is* up and in the bathroom, taking a leak, washing his hands and face, brushing his teeth. Keep moving, keep busy, everything will fall into place, it always does.

He takes a quick look in the mirror. The news isn't good. His face, chalk-white, is plagued with a weird, constantly erupting rash. *This is not acne,* they assured him. What it *was,* they were never able to discover. Typical. He tries to be patient as he waits for his hair to grow out. He had hacked it up badly, cutting it himself the week before he left. "I didn't think they would let you have scissors," his grandmother said to him. "They shouldn't have," he answered her, oh so casual, thereby relieving the listeners of shock and embarrassment while exhibiting his poise, his Sense of Humor, see folks? Everything's okay, he's here, wearing his Levis, boots, and jersey shirt, just like everybody else, all cured, nobody panic.

.   .   .

There is a prickly sensation at the back of his throat. He turns away from the window, picking up his books from the desk. Then he puts them down again. No. Follow routines. First the bed; then line up the towels in the bathroom; then pick up books; then eat breakfast; then go to school. Get the motions right. Motives will follow. That is Faith. Vainly, he has taken to reading bumper stickers again, but they belong to other people. They are not his statements. *I Am a Hockey Nut. Christ Is the Answer—What Was the Question?*

Vaguely he can recall a sense of calm, of peace, that he had laid claim to on leaving the hospital. There were one or two guiding principles to get him through the day. Some ambitious plans, also, for putting his life in order. But the details have somehow been lost. If there ever were any.[6]

Conrad's breakdown came, of course, as the result of a traumatic loss and the wrenching disruption of his family. It devastated Conrad to the extent it did, however, because developmentally it caught him poised in a very vulnerable position. Psychosocially he was, at the time of the accident, living the fragile new identity of the adolescent, the first consolidation of his own variation of his family's and peer world's images of young manhood. From the perspective of the faith development theory to be presented here, Conrad's identity was forming in the context of a world of meaning and value that for him was still mainly tacit and unexamined. He dwelt in a shared reality with family and friends that had not yet become problematic and therefore the object of examination and evaluation. He had not yet "distanced" himself from the meaning-value ethos that nurtured and helped form him. When the accident came it not only brought the grief of losing his only brother, the burdens of survival guilt and of meeting doubled parental expectations. It also punctured the taken-for-granted world of meaning and value that sustained his newly forming identity. Not only were his images of himself and of reality shaken, but for the first time in his life the very possibility of meaning became a searing question. There were no more bumper stickers to sloganize his meanings. His faith and identity, disrupted in a "natural" time of transition, fell into a profound crisis.

2. Faith, Religion and Belief

Tillich and Niebuhr give us a way of asking about faith that widens our focus beyond the specific domains of religion and belief. This broader view of faith opens up some problems we have to address as we go further. As a way of clarifying these issues some of the more recent work of the comparative religionist Wilfred Cantwell Smith claims our attention. Smith is one of the very few students of the history of religion who has the linguistic competence to study most of the major religious traditions in the languages of their primary sources. For nearly two decades he has devoted himself to, among other things, the task of researching and interpreting the contribution each of the central world religious traditions makes to our understanding of faith. As his student, and then later as his colleague at Harvard, I have been enriched and encouraged in my own investigations of faith by his work and person.

In *The Meaning and End of Religion* Smith makes his first, seminal distinction between religion and faith.[7] Speaking of religions as "cumulative traditions," he suggests that we see a cumulative tradition as the various expressions of the faith of people in the past. A cumulative tradition may be constituted by texts of scripture or law, including narratives, myths, prophecies, accounts of revelations, and so forth; it may include visual and other kinds of symbols, oral traditions, music, dance, ethical teachings, theologies, creeds, rites, liturgies, architecture and a host of other elements. Like a dynamic gallery of art, a living cumulative tradition in its many forms addresses contemporary people and becomes what Smith calls "the mundane cause" that awakens present faith. Faith, at once deeper and more personal than religion, is the person's or group's way of responding to transcendent value and power as perceived and grasped through the forms of the cumulative tradition. Faith and religion, in this view, are reciprocal. Each is dynamic; each grows or is renewed through its interaction with the other.

The cumulative tradition is selectively renewed as its contents prove capable of evoking and shaping the faith of new generations. Faith is awakened and nurtured by elements from the tradition. As these elements come to be expressive of the faith of new adherents, the tradition is extended and modified, thus gaining fresh vitality.

Smith knows that this account represents an ideal—the interaction of faith and religion as it occurs under the best of circumstances. As an astute observer and participant in the contemporary religious situation, however, he knows how infrequently things operate according to this ideal. He recognizes with other keen observers that for many moderns the relationship between faith and religion has become problematic. Smith says, somewhat wistfully, "Faith is meant to be religious."[8] But in fact, faith struggles to be formed and maintained in many persons today who feel they have no usable access to any viable cumulative religious tradition.

This situation, Smith believes, results in part from certain confusions that have arisen in our understandings of religion, faith and belief. Having demonstrated that faith needs to be distinguished from religion, Smith turns, in more recent writings, to the task of exposing as an error the widespread modern identification of faith with *belief*. This is an error both in an accurate reading of the history of religious traditions and in any adequate effort to describe the nature and functions of faith.[9]

In his many writings on faith Smith has so far resisted the temptation to try to define the term. I suspect he does this to keep off balance those readers (and that part of all readers) who want to get the matter into a nutshell and go on to other things. Smith wants to arrest us for real thought about faith and its role in personal and corporate life. He wants us to meditate deeply (his word is "ponder") on how crucial a matter the shape and direction of faith is in our lives. He wants us to feel in our bones how essential a part of the human marrow faith is. "Standard man," whenever you find him or her, Smith declares, has been man sustained by faith and knit into communities of faith.[10]

If we examine major and minor religious traditions in the light of contemporary religio-historical knowledge, Smith says, we recognize that the variety of religious *belief* and practice is far greater than we might have imagined. But in like manner we find that the similarities in religious *faith* also turn out to be greater than we might have expected. In explaining why, he characterizes faith in contrast to belief:

Faith is deeper, richer, more personal. It is engendered by a religious tradition, in some cases and to some degree by its doctrines; but it is a quality of the person not of the system. It is an orientation of the personality, to oneself, to one's neighbor, to the universe; a total response; a way of seeing whatever one sees and of handling whatever one handles; a capacity to live at more than a mundane level; to see, to feel, to act in terms of, a transcendent dimension.[11]

Belief he takes to be "the holding of certain ideas." Belief, in religious contexts at least, arises out of the effort to translate experiences of and relation to transcendence into concepts or propositions. Belief may be one of the ways faith expresses itself. But one does not have faith *in* a proposition or concept. Faith, rather, is the relation of trust in and loyalty to the transcendent about which concepts or propositions—beliefs—are fashioned. Smith again writes:

Faith, then, is a quality of human living. At its best it has taken the form of serenity and courage and loyalty and service: a quiet confidence and joy which enable one to feel at home in the the universe, and to find meaning in the world and in one's own life, a meaning that is profound and ultimate, and is stable no matter what may happen to oneself at the level of immediate event. Men and women of this kind of faith face catastrophe and confusion, afflu-ence and sorrow, unperturbed; face opportunity with conviction and drive; and face others with cheerful charity.[12]

In his two most recent books, *Belief and History* and *Faith and Belief* (from which I have already quoted), Smith gives a persuasive demonstra-tion that the language dealing with faith in the classical writings of the major religious traditions never speaks of it in ways that can be translated by the modern meanings of belief or believing. Rather, faith involves an alignment of the heart or will, a commitment of loyalty and trust. His treatment of the Hindu term for faith, *sraddha,* perhaps puts it best: "It means, almost without equivocation, *to set one's heart on.*" To set one's heart on someone or something requires that one has "seen" or "sees the point of" that to which one is loyal. Faith, therefore, involves vision. It is a mode of knowing, of *acknowledgment.* One commits oneself to that which is known or acknowledged, and lives loyally, with life and character being shaped by that commitment.[13]

The Hebrew (*āman* he' mîn, 'munăh), the Greek (pistuō, Pistis), and the Latin *(credo, credere)* words for faith parallel those from Buddhist, Moslem and Hindu sources.[14] They cannot mean belief or believing in the modern sense. For the ancient Jew or Christian to have said, "I believe there is a God," or "I believe God exists," would have been a strange circumlocution. The being or existence of God was taken for granted and therefore was not an issue.

Smith's treatment of the Latin term *credo,* usually translated in Christian credal statements as "I believe," illumines a more adequate understanding of classical and biblical declarations of faith. *Credo,* he finds,

> is a compound from *cor, cordia,* "heart" (as in English "cordial," "accord," "concord," and the like; compare also, from the closely parallel Greek cognate *kardia,* the English derivatives "cardiac," "electrocardiagram," etc.), plus *do,* "put, place, set," also "give." The first meaning of the compound in classical Latin had been and its primary meaning continued to be "to entrust, to commit, to trust something to someone," and of money, "to lend." . . . A secondary meaning in secular usage was "to trust in," "to rely upon," "to place confidence in." . . .
>
> There would seem little question but that as a crucial term used at a crucial moment in a crucial liturgical act of personal engagement—namely Christian baptism—*credo* came close to its root meaning of "I set my heart on," "I give my heart to" ("I hereby give my heart to Christ"; "I herein give my heart to God the Father" . . .); or more generally: "I hereby commit myself ("to . . ."), "I pledge allegiance."[15]

In a fascinating study of the evolution of the English words *believe* and *belief* Smith shows that the early translations of *pistuō* and *credo* into "I believe" were not essentially mistaken. For until the early modern period (sixteenth century on) "believe" carried much the same range of meaning as that associated with "to set the heart upon." He writes, "Literally and originally, 'to believe' means 'to hold dear': virtually, to love." Modern German usage of *belieben* still means "to cherish," or "to hold dear," and the modern German term for faith *(Glaube)* can be traced back to common roots with a family of Old English words *leof, liof* (dear, beloved) that formed the verb *geleofan, gelafen, geliefen,* "to hold dear, to love, to consider valuable or lovely"; this parallels the Old High German *gilouban,* which has the same meanings. This word developed into *glauben* (to have faith).[16]

Gradually after the sixteenth century (especially in the seventeenth and eighteenth centuries), secular usage of the words *belief* and *believe* began to change. Following by about a century, religious and ecclesiastical usage underwent the same changes. "By the nineteenth century,"

Smith asserts, "the change was virtually complete."

The "change" Smith has in mind is summarized in one of his most pithy paragraphs:

> There was a time when "I believe" as a ceremonial declaration of faith meant, and was heard as meaning: "Given the reality of God, as a fact of the universe, I hereby proclaim that I align my life accordingly, pledging love and loyalty." A statement about a person's believing has now come to mean, rather, something of this sort: "Given the uncertainty of God, as a fact of modern life, so-and-so reports that the idea of God is part of the furniture of his mind."[17]

He sees three broad movements in this transition in the cultural meaning of *believe* and *belief*. First, the *object* referred to with the word almost always was understood as personal when *believe* was first used to translate *credo* and *pistuo*, but in the nineteenth and twentieth centuries it far more frequently has a proposition as its object. Second, in the early usage, the subject of the verb "to believe" was almost always in the first person singular or plural: "I believe, we believe." In the present era statistically it is far more likely to be found with third person subjects: "He or she believes, they believe." Third, there has been a shift in reporting from what is believed as true, to what is believed as of neutral or noncommittal import, to what is believed as likely to be erroneous or false.

These linguistic shifts to which Smith points are causally and symptomatically related to a larger cultural shift or movement. Termed variously as "secularization," "religious disenchantment" or "modernism," this movement has given rise to an essentially new form of consciousness. It has construed knowledge as empirically demonstrable facts; it has subordinated ethics and aesthetics to what works or is workable; it has reduced intimacy to sexuality and inflated sexuality to a fetishism. It has come to see faith as belief or a belief system and, in what passes for tolerance or "understanding," maintains a dogmatic attitude of relativism regarding the truth or appropriateness of all such "systems of belief."

I caricature here, but the point I am trying to bring out is one Smith develops more thoroughly: so pervasive is the impact of the secularizing consciousness that even religionists and persons of faith have tended to accept the culture's truncation of belief into assent to a set of propositions or commitment to a "belief system." Many modern Westerners when encountering someone from another religious tradition are likely to ask what do you (they) 'believe?' as if that were the key question. Smith's careful work, with a cumulative impact I can scarcely hope to communicate here, helps us see that curiosity about what "they believe," to reach any significant level of depth, has to become the question of *faith:* "On what or whom do you set your heart? To what vision of right-relatedness between humans, nature and the transcendent are you loyal? What hope and what ground of hope animate you and give shape to the force field of your life and to how you move into it?"

The failure to probe beneath this shallowing of faith, equating it with the modern understanding of belief, means to perpetuate and widen the modern divorce of belief and faith. If faith is reduced to belief in credal statements and doctrinal formulations, then sensitive and responsible persons are likely to judge that they must live "without faith." But if faith is understood as trust in another and as loyalty to a transcendent center of value and power, then the issue of faith—and the possibility of religious faith—becomes lively and open again. Smith's work makes an extraordinary contribution to our grasping the need for re-imaging faith. No summary can adequately evoke the rich new perspective that results from a meditative reading of these writings, but perhaps I have shared enough to enable us to benefit from a review of his major conclusions:

1. *Faith,* rather than belief or religion, is the most fundamental category in the human quest for relation to transcendence. Faith, it appears, is generic, a universal feature of human living, recognizably similar everywhere despite the remarkable variety of forms and contents of religious practice and belief.

2. Each of the major religious traditions studied speaks about faith in ways that make the same phenomenon visible. In each and all, faith involves an alignment of the will, a resting of the heart, in accordance with a vision of transcendent value and power, one's ultimate concern.

3. Faith, classically understood, is not a separate dimension of life, a compartmentalized speciality. Faith is an orientation of the total person, giving purpose and goal to one's hopes and strivings, thoughts and actions.

4. The unity and recognizability of faith, despite the myriad variants of religions and beliefs, support the struggle to maintain and develop a theory of religious relativity in which the religions—

and the faith they evoke and shape—are seen as relative apprehensions of our relatedness to that which is universal. This work toward a "universal theory as to the relation between truth itself and truth articulated in the midst of the relativity of human life and history"[18] represents a rejection of faith in "relativism," (the philosophy or common sense view that religious claims and experience have no necessary validity beyond the bounds of the communities that hold them) and serves a commitment to press the question of truth in the living and in the study of faith.

3. Faith and Relationship

The English language handicaps us when we try to speak of faith. It gives us no verb form of the word. As we have seen, the Greek verb *pistuō* and the Latin verb *credo* permitted writers and speakers to say, "I trust, I commit myself, I rest my heart upon, I pledge allegiance." All of these paraphrases show us that faith is a *verb;* it is an active mode of being and committing, a way of moving into and giving shape to our experiences of life. They also show us that faith is always *relational;* there is always *another* in faith. "I trust *in* and am loyal *to* . . . "

Our first experiences of faith and faithfulness begin with birth. We are received and welcomed with some degree of fidelity by those who care for us. By their consistency in providing for our needs, by their making a valued place for us in their lives, those who welcome us provide an initial experience of loyalty and dependability. And before we can use language, form concepts or even be said to be conscious, we begin to form our first rudimentary intuitions of what the world is like, of how it regards us and of whether we can be "at home" here.

Notice that even in this rudimentary form faith exhibits what we may call a covenantal pattern of relationship. In the interaction of parent and child not only does a bond of mutual trust and loyalty begin to develop, but already the child, albeit on a very basic level, senses the strange new environment as one that is either dependable and provident, or arbitrary and neglectful. This covenantal pattern of faith as relation comes clearer as we reflect on what the parent or parents bring with them to the care and nurture of the child. They bring *their* way of seeing and being in the world. They bring *their* trusts and loyalties. They bring *their* fidelities—and infidelities—to other persons and to the causes, institutions and transcending centers of value and power that constitute their lives' meanings. Long before the child can sort out clearly the values and beliefs of the parents, he or she senses a structure of meaning and begins to form nascent images (a matter we will discuss more fully later) of the centers of value and power that animate the parental faith. As love, attachment, and dependence bind the new one into the family, he or she begins to form a disposition of shared trust and loyalty to (or through) the family's faith ethos.

If we diagram this covenantal pattern in a family it takes on a triadic shape:

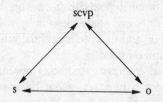

Along the base line of the triad we see the two-way flow between the self *(s)* and others *(o)* of love, mutual trust and loyalty that make selfhood possible. Above the base line, at the point of the triad, we see a representation of the family's *shared center(s) of value and power (scvp).* This includes the family's "story," its recognized and unrecognized collection of formative myths. Both self and others invest trust and loyalty in ("rest their hearts upon") this center or these centers. Of course it is never quite this simple. Family members' degrees of awareness of the central myths and values they serve will vary greatly. Each member of a family probably participates in other, nonfamilial faith triads with their different value and power centers. Moreover, all human associations, including the family, are dynamic. The members change and their personal and corporate center(s) of value and power must evolve and be renewed. Nonetheless, the triad, with its depiction of the structure of mutual trusts and loyalties, discloses the essential covenantal pattern of faith as relational.

I can think of no lasting human association that does not exhibit something approximating this fiduciary or covenantal pattern. The intangible factor "good will," sometimes included in the sale of a business or corporation, symbolizes the shared loyalty to fairness and right-dealing the company has built up with its clientele. The vast web of commercial interdependence by which an urban society provides basic necessities for its population depends upon at least tacit fiduciary covenants at many levels. That these covenants blend pragmatism and self-interest with fairness, dependability and honesty in their shared value centers makes them no less covenantal in structure. A university has its principle of unity in a shared commitment to knowledge and truth. Administration, faculty, students and trustees "keep faith" insofar as the search for knowledge, and the truthful sharing of it constitute the central value of the whole, complex, multidimensional enterprise. A nation-state, at least insofar as it can rightfully claim the name "democratic republic," is a covenantal community. Though we may never know personally more than a few hundred of our fellow citizens, we are bound together in a degree of shared identity and shared loyalty by virtue of our common allegiance to the nation and to its foundational values of justice, order, freedom and the common good.

Faith is a relational enterprise, triadic or covenantal in shape. We have said nothing so far, however, about the interplay of *faith* and *identity* in the triadic pattern of faith. When I speak of commitment to centers of value and power I use a highly formal language to speak about intensely personal relationships. We do not commit ourselves— "rest our hearts upon"—persons, causes, institutions or "gods" because we "ought to." We invest or devote ourselves because the other to which we commit has, for us, an intrinsic excellence or worth and because it promises to confer value on us. We value that which seems of transcendent worth and in relation to which our lives have worth. Further, in a world of powerful forces that have an impact on us, enlarging and diminishing us, forming and sometimes destroying us, we invest loyalty in and seek to align ourselves with powers that promise to sustain our lives and to undergird "more being." The centers of value and power that have god value for us, therefore, are those that confer meaning and worth on us and promise to sustain us in a dangerous world of power.[19] Here we are back to Tillich's insistence that faith is the relationship to that which concerns us ultimately. Real idolatry, in the Jewish and Christian traditions, does not have to do with the worship of statutes or pagan altars. Idolatry is rather the profoundly serious business of committing oneself or betting one's life on finite centers of value and power as the source of one's (or one's group's) confirmation of worth and meaning, and as the guarantor of survival with quality.

Our commitments and trusts shape our identities. They determine (and are determined by) the communities we join. In a real sense, we become part of that which we love and trust. "Where your treasure is, there will your heart be also," Jesus said.

As we reflect on our lives of faith—using faith in the broad sense I have been discussing—we recognize that we are members of many different faith-relational triads. In each of the roles we play, in each significant relationship we have with others, in each institution of which we are part, we are linked to others in shared trusts and loyalties to centers of value and power. In each of these contexts we serve common goals, we hold shared meanings, we remember shared stories, we celebrate and renew common hopes. Our identity and our faith must somehow bring these diverse roles, contexts and meanings into an integrated, workable unity.

How do our faith and identity integrate the many triads to which we belong? Are we each, in effect, "many selves," adapting and reshaping our identities as we move from one role, relationship or context to another? Do we have one "master identity," correlated with one dominant center of value and power and its community, which so overshadows our other triadic involvements as to make them unimportant for shaping our identity and faith? Or can we authentically claim faith in an infinite source and center of value and power, in relation to which we are established in identities flexible and integrative enough to unify the selves we are in the various roles and relations we have?

These three possibilities suggest three major types of faith-identity relations. I first encountered a discussion of these types in the writings of H. Richard Niebuhr.[20] Although in what follows I build on his analysis, he should not be held responsible for how I develop it here.

Some years ago a *New Yorker* cartoon showed one blue-jeaned coed talking with another. The subject was the latest male object of her enthusiasm. Describing him she gushed, "He's into scuba diving, motorcycle scrambling, bluegrass banjo picking, pottery making, Haiku poetry, and Gupta Yoga! He's a real Renaissance Man!" Whatever else he may be or become, I'll wager her boyfriend is a *polytheist*. Here I use this anthropological term to characterize a pattern of faith and identity that lacks any one center of value and power of sufficient transcendence to focus and order one's life. For the polytheist not even the *self*—one's myth of one's own worth and destiny—can lay a compelling enough claim to unify one's hopes and strivings. The polytheist has "interests" in many minor centers of value and power. He or she may exhibit the pattern described by Robert J. Lifton's image of the *protean man,* a personality pattern he found in postwar Japan and in the United States in the sixties.[21] Proteus was a minor sea god in the court of Poseidon who could readily adopt any form or guise he desired, but who found it impossible to maintain any particular identity or commitments. Protean people make a series of relatively intense or total identity and faith plunges, but their commitments prove to be transient and shifting. They thus move from one faith-relational triad to another, often with sharp discontinuities and abrupt changes of direction.

Other polytheists live with a *diffuse* pattern of faith and identity. These people never bring all of their passion to any relationship or value commitment. They tend to preserve a kind of laid-back, cool provisionality regarding commitment or trust. Most of us are more polytheistic than we might like to think. The practical impact of our consumer society's dominant myth—that you should experience everything you desire, own everything you want and relate intimately with whomever you wish—is to make the polytheistic pattern, in either its protean or diffuse form, seem normative.

Let's consider a second faith-identity pattern.

The top-flight surgeon, always in heavy demand, allowed himself to let down one day in a chance, hospital corridor meeting with his minister. He talked of the pressures in his life, the professional burdens he carried, and the family strains he lived with. After a time his clergyman put to him a frank question.

"Doctor," he said, "who are you when you're not an M.D.?"

Stunned, but only for a moment, the surgeon replied, "By God, I'm *always* an M.D.!"

"Yeah, and that's just the problem," the minister responded.

Insofar as his minister's question accused, it accused the surgeon of spending and being spent in the service of a *henotheistic* faith-identity pattern centering in his work. That particular minister knew that he, too, should be asked, "Reverend, who are you when you're not a minister?" If *polytheism* means "having many gods," henotheism (Greek, *heno*, "one" + *theos*, "god") suggests trust in and loyalty to one god. The nineteenth-century student of comparative religion, Max Müller, used the word to describe faith "in one god, as the deity of the individual family or tribe, without asserting that (it) is the only god."[22] I shall use the term *henotheistic* to characterize a pattern of faith and identity in which one invests deeply in a transcending center of value and power, finding in it a focal unity of personality and outlook, but this center is inappropriate, false, not something of ultimate concern. The henotheistic god is finally an idol. It represents the elevation to central, life-defining value and power of a limited and finite good. It means the attribution of ultimate concern to that which is of less than ultimate worth.

Ernest Becker in *The Denial of Death*[23] makes a compelling contribution to our understanding and experience of henotheistic faith. Becker, whose book (and whose life) struggled with death as the central power with which we must deal, pointed out that our most heroic human projects are likely to be devoted to the effort to deny death its victory. We engage in what he called *causa sui* projects—projects in self-vindication, projects of self-justification. These are projects that seek to guarantee, in some fashion, a kind of immortality for us. And on the way to that, we trust our *causa sui* projects to demonstrate and validate our value and power as persons. *Causa sui* henotheism finally ends up in our worshiping at an altar on which sits the faintly smiling image of our own ego. Its centers of value and power have to do with the extensions and guarantors of the self as center. Success, power, prestige, wealth, fame and the like are not ends in themselves. They serve, rather, as guarantors of the worth and significance of the self. John Dean's honest book about Watergate, *Blind Ambition,* 24 is a poignant if somewhat banal documentary of a nightmare of tangled ego extensions in a season of henotheism gone to seed.

Henotheism also has more noble forms. Institutions and causes that elicit selfless sacrifice and virtually total commitment are often worthy tribal gods. For some good causes to make their proper impact on history, Nietzsche somewhere suggests, they have to be loved by a few people for far more than they are worth. Nations, churches, universities, political parties, the liberation and empowerment of minorities, even (or especially) philosophies and ideological movements, are all potential henotheistic centers of value and power. There are many others. In this more noble form of henotheistic faith, identity is found in losing the self in the service of a transcendingly important, if finite, cause.

The most extreme form of henotheistic faith is fetishism. Fetishistic faith focuses on an extremely narrow and exclusive center of value and power. Religions that make cardinal virtues of certain avoidances can be fetishistic. Some extreme cases of careerism and workaholism border on fetishism. Sex and money readily become gods in this form of henotheism.

Edward Wallant's searing novel, *The Pawnbroker,* 25 made into the movie of the same title, gives us a vivid portrayal of the dynamics of a fetishistic faith and identity pattern. Sol Nazerman survived the Nazi death camps, but they stripped him of every extension of his ego, including wife and children, parents, profession, country and social status. He apparently makes a good living for himself and a few other survivors by managing a seedy pawnshop in a grim New York ghetto. Nazerman impresses his customers, his assistant, and the few persons who reach out to him in human warmth and friendship as a man of self-contained strength. Seemingly reserved, even arrogantly private, he seems to be secretly full and powerful. As the story unfolds we see Nazerman plagued by flashbacks to his previous life. Slowly it dawns on us that Nazerman's apparent strength is a hollow shell. As Ernest Becker says in his extraordinary commentary on the film,[26] it becomes clear that Nazerman is a man whose meanings have all been "scooped out." Because he is seemingly condemned to live when he feels he should have died, his survival—and that of the few other refugees he helps support —has come to center in the exceedingly narrow but compelling theme of money. At one point in the film he tells his young Puerto Rican assistant, who thinks of himself as an apprentice learning from Nazerman's rich knowledge of the business, "Next to the speed of light, which Einstein tells us is the only absolute in the universe, second only to that I would rank money. There, I have taught you the Pawnbroker's Credo, Ortiz."[27] The disintegration of identity becomes complete when Nazerman learns that the salary he is paid for running the shop comes not from the meager profits of the business, and not from other legitimate enterprises owned by his boss, but from the whorehouse up the street, for which the pawnshop is a front. Now even money, this narrow but life-giving center of value and power, is tainted by the living deaths of the women who bring it in. Nazerman's attachment to money should not be confused with the miser's fetish, though. He takes no delight in the contemplation or fondling or accumulation of money. Rather it is a fetish born of desperation, a last symbol of a reason to live for a man who already feels himself dead. It is the slender straw supporting the broken Nazerman in a seared vacuum of faith.

The third faith-identity relational pattern we need to consider can be called *radical monotheism*. Before I proceed any further in developing this third type, let me make a clarification. The terms *polytheism* and *henotheism*, taken from anthropology and comparative religion, originally applied specifically to forms of religious faith. In our discussions, however, we used the terms as descriptive of patterns of identity and faith not limited specifically to religious instances. *Monotheism* has traditionally meant "the doctrine or belief that there is only one God."[28] In contrast to henotheism nineteenth-century comparative religionists saw monotheism as commitment to one God, the transcendent creator, ruler and sustainer depicted in the Jewish, Christian and Islamic traditions.

Monotheism therefore came to be identified with these particular theistic traditions and with the implication of their superiority over others.

In keeping with our use of the two previous terms I want to broaden our understanding of monotheism. By it I shall mean a type of faith-identity relation in which a person or group focuses its supreme trust and loyalty in a transcendent center of value and power, that is neither a conscious or unconscious extension of personal or group ego nor a finite cause or institution. Rather, this type of monotheism implies loyalty to the *principle of being* and to the *source and center of all value and power.* This transcendent center of value and power has been symbolized or conceptualized in both theistic and nontheistic ways in the major religious traditions of the world. It is not limited to Western culture or predominantly Western religion.[29]

Monotheism, as understood here, does not mean the *negation* of less universal or less transcendent centers of value and power, but it does mean their *relativization* and ordering. In radical monotheistic faith persons are bound to each other in trust and loyalty—to each other and to an inclusive center of value and power—in relation to which our tribal gods and finite goods must be seen for what they are. Radical monotheistic faith calls people to an identification with a universal community. Again this does not negate or require denial of our membership in more limited groups with their particular "stories" and centering values. But it does mean that our limited, parochial communities cannot be revered and served as though they have ultimate value. Our potentially henotheistic centers of value and power can be loved with a proper and proportionate devotion.

Radical monotheistic faith, as understood here, rarely finds consistent and longlasting actualization in persons or communities. People too easily lapse into a confusion of our *representations* of a transcendent center of value and power with that reality itself. We continually feel the pull towards henotheistic and polytheistic forms of faith. But as a regulative principle, as a critical ideal against which to keep our partial faiths from becoming idolatrous, radical monotheism is of tremendous importance. If we regard the future of humankind as requiring our learning to live in an inclusive, global community, then in a sense, radical monotheistic faith depicts the form of our universal "coming faith." It becomes terribly important for us to work with this understanding of faith and to try to formulate and symbolize it so that it exerts truly transformative power over our more parochial faith orientations.

4. Faith as Imagination

In German one of the terms for *imagination* is the compound word *Einbildungskraft:* literally, the "power *(Kraft)*" of "forming *(Bildung)*" into "one *(Ein)*."[30] Here I want us to reflect about faith as a kind of imagination. Faith forms a way of seeing our everyday life in relation to holistic images of what we may call the *ultimate environment.* Human action always involves responses and initiatives. We shape our action (our responses and initiatives) in accordance with what we see to be going on. We seek to fit our actions into, or oppose them to, larger patterns of action and meaning. Faith, in its binding us to centers of value and power and in its triadic joining of us into communities of shared trusts and loyalties, gives form and content to our imaging of an ultimate environment.

I remember the day my eighth-grade science teacher brought the electromagnets and little jars of iron filings to our mountain classroom. Scattered over a piece of white notebook paper, the black filings ("Superman's shavings," we called them) lay in random disarray. Then we brought two electromagnets into place, one at either end of the paper, and connected the current. Impressively, the iron filings danced into a symmetrical oval pattern. As we tapped the paper lightly they formed force lines running smoothly from one magnet to the other, spreading in the middle like the seams of a cantaloupe. The lines graphically revealed the pattern of the magnetic force field.

We live our lives in dynamic fields of forces. In contrast to the bipolar orderliness shaped by the pull of the magnets, we are impinged upon, pulled at and moved from many directions. Part of what we mean when we say that humankind—*Homo poeta*—lives by meaning is that from the beginning of our lives we are faced with the challenge of finding or composing some kind of order, unity and coherence in the force fields of our lives. We might say that faith is our way of discerning and committing ourselves to centers of value and power that exert ordering force in our lives. Faith, as imagination, grasps the ultimate conditions of our existence, unifying them into a comprehensive image in light of which we shape our responses and initiatives, our actions.

Now we must unpack this idea a bit. Notice that we continue to speak of faith as a verb. Here we see that aspect of faith in which it composes a felt image of the conditions of existence grasped as a whole. Faith, in this sense, is a dynamic process arising out of our experiences of interaction with the diverse persons, institutions, events and relationships that make up the "stuff" of our lives. Faith as an imaginative process is awakened and shaped by these interactions and by the images, symbols, rituals and conceptual representations, offered with conviction, in the language and common life of those with whom we learn and grow. Faith, then, is an active mode of knowing, of composing a felt sense or image of the condition of our lives taken as a whole. It unifies our lives' force fields.[31]

Our use of the word *image* requires some explanation. I maintain that virtually all of our knowing begins with images and that most of what we know is stored in images. Several points must be developed here. First, evidence from a variety of sources suggests that our knowing registers the impact of our experiences in far more comprehensive ways than our own conscious awareness can monitor. Experiences in infancy and early childhood, before the emergence of what Julian Jaynes calls the "narratizing consciousness"[32] makes conscious memory possible, give powerful form to our knowing of self, others and our forming of "the world." Sometimes through careful use of hypnosis, guided reflection or "regression" therapies, these powerful experiences and their impacts upon our knowing can be remembered or "re-membered." Regardless of our possible remembering of such experiences, their impacts or meanings for us are part of our imaginal knowing. Second, the spectrum of knowing taking place in us is always wider and more inclusive than the band of our conscious awareness or attention apprehends. Subliminal knowing registers the impacts and meanings of occurrences we experience without our narratizing our examining them. Such impacts or meanings become part of our dynamic storehouse of potential imaginal material, coalescing with previous knowing, augmenting and extending it. Third, even when we consciously attend to events or to the communication of others, and are consciously narratizing what we are "learning," we do not yet "know" what we are seeing or being told until it has found linkages with our previously formed images. Significant learnings both resonate with previous images and extend them, possibly reorganizing and re-valencing them with feeling.

An *image,* as I use the term here, begins as a vague, felt inner representation of some state of affairs and of our feelings about it.[33] As we have suggested, the forming of an image does not wait or depend upon conscious processes. The image unites "information" and feeling; it holds together orientation and affectional significance. As such, images are prior to and deeper than concepts. When we are asked what we think or know about something or someone, we call up our images, setting in motion a kind of scanning interrogation or questioning of them. Then in a process that involves both a forming and an expression, we narrate what our images "know." The narration may take story form; it may take poetic or symbolic form, transforming nascent inner images into articulated, shared images; or it may take the propositional form of conceptual abstractions.

Let me offer an illustration of this movement from the image as a vague internal representation of a state of affairs to the "narration" of the image—in this case in poetic form. A friend of mine endured several years of persistent depression. Finally he took some rather decisive steps to alter his professional and personal life in an attempt to put the depression and its causes behind him. He and I were a long distance from each other when I heard of his actions. The news of what had happened made considerable impact on me. As I thought over what he had been through and what he now experienced I felt the forming of an image that seemed to grasp his situation and my feelings about it. I attended to the image, feeling the internal pressure it exerted and became aware that it called for expression and communication. As I sometimes do in that kind of situation I felt moved to let it find expression in a kind of poetic blank verse. With disclaimers about its quality, I share the "analogues," the specifying images, that my forming image of my friend and his situation—and its future—"chose":

The grosbeak sits in solitude
An island, girdled with heavy mist
Moist, dank-shored, empty
The mainland murky.
Energyless, the head hangs
Skullpiece pounding
Beak clenched

Isolated
Wings wampled
Waiting.

In its autonomy and creativity the image chose the analogue of a lonely,
weary, sea-locked, spiritless and muted bird to bring itself to expression.
I certainly had never thought of my friend in these terms, nor did I
consciously know anything about grosbeaks. But then the image had
more to express. Coupled with its grasp of my friend's desolation were
also portents of hope and restoration. It continues,

Heart,
Take heart.
The faint shudder
Of activated adrenalin
The heart-chest nudge of firing nerve
The foreign forgotten feel
A tide-burst of hope.
Beat sustained, beat accelerated
Readiness returning
Wampled wings waking
Sinews tightening
Muscles knitting with strange
New power.
Up Up Up Up Up Soar Pound Climb
SEE!
The Mainland lures.

"Brought outside of me" in poetic form, the image is no longer simply
private and unformed. We know something of what I, as the locus of
the forming image, felt and sensed in my friend's state of affairs and its
future. But no narration of a nascent image, whether in story, poem or
conceptual form, exhausts the content of the image. Michael Polanyi is
right when he says that we know more than we can express.[34] Faith, in
its forming of images of the ultimate environment, never finds analogues
that fully or with complete accuracy bring out and express its knowing.
This is the practical reason why our earlier distinctions between faith,
belief and religion are of critical importance. Belief or beliefs try to bring
to expression what faith sees as it images an ultimate environment.
Religion is constituted by the forms faith shapes for expressing, celebrat-
ing and living in relation to the ultimate environment as faith has
imaged it in the past and images it now.

Well aware that our brief excursion into a theory of the image may raise more questions than it settles, let us return to our main line of thought. Faith, we have seen, composes powerful felt images of the conditions of existence grasped as a whole. In its imaginal mode, faith "forms into one" a comprehensive image of an ultimate environment, an environment of environments, in relation to which we make sense of the force field of our lives. In this forming into one faith's image of the ultimate environment grasps its "character," the disposition of value and power in it toward self, others and world. If the term ultimate environment gets in the way, let us speak of a comprehensive frame of meaning that both holds and grows out of the most transcendent centers of value and power to which our faith gives allegiance. The point is, faith affects the shaping of our initiatives and responses, our relationships and aspirations in everyday life, by enabling us to *see* them against the backdrop of a more comprehensive image of what constitutes true power, true value and the meaning of life. This overall image may be largely tacit and unexamined, functioning without one's being aware of or reflective about it. On the other hand, significant parts of it may have found expression or been made explicit in ritual, myth, symbol or story, or in the more systematic conceptual elaboration of a theology or philosophy.

I must be patient with myself and my readers if this notion of faith's composing an image of the ultimate environment still seems a bit murky. Grasping it takes some time and thought. When I moved to Boston College in 1976 I had the first opportunity in my academic career to teach undergraduates. Seventy freshmen and sophomores registered for my first course, "Faith and the Life Cycle." While my course was not required, as such, students did have to take two courses in theology. These students, without knowing their new "captor," had elected my course to fulfill their requirement. That fall I learned a couple of things very quickly. The first is that undergraduates don't *feign* interest. There is nothing more chilling than seventy pairs of eyes randomly going glassy when you are trying to get across one of your favorite—if very abstract —notions! The second thing I learned is that the antidote for glassy eyes is to tell a story. Couple that with walking down off the professor's platform and into the aisles of the lecture hall, penetrating their space, and you are sure to regain their rapt attention.

On the day I lectured on faith's composing images of the ultimate environment I began to see the glassy-eye syndrome setting in. Without waiting to tell a story I strode into the aisles and put a question to them.

"What do you think I'm trying to get at when I speak of an *ultimate environment*? What sense do you make of this idea?" A brash young fellow on the right side spoke up quickly.

"I think you mean that environment we will enjoy when we're successful, rich, happily married, with children, about age forty. It's that environment we dream about and work for."

Admitting a certain plausibility to what he'd said, I told him that was not, however, exactly what I had in mind. Another lad spoke up from the middle of the class.

"I think I've got it, Professor. The ultimate environment is our *ideal* environment; it's our *utopia*. It's what we wish and hope our lives and the lives of others might be."

I acknowledged that he was getting closer; our images of the ultimate environment might in fact have some utopian dimensions. But then I pressed the question again. After a time a young woman in the back of the hall, whom I had thought mentally absent from that class, looked up from her knitting and spoke.

"I think you mean, Professor, our images of that largest theater of action in which we act out our lives. You might say that our images of the ultimate environment determine the ways we arrange the scenery and grasp the plot in our lives' plays." And then she added, "Furthermore, our images of the ultimate environment change as we move through life. They expand and grow, and the plots get blown open or have to be linked in with other plots."

With that answer this young woman saved my day. She had begun to compose for herself the felt image that was trying to find shared expression in all my talk about imaging an ultimate environment. I was grateful.

Metaphors, symbols, concepts—and many, many other kinds of representations—serve to bring our shared images of an ultimate environment to expression. The lasting world religious traditions prove again and again to be the lively custodians of *truthful* images of the ultimate environment. They awaken persons to an imaginal grasp of the ultimate conditions of existence and enable them to celebrate or assent to the visions of transcendent value and power they mediate. The Jewish and Christian symbol of "the Kingdom of God," for example, awakens images of the ultimate environment as unified and as having character by virtue of God ruling as creator, righteous judge and redeemer-liberator.

But there are images of the ultimate environment other than religious ones. In my part of the little book *Life-Maps*[35] I tell of a memorable conversation I had in a taxicab with a witty and articulate lawyer-playwright. After an exchange in which we probed each other's outlooks on life in more than usual depth, he summed up his perspective on things.

"The way I see it, if we have any purpose on this earth, it is just to keep things going. We can stir the pot while we are here and try to keep things interesting. Beyond that everything runs down: your marriage runs down, your body runs down, your faith runs down. We can only try to make it interesting."[36]

The image of the ultimate environment that comes to expression here would seem to be summed up with the word *entropy*—irreplaceable loss of energy, the consumption and sure exhaustion of life's resources. Everything runs down. The label stamped on us is "perishable" or perishing. No center of power or value conserves, renews or takes notice of our steady erosion. Beyond the temporarily distracting diversion of keeping it interesting, life has no meaning or purpose. Another playwright more than two millennia before gave words to the same image on the lips of Oedipus:

> To the Gods alone
> belongs immunity from death and age:
> All else doth all-consuming time confound.
> Earth's strength decays, the body's strength decays,
> Faith dies, and faithlessness bursts into flower.[37]

By now I hope it is clear that imagination is not to be equated with fantasy or make-believe. Rather, imagination is a powerful force underlying all knowing.[38] In faith, imagination composes comprehensive images of the ultimate conditions of existence. If it is "faithful" in this imaging it does not fall into solipsism and subjectivity. "Reality" has character and shape. That which we designate with the name "ultimate environment" *is* reality. We compose, therefore, in the direction of adequacy, fit or truthfulness in representation. Others before us have composed, giving us language, symbols, myths and concepts which both awaken and guide faith's composing. We are accountable to them and to other contemporary companions, the heirs of other faith traditions. We do not compose alone; events and moments of disclosure (revelation) occur to us, striking us as powerful clues for composing truthfully and accurately.

The images faith composes are not static. By virtue of our research and observation I believe that we can identify reasonably predictable developmental turning points in the *ways* faith imagines and in the ways faith's images interplay with communal modes of expression. Less predictable are those more momentous changes in the life of faith when one's image of the ultimate environment undergoes a shift of center. When one of our deeply invested henotheistic "gods" fails us or collapses, it results in dislocation, pain and despair. When we are grasped by the vision of a center of value and power more luminous, more inclusive and more true than that to which we are devoted, we initially experience the new as the enemy or the slayer—that which destroys our "god." Alfred North Whitehead wrote, "Religion is the transition from God the Void to God the Enemy, and from God the Enemy to God the Companion."[39] Only with the death of our previous image can a new and more adequate one arise. Thus "substantive doubt" is a part of the life of faith.[40]

Then there are times when our images of an ultimate environment, focused on our shared trust in and loyalty to a transcendent center of value and power, seem to fail or be destroyed without the possibility of replacement. Richard Rubenstein's book *After Auschwitz*[41] brings this kind of dilemma into sharp focus: after six million Jews have died in the holocaust can the survivors any longer rest their hearts in a God who is purported to rule history and who has called Israel into a covenant relationship to which that God is faithful? At such times faith's primal images are deeply tested and many find that their images of faith have atrophied or died.

Some of you who read these pages will protest that there are those —and perhaps you include yourself in that number—who have no unifying image of an ultimate environment. You may add that far from being ultimately concerned about such matters, you don't really have much concern about them at all. In response to this commonly stated position I have to reply that the fact that an image of the ultimate environment is largely unconscious or tacitly held makes it no less influential or operative in a person's initiatives and responses in life. Similarly, the fact that one images the ultimate conditions of existence as impersonal, indifferent, hostile or randomly chaotic, rather than as coherent and structured, does not disqualify his or her image as an operative image of faith. The opposite of faith, as we consider it here, is not doubt. Rather, the opposite of faith is nihilism, the inability to image any transcendent environment and despair about the possibility of even negative meaning.

5. On Seeing Faith Whole

||||||||||||||||||||||||||||||||||||||||||||||||||||||||||||||||||||||||||||||||||||||||||||||||||||||||||||||||||||||||||||||||||||||||||||||||

Archie Bunker once got some laughs with a spiced-up version of a quip stolen from Mark Twain: "Faith," he said, "is believing what any damn fool knows ain't so."[42] My hope, at this point, is that the reader's chuckle is immediately followed by a kind of sadness at the impoverishment of that notion of faith and at the awareness of just how widely Bunker's writers expected it to be shared. Our effort in Part I has been to reflect upon several dimensions of this complex, dynamic phenomenon we call faith. Frequently I remember something H. Richard Niebuhr wrote after having spent a number of years trying to formulate a comprehensive perspective on faith. He likens faith to a cube. From any one angle of vision, he points out, the observer can see and describe at least three sides of the cube. But the cube has back sides, a bottom and insides as well. Several angles of vision have to be coordinated simultaneously to do any real justice in a characterization of faith. Niebuhr was also well aware of another complicating factor. Unlike some other topics on which we might do research and reflect, we cannot easily externalize faith and make it the detached object of our inquiry. As in Gabriel Marcel's distinction between a problem and a mystery, faith, as a mystery, is perplexing because we are *internal* to it. We are involved, in ways that matter greatly, in the phenomenon we try to understand.

But carry this reflection on faith's complexity one step further. In what we have said so far we have focused on the human side of faith —on persons engaged and involved in shaping their lives in community and in relation to shared visions of transcendent value and power. In the main we have—as we will throughout this book—avoided doing *theology*, systematic inquiry into and reflection on the transcendent to whom (or which) persons in faith are related. Our concern here is primarily with the *human* side of faith. But as we look at the data of lives of faith, our own and those of others, we are struck by the recog-

nition that faith is *response* to action and being that precedes and
transcends us and our kind; faith is the forming of images of and
relation to that which exerts qualitatively different initiatives in our
lives than those that occur in strictly human relations. While this "X-
factor" in faith is not our primary focus, it continues to impinge upon
our work and to keep us modestly aware that we are encompassed in
mystery.

The fact that we deal with a complex subject matter, edged around
with mystery, provides no excuse for not being clear where we can be
clear. In this part I have tried to combine analysis and exposition of
aspects of faith with some stories and questions aimed at drawing the
reader into reflection and self-examination. My goal has been to call
attention to some major movements in the activity that is faith and to
make some distinctions between faith and other phenomena often confused with it. We have considered faith as a *human phenomenon, an
apparently generic* consequence of the universal human burden of
finding or making meaning. Following W. C. Smith, we have differentiated religion and faith, hinting at their reciprocal enrichment in times
of vital religious faith. We addressed Archie Bunker's problem—the
unthinking modern identification of faith with belief—and again following Smith, tried to clarify how we got into this predicament and to
recognize the seriousness of its consequences. Building on insights of H.
Richard Niebuhr, we called attention to the fact that faith is everywhere
a relational matter. The *patterns* of faith that make selfhood possible
and sustain our *identities* are *covenantal (triadic) in form.* Our relations
of trust in and loyalty to our companions in community are deepened
and sanctioned by our shared trusts in and loyalty to transcendent
centers of value and power. Lasting human associations at every level
exhibit this triadic form, though often our covenants are tacit and taken
for granted rather than explicit. Though I have not said it before now,
the covenantal structure of our significant human relations is often made
visible as much by our betrayals and failures of "good faith" as by the
times when we are mutually loyal and faithful.[43]

Having examined three major patterns of faith-identity relationships
we turned to consider how faith images a unifying grasp of the ultimate
conditions of existence. Faith is imagination as it composes a felt image
of an ultimate environment. We image from our experiences of relatedness in the covenantal contexts of our lives. We enter into, form and
transform our covenantal relationships in reciprocity with the transcen-

dent backdrop of meaning and power in relation to which we make sense of our lives. As this reciprocal relationship between imaged ultimate environment and everyday living suggests, faith's imaginal life is dynamic and continually changing.

We closed the part with hints about *evolutionary* changes in the way faith imagines (development), and *revolutionary* changes in its "centering" (conversion). These considerations open the way for what must come next. Having begun to image—even to conceptualize faith—how shall we bring our understanding of it into relation with what we can know of human development? How shall we approach human development? How shall we see human faith as a powerful aspect of human growth and transformation?

NOTES

1. An introductory remark Erikson made at the beginning of his 1972 Godkin Lectures at Harvard. The lectures were subsequently published under the title *Toys and Reasons* (New York: Norton, 1977).
2. Ernest Becker, *The Structure of Evil* (New York: Macmillan, 1968), p. 210.
3. Paul Tillich, *Dynamics of Faith* (New York: Harper & Row, 1957).
4. H. Richard Niebuhr, "Faith on Earth," unpublished manuscript of seven chapters, intended originally for publication with what became Niebuhr's *Radical Monotheism and Western Culture* (New York: Harper & Row, 1960). For a summary of "Faith on Earth" see James W. Fowler, *To See the Kingdom: The Theological Vision of H. Richard Niebuhr,* (Nashville, Tenn.: Abingdon Press, 1974), chap. 5.
5. Judith Guest, *Ordinary People* (New York: Viking Press, 1976).
6. Guest, *Ordinary People,* pp. 1–5. Used by special permission from Viking Press.
7. Wilfred Cantwell Smith, *The Meaning and End of Religion* (New York: Macmillan, 1963), chaps. 6, 7.
8. In an early draft of chapter 1 of *Faith and Belief* Smith had written, "Faith is deeper, richer, more personal. It is usually engendered and sustained by a religious tradition, or at least is meant to be; but it is a quality of the person, not of the system." In *Faith and Belief,* as published (Princeton, N.J.: Princeton University Press, 1979), the sentence in question was altered to read: "It is engendered and sustained by a religious tradition, in some cases and to some degree by its doctrines; but it is a quality of the person, not of the system" (p. 12).
9. See Smith, *Belief and History* (Charlottesville, Va.: University Press of Virginia, 1977) and Smith, *Faith and Belief* (Princeton, N.J.: Princeton University Press, 1979). An exposition of Smith's major themes follows in this present book.

10. Smith, *Faith and Belief*, p. 135.
11. Ibid., p. 12.
12. Ibid., p. 12.
13. Ibid., p. 61.
14. Smith, *Belief and History*, pp. 71ff.; *Faith and Belief*, pp. 69ff.
15. *Faith and Belief*, p. 76.
16. Ibid., pp. 105–106.
17. Ibid., p. 118.
18. Ibid., p. 208, footnote 41.
19. See Richard R. Niebuhr, *Experiential Religion* (New York: Harper & Row, 1972), pp. 28ff.
20. H. Richard Niebuhr, *Radical Monotheism and Western Culture* (New York: Harper & Row, 1960).
21. Robert Jay Lifton, *History and Human Survival* (New York: Random House, Vintage Books, 1971), pp. 311–331.
22. *The Compact Edition of the Oxford English Dictionary*, vol. 1, s.v. "henotheism."
23. Ernest Becker, *The Denial of Death* (New York: Free Press, 1973).
24. John W. Dean, III, *Blind Ambition* (New York: Simon & Schuster, 1976).
25. Edward Wallant, *The Pawnbroker* (New York: MacFadden-Bartell, 1966).
26. Ernest Becker, *Angel in Armor* (New York: Free Press, 1975).
27. Quoted in Becker, *Angel in Armor*, p. 82.
28. *The Compact Edition of the Oxford English Dictionary*, vol. 1, s.v. "monotheism."
29. For a Western but nontheistic perspective that sets forth important elements of the ethical nomativity of radical monotheism, see Roderick Firth's account of "ideal-observer theory," in "Ethical Absolutism and the Ideal Observer," *Philosophy and Phenomenological Research*, vol. 12 (1952).
    For an Eastern and nontheistic parallel, see the account of Zen Buddhist spirituality in William Johnston, S.J., *The Still Point: Reflections on Zen and Christian Mysticism* (New York: Harper & Row, 1971).
30. I am indebted for this point to Sharon Parks in her doctoral dissertation entitled "Faith Development and Imagination in the Context of Higher Education" (Th.D. diss., Harvard Divinity School, 1980).
31. See Richard R. Niebuhr, *Experiential Religion*.
32. Julian Jaynes, *The Origins of Consciousness in the Breakdown of the Bicameral Mind* (Boston: Houghton Mifflin, 1976).
33. For a similar though expanded analysis see Susanne K. Langer, *Mind: An Essay on Human Feeling*, vol. 1 (Baltimore: Johns Hopkins University Press, 1967), pp. 58ff.
34. Michael Polanyi, *The Tacit Dimension* (Garden City, N. Y.: Doubleday, 1966).
35. Jim Fowler and Sam Keen, ed. Jerome Berryman, *Life-Maps: Conversations on the Journey of Faith* (Waco, Tex.: Word Books, 1978).
36. Ibid., p. 36.
37. Quoted in Ronald Blythe, "Living to Be Old," *Harper's Magazine*, vol. 259, no. 1550 (July, 1979), p. 51.

38. See William F. Lynch, S.J., *Images of Faith: An Exploration of the Ironic Imagination* (Notre Dame, Ind.: University of Notre Dame Press, 1973); Urban T. Holmes, III, *Ministry and Imagination* (New York: Seabury Press, 1976); and Ray L. Hart, *Unfinished Man and the Imagination* (New York: Herder and Herder, 1968).

39. *Religion in the Making,* Cleveland: World Publishing Co., [1926] 1960, p. 16.

40. Norman Lamm, *Faith and Doubt: Studies in Traditional Jewish Thought* (New York: Ktav, 1971), p. 13.

41. Richard Rubenstein, *After Auschwitz* (Indianapolis, Ind.: Bobbs-Merrill, 1966).

42. Archie Bunker, as quoted by one of my students. Mark Twain, *Mark Twain's Notebook,* ed. Albert Bigelow Paine (New York and London: Harper Bros., 1935), p. 237: "There are those who scoff at the schoolboy, calling him frivolous and shallow. Yet it was a schoolboy who said: 'Faith is believing what you know ain't so.'"

43. See Fowler, *To See the Kingdom,* chap. 5.

Part II

Windows on Human Development: A Fictional Conversation

‖‖

My first full-time job was as associate director of an unusual religious and cultural center called Interpreters' House. Located in the mountains of western North Carolina, Interpreters' House was intended by its founder, Carlyle Marney, to be a place of conversation—a meeting place where interreligious, interracial, interpersonal engagements of real depth and honesty could occur. Marney took the name from Bunyan's *Pilgrim's Progress*. He liked the pilgrimage image, the journey motif. In Bunyan's book the house of the interpreter was a place where pilgrims could stop awhile and receive things that would help them on their journey. We spelled Interpreters' with a plural possessive. In intense, intimate conversations one never knew who the interpreter might be: it could be one of the "hired-hands" on the residential staff; just as likely it would be one of the other pilgrims.

During that demanding year I found myself providing group leadership, lecturing occasionally and counseling people often twice my age. Most of all I found myself listening—listening in the acutely active way that makes dialogue a truly hermeneutical act. *Hermeneutics* is the science of the interpretation of texts. Hermeneutics helps bring the meanings in texts to expression. Conversation as a hermeneutical enterprise helps persons bring their own meanings to expression. With sensitive, active listening we "hear out of" each other things we needed to bring to word but could not, and would not, without an *other*. This is Martin Buber's "I-Thou" relationship with its dialogical transcendence; this is Reuel Howe's "miracle of dialogue."[1]

The listening at Interpreters' House usually began with our hearing something of each person's life journey. As I listened to some two hundred men and women that year I began to hear patterns. The particular relationships and events of their lives differed, to be sure, but there did seem to be some important commonalities in the stories. I shall never fully know to what degree my search for and attention to common turning points in life stories were shaped by my immersion in the writings of Erik Erikson. What is certain is that I devoured his work that year, finding him to be an extraordinary teacher and companion as I tried to process the overwhelmingly rich data people shared.

A year later, somewhat unexpectedly, I found myself teaching graduate students at Harvard Divinity School. In my own graduate study I had focused on theological ethics and sociology of religion. My dissertation had studied the development of H. Richard Niebuhr's theological position.[2] At Harvard I was given the opportunity to teach in the field of applied theology, theology as it informs—and is informed by—the practice of ministry. Filled with my Interpreters' House experience and informed by my captivation in Erikson's developmental psychology, I determined to offer courses that were at once theological and experiential, concerned with faith and with human formation and transformation. I wanted students to take seriously the fact that they began as infants and children and that in their present efforts to shape adult identity and faith they needed to revisit their earliest years and relationships. I wanted to offer them the beginnings of an ordering of the predictable phases of growth in faith, taking full account of the dynamics of doubt and struggle it entails.

Blessed with able and honest students who were ready to be engaged, the outlines of a broad developmental approach to faith began to take shape. Hearing my exposition of stagelike positions in faith, which drew on Niebuhr, Erikson, Robert Bellah, Carl Jung and others, some of my students began to ask me if I knew the work of Lawrence Kohlberg on moral development or if I was aware of Jean Piaget's rigorous research on cognitive development. In my effort to become literate in these new areas I found the friendship and colleagueship of Kohlberg. In the circle of associates that I met through his work my tourist's approach to developmental psychology began to become more systematic and committed. A citizen reared in the land of theology began to try to earn dual citizenship in the new world of the psychology of human development.

As a background for our conversation on faith and human development I want to communicate some of the immense richness I have found in the worlds of Jean Piaget, Lawrence Kohlberg and Erik Erikson. I have read and learned from many other theorists of human development, but as regards the timbers and foundations of my own work these three keep proving most fundamental. Many secondary interpretations of their respective theories are available. I do not need to offer you another conventional introduction to these figures. What I do want to show is the rich interplay of their perspectives as we consider the major developmental eras of the life cycle. This will provide direct preparation for our introduction of stages in faith in Part IV.

6. The Fictional Conversation

||||||||||||||||||||||||||||||||||||||||||||||||||||||||||||||||||||||||||||||||||||||||||||||||||||||||||||||||||||||||||||||||

In that spirit of playful seriousness and serious playfulness with which we began this conversation I want to propose an experiment in imagination—a fictional discussion between Lawrence Kohlberg, Erik Erikson and Jean Piaget. I count Lawrence Kohlberg as a good friend. I have worked closely with him. I have met Erik Erikson, have heard him lecture, and I teach a graduate seminar on his thought. Jean Piaget I knew only through fairly extensive readings in his theoretical and autobiographical writings, and from seeing him in a movie and in pictures. Erikson and Piaget have met and worked together at international conferences. Kohlberg and Erikson have met and shared ideas. Kohlberg and Piaget did not meet. In the year I finished this book Piaget died. Thus, in that genre of conversations that *ought* to have occurred,[3] I propose to bring these three men together in our imaginations so that we can overhear them talking about stages of human development from their various points of view.*

Our conversation partners are pioneering, creative figures. They bring well-researched and elaborated theoretical perspectives to the table. They have somewhat different starting points and foci in their work. Nonetheless, they have accepted the terms of our invitation, which stipulate that we will talk our way together through the major develop-

---

*Most of the conversations these men have in the coming pages are written in my own prose. Their statements in these fictional exchanges are meant to express their central ideas and findings, which have been written or said in their own words in other contexts. I have footnoted the principal sources where their own formulations on these matters can be found. In the few instances where I have quoted them directly I note this and give the source. In the occasional places where I have caused one of these men to make a point that either I think he would or should make—but didn't or hasn't—I indicate this fabrication in a footnote. In this interpretation of their positions I do not become involved in critical assessments of either their research methods or their theoretical positions.

mental eras of the life cycle. Using as little technical jargon as possible each member of the conference will offer insights into the successive developmental eras from the perspective of his particular research and theory. While other occasions have been used to highlight differences and to argue disputed points, our avowed goal is to examine the complementarity of these perspectives and to try to glimpse the more comprehensive understanding of human development that they, together, promise.

Shall we begin?

Convener: Friends, we welcome you to this symposium and express our gratitude for your participation. May I ask each of you to introduce yourself and briefly say something about the distinct focus of research and theory from which you will be speaking? Let's simply move around the table. The microphones are suspended in such a way that our audience will be able to hear if you use a normal conversational voice. Would you begin, Mr. Erikson?

[*A tall man, his ruddy Nordic face a contrast with the white of his moustache and mane of hair, clears his throat and begins to speak. His voice is a soft, husky baritone; his words are clipped a bit with the accents of his first language.*]

Erikson: I am Erik Erikson. In my youth and early adulthood I set out to be an artist. During my mid-twenties (which were also the mid-twenties of this century) I began teaching art and social studies to young children in a special school started in Vienna. The school was begun for the children of Americans and Canadians who came to undergo psychoanalysis with Sigmund Freud, his daughter Anna, and other members of the growing circle of Viennese psychoanalysts. That teaching experience led to two determinative kinds of professional training: I earned a certificate as a Montessori teacher, and I underwent a training analysis and other supervision with Anna Freud that qualified me in the new field of child psychoanalysis. The rise of Hitler in Germany, with its escalation in anti-Semitism, meant that I, my Canadian-born wife and our children had to leave Austria. After a brief stay in Denmark we emigrated to Boston where I became that city's first child psychoanalyst. The temptation must be resisted to try to say exactly how I came to the particular focus of my work. Suffice it to say that during my years of psychoanalytic practice and continuing into the decades in which I have come to think of myself more as a writer and a teacher, a particular cluster of interests have held my attention. Building on Freud's theoretical work on psychosexual growth, I have wanted to extend his seminal insights in two directions. First, I have wanted to see the interplay of psychic and somatic development extended to take account of its interaction with social and cultural environments. Second, I have wanted to extend our perspectives on what I call psychosocial development beyond puberty to adulthood in its various phases. As a kind of corrective to my discipline's tendency to focus on pathology, I have been fascinated with human strength and health. My work, sometimes characterized (unfairly I think) as too optimistic, has sought to illumine the growth and crises of the healthy personality. In this connection I have found it necessary to introduce some new concepts which seem to have proven useful. The idea of *identity* particularly has proven to be a fertile one in a land of immigrants and ex-pioneers. And in the study of adolescence and young adulthood I have learned to speak of a *moratorium,* a time when the near young adult avoids premature overcommitment either by taking time out, or by committing him- or herself to an arduous apprenticeship in some field of endeavor unexpected by those who hold urgent and hopeful expectations for the youth. In addition to my psychoanalytic practice I have engaged in several anthropological studies of childhood and human development in other cultures. I have tested the usefulness of our theoretical formulations in the study of biographies. Too simply, I can say that I have sought to extend and expand that part of the psychoanalytic vocation which undertakes to contribute to ethical clarification and to the renewal of widened reason and passion for social justice and world peace. And as readers of my work will know, I have considerable interest in the understanding of religion and faith and their contributions in the ongoing cycle of the generations. Perhaps I should stop with that.[4]

[*A smaller man with dancing eyes behind large, black-framed glasses puts down his pipe. Sparse on top, his white hair frames the square features of his face. He speaks somewhat slowly. His English betrays that he is more at home in French.*]

Piaget: I am Jean Piaget. My colleague Erikson began as an artist. Perhaps I may be excused if, speaking from a standpoint decisively shaped by *my* first professional training, I suggest that the illuminative, broad vision on human development that Erikson proposes is better thought of as part of the domain of art or philosophy—or even of theology—than of the domain of science. I say that with a certain playfulness as one who almost, in my late adolescence, succumbed to the seductions of both philosophy and psychoanalysis. That I was saved from both and turned to genetic epistemology instead may be credited, among other factors, to my early grounding in biology and my commitment to the rigor of the scientific method. Actually my career has focused at the intersection of biology and philosophy and has yielded, if I may say so, a distinct method of inquiry and body of theory in psychology. My central question across nearly sixty years of work may be stated in terms of the decisive legacy of Kant's critical philosophy. What operations of mind can be scientifically demonstrated to underlie the achievement of rationally certain knowledge and how do those operations take form in human beings? To Kant's interest in the *a priori* forms and categories by which we shape and reflect on experience, I bring the question of development. How, in individuals and in the species as a whole, do the operational forms of thought required for successful use of the scientific method emerge and take form? To this question I bring a decisively important metaphor that seized me early in my biological-philosophical explorations. All organisms or entities—from the mollusks I studied in Lake Geneva to the social life of rural French villages, to the organization of operations of thought in formal logic—exhibit patterns in the relationship of their elements that may be called "structures of the whole." So in relation to our problem of the development of the forms of thought that make scientific reason possible I asked, What operational "structures of the whole" characterize the thinking of the child? The infant? The adolescent? What transformations in these "structures of the whole" occur on the way from the infant's thought world to that of the scientist? Basing our research on categories similar to those of Kant—space, time, causality, the object, number and so on—we have demonstrated a succession of four different "stages" or logics characterized by developmentally related "structures of the whole." As our discussion proceeds I will offer what I can from our understanding of these logics to clarify how the child or adolescent, if typical, may be going about the important business of thinking and reasoning.[5]

[Piaget picks up his large pipe again, tamping its bowl with his finger. As he lights it the younger man beside him begins to speak. His angular features are crowned with unruly brown hair. The faded checked shirt and

baggy trousers give an overall impression of a somewhat disheveled intensity. He begins a little haltingly.]

Kohlberg: My name is Lawrence Kohlberg. My senior colleagues have told us something about how they got into their respective intellectual and professional adventures. Perhaps I should make a similar start. Some years ago now I attended the twenty-fifth reunion of my prep school class. Among others I was invited to address the group from the standpoint of my research on moral development. After the talk several of my old teachers and classmates expressed dismay that I should be working in this field. Their memories of me as an adolescent in the school made it seem a highly unlikely field for me!

How did I get into the study of moral development? Immediately upon graduation from high school I signed on as a crewman on a freighter that was part of the effort by certain Zionist groups after World War II to get Jewish refugees out of Europe and into Israel. Restricted by United Nations regulations, this emigration was illegal. My ship flew a Panamanian flag; the human cargo was packed in the wooden shelves where normally boxes of bananas would have been carried. As we neared Cypress our ship was intercepted by a British destroyer and boarded. Crew and passengers were taken to the island for confinement in a stockade. In the bus on the way to the stockade I was faced with a moral dilemma. Should I stay with the passengers, go to the stockade and do what I could to aid and assist them, or should I try to escape so that I could make my way back and join the crew of another "banana boat"? Actually this was only the latest of many moral dilemmas I had encountered in the course of this service. In all of them I found that I was utterly unprepared to deal with moral issues in any consistent or rational manner.

I did escape and sailed on several other such ships. After it was over I returned to the United States and enrolled in the University of Chicago. In those days, under the influence of Robert M. Hutchins, every University of Chicago student read Plato and John Dewey. There I began to find some lasting help on ethics and moral reasoning. When I enrolled in a Ph.D. program in clinical psychology I soon learned something of Piaget's early work in *The Moral Judgment of the Child.* Piaget, who had also been influenced by John Dewey, and another American, J. Mark Baldwin, had combined philosophy and psychology in an empirical approach to the development of moral reasoning that excited me. When it came time to do my doctoral dissertation I undertook a cross-sectional study of moral reasoning in seventy-five boys distributed in age from early childhood to late adolescence. From this emerged an extended hypothesis of six stagelike positions in the development of moral reasoning. In the intervening twenty-two years I and a number of younger associates at Chicago and Harvard have continued my original study longitudinally and have supplemented it with extensive investigations in other cultures. More recently we have turned to the challenges of moral education. Following Dewey, I have been concerned with how effective moral education can be conducted while respecting the constitutional separation of church and state in this country.

Piaget's work has strongly influenced mine. His focus on an active knowing subject interacting with a dynamic environment has shaped our approach. His concern to harness empirical psychological inquiry for dealing with philosophical issues I have carried over into ethics. Where Piaget has been content in his later work to restrict himself to how persons construct and know the world mathematically and scientifically, however, I and my associates have studied how persons structure their experiences of and judgments about the *social* world. Further, taking a rational understanding of justice as the norm for moral judgment, I have not hesitated to argue, both empirically and philosophically, that moral reasoning develops through a succession of stages. I hold that the sequence of these stages is invariant and universal (in formal terms), and that "higher" stages are more adequate—more "true," if you will—than the earlier ones. Needless to say, I have not experienced any lack of critics or debate partners! In my contributions to our discussion I will speak about how the person is likely to reason about moral dilemmas in different stages. As part of this I will give attention to how, in different stages, persons construct and take account of the social perspectives of other people and groups.[6]

Convener: "Our thanks to each of you for these introductory remarks. Perhaps before we begin to build a shared understanding of stages of human development we had better take notice of some differences in your respective approaches. As a way of highlighting some of these let me ask each of you to speak briefly about what you mean when you refer to a "developmental stage."

Erikson [*indicating that he wants to speak first*]: The origins of the stage concept in the psychoanalytic and ego psychology traditions in which I stand derive from Freud's suggestive work on psychosexual stages. His important discoveries concerning the unconscious influences of infantile sexuality are key here. With ingenious insight Freud saw psychosexual development proceeding by way of the successive energizing and sensitization of erogenous zones and the emergence of their characteristic modes. In the first year of life libidinal energy (Freud's term for life-energy as a whole) focuses in the oral zone. The oral modes associated with feeding—taking and receiving, later biting—are generalized and become characteristic of the infant's ways of relating to its environment as a whole. As I will want to say a little later, the great achievement of this oral period—for both child and mother (or her surrogate)—is the mutual regulation of giving and taking, a fitting of the child's need with the parent's need to be needed. For the child from eighteen months to two years, with the maturation of the sphincter muscles, Freud saw the new focus of libidinal energy centering in the now sensitized anal area. During the time when toilet training becomes possible, the modes of this zone, holding on and letting go we will suggest, become generalized in the two-year-old's vigorous ability to assert that things are "mine" and the ability to say a stubborn "No!" A third psychosexual stage Freud saw emerging with the Oedipal period, an period from age three to five or six, in which there is a first energizing and sensitization of the genital zone in infantile sexuality. In fantasy and everyday life the child experiments with initiatives that are generalizations from genital modes, including aggressive intrusiveness and the aggressive and seductive holding onto or recruitment of adults and other children into his or her activities. Freud saw the elementary school years as a time of psychosexual latency when libidinal energy could be directed toward the mastery of physical and mental skills and in the forming of cooperative relationships. Then puberty, with its explosive changes in body size and glandular functions, marked the adolescent return of libidinal energy to focus in the now maturing genital zone.

I have found the biological notion of epigenetic stages helpful in trying to convey how I want to build on and extend Freud's introduction of the psychosexual stage concept. Epigenesis combines an understanding of development as the unfolding or emergence, on schedule, of new organ modes or capacities with an additional dimension. In pre-natal development if an organ or limb misses its critical time of emergence, the fetus continues development though all its future growth will be marked by this failure. Epigenesis as a concept also refers the innovative or adaptive responses a post-natal organism makes to the challenges and opportunities its environment provides. Epigenetic stages, then, describe the emergence of new capacities and the leeway they provide for individuating organismal adaptation, and point to the limits or distortions to which the failure to appear on schedule give rise. As I mentioned earlier I have expanded Freud's drama of the nuclear family to include more consistently the person's interaction with—and the family's participation in—the institutions and cultural symbols of the larger society. Therefore, when I speak of a psychosocial stage, I refer to a phase of development marked by significant bodily changes, accompanied by emotional and cognitive growth, giving rise to new relational modes and roles in the context of institutional arrangements geared to meet, form and utilize the person's new capacities and accompanying new "sense of self."

As I will make clear later, each new stage is initiated by a crisis; a struggle between the optimal possibilities presented by one's emerging new capacities, on the one hand, and the failure to integrate them into one's being and well-being on the other. The stages are cumulative in that one brings to each new crisis the mixed residue of past solutions. Each new stage requires the reworking of those past solutions and contains in it an anticipation of the issues of crises in future stages. The adult stages, I might add, are less closely tied to biological maturation than are the stages of childhood and adolescence.[7]

Piaget [*stirring, and with a slight frown clouding his brow, moves into the pause*]:   I am always somewhat bothered by the rather imprecise way Erikson, and Freud before him, use the concept "stage." By making the scope of my own theoretical focus narrower, so as to center on the operational structures employed in thought, we can gain a formal precision in the description of stages that ego psychology will never achieve. Erikson speaks of a "sense of basic trust" or a "sense of industry." These are unfortunetly vague notions that, while undoubtedly useful in the broad context of therapeutic diagnosis and treatment, lack the rigor we need to investigate and clarify the mechanisms of transformation in intellectual development. Since the late thirties I and my associates have moved decisively in the direction of characterizing the formal structures of knowing in terms of mathematical and logical models. While our discussion here will not call for a great deal of elaboration of these models, they do make it possible for us to stipulate a series of cognitive stages that are logically and empirically sequential and invariant. We also claim, with considerable empirical justification, that these stages in their formal (content-free) descriptions are universal.

A stage then, we may say, is an integrated set of operational structures that constitute the thought processes of a person at a given time. Development involves the transformation of such "structures of the whole" in the direction of greater internal differentiation, complexity, flexibility and stability. A stage represents a kind of balanced relationship between a knowing subject and his or her environment. In this balanced or equilibrated position the person *assimilates* what is to be "known" in the environment into her or his existing structures of thought. When a novelty or challenge emerges that cannot be assimilated into the present structures of knowing then, if possible, the person *accommodates*, that is, generates new structures of knowing. A stage transition has occurred when enough *accommodation* has been undertaken to require (and make possible) a transformation in the operational pattern of the structural whole of intellectual operations.[8]

Kohlberg [leaning forward and taking up the conversation]: "Let me build on what M. Piaget has been saying. A central thrust of my work is the claim that moral judgment and action have a rational core. Moral choice is not just a matter of feelings or values. It involves the interpretation of a moral dilemma situation, the construction of the points of view of the various participants and affected parties, and the weighing of their respective claims, rights, duties and commitments to the good. These are all cognitive acts. Similar to M. Piaget's position, therefore, we see a stage of moral judgment as characterized by a formally describable (describable apart from any particular content) pattern of thought or reasoning employed by a person in the adjudication of moral claims. And just as Piaget sees formal operational thinking as the most developed stage of cognition, so we see the universalizing exercise of the principles of justice as the most developed stage of moral reasoning. The process of development of this cognitive core of moral judgment occurs in the interaction of persons with the social conditions of their lives. With Piaget we see a succession of stagelike equilibrations that are, in effect, more or less comprehensive "moral logics." These stages, our research indicates, are *hierarchical;* that is, each builds on and integrates the operations of the previous stages. They are *sequential,* one coming after the other in logically necessary fashion; and the sequence is *invariant.* You can't skip over a stage. Based on cross-cultural research we believe this sequence to be *universal.* The rate at which persons in different societies move from one stage to another, and the point of arrest or final equilibration that is "average" for adults in given cultures will vary. But the same series of stages—if *formally* described—seem to characterize the path of development in moral judgment in each society.[9]

Convener: I think it is clear from what each of you has said that Professors Piaget and Kohlberg focus their stage analyses on the structures of thought and reasoning in their respective domains. Let us designate this approach as the "structural-developmental" school. Professor Erikson, on the other hand, attends more broadly to the development of personality as a whole, in interaction with the persons, institutions and cultural meanings at hand. And although we have not yet brought it out here, Professor Erikson, standing in the psychoanalytic tradition, attends to the functioning of the "depth unconscious" and to the dynamics of repression and defense which Freud's heirs have received as part of their rich legacy. The structural developmentalists point out that the structures of thought are themselves a kind of unconscious, different from the dynamic unconscious of Freud and Jung, to be sure, but to be seen in relation to it.[10]

These differences will undoubtedly call for further clarification as we proceed with our main task. But now, in order to get on with our goal of asking each of you to comment succinctly on the main features of lifespan developmental eras, let me offer one final clarification: Professor Erikson's "eight ages" of the life cycle, as he has pointed out, correlate closely with biological maturation and chronological age —particularly in the first five stages. The structural developmentalists, on the other hand, have affirmed in other writings that their stages, while dependent upon maturation and time, are not tied to them. Movement from one structural-developmental stage to another is not automatic or inevitable. As the wisdom of our television advertising industry demonstrates, many American adults do not attain Piaget's formal operational stage of reasoning. Kohlberg's research has consistently shown that a majority of persons in this society are best described by the conventional stages of moral judgment. One can "arrest" or equilibrate in one of Piaget or Kohlberg's intermediate stages.

Yet the person who so arrests, in cognitive or moral developmental terms, still must meet the life challenges or crises described in Erikson's stages. We might say that the psychosocial crises come "ready or not." This means, gentlemen, that in asking you to share your perspectives on successive developmental eras we are making an assumption of parallelism in cognitive, moral and psychosocial development that, if optimal, may also be the exception rather than the rule. This will be a useful procedure, then, so long as we do not forget *that persons' ways of meeting and dealing with the developmental crises Erikson delineates may differ in significant ways, depending upon their operative stages of cognitive and moral judgment development.*

Now let's move ahead. I think it makes sense to organize our discussion under fairly traditional divisions of developmental eras. I propose that we deal with infancy, early childhood, childhood, adolescence, young adulthood, adulthood and maturity. We cannot aim for comprehensiveness in the presentations of each of your theories. The values of our discussion will derive from your indicating the main contours of each era and then our seeing the rich interplay of perspectives. Let's place this composite chart (Table 2.1) in a position where our audience can see it. It lists your respective stage sequences, showing the ideal or optimal correlations between them. The numbers I have placed alongside the eras are meant merely to indicate average ages.

Table 2.1 Stages of Human Development: Optimal Parallels

Eras and Ages	Erikson	Piaget	Kohlberg
Infancy (0–1 1/2)	Basic Trust vs. Basic Mistrust (Hope)	Sensorimotor	—
Early Childhood (2–6)	Autonomy vs. Shame and Doubt (Will)	Preoperational or Intuitive	*Preconventional Level* 1. Heteronomous Morality 2. Instrumental Exchange
Childhood (7–12)	Initiative vs. Guilt (Purpose) Industry vs. Inferiority (Competence)	Concrete Operational	
Adolescence (13–21)	Identity vs. Role Confusion (Fidelity)	Formal Operational	*Conventional Level* 3. Mutual Interpersonal Relations 4. Social System and Conscience.
Young Adulthood (21–35)	Intimacy vs. Isolation (Love)	—	*Postconventional Principled Level* 5. Social Contract, Individual Rights
Adulthood (35–60)	Generativity vs. Stagnation (Care)	—	
Maturity (60—)	Integrity vs. Despair (Wisdom)	—	6. Universal Ethical Principles

Handwritten margin annotations (left): Facts / Feelings (Infancy); Feelings (Early Childhood); Facts (Childhood); Feelings (Adolescence); Facts (Young Adulthood); Feelings (Adulthood); Facts / Feelings (Maturity).

Handwritten annotations (Kohlberg column): "punishment related" (1. Heteronomous Morality); "self-image good girl / good boy" (3. Mutual Interpersonal Relations); "law/conscience for morals" (4. Social System and Conscience); "(gray)) skeptical" ; "one step limited perspective / black & white" (5. Social Contract, Individual Rights).

7. Infancy

‖‖

Piaget: Let me begin. The human infant is born with very few innate reflexes. Among these are the sucking reflex and the so-called palmar reflex, the latter being the baby's tendency to close the fingers on any object pressed against the palm of its hand. The baby's first thinking or intelligence arises out of its actions. In this first stage thought *is* the coordination of actions and the gradual elaboration of action schemata by which the baby orients itself to the world. In the early months of life an infant experiences the world as a relatively formless and fluid sequence of stimuli, having no permanence or reality apart from the infant's attending to it. If the psychoanalysts speak of this phase as characterized by feelings of narcissistic omnipotence in the child, we must say it is a narcissism without Narcissus. As yet there are no "self" and "other." Throughout the first year to eighteen months the child is involved in the gradual decentration of self; that is to say, the gradual differentiation of self from a world coming to be experienced as separate, permanent and having its own regularities of spatial, temporal and casual relationships. The child comes to "know" that world by physical interaction with it. Its knowledge is of a practical kind: its action schemata enable the child to move and maneuver in a world of permanent objects. By around seven or eight months babies begin to search for objects they have seen and handled when they are removed from them and hidden by researchers in experiments. At four months, typically, they do not search for the hidden objects. "Out of sight is out of mind." By the age of seven to eight months we may infer that the child has developed structures of thought that enable him or her to construct and retain a mental image of the misplaced object. Many observers have also reported the emergence at about that same time of a new quality of anxiety in babies. It is as though the absence or coming and going of those who give primary care is now experienced as more threatening and disturbing than before. Undoubtedly Erikson will have more to say about the anxiety arising from the development of object permanence when the "objects" in question are persons.

Sensorimotor thought shows the marks of genuine intelligence, including the construction of rudimentary schemata of space, time, causality and the permanence of objects. Infants experiment, draw causal connections, invent means-ends procedures and frequently give indications of insight. But sensorimotor intelligence is prelinguistic and presymbolic. The roots of intelligence and speech in the infant are separate. When they begin to converge, between twelve and eighteen months on the average, we are ready for a new stage in cognitive development.[11]

Erikson: We have just heard the barest outlines of a very rich theory of the genesis of cognitive operations in infancy. Piaget frequently calls attention to the fact that cognitive development does not occur apart from emotional or affective development, but his attention, of course, primarily remains drawn to the emergence of cognitive structures. Yet, the very processes of differentiation of self and other and of decentration of self from environment, which he has so adroitly described, are occasions of great emotional moment in the child's forming sense of self and world. The student of psychosocial development cannot afford to forget the infant's *first* traumatic experience of separation, that of birth. To use one of Dr. Piaget's concepts for a moment, we may say that birth is a radical experience of disequilibrium. The symbiotic mutuality of prenatal life is interrupted and the child is thrust into a new and alien environment. The first order of business for the neonate (newborn) and the one (or ones) providing primary care is the (re-) establishment of a mutuality in which the unequilibrated neediness of the child can be met by the readiness and capacity of the adult(s) to provide nurture. At stake in this effort at mutuality between infant and provider is the baby's forming, rudimentary sense of basic trust, in tension with feelings of basic mistrust. I must use the imprecise word "sense" here because as Piaget has pointed out, initially there is no separation of self and other, nor is there "consciousness" in the sense of a reflective experience. It *is* a sensorimotor stage.

The establishment of a dependable mutuality between providers and baby, expressed and renewed daily in rituals of care and interplay, provides a foundation that enables the infant to maintain trust in face of the separations and diluted maternal attentions of the second half of the first year. Of particular interest to the psychoanalyst is the separation that comes about with the onset of teething. Whether weaning is from breast or bottle, it occurs in earnest as the teeth begin to break through. Teething feels like a kind of painful explosion of the gums. When the baby vigorously pursues the only activity that promises relief, namely biting, the previously available sources of oral succor—fingers and nipples—are likely to be withdrawn. There is reason to suppose that primal myths of separation from paradisial, nurturing gardens due to the biting of forbidden fruit may have their psychological roots in this separation from the primary nurturer during the second oral stage. That this corresponds with the time when Piaget sees the emergence of the schema of the permanent object, bringing with it a new awareness of "otherness," I find quite suggestive.

Parents convey a sense of trustworthiness and rely-ability not so much by the quantity of food or demonstrations of love they provide, but by the quality and consistency of their care. By the ways they hold and handle the child, by the guidance, permissions and prohibitions they give, they convey to the child a deep, almost bodily conviction that there is meaning to what they are doing. The child, feeling cherished and included in the parent's meanings, feels an inner sense of trustworthiness and reliability that can balance the terrors of separation and abandonment.[12]

Piaget finds the prelinguistic foundations of the structures of future operations of thought taking form in the sensorimotor action schemata of the infant. It is not too much to say that the child's first profound experiences of mutuality (or their failure) in the first year of life provide a beginning ratio of trust to mistrust that funds his or her movement into the challenges of subsequent stages. Further, the quality of the child's first mutuality is likely to exert paradigmatic or patterning power in his or her ways of approaching future relationships. When the ratio of trust to mistrust is favorable there emerges the ego virtue or strength we call *hope*.[13]

8. Early Childhood

||||||||||||||||||||||||||||||||||||||||||||||||||||||||||||||||||||||||||||||||||||||||||||||||||||||||||||||||||||||||||||

Convener: M. Piaget, let's ask you to begin again as we now look at the years from two to six, or early childhood. Professor Kohlberg's research begins with children in this age span, so he will join you and Dr. Erikson in helping us to see the contours of development in this era.

Piaget: In terms of cognitive development the era we now examine really should be thought of as a long transition, initiated by the joining of language and thought, toward the emergence of the first real logical operations around the ages of six or seven. Yet it is more than a transition. The young child's characteristic patterns of thought have a kind of integrity of their own that justifies our speaking of this as a stage. We call it *preoperational* or *intuitive* thinking.

The differentiation of self from world effected in the sensorimotor stage undergoes another decisive step as the child begins to use language to express and explore experience. Language makes possible the "socialization" of action schemata. They can be named, remembered and spoken about with others. Also, inner states and feelings can be expressed. Observations of young children's conversations and group play, however, remind us of the ongoing egocentrism of the child in this era. In speaking of egocentrism I am not making a moral judgment, suggesting that the child is selfish or immoral. Rather, I mean to point out that the child, for the most part, is limited to his or her own perspective on and feelings about things. He or she has not yet developed the next stage's ability to differentiate the self's perspective from that of others and to coordinate the two different outlooks simultaneously. The child may have keen empathy and identification with the feelings of others and may from time to time give evidence of really seeing the point of view of another, but these are not consistent or reliable achievements in the preoperational child. Thus when young children play together their talk and play frequently take the form of parallel monologues. The rules of their games are fluid and egocentric and often both or all win, if winning is important at all.

In early childhood thought is dominated by perception. This means that the child thinks by way of mental pictures that are imitations of reality as perceived. As yet the child lacks the mental capacity to prolong actions or to reverse them, so as to test the inferences he or she makes on the basis of perception. Causal relations and connections, therefore, are poorly understood. The child's feelings and fanciful imagination have free rein to fill in the gaps in understanding that perception leaves.[14]

Perhaps a well-known example from our research will help to illustrate some of the patterns of preoperational thought. In order to test children's constructs of conservation when the form or shape of a substance is changed we gave four- and five-year-olds the following problem. We presented a child with two plasticene balls of the same size and weight. Allowing the child to feel and compare the balls, we asked if each had about the same amount of plasticene. The child readily answered yes. Then, with the child observing, we took one of the balls and rolled it out into the elongated shape of a hot dog. We asked him or her if the two pieces still had the same amount of plasticene. Most frequently the answer was no. Asked which form had more, about 80 percent of the children pointed to the sausage-shaped piece. They explained that it was longer or bigger. About 20 percent of them pointed to the round ball, saying that it was bigger or rounder. Then we re-formed the elongated shape into a sphere. Once again the children said they were the same. Then after watching it being rolled out again, they affirmed once more that one or the other was "more." This example illustrates the inability to coordinate two dimensions of magnitude—length and thickness—at the same time. It also illustrates the preoperational inability to mentally reverse the operations performed on the ball, imaginatively restoring it to its previous shape. Unable to coordinate the two shapes as different conditions of the same substance, the children drew conclusions based on their perceptions and intuitive hunches. Many other such examples could be given.[15]

Kohlberg: M. Piaget's description of some of the features of preoperational thinking provides a good way into understanding the first steps toward moral reasoning in young children. Moral judgment requires the construction and coordination of the points of view of self and others. It involves balancing self-interests with the interests, rights and needs of others. Given Piaget's account of the egocentrism of the young child, you can readily see why I frequently say that our first stage really describes a premoral position. The inability yet to coordinate the perspectives of self and others and the domination of thought by perception and feeling mean that the child will look primarily to external cues to determine the rightness or wrongness, the goodness or badness of actions. Therefore, we find that persons best described by stage one (and these are not, by the way, always preschoolers) determine the rightness or wrongness of actions in terms of anticipated punishment or reward. Largely inattentive to the subjective intentions of actors, stage one looks to the consequences of an act and the probable degree of punishment it would entail. As Piaget's studies and our work have shown, in the preoperational stage children consistently weigh magnitude of consequences over motives for action in assessing moral blame. They regularly see the child who accidentally breaks five glasses while trying to help a parent as deserving more punishment than a child who breaks one glass while trying to steal a forbidden cookie. Criteria such as physical size and visible symbols of authority are employed to determine who should be listened to and obeyed.[16]

Erikson: As will become more and more evident, I'm sure, we really do move between markedly different thought worlds when we put these structural-developmental theories with their rigorous attention to cognitive processes alongside the psychosocial approach. We must remember that neither Piaget nor Kohlberg claims that his theory accounts for personality development as a whole—or in Kohlberg's case, for the full process of moral development. Keeping this limitation of scope in mind, I think we will find considerable complementarity between the structural-developmental and psychosocial viewpoints.

My comments on the early childhood era will have to be somewhat fuller than those of my conversation partners, for my observations and training lead me to distinguish two periods or stages in early childhood. The first, which I designate as the crisis of *autonomy vs. shame and doubt,* depicts the struggle of the two- and three-year-old. The second, emerging and finding resolution roughly between four and six, I call the crisis of *initiative vs. guilt.*

The differentiation of self from others and the joining of thought and language, of which Piaget has spoken, combine with certain features of physical maturation around age two to make possible (and necessary) a new stage of psychosocial growth. Physically, the child has learned to stand up (to stand on his or her "own two feet") and to walk. By virtue of this a child becomes one who could go far, or indeed go too far. In addition, control of the sphincter muscles is developing and, in an achievement which has considerable social meaning, at least in this culture, the child is becoming one who can "hold on" or "let go." As we hinted earlier in the conversation, these new physical modalities have their correlates in the child's ways of relating socially to others. Further, the child with these new capacities, including language, encounters a more challenging and complex range of expectations from the significant others around him or her. Taken together, these new capacities and the child's experience of self in relation to others' reactions to him or her, give rise to the ability to say "I," "my," and "mine" with conviction. There is now an experienced and named sense of self as separate from others. The child now frequently uses the word "no," also with conviction. Her or his new-found readiness to appropriate demandingly and resist forcefully signal the emergence of felt boundaries of the self. This we may call a growing sense of *autonomy*.

Let me insert a brief parenthesis at this point. Here again, as I shall throughout this conversation, I use the phrase a "sense of." M. Piaget has referred to this usage as vague and as symptomatic of a wider imprecision in my thinking and writing. When I speak of a "sense of autonomy" or a "sense of shame" such "senses," as in the phrase "a sense of health," pervade surface and depth, consciousness and the unconscious. They are, then, at the same time ways of *experiencing* accessible to introspection, ways of *behaving* observable by others, and unconscious *inner states* determinable by test and analysis. It is important to keep these three dimensions in mind as we proceed.[17]

The same child who is learning to stand and walk alone becomes quickly aware of the great discrepancy in height and size between him- or herself and adults. In addition to this awareness of smallness, he or she must face the relative ease with which the assertions of infantile autonomy can be overwhelmed or "shamed" by adults or older children. Shame is a visual phenomenon. It derives from a sense of being seen or exposed before one is ready. Exposure means revealing one's vulnerability or one's deficiency. The vulnerability or deficiency connected with shame is not a matter of moral failure. It involves something deeper and more essential to self. The person (or child) who feels shame experiences an exposure to others in which a deficiency in being, an inadequacy intrinsic to self, is on display. Psychoanalytic insight alerts us to likely connections between the emergence of shame and its twin brother, doubt, in the child's awareness of having a backside. The experience of evacuating the bowels —praiseworthy when done on schedule and in appropriate places— is followed by prohibitions of contact with that which felt good as it passed, but now is said to be dirty, filthy and eminently disposable. That objectionable material, which after all forms within me and is part of me, emerges from that visually inaccessible and physically vulnerable "dark continent" of my backside. Shame and doubt, from a clinical standpoint, have their psychological origins in the child's experiences of the culture's responses to these physiological processes and features.

The outer control exerted by parents and others at this stage must be firmly reassuring. The child must come to feel that the basic faith in existence, which is the lasting treasure saved from the rages of the oral stage, will not be overthrown by these sudden, violent wishes to have a choice, to grasp and claim things and to eliminate stubbornly. Consistent affirmation coupled with firm guidance must protect the child from the potential anarchy of the as yet untrained sense of discrimination, the inability to hold on and let go with discretion. As the environment encourages the child to "stand on his or her own feet," it must protect him or her against meaningless and arbitrary experiences of shame and of early doubt. The fruit of such guidance and of the growth it nurtures is the emergence of the ego strength or virtue of *will*. [18]

Convener: Before you continue, Professor Erikson, it may be useful to remind ourselves and our audience that, in contrast to that of the structural developmentalists, your account does intend to deal with the growth of personality taken as a whole. Professors Piaget and Kohlberg have described the patterns of thought accessible to the young child in constructing and reasoning about aspects of the environment, including other persons as moral actors. But you are delineating a series of developmental crises that arise with some predictability, both because of the maturational schedule of human beings and because of the related social expectations, roles and supports with which societies greet our emerging new capacities. Presumably, the developing structures of thought and reasoning constitute an important dimension of that larger maturational process. But your concern is with this larger interactive process and with the evolving integrity or integration of the emerging personality.

Erikson: Yes. You might add to that the concern for giving an account of the growing consciousness of self, which is a feature of personality development as a whole. By this I mean the gradual forming of a self-aware sense of *identity,* which again has important cognitive as well as physical, emotional and social dimensions.

But now perhaps we should return to the era of early childhood. I had just come to the point of discussing the stage that centers in the crisis of *initiative vs. guilt.* By the age of four or five, children have mastered the use and coordination of arms and legs. They experience a new quality of abandonment and ease in movement; they seem to "grow together" both in their persons and in their bodies. In accompaniment with these developments initiative adds to autonomy the quality of undertaking, planning and "attacking" a task for the sake of being active and on the move. This ambulatory stage and the emergence of infantile genitality add to the inventory of basic social modalities that of "making," first in the sense of "being on the make." Though new patterns of sex role socialization may have some effect in this regard, we must still say that this "making," this pleasure in attack and conquest, has somewhat different emphases in boys and girls. In the boy the emphasis remains on phallic-intrusive modes; in the girl it turns to aggressive modes of "catching" or to the milder forms of making oneself attractive and endearing.[19]

In relation to older siblings initiative brings with it anticipatory rivalry. And in the child's desires for and fantasies of an exclusively privileged relationship with the parent of the opposite sex, the results can be secret fears and dreams of mutilating retribution. This brings us to the issue of *guilt.* In this stage a fateful split occurs in the emotional life of the child. Under the impact of emerging infantile sexuality with its fantasies and the answering terrors of incest taboos and other prohibitions, a child internalizes the constraining voices of parental judgment, setting them over against the instinct fragments that have heretofore fueled bodily and psychic growth and exuberance in relatively unconflicted ways. If shame is a visual phenomenon, *guilt* is auditory. With an inner ear the child hears the admonitory or judging voice of the now internalized set of parental injunctions and prohibitions, curbing or circumscribing the child's thrustings and seductions. The problem is the infantile conscience or superego can be more primitive, cruel and uncompromising than the parents or other adults ever intended. A pervasive sense of guilt and self-judgment can lead children to overcontrol and overconstrict themselves to the point of self-obliteration. This is the danger of the stage. Where parental and other adults' guidance can contribute to a mutual regulation of instinctual energy and controlling conscience, the child experiences the emergence of the virtue or ego strength we may call *purpose.* [20]

In closing, having said some things, however briefly, about conscience, I must point out to Professors Piaget and Kohlberg how complicated a matter punishment and reward in moral development can turn out to be when one looks at it in broader than cognitive terms.[21]

Convener: Let me thank our participants for the balance they are striking between comprehensiveness and economy of presentation in their remarks. As these varying windows on childhood are set forth I'm struck by the necessarily formal nature of both the structural-developmental and psychosocial accounts. In order to describe developmental stages, it seems, we must speak in terms that have the possibility of "containing" the varied experiences of each of us. Perhaps one of the ways we derive benefit from this kind of discussion is by letting the descriptions evoke the concreteness of our own childhood memories, testing the theoretical categories against our own experiences.

Kohlberg: That's right. But I would also urge you to let the descriptions given by the theories guide you to a new quality of observation of and listening to children. Each of the theoretical perspectives we are sharing grew out of systematic and careful observation of the language, thought, play and behavior of children. Both the strengths and limitations of the theories will become apparent in the most lively ways if we let them lead us to some attentive observations of and interaction with children.

Convener: Good. But these theories also deal with adolescence and adulthood. I think we'd better move on to the next era, that of childhood proper—the elementary school years.

9. Childhood

||||||||||||||||||||||||||||||||||||||||||||||||||||||||||||||||||||||||||||||||||||||||||||||||||||||||||||||||

Piaget: Since I have been quiet in this discussion for an uncharacteristically long time I would like to open up the discussion of this era. Around age seven, give or take a year, a typically rather rapid and pervasive transformation in the thought patterns of children occurs. The domination of thought by egocentrism and perception begins to give way to what may be designated as the first truly logical operations of thought. The previous stage's tendency to give magical explanations of causal relationships and its inability to think in terms of processes that can be mentally prolonged or reversed are overcome in this period. The emerging stable and flexible system of logical operations we call *concrete operational* thinking.

Let's deal for a moment with what we mean by "operations." When we spoke before about the *action schemata* of the sensorimotor period (an example would be the coordination of arm, hand, fingers and mouth required for sucking the thumb), we were referring to the precursors of operations. The action elements involved in thumb-sucking are generalizable. The same schema of action can be used, with slight modifications, to lift any number of objects to be "known" by the mouth. The next stage, that of preoperational thinking, through its use of language brings the beginning of the internalization of the action schemata of the sensorimotor period. The child can now think or talk about actions, representing or rehearsing them to him- or herself internally without actually having to perform them. Language and the socializations of action, however, present the child with a far more vast and complex universe of physical objects, concepts, symbols and persons. The now internalized sensorimotor schemata, while dependable in the coordinates of movements and physical interactions, have limited utility in organizing, ordering and conceptually mastering other dimensions of this more complex world. Hence the dominance of intuition, affect and perception in the preoperational phase, and the child's "entrapment" in an egocentric perspective. He or she can only assume that others' experiences and understandings are identical with his or her own. In order to move beyond the fluid, unpredictable and magical world of preoperational thought a new system of stable and internally integrated schemata of mental transformations has to emerge. This is what we mean by operations.

Operations, like action schemata before them, are patterned acts of transformation exercised on the objects of knowing. They are *generalizable;* that is, they can be employed in the knowing of a wide range of possible objects. For example, operations such as the union of two classes (fathers united with mothers constitute parents) or the addition of two numbers are actions characterized by very great generality since the acts of uniting, arranging in order and so on enter into all coordinations of particular actions. Further, operations are *reversible* (the reverse of uniting is separating, the reverse of addition is subtraction, and so forth). Another feature of true operations is that they are never isolated but are always *capable of being coordinated into overall systems.* For example, many kinds of combinations or separations can be performed within a larger system of classifications. Finally, true operational structures are not peculiar to a given individual; they are *common to all persons* on the same mental level or stage.

The operational logic of childhood gives rise to a construction of reality that is increasingly orderly, predictable and temporally linear. The child soon is able to create and use schemes of classification and seriation. Conservation problems, of the sort we described earlier involving the plasticene balls, now present no problem due to the child's ability to mentally reverse the action of rolling the ball into a sausage. In addition, the child can coordinate the several dimensions of magnitude involved simultaneously: being longer the plasticene must also be thinner, and so forth. Moreover, the child begins to learn the operations of arithmetic and with this comes an operational mastery of the system of numbers.

With the assembling of these operational "groupings" there develops an ability that has great significance for social and moral development. The composing of a more stable and predictable physical universe enables the child to begin to take account of differences of perspective between the self and others. Operational structures of space, time and causality provide a firm enough grasp on the world of objects (childhood's version of the permanence of objects!) that he or she can now attend to and coordinate the effects on perspective of occupying vantage points different from his or her own. I am sure that Professor Kohlberg will want to build upon this mention of the differentiation and coordination of perspectives in his account of the development of social perspective taking and moral judgment.

We must remind ourselves, however, that the operational logic of childhood remains concrete. Its perspective taking is largely limited to those flesh and blood others with whom the child interacts. Its use of operational structures is sophisticated and becomes increasingly sure across the years from six or seven to eleven or twelve. But the elaboration and use of the operations arise out of action on and interaction with objects and persons that are concretely present, visible and accessible. We might say that the concrete operational mind reflects *with* the operations of logical thought, but it does not yet reflect *upon* these operations. It is a logic of objects and not yet a logic of propositions about objects. Similarly, concrete operational thinking is oriented toward reality. Working to achieve a qualitatively new "objectivity," or decentration of self from other, concrete operational thinking focuses on what *is*. Its constructions of possible future conditions represent mere extensions of what is. For concrete operational thought, we might say, possibility is a function of reality. The propositional logic of the next stage, however, with its ability to imagine theoretically all possible perspectives, transcends the real, subordinating reality to possibility. But that is to leap ahead in the story.[22]

Kohlberg: The logical operations appearing typically at seven or eight do have important implications for the child's approach to making moral judgments. Perhaps before I sketch these implications, however, I should provide a bit of orientation to the relations we find between logical operations in cognitive development per se and their extension to the moral domain. Stage two in moral development we call *instrumental exchange.* Concrete operational thinking is *necessary but not sufficient* for this stage and for the form of social perspective taking it assumes. To say that a given level of cognitive development is necessary but not sufficient for a stage of social perspective taking or moral judgment, is to recognize that a different (or additional) range of interactions and experiences is required for moral development beyond those required for cognitive development alone. Opportunities for taking the perspectives of others, for facing and conversing about situations of moral conflict and perhaps for observing and hearing others' ways of dealing with moral dilemmas are some of the requisite experiences for the development of new structures of moral judgment and social perspective taking.

Now back to moral thinking in stage two. The person whose moral judgment is dominantly stage two (and I remind you it could be an adolescent or an adult as well as a school child) is no less self-interested than the person of stage one. In a special sense we may say that he or she is *more* self-interested. Having begun, as M. Piaget suggested, to be able to differentiate the self's perspective from and to coordinate it with those of others, we may say that those in stage two are more clearly aware of and therefore more effectively able to pursue their own interests and desires. The differences from stage one's egocentrism, however, are very significant. Now the moral actor is aware of and must take account of the interests, needs and claims of others. There is the recognition that in order to get others to assent to or even to cooperate in the achievement of one's own goals, one must be prepared to reciprocate. For a time we subtitled stage two "You scratch my back and I'll scratch yours," but this makes it sound more cynical than it need be. A very significant step toward the understanding of (and acting upon) justice involves coming to feel and honor the force of reciprocal rights and claims. We should recognize, moreover, that this moral logic informs all theories of punishment and retribution of the type "an eye for an eye and a tooth for a tooth." In this concrete reciprocity we find the roots of justice as fairness. The perspective taking underlying justice as reciprocal fairness is concrete and individualistic. It does not yet generalize beyond particular face-to-face situations. It does not yet formulate moral propositions governing whole classes of reciprocal relations. In this we are again reminded of the concrete nature of concrete operational thought. And we see why the school boy or girl (or older person best described by stage two) remains heavily dependent upon specific sets of rules, guidelines or directives for shaping moral behavior more generally.[23]

Erikson: My colleagues' descriptions of the appearance in the school age of logical operations and of patterns of reciprocity in moral decision making make me freshly aware that, after all, our theories are unified and complementary, at least to the degree that we keep an honest and accurate focus on the growing person.

Having found that he or she will have no lasting place in the home or as a marriage partner for a parent, the child of school age has energy and interest to turn outward. All societies provide some form of educational preparation for adult membership in the group. That this is begun universally at about the ages of six or seven is powerful testimony that some new level of emotional and intellectual, not to mention physical, readiness can be counted upon in dealing with a qualitatively new set of challenges and expectations. In more or less formal settings children are led in the development of skills and the use of tools they will need as adults. This era and its challenges focus on the crisis I call *industry vs. inferiority.*

A sense of industry accrues as the child learns to utilize her or his physical and intellectual capacities in potentially productive work. In becoming a "worker" the growing person must learn to contribute as a productive unit in cooperative enterprises. This involves, in addition to developing particular cognitive and physical skills, learning the disciplines of group life and the expression and integration of emotions.

The danger of this stage lies in a sense of inferiority and inadequacy. If one despairs of one's tools and skills—or of one's status among partners in cooperation—then the person may pull back into the more isolated, less tool-conscious familial context of the Oedipal time. The child may despair of his or her equipment in the tool world or in anatomy and consider him- or herself doomed to mediocrity or inadequacy. Where good modes of leadership and not too severely interrupted opportunities for learning and growth enable children to avoid these dangers, a lasting sense of *competence* results. This virtue or ego strength contributes an abiding confidence that one *can do* and *learn* and that one is capable of performing a valued service in the community's economy of work.[24]

Convener: You men have given us a lot to digest as we try to grasp the contours of cognitive, moral and psychosocial development in the elementary years. There truly is a decisive revolution in both thought and emotional life as the child moves from the preschool to the elementary period. Once I was trying to describe some of these changes in a lecture. I expressed a kind of vicarious grief I feel for the child as he or she leaves the imaginatively rich, mythical world of early childhood and begins to live in the more prosaic, linear and predictable era of the school years. A woman in my audience offered an insightful response.

"But think of the exhilaration the child must experience," she said, "precisely in being more sovereignly able to distinguish fact from fantasy and in being able more reliably to predict the behavior of persons and objects. To really *know*, when previously you've only been able to intuit, can bring a powerful sense of satisfaction."

As we turn now to the era of adolescence I am certain that we can expect to hear about an equally dramatic confluence of developmental changes.

10. Adolescence

||||||||||||||||||||||||||||||||||||||||||||||||||||||||||||||||||||||||||||||||||||||||||||||||||||||||||||||||||||||||||||||||||||||||

Piaget: I suspect that this discussion of adolescence from our several points of view may prove particularly valuable, in that it will show how significant a part cognitive development plays in the crises of adolescence and their resolutions. Earlier in this century authorities on adolescence wrote to the point of trivialization about the emotional upsets of puberty. They ran the risk of overemphasizing the impact of adolescent sexuality and its accompanying affective disequilibrium. It is important to recognize that while the transition from the patterns of thought that ripen in late childhood to those of adolescence does bring disequilibrium and disruption, the emerging new cognitive structures provide markedly increased capacity, flexibility and stability. In fact, as I shall try to show, the formation of personality, as a matter of reflective personal engagement, only emerges with the development of formal operational thinking.

In examining the course of cognitive development it is useful to observe a phenomenon that occurs in some form with each of the major transitions. The operations that were constitutive of the previous stage become, to some degree, the objects of reflection for the next stage. Put another way, the operations of the previous stage come to be part of the "theory" of the next stage.[25] Preoperational thinking, for example, brings the world, constructed in accordance with the sensorimotor action schemata, into language and symbolic representation. Similarly, concrete operational thought takes the mental imitations of reality composed by the preoperational stage and manipulates them in accordance with its now more stable and reversible operational structures. Pre-eminently, formal operational thinking makes the concrete operations both the *objects* of its thought as well as the *instruments* of its thinking. Formal operational thought *is thinking about thinking.* Put another way, whereas concrete operations constitute a logic of objects and of the relationships between objects, formal operations constitute a logic of propositions. If concrete operations manipulate objects, formal operations manipulate *concepts* about objects and their relationships.

Consider an example. Subjects of various ages were presented with a number of metal rods of varying length, thickness, shape (cross-section would appear square, rectangular, or round) and material (in this experiment, steel and brass, which differ considerably in elasticity). The subjects were given the problem of explaining the rods' differences in flexibility. Concrete operational subjects did not attempt to inventory separately the possible factors that might have an influence. Rather, by arranging the rods in order of descending or ascending lengths they began to see whether the rods were increasingly flexible. When other variances, such as thickness or material were perceived to interfere with factors of length, these latter factors were analyzed in turn by the same method. But there was neither a systematic isolation of each separate factor, nor any recognition of the necessity of creating a synthetic perspective or theory that could coordinate the effects of all various factors. When pressed to provide proof for their conclusions subjects of nine or ten typically chose a long thin rod and a short thick one to demonstrate the role of length, because in this way, as a boy of nine and a half told us, "you can see the difference better!"

In contrast, subjects of eleven or twelve or beyond (with a leveling off at fourteen to fifteen), after some initial groping, made a list of factors by way of hypothesis and then studied them one by one. In this step, which represents the advance over the previous stage, they separated each variable factor, testing each one while controlling or keeping constant all the others. For example, they would choose two rods of the same length, same width and same cross-section but of different substances. This enabled them to attend to the impact of this last variable alone. When asked to give proof of the validity of their conclusions the subjects could show that these variables and only these could singly and in combination account for the differences, and that by systematically testing each variable, holding all the others constant, one could determine which affected flexibility and which did not. In short they could give you a method, comprehensive and exhaustive, for solving the problem and could demonstrate that it covered all possible relations between factors. We call this *hypo-*

thetico-deductive thinking. It is second-level thinking, thinking about method in thinking. This method, which we found fairly general at about fourteen, is all the more remarkable in that none of the subjects we interviewed had received instruction in it at school.[26]

In the problem I just described concrete operations were sufficient for separating the factors and for considering the variations of one of them or two of them at a time. But in such a complex system of influences the concrete operations of classification, seriation, correspondence and measurement are not sufficient. The solution requires implications, disjunctions, and exclusions, which belong to propositional operations and which presuppose both a combinitorial system and coordinations of inversion and reciprocity. As these new transformations take form the adolescent is acquiring the fully developed operations he or she will require for adult thought and for the ability to use, in principle, the scientific method.[27]

Earlier we contrasted concrete and formal operational thinking in the following way: for concrete thinking, we said, *possibility* is a subset of *reality;* for formal thinking, on the other hand, *reality* is a subset of *possibility.* In the formal operational stage thought takes wings. Able imaginatively to transcend empirical experience, formal thinking can construct ideal states or regulative norms. In social terms, formal operational thinking can be utopian. With its ability to extrapolate or imagine perfection, the adolescent mind can be quite harsh in judging friends, parents, social or political conditions generally or the self. Now able to conceive of the possibility of an infinity of perspectives on a problem, the adolescent shows both a marked improvement in taking the perspectives of others and a tendency to an overconfident distortion of others' perspectives through overassimilation of them into his or her own.

The intellectual transcendence we have just described also makes possible a new kind of reflection on the course of one's own life. The concrete operational child is *carried* by the flow of his or her life and reflects on events and relationships from *within* that flow. In contrast, the adolescent begins to be able to reflect on the life course from "above" or "beside" it. Formal operations bring the ability to construct a personal past and to anticipate a personal future, based on expected or projected developmental transformations of the self. Thus, in a qualitatively different sense than before, the youth begins to exhibit personality, that is, the disciplining and conscious effort at

shaping one's life in accordance with self-discerned patterns and aspirations.[28]

Kohlberg: M. Piaget's discussion of the implications of formal operational thought for social relations leads well into a look at corresponding advances in moral judgment and in social perspective taking. The
"transcendence" of thought from its embeddedness in the concrete
world of objects and relationships manifests its impact in three decisive steps in social perspective taking. I and my associates have studied
these developments and as I tell about them I want particularly to
draw on the work of my associate Robert Selman.[29]

Almost parallel with the appearance of early formal operations
(usually about eleven) there can emerge a qualitatively new dimension
in taking the perspectives of others. With the earlier concrete operational form of social perspective taking a person develops a proficiency
for constructing the perspective of another or others upon a third
object or person. I can show this by means of a diagram:

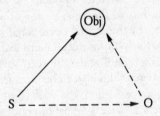

Let *S* be "self," *O* be "other," and *Obj* be a third object or person
to which self and others relate from these different positions. In
simple perspective taking I see you seeing a third object and I
imaginatively construct your perspective on it. My knowledge of both
you and the object is enhanced, for as I coordinate our two perspectives on it, I can compare and contrast our ways of seeing it and arrive
at a more "objective" knowing of the object. I also have an expanded
awareness of your standpoint.

But with the transcendence that formal operational thinking brings
I am ready for both a more complex act of construction of another's
perspective and a more difficult act of self-transcendence. With this
new step the subject begins to construct the perspective of the other
on the *self.* Put in personal terms again, "I see you seeing me; I
construct the *me* I think you see." It can be diagrammed in this way:

Let *S* be self, *O* be other, and *S'* be other's image of self as self constructs it. We may call this step *interpersonal perspective taking*. We take a decisive step toward understanding the revolution that can occur in social relations with adolescence if we see that interpersonal perspective taking quickly becomes *mutual* and is understood as such. Let me explain. When I begin to construct your perspective on me, I soon recognize that you, likewise, are constructing my perspective on you. Hence, "I see you seeing me; I see you seeing me seeing you." Or diagrammatically:

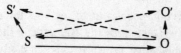

This is *mutual interpersonal perspective taking*. Understanding this helps us grasp more fully some of the mechanisms underlying M. Piaget's account of the adolescent's new ability to make the self and the course of his or her own life objects of reflection. It also contributes to our understanding of his reference to the adolescent emergence of "personality" as the formation of a more or less conscious life project. I am certain that Professor Erikson will build on this in his discussion of identity in adolescence.

But before we can fully appreciate the potential of formal operational thought's contribution to the third stage of moral reasoning, there is one further step in the development of perspective taking which I must describe. Mutual interpersonal perspective taking creates a qualitatively new kind of objectivity, both regarding self and regarding the other or others with whom one has significant and sustained interactions. The coordination or holding together of those two more objective perspectives on self and others makes for the creation of what may be called a *"third-person"* perspective. By this we mean a more dispassionate perspective, inclusive of the perspectives of both the self and other(s), but not identical with or under the control of either. If we diagram third-person perspective taking it looks like this:

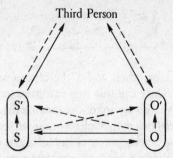

I have drawn this in such a way as to suggest that the third-person perspective is potentially a shared construction, something both or several partners cooperate in. In practice, however, it may not always have this shared quality.

A bit of reflection enables us to see how the capacity for third-person perspective taking greatly strengthens the possibility of an actor's determining what justice requires in a situation of interpersonal conflict. The distancing or transcendence it makes possible enables one to approximate the weighing of another's rights, claims and interpretations with the same scale by which one weighs one's own. The development and consistent use of third-person perspective taking would constitute a remarkable evidence of moral growth. It is not required for our third stage of moral development, though mutual interpersonal perspective taking is. In practice the third-person perspective is often appealed to in more conventional forms, namely by way of appeal to the sanction of generally accepted social expectations (G. H. Mead's "generalized other") or to a shared understanding of God as a transcendent third person.[30]

With this necessarily somewhat complex account of the formal operational developments in interpersonal perspective taking, we can now focus on the third moral stage. Stage three marks the beginning of the *conventional level* of moral judgment. We call it *mutual interpersonal expectations, relationships and interpersonal conformity.* In stage three actions are right if they conform to the expectations of one's "significant others." A powerful motive of stage three moral action is to please those persons who matter greatly and not to disappoint their opinions and expectations of us. Another criterion for the rightness of actions at stage three involves doing what people generally expect of a person in the role or relation one occupies toward others, that is, doing what a good husband, or a good daughter or a loyal friend would generally be expected to do. Relying on either a meeting of the expectations of those whose opinions about one matter a great deal, or on promise making and promise keeping or on fulfilling the customary expectations of persons in one's social role or relationship, stage three represents a conformist mode of moral decision making. The complex steps in cognitive development and social perspective taking that this stage requires, however, remind us that "conventional" moral thinking is not to be taken for granted or to be thought of as an automatic or simple achievement. This moral orientation and its view of social relations must be constructed by each person in the context of his or her interaction with others and with the help and guidance of the available contents of common-sense moral thought.

Though stage three may compose a unified set of social expectations which become part of (or constitute) a third-person perspective (the generalized other), it does not yet take a true societal perspective. It is limited to an interpersonal construction of the moral domain and formulates its moral tenets, however inclusively, primarily on the basis of an extension from face-to-face relationships. A true societal perspective awaits the next stage.[31]

Erikson: My colleague Piaget, in speaking here of the emergence of formal operations, has emphasized in a way I find helpful the consequences of this development for social interaction and personality formation. If I prefer to speak of the latter in terms of *identity* formation, it is with an awareness that our accounts overlap in interesting ways and that the cognitive developments he describes are central in the identity crisis of adolescence. Professor Kohlberg's additional explication of the dramatic new steps in social perspective taking made possible by formal operational thought indeed help us to see quite clearly what I might call the cognitive bases of the identity crisis.[32]

With the ability for entering into "mutual interpersonal perspective taking" the boy or girl suddenly becomes "self-conscious" in new and potentially confusing ways. His or her range of significant others is widened and may be somewhat diverse. The views of self that emerge in relations with peers, parents, teachers and others, therefore, like reflected images in a house of distorting mirrors, may not fit together. The young person can say as did St. Augustine somewhere in the *Confessions*, "And I became a problem to myself!" But we must add one dimension more from among these cognitive complexities contributing to the identity crisis. M. Piaget's indication that formal operational thought brings the capacity to compose a personal past and to anticipate a personal future is an important note. Now one's sense of self—one's felt identity—must try to fit together images of a personal past and its continuities with the images of a personal future and its possibilities.

To grasp the full range of challenges the adolescent faces we must see these cognitive dimensions in the context of broader psychosexual and psychosocial changes. Even as the young person is involved in dealing with new capacities for self-awareness and for interpersonal relations, he or she is experiencing physiological transformations of a dramatic sort: changes in body size and musculature, deepening of voice timbre, the growth of body hair, the enlargement toward maturity of genitals and breasts, the onset of menstruation and the ejaculation of semen and sperm. One's body image is in flux and for a time the youth must incorporate almost daily new features in her or his physiology.

The evidences of new thought processes and reflectiveness as well as the more tangible evidences of physical change are not missed by the persons and institutions with which youth interact. New expectations, qualitatively different disciplines and a host of difficult decisions are the requirements with which societies greet the now more womanly or manly adolescent. In trying to meet and fulfill these requirements youth will call on the available and personally resonant ideological resources of their environments, particularly those that are embodied in charismatic and convincing leaders. They will seek sponsoring groups and figures and will appoint otherwise well-meaning persons as temporary enemies over against whom their identities may be clarified. They may band together in tight cliques, overemphasizing some relatively trivial commonality as a symbol of shared identity. In this cliquishness they can be quite cruel as they exclude those who do not share this common element. In a more constructive mode of approach adolescents may enter a stage of "falling in love," which is by no means entirely, or even primarily, a sexual matter—except where the mores demand it. To a considerable extent adolescent love is an attempt to arrive at a definition of one's identity by projecting one's diffuse ego image on another and by seeing it thus reflected and gradually clarified. This is why so much of young love is conversation.

I call this developmental crisis of adolescence the struggle for *identity vs. role confusion.* By identity I mean an accrued awareness of oneself that maintains continuity with one's past meanings to others and to oneself and that integrates the images of oneself given by significant others with one's own inner feelings of who one is and of what one can do, all in such a way as to enable one to anticipate the future without undue anxiety about "losing" oneself. Identity, thought of in this way, is by no means a fully conscious matter. But when it is present it gives rise to a feeling of inner firmness or of "being together" as a self. It communicates to others a sense of personal unity or integration.[33]

The danger of this stage is role confusion. This can be exacerbated by strong previous doubt about one's sexual identity or about one's place or value in the primary relationships of the family. It can also be heightened by anxieties about the impossibility of finding adult roles in work or love or social-political status that can sustain present and future identity.

Where social conditions and favorable personal relationships support young persons in building a firm enough sense of identity to feel ready to *commit* themselves—in friendship, to future work roles or in loyalty to religious or other ideological visions and communities— we may expect the emergence in them of the ego strength or virtue we call *fidelity.*[34]

11. Adulthood

||||||||||||||||||||||||||||||||||||||||||||||||||||||||||||||||||||||||||||||||||||||||||||||||||||||||||||||||||||||||||||||||||

Convener: Friends, we come now to a new point in our conversation, one that requires something of a change in our procedure. With his remarks about formal operations and their significance, Professor Piaget has completed his account of the cognitive developmental stages. For Professor Kohlberg there remains another stage at the conventional level of moral judgment, and then we want to hear his discussion of the postconventional or principled level, stages five and six. To complete his presentation of ages of the life cycle, Professor Erikson owes us overviews of the three adult eras he has identified.

In order to stay within the time we have allotted for this exchange I propose the following strategy. We will ask Professor Kohlberg to resume the conversation with a discussion of moral stage four. Then Professor Erikson will speak about the crisis of young adulthood. Following that, Professor Kohlberg can deal with the principled stages of moral development. Then we will conclude with a look at the psychosocial stages of adulthood and maturity."

Kohlberg: Let me begin by saying something about the conventional moral level taken as a whole. At this level persons perceive the maintenance of the expectations of their family, group or nation as valuable in its own right. The attitude is not only one of *conformity* to personal expectations and social order but of loyalty to them. As Professor Erikson might say, one's identity is founded in important ways by one's identifications with family, groups and a social-institutional order that protects them. Conventional moral reasoning, therefore, grows out of one's actively maintaining, supporting and justifying this order and identifying with the persons or groups involved in it.

We have already spoken about stage three, *mutual interpersonal relations.* We gave a rather detailed account of the development of the mutual interpersonal form of social perspective taking that is required for that stage. Let me point out here that each stage of perspective taking and moral reasoning incorporates and builds on the structures of the previous stages, integrating them into a more comprehensive and versatile new stage. Moral stage four, which we call *social system and conscience,* requires a further step in social perspective taking. Whereas stage three was limited to interpersonal modes, stage four includes those but widens them to take the perspective of the social system or order as a whole. Stage four sees society as a network of rules or laws and of roles and relationships constituted by them. Therefore in the adjudication of differences between persons one must consider not only the rights, claims, desires and promises that shape their particular relationship and not only the goodness or sincerity of their motives. One must see all those in relation to the more comprehensive interests and requirements of the social system taken as a whole.

Stage four, which in our earlier writings was called the "law and order" orientation, determines the final rightness or wrongness of actions by reference to authority, fixed rules, the social-legal regulations of roles and the maintenance of social order. Stage four emphasizes doing one's duty as defined by law or the rules governing roles. It is prepared to subordinate personal and interpersonal interests and sentiments to duty understood in these ways.

Stage four and the conventional level as a whole have no way of shaping moral decisions beyond interpersonal concord, societal expectations and the legal point of view. Justice, for the conventional level, is inseparable from compliance with these sources of norms. Strictly speaking, civil disobedience, in the service of a principle of justice that transcends and could correct law or social custom, does not emerge in the conventional level. I will deal with the principled moral stages in my concluding remarks.[35]

Erikson: Earlier in this conversation M. Piaget remarked that in cognitive development the operations of the previous stage become the objects of reflection or are integrated into the "theory" of the next stage. In psychosocial development we may offer a similar dictum. "The strength acquired at any stage is tested by the necessity to transcend it in such a way that the individual can take chances in the next stage with what was most vulnerably precious in the previous one."[36]

When the person, chronologically a late adolescent or young adult, carries within the self that firm sense of congruence between his or her meaning to self and to others that we have called *identity,* there is a readiness for risking that unity of self in relations of closeness with another. The young adult is ready for *intimacy,* that is, the capacity to commit oneself to concrete affiliations and partnerships and to develop the ethical strength to abide by such commitments even though they may call for significant sacrifices and compromises. The prototypical relationship of such intimacy occurs in the full genital union of a man and a woman in the context of mutual commitment. To be sure, the exercise of sexual closeness in many instances does not wait for that formation of identity that brings readiness for commitment and fidelity. Much of the sex life preceding these commitments is of the identity-searching kind or is dominated by patterns of genital self-assertion that makes of it a kind of erogenous combat zone.

While sexual intimacy provides the prototype, the capacity for intimacy is called upon in quite other contexts as well. Intimacy is required in experiences of the solidarity of close group associations, in close friendships, in physical combat and other forms of conflict, in experiences of inspiration by teachers and in times of intuition or mystical insight. Avoidance or withdrawal from such situations because of a fear of the loss of the self may lead to the counterpoint of intimacy—and the danger of this stage—namely a deep sense of *isolation* and a resulting self-absorption.

Isolation or *distantiation,* to use a more extreme term, involves not only a withdrawal from or avoidance of intimacy. When the prospect of closeness to another or others is too threatening it may give rise to a readiness to isolate and, if necessary, to destroy those persons or forces whose essence seems dangerous to one's own.*

The capacity for intimacy, as developed in the context of the mutual regulation of two beings in orgasm or in the mutual interpenetration of emotion and will in friendship, as well as in other situations of closeness based on commitment, gives rise to the ego strength or virtue of *love.* [37]

---

*The apparently random killings and mutilation of attractive young women by the "Hillside Strangler," the "Son of Sam" or England's new "Jack the Ripper" can partially be explained by this kind of distantiation under threat. These young women victims are composite symbols to the murderers of a feminine essence that is overwhelmingly threatening and has to be destroyed. The accompanying notoriety, successful evasion of the police and resulting panic in the population perversely serve to justify the killers in the isolated sense of inverse superiority.—J.W.F.

Kohlberg: There was a time earlier in my research when I would have taken the position that the attainment of stages five or six in moral reasoning did not require reaching adulthood, in psychosocial terms. In the earliest years of our work I assumed that postconventional moral development, like the stages before it, grew primarily out of experiences of cognitive conflict regarding moral issues. I supposed that in an environment rich enough with such conflict and with opportunities for social perspective taking postconventional moral reasoning could follow soon after the appearance of formal operational thinking. Our early scoring procedures, which failed to make sharp enough distinctions between the *contents* and the *forms* of moral judgment, made us believe that we found at least stage five reasoning in late adolescence and before graduation from high school.

In the early 1970s, however, we began to have to question these assumptions and that scoring. We began to see subjects whom we had scored at stage five in their last years of high school seemingly "regress" in their moral judgment scores during their college years to a relativist position that seemed a lot like stage two. This was theoretically very disquieting. It seemed as though our claims about moral stage development being hierarchical and invariantly sequential might have to be revised, at least for the postconventional stages. As we began to work with these issues more closely three factors which have importance in this conversation became part of our thinking.

First of all, we gathered a new "wave" of longitudinal data. This showed that by age twenty-five everyone of the apparent "retrogressors" had returned to stage four and five moral reasoning, with most showing more of stage five than when they were in high school.

Second, research by Eliot Turiel on the process of stage transition enlarged our understanding of the disequilibrating effects of transition. This enabled us to see that what appeared at first to be regression might better be understood as a kind of transitional moral relativism, which necessarily emerges as persons dis-embed themselves from conventional moral thinking and begin to be critical of it. Moreover, careful reexamination of our apparent college-aged stage two's showed us that their relativism was quite different from the relativism of stage two children or adults. True stage two relativism grows out of the experienced differences of individual outlooks and desires and the inability to generalize or unify them. The stage four-five relativism, however, arises out of the person's recognition of the relativity of law, customs and group experiences from one society or group to the next.

The post stage four relativists did not really relinquish stage four and regress to stage two, but developed relativisitic outlooks and an "enlightened hedonism" that grew out of trying to go beyond the limits of stage four moral reasoning.

Third, in dialogue with the work of Erikson we began to restudy the question of the relation of moral development and personal experience. With new scoring criteria that more clearly distinguished the *form* from the *content* of moral reasoning we reexamined our data. By these new criteria we found no true stage fives in our longitudinal sample before age twenty-four. This caused us to look closely at Erikson's thinking about adult ethical perspectives. Erikson's account of moral development sees three broad phases. The first, the moralistic era of childhood, derives from the internalization of cultural norms and expectations as taught by parents or other adults. Adolescence, with the emergence of formal operations, makes it possible to grasp the universal good in ideological terms. But the ideological "ethical sense" of adolescence can be inconsistent and reflective of the search *for* identity rather than an expression *of* identity. For a true ethical orientation of adulthood to develop, the identity crisis must have been resolved sufficiently enough to make possible adult commitments that establish relations of care or generativity toward others.

Based on our longitudinal data and in light of Erikson's suggestions we hypothesize that two kinds of experiences, both of which usually come only after high school, are required for the development of consistent postconventional moral reasoning. First, the young person must leave home emotionally and perhaps physically, and encounter experiences of conflicting values in a context of moratorium. Then, second, the young adult, to develop a true postconventional moral orientation, must have undertaken two further steps that typically being a student does not require: the experience of *sustained responsibility for the welfare of others* and the experience of making and living with irreversible moral choices which are the marks of adulthood personal moral experience.

Not all young adults have had these experiences. Not all young adults who have had these experiences develop postconventional moral orientations. But our research suggests that all young adults, or older adults, who *do* develop postconventional moral outlooks and commitments have experienced and resolved the adolescent identity crisis. They have had experiences of sustained responsibility for the welfare of others and they have had to make and live with irreversible

moral choices. These, it seems, are necessary psychosocial prerequi-
sites for the development of a principled moral orientation.[38]

Now what do we mean by postconventional or principled moral
reasoning? At this level persons make a clear effort to define guiding
moral values and principles that have validity and applicability apart
from the authority of the groups or people holding them and apart
from the individual's own identification with these groups. We distinguish two stages in the postconventional level.

"Stage five we call *social contract or utility and individual rights.*
The social perspective taking on which stage five is based we call the
"prior-to-society" perspective. Oriented to human rights that exist
prior to social contracts, law or society, this perspective gives added
depth to stage four's appreciation of social order and due process by
clarifying the purposes for which they have evolved. But beyond stage
four, in its attunement to the ends for which governments are created
and maintained, the prior-to-society perspective serves as a critical
principle that can, under certain circumstances, justify civil disobedience and principled efforts to alter or overthrow unjust laws and social
policies.

Stage five recognizes the relativity of most social rules and laws but
affirms the importance of upholding them in the interest of impartial-
ity and because they are the social contract. Some values and rights,
however, are not relative and must be upheld in any society and
regardless of majority opinion. These include life, liberty and freedom
from arbitrary personal or class oppression. Stage five is oriented to
overall principles of utility, committed to "the greatest good for the
greatest number." But because of its concern for human rights it
qualifies the utility principle with an equality principle that rejects any
maximization of the general good at the expense of a minority or
minorities.

This brings me now to stage six, the *universal ethical principle*
orientation. Building on all that came before, stage six adds an operational commitment to principles of justice that can claim universal
validity. Principles, of course are different from rules, customs or laws.
Principles, we might say, are the abstract, generalizable guidelines and
tests by which particular actions, laws or social policies may be made
or evaluated. The golden rule in its various forms is such a principle.
Kant's categorical imperative in its three forms constitutes a universal
moral principle.

The social perspective taking required for stage six adds to the previous stages' contributions a rather decisive new step. I sometimes characterize this as an ability to play "moral musical chairs." A principle for adjudicating moral disputes or establishing social policy is just if and only if a rational, autonomous, interested person could assent to it, no matter which "chair" (social, economic, racial, or political status or group) he or she might occupy. The formulation of and action in terms of universalizable moral principles, therefore, require a moral imagination informed enough and detached enough from one's own interests to accurately take the perspective of every person or group affected by a policy or action being considered. The principle is just only if from each of those standpoints its application in law or policy would yield an outcome that is manifestly fair and equal in terms of resulting burdens and benefits.

While stage six moral reasoning is quite rare in our empirical sample, it underlies the leadership policies of persons universally acknowledged as the greatest of moral leaders. Most notable in this century are Mahatma Gandhi and Martin Luther King, Jr. In rather different situations of struggle against oppression both of these men articulated and acted on universal principles of radical love and nonviolent action in the service of justice. I maintain that stage six provides the most adequate and "true," if you will, form of moral reasoning. I claim that both logically and psychologically it is the end point toward which moral reasoning in its sequence of formal stages develops.[39]

Erikson: In this conversation with Professors Piaget and Kohlberg it is a somewhat unexpected privilege to have the last word! Professor Kohlberg's account of his growing recognition of the contributions of psychosocial and ego development to the development of adult structures of moral reasoning heartens me. The direction of his thought moves toward the kind of responsible theoretical synthesis we need in order to grasp the interrelatedness of reason and emotion, of moral judgment and identity, and of individual and society. I would only urge him to go further and to take seriously self-hood and life history as well as the structures of consciousness and the unconscious. And with these we would need to attend to ideology and the "world images" that inform and support people's moral choice and action. But, then, I fall again into that ambitious comprehensiveness that M. Piaget calls philosophical and unscientific![40]

In my remarks about the last two stages of adulthood I can be brief.

The crisis of middle adulthood I characterize as *generativity vs. stagnation*. It has taken psychoanalysis some time to realize that the ability to lose oneself in the meeting of bodies and minds in intimacy leads to a gradual expansion of ego interests and to the investment of life-energies in that which is being generated. Generativity marks a culmination of the virtues or strengths of previous stages in an adulthood that is ready to care for what has been and is being created. Our common attention to the child's dependence upon adults often blinds us to the dependence of the older generation on the younger one. Mature men and women need to be needed, and maturity needs guidance as well as encouragement from what has been produced and must be taken care of. The joining of minds and bodies produces other "offspring" in addition to children. Generativity is the readiness to care for and nurture the next generation and the life conditions and resources of all kinds they will need to become generative in their generation. This play on words means to suggest a cogwheeling of the generations in which adults play their parts in such a way as to renew and contribute strength to the ongoing cycle of the generations.

The danger in this stage is stagnation. The adult who fails to find ways of contributing to the nurture of culturally significant strength in the species forfeits his or her place in the cycle of the generations. This can bring the regression to an obsessive need for pseudo-intimacy, often with a pervading sense of stagnation and personal impoverishment. Such individuals often begin to indulge themselves as if they were their own—or one another's—one and only child. The mere fact of having or even wanting children, however, does not "achieve" generativity. In fact, some young parents suffer, it seems, from the retardation of the ability to develop this stage. The reasons are often to be found in early childhood impressions or in excessive self-love based on a too strenuously self-made personality. Most fundamentally such adult "narcissism" (and here we return to the beginnings) derives from the lack of some faith, some "belief in the species," which would make a child appear to be a welcome trust of the community.[41] The composite virtue or ego strength that emerges in generative adults is that of *care*.

Now let me turn, in conclusion, to the crisis of old age. Only those persons who have in some way taken care of things and people, and who have faced the triumphs and disappointments that come with being originators of others or the generators of products as—only in such persons does the fruit of the other seven gradually ripen into what I want to call *ego integrity*. Ego integrity is the ego's accrued assurance of its investment in order and meaning. It is the experience of a post-narcissistic love of the human ego—not of the self—as part of a world order and grounded in spiritual depth. It is an acceptance of one's one and only life cycle as something that had to be and that, by necessity, permitted of no substitutions. It thus means a new, a different love of one's parents. Although aware of the relativity of all the various lifestyles that have given meaning to human striving, the possessor of integrity is ready to defend the dignity of his or her own lifestyle against all physical and economic threats. For this person knows that all human integrity is at stake in the one style of integrity of which he or she partakes.

The absence of integrity and the danger in this stage is a sense of *despair*. The lack or loss of integrity is signified by the fear of death. Despair expresses the feeling that the time is now short, too short for the attempt to start another life and to try out alternate roads to integrity. Disgust hides despair.

The virtue old age contributes to cultures out of its integrity is *wisdom*. In the embodied wisdom of genuine integrity the courage and visions of wholeness that animate persons in other stages are renewed and sanctioned. The integrity of old age thus contributes to the possibility of trust in the first stage. Webster's dictionary defines trust as "the assured reliance on another's integrity." Undoubtedly Webster had business in mind rather than babies, credit rather than faith, but the formulation stands. And it seems possible to further paraphrase the relation of adult integrity and infantile trust by saying that healthy children will not fear life if their elders have integrity enough not to fear death.[42]

Convener: Thank you, all three.

NOTES

1. Martin Buber, *I and Thou*, trans. Ronald Gregor Smith (New York: Scribner's, 1955). Reuel L. Howe, *The Miracle of Dialogue* (New York: Seabury Press, 1963).
2. Published in expanded and revised form as *To See the Kingdom: The*

Theological Vision of H. Richard Niebuhr (Nashville, Tenn.: Abingdon Press, 1974).

3. For an early example of this genre see Walter Savage Landor, *Classical (Imaginary) Conversations* (Washington, London: M. Walter Dunne, 1901).

4. For Erikson's own autobiographical reflections see *Life History and the Historical Moment* (New York: Norton, 1975), chap. 1 " 'Identity Crisis' in Autobiographic Perspective." For a biographical treatment see Robert Coles, *Erik H. Erikson, The Growth of His Work* (Boston: Little, Brown, 1970).

5. For autobiographical statements by Piaget see Richard I. Evans, *Jean Piaget: The Man and His Ideas* (New York: Dutton, 1973), chap. 1; and Jean Piaget, *Insights and Illusions of Philosophy*, trans. Wolfe Mays (New York: World, Meridian Books, 1971), chap. 1.

6. See Lawrence Kohlberg, "Beds for Bananas," *Menorah Journal*, vol. 36, no. 4 (1948), pp. 385–400.

7. Erik H. Erikson, *Childhood and Society*, 2d ed (New York: Norton, 1963), pp. 269–274.

8. Jean Piaget, "Piaget's Theory," in Paul Mussen, ed., *Carmichael's Manual of Child Psychology*, 3d. ed., vol. 1 (New York, John Wiley & Sons, 1970), pp. 710–713. Jean Piaget, *Six Psychological Studies* (New York: Random House, Vintage Books, 1967), pp. xxii and 3–8. See also Herbert Ginsberg and Sylvia Opper, *Piaget's Theory of Intellectual Development* (Englewood Cliffs, N. J.: Prentice-Hall, 1969), chap. 1.

9. See Lawrence Kohlberg, "Stage and Sequence: The Cognitive Developmental Approach to Socialization," in David A. Goslin, ed., *Handbook of Socialization Theory and Research* (Chicago: Rand McNally, 1969), pp. 347–480.

10. See Jean Piaget, *The Child and Reality* (New York: Penguin Books, 1976), chap. 2.

11. See Piaget, *Six Psychological Studies*, pp. 8–17. See also Jean Piaget and Bärbel Inhelder, *The Psychology of the Child* (New York: Basic Books, 1969), pp. 1–27.

12. Erikson, *Childhood and Society*, pp. 247–251; Erik Erikson, *Identity, Youth and Crisis* (New York: Norton, 1968), pp. 96–107.

13. Erik Erikson, *Insight and Responsibility* (New York: Norton, 1964), pp. 115–118.

14. Piaget, *Six Psychological Studies*, pp. 17–38. See Jean Piaget, *Play, Dreams and Imitation in Childhood* (New York: Norton, 1962).

15. Ginsberg and Opper, *Piaget's Theory of Intellectual Development*, pp. 163ff.

16. Lawrence Kohlberg, "The Child as Moral Philosopher," *Psychology Today* (September, 1968), pp. 25–30.

17. See Erikson, *Identity, Youth and Crisis*, p. 97.

18. Erikson, *Childhood and Society*, p. 252; *Insight and Responsibility*, pp. 118–120.

19. Erikson, *Childhood and Society*, p. 255.

20. Erikson, *Identity, Youth and Crisis*, pp. 115–122; *Childhood and Society*, pp. 255–258; *Insight and Responsibility*, pp. 120–122.

21. See especially Erikson, *Identity, Youth and Crisis*, p. 119.

22. Piaget, *Six Psychological Studies*, pp. 38–60; Piaget and Inhelder, *The Psychology of the Child*, pp. 92–129. See also Piaget, "Piaget's Theory."

23. Lawrence Kohlberg, "The Child as Moral Philosopher," *Psychology Today* (Sept., 1968), pp. 25–30; Lawrence Kohlberg, "Moral Stages and Moralization," in Thomas Lickona, ed., *Moral Development and Behavior* (New York: Holt, Rinehart and Winston, 1976), pp. 31–32.

24. Erikson, *Childhood and Society*, pp. 258–261; *Identity, Youth and Crisis*, pp. 122–128. *Insight and Responsibility*, pp. 122–124.

25. A point made forcefully in conversations by both John Gibb and Robert G. Kegan.

26. See Piaget, *Six Psychological Studies*, pp. 60–70; Bärbel Inhelder and Jean Piaget, *The Growth of Logical Thinking from Childhood to Adolescence* (New York: Basic Books, 1958), pp. 46–66.

27. Inhelder and Piaget, *The Growth of Logical Thinking from Childhood to Adolescence*, pp. 46–66.

28. Piaget, *Six Psychological Studies*, pp. 64–70.

29. Robert L. Selman, "The Developmental Conceptions of Interpersonal Relations," publication of the Harvard–Judge Baker Social Reasoning Project, December, 1974, vols. 1 & 2. See also Robert L. Selman, "Social Cognitive Understanding," in T. Lickona, ed., *Moral Development and Behavior*, pp. 299–316.

30. Lawrence Kohlberg, "Education, Moral Development and Faith," *Journal of Moral Education*, vol. 4, no. 1 (1974), pp. 5–16.

31. Kohlberg, "Moral Stages and Moralization," pp. 38–39.

32. This is a point I have never seen Erikson explicitly make in any of his writings, but one to which I think he would agree.

33. Erikson, *Childhood and Society*, pp. 261–263; *Identity, Youth and Crisis*, pp. 128–135.

34. Erikson, *Insight and Responsibility*, pp. 124–127.

35. Kohlberg, "Moral Stages and Moralization."

36. Erikson, *Childhood and Society*, p. 263.

37. Erikson, *Childhood and Society*, pp. 263–266; *Identity, Youth and and Crisis*, pp. 135–138; *Insight and Responsibility*, pp. 127–130.

38. Lawrence Kohlberg, "Continuities in Childhood and Adult Moral Reasoning Revisited," in Paul B. Baltes and K. Warner Schaie, eds., *Life-Span Developmental Psychology* (New York: Academic Press, 1973), pp. 179–204.

39. Lawrence Kohlberg, "From Is to Ought: How to Commit the Naturalistic Fallacy and Get Away with It in the Study of Moral Development," in T. Mischel, ed., *Cognitive Development and Epistemology* (New York: Academic Press, 1971), pp. 151–284; Kohlberg, "Moral Stages and Moralization."

40. See Piaget, *The Insights and Illusions of Philosophy*, especially the first and concluding chapters.

41. Erikson, *Childhood and Society*, pp. 266–268; *Identity, Youth and Crisis*, pp. 138–139; *Insight and Responsibility*, pp. 130–321.

42. Erikson, *Childhood and Society*, pp. 268–269; *Identity, Youth and Crisis*, pp. 139–141; *Insight and Responsibility*, pp. 132–134.

Part III

Dynamics of Faith and Human Development

||||||||||||||||||||||||||||||||||||||||||||||||||||||||||||||||||||||||||||||||||||||||||||||||||

Though our imaginary symposium with Piaget, Kohlberg and Erikson has disbanded, in this part we shall need to continue our conversations with them. Here our task and invitation is to move toward describing stages of faith. One evening in the 1950s the great American Jesuit theologian, Gustav Weigel, and the influential German-American Protestant theologian, Paul Tillich, engaged in a two-and-a-half hour debate in a commons room at Harvard. As reported by one observer, "Tillich was saying of Gustav Weigel that his theology was so static it was embalmed! And Weigel was saying that Tillich's theology was so dynamic it was fluid, if not loose!" After the debate the two men embraced as the warm friends they were and agreed that the truth lay somewhere between their two positions.

Developmental theories give us a way of claiming that kind of in-between position. They allow us to speak of the dynamics of change and transformation. They also allow us to focus on equilibrium and continuity.

As we focus here on the developmental dynamics of faith we must keep in mind that the story of "stages" of faith and human development can give us only half of a much larger and richer picture. Stage theories, such as Piaget's, Kohlberg's or Erikson's, gain their great power by describing predictable changes in human thought and adaptation *in largely formal terms.* That is to say, they present to us the characteristic patterns of knowing, reasoning and adapting in ways that describe general features of human growth, applicable to all of us, despite the vast differences we recognize in our temperaments, our unique experiences and the contents and details of our particular life stories. Developmental theories necessarily depict "every persons'" stories. Therefore their categories of description are necessarily formal and without specific content, general and not particular. So, as we join the company of those who are trying to chart and map the human life cycle, as we share our effort to clarify the developmental dynamics of faith as part of the human story, I ask you to keep in mind this necessarily formal character of our descriptions of faith stages. As we consider aspects of the lives of people we have interviewed, using the stage descriptions to illumine and clarify their patterns of faith, we will constantly be reminded that the stages tell only part of the story. In later sections I try to redress the balance, looking much more carefully at what is particular and unique in each life story. We will consider how powerful in the shaping of our lives are the particular images, beliefs, symbols and themes of our faiths.

Our task now involves laying the groundwork for understanding the formal descriptions of faith stages. To do this we need to refocus our approach back to faith. Then we must account for how we have selectively built on the foundations of Piaget, Kohlberg and Erikson. That done, the theory of faith stages can be described.

12. The Dynamic Triad of Faith

||||||||||||||||||||||||||||||||||||||||||||||||||||||||||||||||||||||||||||||||||||||||||||||||||||||

Wherever I lecture or speak about faith development research I meet people who suggest that I should choose some other term to describe the focus of this work. I find the variety of substitutes they suggest interesting; I find their protests against using the word *faith* instructive. Several groups of critics have a deep suspicion that the concept of faith is really inseparable from religion and belief, Wilfred Cantwell Smith's work notwithstanding! They reject the claim that faith is a generic feature of the human struggle to find and maintain meaning and that it may or may not find religious expression. Their proposed substitutions for faith go in two directions. Those who are favorable to religion and who would like to see this kind of work be fully identified with the scientific study of religion feel that I would be more honest if I simply described it as research on religious development. On the other hand, persons who fear that the linkage of faith and religion taints or limits the usefulness of an otherwise promising body of theory urge that I take the opposite direction. They suggest the use of some more strictly secular term for our focal concern. They have proposed "world view development," "belief system formation," or, on occasion, the "development of consciousness" as categories that would help us avoid confusion.

Two other quite different groups oppose our use of faith for understandable reasons. One of these groups are the Christian critics, particularly those who are heirs of Protestant neo-orthodoxy's stringent commitment to the Reformation's stress on faith as solely the gift of God's grace, given uniquely in Jesus Christ. They protest that we are misusing the term. They claim that faith is an indigenously Christian category and that it owes its proper understanding to Luther and Calvin's reinterpretation of St. Paul's theology.[1] Psychological critics, on the other hand, argue that what we call faith and the stages we present here might with less confusion be designated as *ego* and as stages of *ego development*. They cite broad parallels between our stages and those of Professor Jane Loevinger and point to our common reliance on Erikson and Kohlberg as reasons for this suggestion.[2] They tend to believe, as do the Christian critics, though for contrasting reasons, that our concept of faith is too broad and inclusive.

Our use of the term *faith* does make many people uncomfortable. As Harvey Cox once said to me, "There is something to offend everyone in this way of talking about faith!" Yet I think we cannot afford to give up faith as our focal concept despite its complexity, its likelihood of being misunderstood, and the difficulty of pinning it down precisely. There simply is no other concept that holds together those various interrelated dimensions of human knowing, valuing, committing and acting that must be considered together if we want to understand the making and maintaining of human meaning.

In Part I, I spoke of faith as a dynamic existential stance, a way of leaning into and finding or giving meaning to the conditions of our lives. With considerable attention to Smith's research, I distinguished faith from religion and belief, while also showing some of their relations. We named the social and relational dimensions of faith, seeing our trusts in and loyalties to other persons in community—and to centers of value and power to which they are also loyal—as forming triadic or covenantal patterns. We looked at faith as a way of knowing and seeing the conditions of our lives in relation to more or less conscious images of an ultimate environment. All of these movements or dimensions of faith are part of the same complex action. All of these dimensions play critical roles in shaping our actions and reactions in life. They form our initiatives and responses, our interpretations and our guiding goals. As such, faith is an integral part of one's "character" or "personality."[3]

In the most formal and comprehensive terms I can state it, *faith* is:

People's evolved and evolving ways
of experiencing self, others and world
(as they construct them)

as related to and affected by the
ultimate conditions of existence
(as they construct them)

and of shaping their lives' purposes and meanings,
trusts and loyalties, in light of the

character of being, value and power
determining the ultimate conditions
of existence (as grasped in their
operative images—conscious and
unconscious—of them).

This characterization of faith is, I will grant, formidable in its formalism. Immediately I must ask you to recall all that we said earlier about
faith as social and relational. You must give flesh to those definitional
bones by calling to mind the variety of communities with and in which
persons go about composing (or recomposing) self, others and world in
light of their relatedness to shared images of an ultimate environment.
Let your remembering include communities as disparate as the devotees
of Krishna consciousness, the Jonestown cult in Guyana and the committed adherents of an Enlightenment rationalism all convened in a
recent university symposium. Let the flesh you bring to this formal
characterization of faith include the "civil religion" of a veteran's organization, the revolutionary fervor of a black liberation movement in southern Africa and the quiet serenity of a Zen Buddhist monk who has
attained *satori.*

But consider the virtues of our formal characterization. It does, I
believe, capture the essential triadic dynamics of faith. Wherever we
properly speak of faith it involves people's shaping or testing their lives'
defining directions and relationships with others in accordance with
coordinates of value and power recognized as ultimate.

Let me share a story that in a homely yet powerful way gives concreteness both to our characterization of faith and to the triadic movement
that is faith's essential characteristic. Flannery O'Connor had the awe-
some gift of being able to depict the commonplace in such ways that
we see in it universal contours of the human condition. One of her short
stories gives an unforgettable if very local window on the triadic dynamics of faith.[4]

Ruller McFarney, an eleven-year-old boy, is engaged in solitary, imaginative play. Pretending to be a sheriff, taking a crew of bad actors into
custody in the Wild West, suddenly he notices a for-real movement in
the bushes. Investigating, Ruller sees a turkey—a big turkey—head
pivoting, eyes shining wildly, red wattle dangling. The turkey stays. Its
left wing sags. The boy thinks how great it would be to carry that turkey
home. That would show them; that would put to rest all that ambiguous
parental talk about his playing alone too much and his being an

"unusual" boy. He shifts his footing to grab through the brush. Limping and dragging its wing, the turkey eludes his grasp. Around the bushes and into the field the boy pursues the crippled bird. He must catch it before it gets to the woods. Sweaty and breathless he comes close many times. Nearing the woods, sensing that he must make his decisive move now, the intent boy smashes the top of his head into a low-hanging tree branch. Panting and smarting, momentarily confused from the blow, he rolls over in the dust. His shirt is torn, his arms bloody with scratches, his vision of the triumphant capture and hometaking of the bird dashed. Someone has played a bad trick on him. Tentatively he begins to curse. "Hell!" "He-ell!" "God-dammit to hell!" "God-dammit to hell, good Lord from Jerusalem!"[5] The forbidden words make his heart beat with guilty excitement. He imagines himself walking into the house, head bruised, clothes torn, empty-handed, turning back their scornful curiosity with vile assertiveness. He fantasizes a tough life of crime and adventure. He figures he could be a smart jewel thief and have all Scotland Yard chasing him. He gets up:

> God could go around sticking things in your face and making you chase them all afternoon for nothing.
> You shouldn't think that way about God, though. (His grandmother's admonitions reinforce this voice.)
> But that was the way he felt. If that was the way he felt, could he help it?[6]

Then a miracle—There it was! Speckled bronze feathers rumpled, the still turkey lay in a ditch by the woods. Miss O'Connor tells how Ruller cautiously examines the turkey, finds where it was shot and then begins to grasp the meaning of this remarkable event:

> It came down on him in an instant; he was . . . an . . . unusual . . . child.
> Maybe that was why the turkey was there. . . .
> Maybe it was to keep him from going bad.
> Maybe God wanted to keep him from that.
> Maybe God had knocked it out right there where he'd see it when he got up.
> Maybe God was in the bush now, waiting for him to make up his mind.
> Ruller blushed. . . .
> Maybe finding the turkey was a sign.[7]

We see Ruller carrying the heavy bird home. He goes through town the long way so everyone can see his trophy, his sign. He carries his new specialness with thoughtful gladness. He enjoys the envious glances of other boys, the curious questions of adults—including those of a hunter, the probable author of the bird's wound. He resolves to give a beggar a dime and asks God to provide a beggar as a further sign.

This sign too is provided. You must read for yourself how Ruller, so close to the triumphant entry he had imagined, authorized with the sanction of this pair of signs, suffers a separation from his significant burden. Innocent, oblivious to the threat posed by three curious older boys, he lets them hold the bird. They run away with it, laughing derisively. God's unusual child lost his signifying turkey. Miss O'Connor concludes the story:

> He turned toward home, almost creeping. He walked four blocks and then suddenly, noticing that it was dark, he began to run. He ran faster and faster, and as he turned up the road to his house, his heart was running as fast as his legs and he was certain that Something Awful was tearing behind him with its arms rigid and its fingers ready to clutch.[8]

The triadic dynamics of faith? Let's see. Ruller is at play; his solitary make-believe serves as a way of transcending and coping with a world constituted by parents, a "bad" older brother and a religious grandmother. His play space is intruded upon by something more extraordinary than his fantasy. An ambiguous omen, the game bird occasions an expansion and refocusing of Ruller's fantasy. Swiftly re-imaging his situation, he lets himself anticipate the impact of his bringing home the turkey. Now the pursuit and capture becomes a telescoped voyage of heroic quest, a miniature search for the holy grail. As the investment of energy grows, the fanciful possibility becomes a serious endeavor; the boy sees himself as a barehanded hunter of manly and admirable proportions. The low-hanging limb strikes as a hard reminder of a real world that does not automatically accommodate fantasies, even heartfelt ones. The presence of an objective world and the sudden realization of the solipsism of his enmythed condition brings a shameful self-consciousness, a sense of being seen, exposed, tricked by someone or something beyond himself. Out of a vague shame and a sense of being the butt of someone's malicious trick, he (in another playful mood) begins to experiment with words and phrases associated with the filth of that "back side" exposed in shame. The profanity names God as Trickster and expresses his protest. His delight, his mirth, approaches ecstasy in breaking across forbidden boundaries in his wicked words and fantasies. This seductive violation draws him out in such a way that he experiences a sudden, anxious reversal, a shudder, in which he feels vulnerable and exposed before a power whose name he has profaned.

When the miracle occurs despite all wickedness and the grail is delivered into his hands, the whole saga has to be re-mythed. The profaned Trickster, the malicious, teasing manipulator who seduces and exposes, suddenly can be seen as the God who elects graciously, testing and chastising those whom he especially favors. The sought for prize is *given*, not taken, and with it comes a far more significant gift. Ruller now has a way to go home in a double sense. His bringing the bird will gain for him the recognition of manly competence he desires. But more profoundly, the gift of the talisman bird ratifies a specialness—his being an "unusual child"—that may mean being set apart for a great calling or destiny. Now he can go home to the religious ethos mediated by his grandmother without the vague sense of guilt and shame over fantasies and contemplated transgressions that had begun to make him feel alien.

When Ruller, so close to this double victory, has the turkey taken from him, we can only wonder about the cavity left by this torn-out personal myth. His very exaltation led to the naive, trusting thoughtlessness that set him up to lose the bird. First creeping home, then running, he is again in a shrunken world bare of myth, a shrunken emptied boy, stalked by Something Awful. Is this a third sign?

As infants and children our ways of constructing self, others and world —and our ways of imaging the character of the power(s) determining the ultimate conditions of our lives—are more changing and volatile than they will be later. Hierophanies, the giving of signs—both blessed and cursed—are likely to occur more frequently for children than for adults. Though the adult's susceptibility to seduction into fantasy may have lessened, Ruller's experience of being drawn from make-believe into the zone of imaging and re-imaging the ultimate valences and meanings of his life is not foreign to us.[9] At critical junctures in our lives the normal fabric of our everyday patterns can be interrupted, even as the turkey interrupted Ruller's serious play. As we set off pursuing this interruption or preserving the integrity of our lifestyle against it, we too look behind the precipitating instance. We too wonder vaguely who or what has sent *this* into our lives. Our images of the character of the power(s) determining the ultimate conditions of our lives arise out of and are tested in these kinds of experiences. For increasing numbers of us cancer is this kind of interruption. The moving account of his struggle with terminal cancer and of completing his last book in a race with death, told by historian Cornelius Ryan and his wife Kathryn Morgan Ryan in *A Private Battle,* gives us a public instance. Ryan's faith, certainly not orthodox Catholic, turned toward dialogue with the author of life and death as he strove heroically to complete his history of the abortive "Market Garden" plan in World War II *(A Bridge Too Far)*. Out of his dialogue with and acceptance of the challenge of the disease, Ryan came to feel that his four years of dying were the culminating period of his life, bringing it to fulfillment. In the interplay between such invasions of "normality" and the symbolic representations of the transcendent that have grasped us, we compose images (and perhaps beliefs about and concepts of) the ultimate conditions of our existence. We have varying degrees of consciousness regarding these working images of ultimate reality. But conscious or unconscious, they affect the setting of our goals, the relationships we make and maintain and the ways we respond to emergencies and crises. They have an impact upon the ways we make plans and on our efforts to live our lives with integrity. These are the triadic dynamics of faith.

13. Structural-Developmental Theories and Faith

‖‖

My purpose now is to indicate some of the ways the structural developmentalists Piaget and Kohlberg have contributed decisively to our research and theory in the study of faith development. I shall also point out some of the limitations of their approaches for our project and say some things about how we are trying to correct or go beyond these limits.

Among the most important contributions of the Piaget-Kohlberg school to our project is its broadly *epistemological focus*. Epistemology has to do with the study of *how* we know. A strong theme in the theological writings on faith of H. Richard Niebuhr and Paul Tillich has to do with faith as a way of *seeing* the world. Faith for them *is* a kind of knowing, a constructing of the world in light of certain disclosures of the character of reality as a whole that are taken as decisive. Different faiths are alternate modes of being in the world that arise out of contrasting ways of composing the ultimate conditions of existence. Ways of *being* and ways of *seeing* are reciprocal. As Niebuhr puts it in *The Responsible Self*, we shape our actions and responses in life in accordance with our interpretations of the larger patterns of actions that impinge upon us. Communities of faith are communities of shared interpretations. The previous section's discussion of the triadic dynamics of faith should have made clear how crucial a part knowing, as the construction of self, others, world and ultimate environment, plays in faith as we study it. The broad epistemological emphasis in the structural-developmental theories serves us well as a model for understanding faith as a way of knowing and interpreting. To make it serve adequately, however, we have to widen the scope of knowing involved and account for the interrelatedness of several different modes of knowing in faith. Of this widened view of knowing I say more in a moment.

A second major gift to faith development research from the structural-developmental tradition lies in its focus on the structuring of knowing as it gives form to the contents of knowledge. The structural approach suggested a way of focusing on some features of faith that may be universal despite the great variety of particular symbolic, thematic and imaginal contents. I readily grant that my appropriation of the structural approach in the study of faith has added to the difficulty of distinguishing between "structure" and "content." It has also required that we try to incorporate the structuring of affective, valuational and imaginal modes of knowing that Piaget and Kohlberg have sought to avoid. These difficulties notwithstanding, the structural approach has enabled us to find and describe structural features of faith that make comparisons possible across a wide range of "content" differences. No less important, the structural focus has made it possible for us to systematically compare and contrast differing styles or stages of faith among persons who stand in the same faith community or content-tradition.

In the fictional dialogue of Part II, I shared some of the richness of a third significant contribution that the structural-developmental theories make to faith development research. This contribution has to do with their rigorous concept of structural stages and with the actual descriptions of cognitive and moral reasoning stages as they have worked them out. Stages of faith deal with different domains of knowing than either the cognitive stages of Piaget or the moral stages of Kohlberg. Faith stages arise out of integration of modes of knowing and valuing that Piagetian and Kohlbergian stage theories have intended to avoid. Faith stages are not identical with and cannot be reduced either to cognitive or moral stages or to some mixture of the two. Nonetheless, in any holistic approach to the human construction of meaning, account must be given of the relations of reasoning to imagination, of moral judgment making to symbolic representation, of ecstatic intuition to logical deduction. I do not at all mean to imply that we have found adequate ways to model these relationships. But we have found it important to show the correlations we find between Piaget's and Kohlberg's stages (and those of Robert Selman on social perspective taking) with the forms of knowing and valuing that make up a faith stage. Moreover, we believe that the faith stages meet the structural-developmental criteria for stages. They provide generalizable, formal descriptions of integrated sets of operations of knowing and valuing. These stagelike positions are related in a sequence we believe to be invariant. Each new stage integrates and carries forward the operations of all the previous stages. (Piaget and Kohlberg describe this cumulative integration as "hierarchical." For reasons I will make clear later, I propose a different, spiraling model.) I do not feel warranted in making claims of "universality" for our stages, beyond the contention that the formal descriptions of them are generalizable and can be tested cross-culturally.

A fourth contribution of the structural developmentalists to the conception of our work needs to be acknowledged. Piaget, Kohlberg and their followers have resolutely approached the study of development as an *interactional* process. Behaviorist theories in psychology, such as those of B. F. Skinner, tend to see persons as passive and malleable, their patterns of action largely determined by influences from their environments.[10] Maturationist theories, on the other hand, view growth or development as primarily the unfolding of innately programmed organismic capacities. (Arnold Gesell and R. J. Havighurst represent this position.) The latter deemphasize the significance of environmental factors except as supports or hindrances to an essentially self-guiding process. The structural-developmental interactional approach calls us to view development as resulting from the interchange between an active, innovative subject and a dynamic, changing environment. To be sure, the adaptive capacities of subjects are not unlimited. We have a genetic potential for a given range of structuring possibilities, and these—as we saw in our conversations with Piaget and Kohlberg—are intrinsically related to maturation. Nonetheless, *adaptation is invention;* it is the activation and creative employment of our genetically potentiated structuring (knowing and acting) capacities. Similarly, environments have "structure" too. As the tree decisively interrupted Ruller's mythic construction of the turkey chase, so the environment "pushes back" against our structuring activities with pattern and reality of its own. As our discussion of the triadic dynamics of faith sought to show, faith is an interactional process.

Further, for Piaget and Kohlberg structural development occurs when, in the interaction of subject and environment, the subject must construct new modes of knowing and acting in order to meet new challenges of the environment. Development results from efforts to restore balance between subject and environment when some factor of maturation or of environmental change has disturbed a previous equilibrium. Growth and development in faith also result from life crises, challenges and the kinds of disruptions that theologians call revelation.

Each of these brings disequilibrium and requires changes in our ways of seeing and being in faith.

A final important influence from the structural developmentalists on our research has to do with the *normative* directions and implications of their work. Without sacrificing commitment to empirical rigor in the testing of their claims, Piaget and Kohlberg have offered what we may call philosophical psychologies. By this I mean that they have not shrunk back from the implication that more developed structural stages of knowing are, in important ways, more comprehensive and adequate than the less developed ones; that the more developed stages make possible a knowing that in some senses is "more true" than that of less developed stages. Instinctively many of us reared in a pluralistic, democratic ethos and saturated with an implicit values relativism feel offended by claims like these. In the domain of faith the assertion that more developed stages are in significant ways more adequate than less developed ones has to be made with even greater cautions and qualifications than in the cognitive or moral reasoning spheres. Yet we cannot (and will not) avoid making and trying to corroborate that claim.

The research on faith development owes a great debt of gratitude to Piaget, Kohlberg and many of their associates. We shall continue to acknowledge and build on that indebtedness. But the structural-developmental perspective, as they have shaped it, also has some serious limitations that must be faced and dealt with in the effort to treat faith in structural-developmental terms. The first such difficulty arises out of the way Piaget, and Kohlberg following him, have conceptually separated cognition or knowing from emotion or affection. In the context of intellectual development it makes sense to focus inquiry on the emergence of logical operations and to bracket any serious attention to emotional development. Piaget quite freely acknowledges the importance of feeling and the affections in everyday life and as a part of the life of the mind. Only cognitive operations, however, exhibit logicomathematical structures. The development of rational maturity means precisely that capacity for "objectivity" that makes matters of emotion or affective, subjective bias immaterial. While we may want to question the adequacy of Piaget's cognitive theory even for dealing with accounts of the actual processes of scientific discovery and insight,[11] it is quite defensible to separate cognitive and affective structures as he does and to devote one's prime attention to the evolution of logical structures.

This theoretical separation of cognition and affection is less defensible

in the study of the development of moral judgment making. At least this
is the case if one continues to work with as narrow a notion of cognition
as does Piaget. In fact, what we find in both Piaget's and Kohlberg's
theories are accounts that begin (in the earliest stages) with a much
broader and undifferentiated attention to cognitive processes. Successive
stages in their theories represent steps in the differentiation of strictly
logical forms of knowing from other important, if different, modalities
of knowing. Successive stages represent qualitative movements in the
"purification" of reason. Because he studies the evolution of the logical
operations that make scientific inquiry possible, Piaget can differentiate
logical structures from other ways of knowing less ambiguously than can
Kohlberg. In moral judgments the valuations of actions and their consequences as well as evaluations of self in relation to the expectations of
the self and others are difficult to conceive, even in formal and structural
terms, apart from inherent affective or emotive elements in knowing.
My contention is that Kohlberg's theory already begins a fruitful (if
largely unacknowledged) expansion of the notion of cognition in a way
that we must further broaden (and deepen) in a structural-developmental approach to faith. In this broadening and deepening we must not lose
sight of the role of reason, in the more limited sense in which Piaget
describes it, as part of the more comprehensive knowing that is faith.

I have found it useful, in this regard, to make a distinction between
two kinds of reasoning, one that describes the relatively narrow understanding of cognition with which Piaget works and another that characterizes the necessary combination of rationality and passionality that
faith involves. The first I call the *logic of rational certainty*. This mode
of knowing aims at objectivity understood as a knowing free from all
particular or subjective investigation. Its truths need to be impersonal,
propositional, demonstrable and replicable. The logic of rational certainty, however, is a misleading ideal when we speak about forms of
knowing in which the constitution of the knowing self is part of what
is at stake. The model of disinterestedness represented by scientific
inquiry does not fit with the kind of knowing involved in moral reasoning
or in faith's compositions. This is not to say that there is not a form of
disinterestedness or "objectivity" in moral and faith knowing. It is to say
this latter mode of knowing proceeds in a manner in which the knowing
self is continually being confirmed or modified in the knowing. For this
latter, more comprehensive form of knowing I have chosen the term the
logic of conviction. Let me quote myself on this point:

In both faith-knowing and the kind of moral-knowing which gives rise to choice and action, the constitution or modification of the self is always an issue. In these kinds of constitutive-knowing not only is the "known" being constructed, but there is also a simultaneous extension, modification, or reconstitution of *the knower in relation to the known.* To introduce this freedom, risk, passion, and subjectivity into the Piaget-Kohlberg paradigm (as we must in faith development) requires that we examine the relationship of what we may call a *logic of rational certainty* (Piaget's major concern) to what we may call a *logic of conviction.* (I use the term "logic" here in a metaphorical sense, designating two major kinds of structuring activity which interact in the constitutive knowing that is faith.) This relationship between the two "logics" is not one of choice between alternatives. A logic of conviction does not negate a logic of rational certainty. But the former, being more inclusive, does contextualize, qualify, and anchor the latter. Recognition of a more comprehensive "logic of conviction" does lead us to see that the logic of rational certainty is part of a larger epistemological structuring activity, and is not to be confused with the whole.[12]

In widening our understanding of knowing so as to include the logic of conviction, we must not capitulate to critics who see this as representing an anti-rational or irrational understanding of faith.[13] Rather we need to see "reasoning in faith" as a balanced interaction between the more limited and specialized and the more comprehensive and holistic logics we have described.

We encounter a second set of limitations of Piaget's and Kohlberg's approaches as we build on them to understand faith. This has to do with their very restrictive understanding of the role of imagination in knowing, their neglect of symbolic processes generally and the related lack of attention to unconscious structuring processes other than those constituting reasoning. Piaget mainly understands imagination as a function of childhood fantasy. Imagination is the mode of playful fantasy in which the child assimilates the world into his or her schemes without attention to "reality." On the other hand, intuitive thought, for Piaget, is reality oriented. It is the precursor of logical operations in preoperational children, and it is *accommodatory* in the sense that in intuition the child attempts to shape his or her representations of the world in accordance with reality. It is intuition that goes to school in Piaget, not imagination. As the intuition shapes up into (and is superseded by) the reversible operations of concrete thought, the distorting temptations of imagination and fantasy are more strictly relegated to the play world. With the emergence of formal operational thought and its transcen-

dence of the limitations of concrete experience, Piaget recognizes the
return of a form of imagination, though now closely disciplined by the
logical structures and combinatorial processes of formal operations. Piaget makes enticing comments about adolescents' capacities for ideological constructions, their interest in holistic visions of ideal societies and
the like. But those capacities he links to the realm of "faith" and,
following Kant, sees that kind of imaginative construction as having
little to do with knowledge, properly speaking. For Piaget, we might say,
such ideological visions are a form of serious adult "play." The structures
of formal operational logic do make possible the development of propositions and theories. These only lead to knowledge, however, when
focused on phenomena capable of being empirically investigated, proving or disproving one's theoretical claims.[14]

I do not fault Piaget for denying that ideological constructions are
knowledge in his strict sense of the term. Our challenge, however, since
faith in some form is necessary and inevitable for human beings, is to
describe what kind of knowing faith is and to characterize the operations
that constitute it.

This latter domain—the domain of faith and of the logic of conviction—
involves recognizing the role played in faith of the modes of knowing we call
ecstatic and imaginative. As is becoming generally recognized, the mind
employs the more aesthetically oriented right hemisphere of the brain in these
kinds of knowing. To my knowledge none of the Piagetian cognitive-construc-
tivists . . . have given any significant attention to the bihemispheric, bimodal
forms of thought involved in the constitutive-knowing that is faith. To move
in this direction requires coming to terms with modes of thought that employ
images, symbols, and synesthesial fusions of sense and feeling. It means taking
account of so-called regressive movements in which the psyche returns to
preconceptual, prelinguistic modes and memories, and to primitive sources of
energizing energy, bringing them into consciousness with resultant reconstru-
als of the experience world. To deal adequately with faith and with faith's
dynamic role in the total self-constitutive activity of ego means trying to give
theoretical attention to the transformation in consciousness—rapid and dramatic in sudden conversion, more gradual and incremental in faith growth—
which results from the re-cognition of self-others-world in light of knowing
the self as constituted by a center of value powerful enough to require or
enable recentering one's ultimate environment.[15]

In a subsequent section these matters will occupy us in some fascinating ways. For now my primary point is to underscore how we must

necessarily expand the concept of cognition or knowing in order to comprehend faith's imaginal and generative knowing. As Fr. William Lynch writes: "By what and for what shall we be judged more than by and for our images?"[16] We are trying to grasp the inner dialectic of rational logic in the dynamics of a larger, more comprehensive logic of convictional orientation.

Finally, it is no critical remark to point out that neither Piaget nor Kohlberg has offered a theory of the epistemological or moral self. Kohlberg and Selman's elaboration of the development of social perspective taking moves a considerable step in this direction with its clarification of the cognitive bases of self-reflection. Kohlberg took another step toward incorporating a perspective on the developing self in his consideration of the necessity of experiences of leaving home and of the assumption of moral responsibility for others for the development of postconventional moral reasoning.[17] Faith development requires that we push further in this direction. A structural-developmental theory of faith must be a theory of personal knowing and acting. This means neither an individualistic theory, nor one that gives up the commitment to generalizability. Rather, it means a commitment to take seriously that our previous decisions and actions shape our character, as do the stories and images by which we live. It means a commitment to take seriously the fact that we are formed in social communities and that our ways of seeing the world are profoundly shaped by the shared images and constructions of our group or class.[18] It means, further, a commitment to relate structural stages of faith to the predictable crises and challenges of developmental eras and to take life histories seriously in its study.

This last point leads well into a brief consideration of the ways we have drawn on that other major school of developmental psychology, the psychosocial theorists. Erikson is the primary figure for us here, although in recent years we have attended with interest to psychosocial theories of adult development offered by Levinson, Vaillant, Gould and others, and as popularized by Gail Sheehy.[19]

14. Psychosocial Development and Faith

IIIIIIIIIIIIIIIIIIIIIIIIIIIIIIIIIIIIIIIIIIIIIIIIIIIIIIIIIIIIIIIIIIIIIIIIIIIIIIIIIIIIIIIIIIIIIIIIIIIIIIIIIIIIIIIIIIIIIIIIIIIIII

As we showed in our presentation of Erikson in Part II, his theory undertakes the coordination of a dizzying range of factors. In the study of ego development he has tried to relate biological maturation with changes in social role and to coordinate both with an account of persons' conscious and unconscious psychic modes of adaptation. Erikson is frequently criticized for the breadth and inclusiveness—and the resulting lack of precision—of his constructions and interpretations. Efforts to design empirical tests of the claims of his theory have yielded very mixed results.[20] Nonetheless, the central lines of his account of the growth and crises of the healthy personality have much to commend them. They were formed out of the testing and refinement in clinical experience of Freud's pioneering work. They were tested and corrected for bias in the context of several kinds of cross-cultural studies. Moreover, their use and widespread intuitive acceptance by a large and thoughtful audience represents another important, if unscientific, kind of validation.

From the beginning Erikson's account of stages or eras and the emergent crises which typify them has served as an important framework for our studies. Initially I was inclined to hypothesize stages of faith that largely paralleled Erikson's eras. After encountering the structural-developmental theories, however, and after coming to terms with their more rigorous understanding of structural stages, I began to change the focus of my effort to find stages of faith. I and my associates began to rely on Erikson's theory more as a background against which to hear and analyze the life stories that persons shared with us. We began to realize that a time of movement from one of Erikson's eras to another frequently correlated with or helped to precipitate a change in the structural operations of faith. *But not always.* More recently we have come to see that a person's structural stage of faith (correlated with other structural aspects) has important implications for the way the person will construct the experience of crisis that inaugurates a new Eriksonian developmental era. Research by Richard Shulik, for example, has shown that elderly persons best described by faith Stage 3* construct their experience of the process of aging in qualitatively different ways than do those best described by faith Stages 4 or 5.[21]

Any effort to synthesize the perspectives of structural-developmental and psychosocial theories must come to terms with what Shulik's findings help us to see: in terms of the structural stages, normal persons can reach a longlasting or even a lifetime equilibration at any Stage from 2 on. This fact affects the *way* they experience and deal with the psychosocial crises Erikson has identified, but it in no way means that they will avoid or bypass them. Research is likely to show that a person of twenty-two, whose moral and faith structuring is best described by Stage 2, will indeed encounter the physical, social and emotional issues of the crisis of intimacy. But he or she will "construct" and experience them without benefit of a capacity for mutual interpersonal perspective taking, without a self-reflective sense of identity and with a construction of the ultimate environment likely based on intuitions of cosmic reciprocity.** As will become clear in subsequent sections of the book, other twenty-two year olds, structurally operating at Stage 3 or 4, will construct, interpret and respond to the issues of the intimacy crisis in qualitatively different ways than one at Stage 2. In some respects, we might say, *it is not even the same crisis for persons at these three different stages.*

Perhaps a chart will help to visualize the interplay we see between structural and psychosocial stages (Table 3.1). The left-hand column lists structural-developmental stages. Across the bottom are the psychosocial stages of Erikson. The solid segments of the horizontal bar lines indicate the kind of optimal correlations between structural equili-

---

*Faith stages will be distinguished from other stages in this manner.

**Cosmic reciprocity means the projection of a reciprocal sense of fairness—that is, goodness should be rewarded, badness punished; if I do my part you should do yours,— as the guiding image for grasping the character of the ultimate environment. It is a "pre-personal" way of constructing an image of God or reality. A Stage 2 atheist is one whose rejected God is of this sort.

Table 3.1 Interplay Between Structural and Psychosocial Stages

Structural Stages

	Trust vs. Mistrust	Autonomy vs. Shame & Doubt	Initiative vs. Guilt	Industry vs. Inferiority	Identity vs. Role confusion	Intimacy vs. Isolation	Generativity vs. Stagnation	Integrity vs. Despair
6								
5								
4								
3								
2								
1								
0								

| Average Ages | 0–2 | 2–3 | 3–6 | 6–12 | 13–20 | 21–– | 35–– | 60–– |

brations at each stage that would shape the person's experience of all the subsequent psychosocial crises.

In sum, Erikson's eras and crises provide a helpful guide to what Sheehy calls "predictable crises" of the life cycle. From our standpoint, those crises of trust, autonomy, initiative, and so forth, which are reasonably correlated with maturation and age, represent life challenges with which all persons must deal. As a part of their coping, in their adaptation, faith forms, functions and is changed. If Piaget and Kohlberg have given us impetus to study the structuring activity of faith, Erikson has helped us in many ways to focus on the *functional* aspect of faith, the expected existential issues with which it must help people cope at whatever structural stage across the life cycle.

Almost as fundamental for our work as Erikson's theory of the developmental eras and their virtues has been his own understanding of and attention to faith. His account of the crisis of the first stage, basic trust vs. mistrust, avowedly deals with the foundations of faith in human life. Erikson carefully avoids any heavy-handed determinism of the sort that would suggest that everything decisive for faith occurs in the first twelve or the first sixty months of life. But he does make plain how powerful a factor the quality of the child's first mutuality with the conditions of his or her existence and with those who mediate the ultimate environment is for all that comes thereafter in identity and faith. In a remarkably suggestive subtheme of his book *Young Man Luther,* Erikson, carefully avoiding the reductionism that marks the work of Freud and many Freudians on these matters, suggests some of the universal features of religious images of God that have their infantile origins in the child's experiences with his or her parents.[22] His attention to *fidelity* as the virtue emerging in adolescence and the accompanying attention to ideology as the young person's necessary concern for finding a comprehensive "world image" provide access to other central aspects of faith. The study of identity crisis and resolution, through the reshaping of images of faith by young Luther, opens ways to understanding the interplay of faith and culture as well as many other rich issues. Erikson's representation of ethical development in terms of widened care and more inclusive identity contributes an important set of criteria for growth in faith as well as in moral action. Avoiding the trap of identifying faith with religion or belief, Erikson suggests something of his overall orientation toward faith with this statement:

Each society and each age must find the institutionalized form of reverence which derives vitality from its world image. . . . The clinician can only observe that many are proud to be without religion whose children cannot afford their being without it. One the other hand, there are many who seem to derive a vital faith from social action or scientific pursuit. And again, there are many who profess faith, yet in practice breathe mistrust both of life and man.[23]

I have found it easier to put on paper the influence of Piaget and Kohlberg on our work than I have that of Erikson. I believe this is because Erikson's influence on me has been both more pervasive and more subtle; it has touched me at convictional depths that the structural developmentalists have not addressed. As unsystematic and unsatisfactory as it may seem, I simply have to say that Erikson's work has become part of the interpretative mind-set I bring to research on faith development. The explicit references in these pages to aspects of that influence are, I'm afraid, really only suggestive clues to a much greater—and more grateful—indebtedness.

In the late stages of completing this book I had my first opportunity to meet and work with Daniel Levinson. I had read and taught Levinson's thought as expressed in *The Seasons of a Man's Life.*[24] In my reading and teaching, however, I had focused more on Levinson's "periods" and "transitions" in adult development than on the broader framework of "eras" he has proposed. As I heard him speak and then when I conversed with him privately, two new understandings struck me forcefully. First, I began to see that for Levinson, time—chronological time by which we measure aging—has ontological significance. Being and time are profoundly linked in our experiences of self and others and in our ways of responding to our world. Second, I recognized that while the *periods* Levinson has identified may be variable and susceptible of differing rates and intensities of transition, the impact on one's way of being in the world resulting from the transition from one *era* of life to another is inevitable, unvariable and necessarily profound.

Levinson has come to view the life cycle as divided into eras of roughly twenty years duration.

Infancy, childhood and adolescence constitute the life cycle's first broad era. Revolutions in both physical and psychic life are more frequent in this first era than in later ones, due to the rapidity of bodily maturation and of cognitive and emotional development. The years

Table 3.2   Levinson's Eras of the Life Cycle

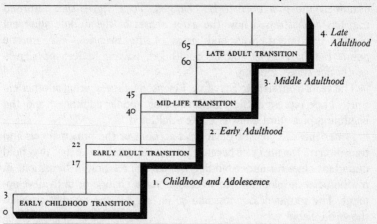

From *Seasons of a Man's Life* by Daniel J. Levinson and others © 1978 by Daniel J. Levinson. Reprinted by permission of Alfred A. Knopf, Inc.

from seventeen to twenty-two, in Levinson's view, represent both the culmination of the first era and the inauguration of the next, the first adult era. In these years a person must complete the tasks of forming a personality, of acquiring basic abilities to think and learn, of shaping values and beliefs and of preparing for separation from the matrix of home and family that has nurtured and sustained growth in the first era.

Overlapping with this work of culminating the first era, the young girl-woman or boy-man must begin the tasks of creating a life structure for the next developmental era, the first adult era. Issues of choice must be faced: the focus of study or apprenticeship, the patterns of intimacy and partners in it, the shaping of a personal and vocational "dream." The young adult takes on the tasks of building a first adult life structure that, with necessary modifications and changes, will carry him or her to mid-life.

The years from forty to forty-five Levinson sees as another major era transition. Here again the tasks of one era need to be brought to culmination and completion, even as the person begins to undertake the construction of a life structure for the second adult era, "middle adulthood." Assessments of the last era's "dream," of its patterns of commitment in work and love, and of its dominant images of self, world and reality demand attention. One's sense of time and timing begins to change. Goals, priorities, relationships, and roles must be examined and may need to be changed. To a degree that surprised me, Levinson stressed how the early phases of the middle adult era parallel the uncertainties and stress of the twenties. We are, he points out, novices at middle adulthood, having to reshape significantly our ways of being.

The years from sixty to sixty-five, Levinson believes, bring another era shift. They represent the culmination of middle adulthood and the beginning of a third adult era, late adulthood.

I offer this overview of Levinson's account of the principal eras and transitions in the life cycle because I am coming to believe that they hold important clues for understanding the natural relation of transitions in psychosocial development to structural stage change in faith development. The results of our research so far suggest the *optimal* parallels shown in Table 3.3

A reflective examination of these parallels suggests that during the rapid revolutions in cognitive, psychosocial and physical growth that occur during the years from birth to twenty-two (Levinson's first era), we recognize four different structural stages of faith. As we shall see, not all children make these faith stage transitions, just as not all children attain the cognitive structures of formal operational thought. Ordinarily, however, Synthetic-Conventional faith does take form during adolescence and represents the culminating form of faith for the first era of the life cycle.

The period from seventeen to twenty-two, the time Levinson sees as marking the transition to the early adult era, corresponds with what appears to be the optimal time for beginning a transition from a Synthetic-Conventional toward an Individuative-Reflective stage of faith. As our subsequent discussion of these stages will show, many young adults, for a variety of reasons, do *not* enter upon a faith stage transition at this point. This group moves into the creation of a first adult life structure guided by their Synthetic-Conventional faiths. As they encounter the various predictable and unpredictable crises of their twenties and thirties some of them will make belated and usually more difficult transitions in faith stage. Some never do. Only with extended longitudinal studies will we gain reliable knowledge on these matters. Our preliminary research suggests, however, that if the transition from Synthetic-Conventional to Individuative-Reflective faith does not occur before or during the mid-life transition, its chances of occurring at all decrease markedly.

Table 3.3 Psychosocial and Faith Stages: Optimal Parallels

Levinson's Eras and Erikson's Psychosocial Stages:	Fowler's Faith Stages
	Undifferentiated Faith (Infancy)
Era of Infancy, Childhood and Adolescence	1. Intuitive-Projective Faith (Early Childhood)
Trust vs. Mistrust	
Autonomy vs. Shame & Doubt	
Initiative vs. Guilt	2. Mythic-Literal Faith (School Years)
Industry vs. Inferiority	3. Synthetic-Conventional Faith (Adolescence)
Identity vs. Role Confusion	
First Adult Era	4. Individuative-Reflective Faith (Young Adulthood)
Intimacy vs. Isolation	
Middle Adult Era	5. Conjunctive Faith (Mid-life and Beyond)
Generativity vs. Stagnation	
Late Adult Era	6. Universalizing Faith
Integrity vs. Despair	

So for some adults Synthetic-Conventional faith becomes a stable, equilibrated, lifelong structural style. For others it gives way, in the early adult era, to an Individuative-Reflective style. The structuring of this latter stage is ideally suited to the tasks and challenges of the first adult era. Again, we find that for a fair number of adults this stage, formed in the twenties or thirties, becomes a permanently equilibrated style of orientation. Although it may suffer buffeting in the middle adult transition, it can persist and sustain persons through the middle adult years. Our knowledge of this is based more on observations and speculation than on longitudinal research. My hypothesis, however, is that the work of the mid-life transition is better done if it includes or corresponds to a transition in faith stages as well.

It appears that at each of the major era transitions the shaping of the new era's life structure is enhanced if we engage in those tasks bringing new and enriched ways of being in faith. Put negatively, to approach a new era in the adult life cycle while clinging too tightly to the structural style of faith employed during the culminating phase of the previous era is to risk anachronism. It means attacking a new agenda of life tasks and a potential new richness in the understanding of life with the limiting pattern of knowing, valuing and interpreting experiences that served the previous era. Such anachronism virtually assures that one will settle for a narrower and shallower faith than one needs.

This preliminary look at optimal relations between psychosocial development and structural-developmental stages of faith may help clarify in what sense faith stages may be said to be normative. The faith stages soon to be discussed are not to be understood as an achievement scale by which to evaluate the worth of persons. Nor do they represent educational or therapeutic goals toward which to hurry people. Seeing their optimal correlations with psychosocial eras gives a sense of how time, experience, challenge and nurture are required for growth in faith. Education and nurture should aim at the full realization of the potential strength of faith at each stage and at keeping the reworking of faith that comes with stage changes current with the parallel transitional work in psychosocial eras. Remedial or therapeutic nurture is called for when the anachronism of a lagging faith stage fails to keep pace with psychosocial growth. Less frequently, but just as important, sometimes precocious faith development outstrips or gets ahead of psychosocial growth. In this situation help may be needed in overcoming or reworking crippled psychosocial functioning.

NOTES

1. For such a position see Gerhard Ebeling, *The Nature of Faith* (Philadelphia: Fortress Press, 1967).
2. See Jane Loevinger, *Ego Development* (San Francisco: Jossey-Bass, 1976).
3. In this position I am indebted—as in many places—to H. Richard Niebuhr. See especially his *The Meaning of Revelation* (New York: Macmillan, 1941) and *The Responsible Self* (New York: Harper & Row, 1962).
4. Flannery O'Connor, "The Turkey," in *The Complete Stories* (New York: Farrar, Straus & Giroux, 1979), pp. 42–53.
5. Ibid., p. 46.
6. Ibid., p. 48, parenthesis added.
7. Ibid., p. 49.
8. Ibid., p. 53.
9. See William F. Lynch, S.J., *Images of Faith* (Notre Dame, Ind.: University of Notre Dame Press, 1973).
10. For a comparison of behaviorist, maturationist and structural-developmental approaches in the study of moral development see L. Kohlberg and R. Mayer, "Development as the Aim of Education," *Harvard Educational Review*, vol. 42, no. 4 (Nov., 1972).
11. For a powerful critique of the postivistic philosophies of science to which Piaget is responding and by which his epistemological focus is largely determined, see Michael Polanyi, *Personal Knowledge: Toward a Post-Critical Philosophy* (Chicago: University of Chicago Press, 1958).
12. James Fowler, "Faith and the Structuring of Meaning" in *Toward Moral and Religious Maturity* (Morristown, N.J.: Silver Burdett, 1980), pp. 61–62.
13. See Ernest Wallwork, "Morality, Religion and Kohlberg's Theory" in Brenda Munsey, ed., *Moral Development, Moral Education, and Kohlberg* (Birmingham, Ala.: Religious Education Press, 1980), pp. 269–297.
14. Jean Piaget, *Insights and Illusions of Philosophy*, trans. Wolfe Mays (New York: World, Meridian Books, 1971).
15. Fowler, "Faith and the Structuring of Meaning," p. 63.
16. William F. Lynch, S.J., *Images of Faith* (Notre Dame, Ind.: University of Notre Dame Press, 1973), p. 19.
17. Lawrence Kohlberg, "Continuities in Childhood and Adult Moral Reasoning Revisited" in Paul B. Baltes and K. Warner Schaie, eds., *Life-Span Developmental Psychology* (New York: Academic Press, 1973), pp. 179–204.
18. See Stanley Hauerwas, "Character, Narrative and Growth in the Christian Life" in *Toward Moral and Religious Maturity* (Morristown, N.J.: Silver Burdett, 1980), pp. 441–484.
19. Daniel Levinson et al., *The Seasons of a Man's Life* (New York: Knopf, 1978); George E. Vaillant, *Adaptation to Life* (Boston: Little, Brown, 1977); Roger L. Gould, *Transformations: Growth and Change in Adult Life* (New York: Simon & Schuster, 1978); Gail Sheehy, *Passages: Predictable Crises of Adult Life* (New York: Dutton, 1976).

20. See Stuart T. Hauser, *Black and White Identity Formation* (New York: Wiley, 1971), pp. 7–20.

21. Richard Norman Shulik, "Faith Development, Moral Development, and Old Age: An Assessment of Fowler's Faith Development Paradigm" and Aging" (Ph.D. diss. Committee on Human Development, Department of Behavioral Science, University of Chicago, 1979).

22. Erik H. Erikson, *Young Man Luther* (New York: Norton, 1958), pp. 263–266.

23. Erik H. Erikson, *Childhood and Society* (New York: Norton, 1963), p. 251.

24. Levinson, *The Seasons of a Man's Life.*

Part IV

Stages of Faith

15. Infancy and Undifferentiated Faith

It is morning. A very young baby awakens. Feeling the discomfort of hunger, a wet diaper and a vague anxiety, she cries out. Nearby, a mother wakes up, attending to the cry. Soon she is in motion. Approaching the baby, she calls out a name. She follows this with verbal greetings and phrases of tenderness. The baby's head turns; its eyes grow animated. Their eyes meet. Face to face now, the greetings are repeated. Then with her face expressive of interest and concern, the mother picks up the child, nuzzling and embracing her, while sniffing and feeling in order to determine the extent of her need. Continuing the verbal caresses all the while, the mother carries out the necessary operations of cleansing and replacing soiled clothes. The baby watches the mother's face as she works; their eyes meet frequently. Picking the baby up again, the mother produces a warm bottle or a breast. As she holds the infant in her arms, perhaps rocking her gently, the baby begins to suck vigorously. As her lips, tongue and palate draw warm milk into her mouth and stomach, her eyes play on the face of the mother. The mother's eyes are bright and attentive, her features mobile. Frequently she speaks, producing familiar, soothing or playful sounds. As the sharp edge of her hunger eases, the baby pauses. Lifting her to her shoulder the mother pats her on the back while continuing words of encouragement. After a burp or two the feeding continues, only now it is a little more relaxed.[1]

We all begin the pilgrimage of faith as infants. Formed in the profound symbiosis of prenatal life in our mother's womb, at birth we are thrust into a new environment for which we have potential but not yet fully viable abilities. For another nine months after birth we are more dependent on the care of those who welcome us than are all but a few of our mammalian companions. We are wonderfully endowed with innate potential for adapting to this new world, but the activation and elaboration of our adaptive capacities depends both on the progress of our overall maturation and on the way the persons and conditions of our environment greet us and beckon us into interaction. If there is not enough holding, rocking or stimulation from communication, our adaptive capacities for relationship and loving attachments can be severely retarded or nonactivated. If our environment presents us with no change, with no novelty or physical objects to call forth and challenge us, our movement and our coordination, our curiosity and operations of knowing may be severely limited. If the quality and consistency of our feeding and cleansing are inadequate and if there is no person (or persons) with whom we can achieve a dependable complementary relationship of mutuality, our trust of the world and in ourselves can be outweighed by distrust and infantile despair.[2]

Only gradually do we begin to know objects in our environment as separate from us and as continuing in existence when out of our sight or attention. Initially it is as though the breast or bottle, the maternal face and the objects we grasp and taste are extensions of us, there at hand miraculously when need or curiosity direct us to them. A kind of primal "fall" into consciousness occurs as our interaction with persons and objects enables us cognitively to construct what Piaget calls the "schema of object permanence." By seven or eight months we form and retain mental images of missing objects—people and things—and we are on the way toward knowing that we are separate from those we love and toward needing to experience ourselves as central in a world of "others." This fall is traumatic. Some think that our primal innocence gives way to the first split of conscious and unconscious as we experience the new anxiety, emerging on the average around eight months, of remembering our mothers when they are absent from us and the panic about whether they will return. This panic is so severe, these observers tell us, that it is repressed by our first psychic defenses and "forgotten."[3] This healthy forgetting is made possible by the timely returns of the mother or other primary giver of care. As she returns, calling the baby's name and blessing it with the gift of her eyes and face, the baby is reconfirmed in being and well-being and restored to a sense of centrality in its world of objects growing increasingly separate. In such a way does trust take form—trust in the caregivers and the environment they provide; trust in the self, its worthiness and its being at home; trust in the larger world of meaning inchoately surrounding the infant and the caretakers, mediated through their bodies and voices and the patterns of their ways of parenting the child, even as a baby, toward their (and their culture's) images of worthy womanhood or manhood.[4]

Those observers are correct, I believe, who tell us that our first *pre-images* of God have their origins here. Particularly they are composed from our first experiences of mutuality, in which we form the rudimentary awareness of self as separate from and dependent upon the immensely powerful others, who were present at our first consciousness and who "knew us"—with recognizing eyes and reconfirming smiles—at our first self-knowing.[5] I call these *pre-images* because they are largely formed prior to language, prior to concepts and coincident with the emergence of consciousness.

Against this background let us look at a more formal characterization of infancy and Undifferentiated faith.

In the pre-stage called Undifferentiated faith the seeds of trust, courage, hope and love are fused in an undifferentiated way and contend with sensed threats of abandonment, inconsistencies and deprivations in an infant's environment. Though really a pre-stage and largely inaccessible to empirical research of the kind we pursue, the quality of mutuality and the strength of trust, autonomy, hope and courage (or their opposites) developed in this phase underlie (or threaten to undermine) all that comes later in faith development.

The emergent strength of faith in this stage is the fund of basic trust and the relational experience of mutuality with the one(s) providing primary love and care.

The danger or deficiency in the stage is a failure of mutuality in either of two directions. Either there may emerge an excessive narcissism in which the experience of being "central" continues to dominate and distort mutuality, or experiences of neglect or inconsistencies may lock the infant in patterns of isolation and failed mutuality.

Transition to Stage 1 begins with the convergence of thought and language, opening up the use of symbols in speech and ritual play.

16. Stage 1. Intuitive-Projective Faith

For several weeks between her fifteenth and eighteenth months my older daughter conducted daily a curious ritual. In our four-room graduate student's apartment she had a small bedroom adjoining that of her parents. In what had been an old New England farmhouse there were long windows, almost from floor to ceiling. As early morning sunlight bathed the room, Joan would awaken, stand up in her crib and through the open door demand her parents' sleepy attention. When she was sure that we were both in attendance she began, in her tentative English, to name the various pictures and objects of furniture in her little room. After she had named each of the eleven or twelve items she knew, waiting after each one to get our confirmation and praise, she then turned to other play and the day could begin.

What was the meaning of this ritual? At the time I had done very little study in developmental psychology and simply assumed that it was a playful step in language acquisition. Certainly it was this, but now I know that it was more. The operations of our thought and the beginnings of language have different roots in infancy. Our first "reasoning" involves sensorimotor knowing—the coordination of movements and the construction of practical schemata of space, object permanence and causal action. The production and repetition of vocal sounds, which elicit response and mutual imitation between parents and child, do not effectively come into the service of thought until the beginnings of the second year of life. At that point, when the convergence of thought and language begins to occur, the child takes hold of a qualitatively new and powerful kind of leverage on the world of experience.[6] I think our daughter's morning ritual had to do with this revolutionary convergence of thought and language. Minimally, I believe, it represented a daily celebration (and reconfirmation) that the external world was made up of dependably permanent objects, that they had names, and that she, in mastering their names, could daily reconstitute a repertoire of shared meanings with her parents.

The Intuitive-Projective child, whose age ranges from two to six or seven, uses the new tools of speech and symbolic representation to organize her or his sensory experience into meaning units. With words and names the child explores and sorts out a world of novelty, daily encountering new elements for which he or she has no previously developed categories or structures. In this era the two- and three-year-old's endless questions of "what" and "why" may drive responsive parents, on some days, to wit's end. Close observation of the parent-child interchange helps one realize that often the logic that formulates the questions works in quite different ways than does the logic that produces the answers. Hence, the questions frequently are not satisfactorily answered. The child's thinking is not yet reversible. Cause-effect relations are poorly understood. The child's understanding of how things work and what they mean is dominated by relatively inexperienced perceptions and by the feelings these perceptions arouse.

Intuitive-Projective children exhibit the cognitive egocentrism we spoke of in Part II. Being as yet unable to coordinate and compare two different perspectives on the same object, they simply assume without question that the experiences and perceptions they have of a phenomenon represent the only available perspective. This means that many conversations between Intuitive-Projective children have the character of dual monologues, each speaking in a way that assumes identity of interest, experience and perception, while neither coordinates his or her perspective with that of the other, testing for fit or aptness. Seen from the cognitive developmental perspective the child's thinking is fluid and magical. It lacks deductive and inductive logic; it has an episodic flavor in which associations follow one another according to imaginative processes not yet constrained by stable logical operations.

Our interviews begin with children at age four. What they articulate in these talks appears to bear out the descriptions of cognitive

processes just presented. We will not make the mistake of assuming
that what children are able to bring to word in these talks with stran-
gers exhausts their faith constructions, but it does provide a beginning
point. I want to let you overhear parts of an interview with Freddy, an
alert six-year-old from a Catholic family. He had been told the outlines
of a simple story about a brother and sister (the boy his age, the girl
somewhat younger) who go on a family picnic in a large park. In the
course of the afternoon the brother and sister wander off from the
family and become lost in the deep woods that border the park. He is
invited to tell some of the things they might see and experience in the
woods.

Freddy: They see—you can see deers, you can get sunshine. You see beautiful trees. You see lakes and you see clear streams.

Interviewer: Well tell me, how did all of these trees and animals and lakes
and things get there?

Freddy: By rain. . . . Mothers get the babies. The sunshine shines through
the clouds and that's a lot of fun. Yeah, the stream and the water lakes.
The lakes—the lakes get um, more—the forest—you have a deep hole and
then it rains and then when it gets full enough they—it's a—it's a lake. But
when it gets stinky you can't swim.

Interviewer: Oh, I see. Well why do you think we have trees and animals?

Freddy: 'Cause God made them.

Interviewer: I see. Why do you think he made them?

Freddy: 'Cause. 'Cause there's two reasons why. Number one is 'cause trees
give off oxygen and number two is animals protect other animals.

Interviewer: I see. I see. Well why are there people?

Freddy: Uh—I don't know.

Interviewer: Can you think what it would be like if there weren't any people?

Freddy: The beautiful world would become ugly.

Interviewer: How come?

Freddy: 'Cause, nobody would be down and the world would be ugly.

Interviewer: Yeah?

Freddy: I think it would be like in the old days and things.

Interviewer: Um-hum. And what was it like in the old days?

Freddy: Like there was big holdups. There was wagons going fast.

Interviewer: But what—but what about even before that? What if there
weren't any people at all anywhere?

Freddy: Just animals? I think it would be like—be like an animal world.

Interviewer: Would that be good?

Freddy: No, if there weren't any people, who would be the animals?

Interviewer: Well, how did people get here?

Freddy: They—they got here from God? That's all I know about the old days.

In Freddy's responses to a classic Piagetian moral dilemma we learn something about both his form of moral reasoning and his location of authority. The interviewer told him about a dinner table incident involving the same two children who had been lost in the woods. The sister, reaching for the margarine across the table, accidentally spills her glass of milk, ruining the front of her dress. Later the brother gets mad because he is not allowed to have a second piece of cake. In his anger he pushes his glass of milk over, but he gets only a small spot on his shirt.

Interviewer: Now which one of those people do you think did the worse thing?

Freddy: The sister.

Interviewer: Why?

Freddy: 'Cause—'cause she got a lot of milk all over her dress.

Interviewer: Yeah, and that's worse?

Freddy: Yeah.

Interviewer: I see. Do you know when you've done something bad?

Freddy: When I break a cup.

Interviewer: How do you know that's bad?

Freddy: 'Cause my mother gets upset and then she starts spanking and she starts screaming. When she sees the rug she screams real loud.

Interviewer: Well, how does your mother know that that's bad? Who told her?

Freddy: Her mother when she—when my—her mother—her mother got mad.

Interviewer: How did her mother find out?

Freddy: From her mother.

Interviewer: Well how did the first mother find out?

Freddy: From her mother.

Interviewer: How about the very first mother?

Freddy: Uh, I bet she was real smart.

At a later point in the conversation the interviewer introduces a series of questions about sickness and death. Freddy tells us that if a person is not getting well ". . . you just go to the hospital." Then he adds, "But the hospital can't fix you up sometimes."

Interviewer: What happens when they can't fix you up?

Freddy: You die.

Interviewer: You just die?

Freddy: Yeah.

Interviewer: What happens to you when you die?

Freddy: I don't know. Never been up in heaven before, only when I was a baby.

Interviewer: When you were a baby you were in heaven?

Freddy: Yeah.

Interviewer: How do you know that?

Freddy: Well, 'cause I felt the cold.

Interviewer: It's cold in heaven?

Freddy: Yeah, no, I think it's warm, real warm.

Interviewer: Where is heaven?

Freddy: Uh, high, high, high up in the sky.

Interviewer: What's it look like?

Freddy: Uh, high mountains, so I know about heaven.

Interviewer: Who is in heaven?

Freddy: God.

Interviewer: Just God? Is he by himself?

Freddy: No.

Interviewer: Who else is there?

Freddy: There's, there's the shepherds—the shepherd man—I mean the wise men that are dead.

Interviewer: Is there anyone else in heaven?

Freddy: Baby—no, not baby Jesus.

Interviewer: No?

Freddy: 'Ca—yeah, baby Jesus is God.

Interviewer: He is?

Freddy: Yeah.

Interviewer: Okay. Is anybody else in heaven?

Freddy: There's Mary. Saint Joe—that's all I know.

Interviewer: So heaven is where people go when they die?

Freddy: Your spirit goes up.

Interviewer: Oh, your spirit. What is your spirit?

Freddy: It's something that helps you—helps you—helps you do everything.

Interviewer: Yeah, where is it?

Freddy: In your body.

Interviewer: Inside you?

Freddy: Yeah.

Interviewer: And what does it help you do?

Freddy: Helps you do lots of things.

Interviewer: Like what?

Freddy: I don't know. Maybe—maybe walking. Maybe seeing around and stuff. That's all I know.

Freddy's account of spirit reminds me of a scene in a frieze on the front of the twelfth-century cathedral in Arles, France. Portraying the death by stoning of the first Christian martyr, St. Stephen, the artist depicted Stephen's spirit in the form of a child-sized body being drawn gently upward by angels from the dying witness's mouth.

I conclude our quotes from Freddy's interview by combining several brief passages where he speaks about God. In one section he is shown a picture of a church. The interviewer asks him how the people in the picture feel about going to church.

Freddy: They feel sad.
Interviewer: How come?
Freddy: 'Cause all the things about God.
Interviewer: What kind of things about God make them feel sad?
Freddy: Well, God dies. God dies and then he comes back to life. That—coming back to life is good but—
Interviewer: But the other part is sad?
Freddy: Yeah, 'cause when you stay dead. That's all I know about that.
Interviewer: All right. Can you tell me what God looks like?
Freddy: He has a light shirt on, he has brown hair, he had brown eyelashes . . .

At this point Freddy brought in two small statues of Christ which he showed to the interviewer. After remarking about the statues she asked him, "Does everybody think that God looks like that?" Freddy's answer, suggesting a typical inability to construct other perspectives, is arresting: "Mmm—not when he gets a haircut." The interviewer follows these questions with one that asks how we can find out about God. The answers, probably a mixture of spontaneous construction and Freddy's efforts to make sense of some things he has heard, are interesting:

Freddy: When you go up—when your spirit goes up to heaven.
Interviewer: Is there any way we can find out before that?
Freddy: I don't know, really . . . when you take off in space.
Interviewer: Well how do *you* know about God?
Freddy: My teacher tells me about him sometimes. Sometimes I see him on cards and I see, uh—all those people up in heaven.
Interviewer: Do people ever talk to God?
Freddy: Yeah.
Interviewer: How?
Freddy: Well, well God can hear them, but he's in signs. He doesn't talk.

Interviewer: [Mis-hearing him]: He doesn't? What kind of songs does he sing?

Freddy: He sings songs about—I don't know, really. But he's in *signs*. Signs like stop signs.

Interviewer: Stop signs? Can you guess what kind of signs he might send?

Freddy: Like peace signs.

Interviewer: Peace signs?

Freddy: Yeah. That's all I know about that.

For a final sample of Freddy's theology we hear him talk about God in a quite different way than the anthropomorphic images of the Christ.

Interviewer: When you do something bad, does God know?

Freddy: Yes. He spreads all around the world in one day.

Interviewer: He does? How does he do that?

Freddy: He does 'cause he's smart.

Interviewer: He's smart? How does he get all around the world in one day?

Freddy: Uh—he can split or he can be like a God.

Interviewer: He can split into lots of things?

Freddy: Yeah.

Interviewer: Can he do anything he wants to?

Freddy: Yeah.

Interviewer: There's not anything he can't do?

Freddy: He can do things, things that are good, not bad. God never tells a lie in his life.

Interviewer: Never?

Freddy: Nope.

Freddy has been exposed to a relatively rich range of symbols for composing his images of the character of an ultimate environment. His eclectic appropriation and extension of some of these help to make clear that children in Stage 1 combine fragments of stories and images given by their cultures into their own clusters of significant associations dealing with God and the sacred. Children from non- or anti-religious homes show similar tendencies, though their sources of images and symbols may be more limited. In an interview with Sally, four and a half, whose parents have made intentional efforts to avoid exposing her to religious symbols, we talked about belief in God.

Sally: Sometimes I believed in God, but my mother and father never believed in God.

Interviewer: Why do you believe in God?

Sally: Because on those shows they believe in God, like on "Leave It to

Beaver" and Davey [the Lutheran Church in America's animated cartoon series, "Davey and Goliath"] you know that? Especially on Davey; there's a lot of that. Saturday morning we wake up kind of early and we watch Davey. And like today I watched Beaver and "Father Knows Best," but they don't have much about God.

Interviewer: Is God real to you?

Sally: Ummm—yeah . . . sometimes I think it's real.

Interviewer: What does God look like?

Sally: He doesn't look like anything. He's all around you.

Other sources of knowledge about God to which Sally referred included wedding and funeral scenes which occasionally occur in TV westerns. Sally's comments underscore the point of Dr. Ana-Maria Rizzuto in her rich psychoanalytic study of the origins of God images. Dr. Rizzuto finds that despite our secularization and religious fragmentation, religious symbols and language are so widely present in this society that virtually no child reaches school age without having constructed—with or without religious instruction—an image or images of God.[7]

Preschool children typically do not yet generate (or faithfully retell) narratives that could give order and a kind of causal connectedness to their image clusters. They appreciate long stories and follow their details, but have limited abilities to retell them. And while the precursors of conceptual abstractions are present (Freddy's statement that God "spreads all around the world in one day"), only concrete symbols and images really address the child's ways of knowing.

One of the questions in our interviews with young children asks them to share what kinds of things make them feel fearful or afraid. Almost invariably, from boys and girls alike, the answer is some variant of "Lions, tigers, bears and monsters!" When I first began to administer the interviews I would frequently respond to this by saying, "But you don't *really* have any of these things around your neighborhood, do you?" And they would say no. Then I would ask again, "What makes you feel afraid or fearful?" The answer would return: "Lions, tigers, bears and monsters!" Puzzling over this with some of my research assistants I was helped when one of the women pointed out to me that these fearsome, archetypal creatures are what the children dream and daydream about, and that "reality" and fantasy interpenetrate for them. Since then I have been helped tremendously by Bruno Bettelheim's book *The Uses of Enchantment: The Meaning and Importance of Fairy Tales.*[8] Drawing on his work as a child therapist, Bettelheim shows how

fairy tales provide powerful symbolizations for children's inner terrors
and for the hidden fantasies of violence or sex that bring them secret
feelings of guilt. They also provide the child with tangible models of
courage and virtue and with conviction-awakening stories showing that
goodness and resourcefulness triumph over evil and sloth. Bettelheim's
position makes a strong case against the effort, in children's literature
or early childhood religious education, to present children only with the
sunny or cheerful sides of life. By the third or fourth year children have
developed an often preoccupying fear of death, particularly fear of the
death of a parent or parents. Similarly, they have begun to internalize
—often with a harshness far greater than parental adults ever intend—
the taboos and prohibitions that surround and make mysteriously attractive things sexual and religious. The useful realism of fairy tales—and
of many biblical narratives—provides indirect yet effective ways for
children to externalize their inner anxieties and to find ordering images
and stories by which to begin to shape their lives. One of Bettelheim's
examples can be shared:

> Encouraged by discussion about the importance fairy tales have for children
> a mother overcame her hesitation about telling such "gory and threatening"
> stories to her son. From her conversations with him, she knew that her son
> already had fantasies about eating people, or people getting eaten. So she told
> him the tale of "Jack the Giant Killer." His response at the end of the story
> was: "There aren't any such things as giants, are there?" Before the mother
> could give her son the reassuring reply which was on her tongue—and which
> would have destroyed the value of the story for him—he continued, "But
> there are such things as grownups, and they're like giants." At the ripe old
> age of five, he understood the encouraging message of the story: although
> adults can be experienced as frightening giants, a little boy with cunning can
> get the better of them.[9]

Testimony of another kind helps us appreciate more fully the immense responsiveness of children in this stage to symbols and images
that awaken and shape conviction. One of our adult respondents, a male
in his thirties, recalls that as a four-year-old he was required to take an
afternoon nap. At the beginning of these naps his mother would sometimes read a story from the Bible. After reading the stories and responding to some of his curious questions, she would leave him "to go to
sleep." Sleep came, he says, less frequently than rich fantasies and
daydreams, often stimulated by the stories. He shared two of these with
us. The first was the Daniel sequence, which tells of the heroic purity,

faithfulness and defiance of Daniel and his three Hebrew friends in face of the king of Babylon. The story culminates, of course, with Daniel and his friends being subjected to a fiery furnace and to dangerous lions and being protected against all harm by God in both instances. Our respondent was particularly fascinated with the trial in the lions' den. He asked his mother many questions about how God "shut-mouthed" those lions. His own image of how it happened, he recalls, had to do with the instantaneous appearance in the lions' mouths of something like dental braces, locking their teeth together. After his mother left the room that day, and for some days to come, he relived that dramatic situation. He remembers that on at least one occasion he thought to himself, as though saying it out loud, "God, I'm brave like Daniel. Put some lions here in this room and I will show you that I am not afraid." Then, he said, he began to feel real fright at the possibility that God might really do what he asked.

The other story this man shared centered on his hearing the account of Samuel's call in the temple (1 Sam. 1–3). As his mother told him the story of the dedication by Hannah of her son Samuel to the work of God, it made a strong impression on him. It seems likely that just as he identified with Daniel in his fantasies, he also saw parallels with Samuel and felt identification with the latter's relation to a religiously serious mother. He felt, he said, a special closeness to the boy Samuel as he served in the temple. As the story continues, Samuel, on two different occasions, hears a call in the night. Two times he goes to Eli, the high priest, responding to what he took to be Eli's call. After the second call, Eli, perceiving that God was addressing the boy, instructed him when the call came again to respond: "Speak, Lord, for thy servant hears." (1 Sam. 3:9). Later in his childhood and adolescence, this man says, he would frequently awaken in the middle of the night and in the pregnant darkness would find himself feeling, "Speak, Lord, for Thy servant hears." It comes as no surprise to learn that today he is a minister and theologian.

In the following passage from Bettelheim I would prefer to substitute for his somewhat pejorative word *fantasy*—which suggests "make-believe" and "unreality"—the stouter word *imagination*. Imagination can indeed be fanciful, but it arises in this stage, for reasons Bettelheim helpfully sets forth, as a powerful and permanent force by which we compose an ultimate environment and orient ourselves toward the being or beings that constitute its character.[10]

A young child's mind contains a rapidly expanding collection of often ill-assorted and only partially integrated impressions: some correctly seen aspects of reality, but many more elements completely dominated by fantasy. [Here the phrases "correctly seen aspects of reality" and "completely dominated by fantasy" point to the limits of Bettelheim's appropriation of his own thesis.] Fantasy fills the huge gaps in a child's understanding which are due to the immaturity of his thinking and his lack of pertinent information. Other distortions are the consequences of inner pressures which lead to misinterpretations of the child's perceptions.[11]

While we reject Bettelheim's bias in this passage that imagination merely fills temporary "gaps" in knowledge and that it "distorts" reality, his statement helps us recognize both the robustness of imaginative processes at this stage and their inevitability. This and our previous examples also help us to see how the imagination and fantasy life of the child can be exploited by witting or unwitting adults. For every child whose significant others have shared religious stories, images and symbols in ways that prove life-opening and sustaining of love, faith and courage, there must be at least one other for whom the introduction to religion, while equally powerful, gave rise to fear, rigidity, and the brutalization of souls—both one's own and those of others. There are religious groups who subject Intuitive-Projective children to the kind of preaching and teaching that vividly emphasize the pervasiveness and power of the devil, the sinfulness of all people without Christ and the hell of fiery torments that await the unrepentant. This kind of faith formation—and its equivalent in other religious traditions—can ensure a dramatic "conversion experience" by the time the child is seven or eight. It runs the grave risk, however, of leading to what Philip Helfaer calls "precocious identity formation" in which the child, at conversion, takes on the adult faith identity called for by the religious group.[12] This often results when the child is an adult in the emergence of a very rigid, brittle and authoritarian personality.

Our research convinces me that education at this age—in the home, in synagogues and churches, in nursery schools and kindergartens—has a tremendous responsibility for the quality of images and stories we provide as gifts and guides for our children's fertile imaginations. Because the child's appropriations of and personal constructions of meaning with these symbolic elements is unpredictable and because insisting on conceptual orthodoxy at this age is both premature and dangerous, parents and teachers should create an atmosphere in which the child can freely express, verbally and nonverbally, the images she or he is forming. Where this expression is allowed and encouraged, the child is taken seriously and adults can provide appropriate help in dealing with crippling, distorted or destructive images the child has formed. Dr. Jerome Berryman's approach to the use of parables with children ("being in parables with children" he calls it) provides an extremely helpful model for the approach I am advocating.[13] Berryman's method builds on developmental theory, Montessori principles and current research on the narrative functions of parables.[14]

Finally, we must warn against a possible misunderstanding of the position taken here. The desirability of children's exposure to death, poverty, treachery and maliciousness in the context of fairy tales and Bible stories, when told to them by trusted adults with whom their feelings can be tested and shared is one thing. It does not, however, translate into approval of hours spent passively before a television, absorbing the mixed bag and unending commercials of the Saturday morning cartoons. Nor does it sanction children's exposure to the superrealistic violence, materialism and sexploitation of prime-time television programming.[15]

I close this discussion of Intuitive-Projective faith with a formal summary.

Stage 1 Intuitive-Projective faith is the fantasy-filled, imitative phase in which the child can be powerfully and permanently influenced by examples, moods, actions and stories of the visible faith of primally related adults.

The stage most typical of the child of three to seven, it is marked by a relative fluidity of thought patterns. The child is continually encountering novelties for which no stable operations of knowing have been formed. The imaginative processes underlying fantasy are unrestrained and uninhibited by logical thought. In league with forms of knowing dominated by perception, imagination in this stage is extremely productive of longlasting images and feelings (positive and negative) that later, more stable and self-reflective valuing and thinking will have to order and sort out. This is the stage of first self-awareness. The "self-aware" child is egocentric as regards the perspectives of others. Here we find first awarenesses of death and sex and of the strong taboos by which cultures and families insulate those powerful areas.

The gift or emergent strength of this stage is the birth of imagination, the ability to unify and grasp the experience-world in powerful images and as presented in stories that register the child's intuitive understandings and feelings toward the ultimate conditions of existence.

The dangers in this stage arise from the possible "possession" of the child's imagination by unrestrained images of terror and destructiveness, or from the witting or unwitting exploitation of her or his imagination in the reinforcement of taboos and moral or doctrinal expectations.

The main factor precipitating transition to the next stage is the emergence of concrete operational thinking. Affectively, the resolution of Oedipal issues or their submersion in latency are important accompanying factors. At the heart of the transition is the child's growing concern to know how things are and to clarify for him- or herself the bases of distinctions between what is real and what only seems to be.

17. Stage 2.
Mythic-Literal Faith

||||||||||||||||||||||||||||||||||||||||||||||||||||||||||||||||||||||||||||||||||||||||||||||||||||||||||

The mind of the ten-year-old is an amazing instrument. It can virtually memorize the *Guinness Book of World Records.* It can guide a pair of hands to victory in a game of chess, sometimes over more experienced adult competitors. It can take an hour and a half to tell, in vastly inclusive detail, what the movie *Star Wars* is about. It can write and tell good stories, perform arithmetical operations, create and use systems of classification and consistently and accurately take the perspective of another on some object or interest in common. The ten-year-old mind can reverse its operations; it therefore understands constancy of volume and weight when objects or liquids are changed from one form to another. It can think in terms of processes—particularly if the processes in question are ones for which it has experienced concrete analogies. It can make inferences regarding the cause and effect relationships linking two "states of affairs" and it can reconstruct plausible intermediate steps in the process to test and refine its inferences.

In contrast with the preschooler, the ten-year-old constructs a more orderly, temporally linear and dependable world. Capable of inductive and deductive reasoning, the ten-year-old has become a young empiricist. Where the Intuitive-Projective child fuses fantasy, fact and feeling, the Mythic-Literal girl or boy works hard and effectively at sorting out the real from the make-believe. Within the range of his or her ability to investigate and test, this youngster will insist on demonstration or proof for claims of fact. The concrete operational boy or girl does not cease to be imaginative or capable of a highly developed fantasy life, but the products of imagination are confined more to the world of play and will be submitted to more logical forms of scrutiny before being admitted as part of what the child "knows." Gone or vastly diminished are the epistemological egocentrism and the "blooming, buzzing confusion" of Stage 1. Replacing them are the ability to coordinate one's own perspective with that of another and the experience of a more predictable and patterned—if more prosaic—world.

The great gift to consciousness that emerges in this stage is the ability to narratize one's experience. As regards our primary interest in faith we can say that the development of the Mythic-Literal stage brings with it the ability to bind our experiences into meaning through the medium of stories. Younger children, as we have seen, depend upon rich stories to provide images, symbols and examples for the vague but powerful impulses, feelings and aspirations forming within them. Stories for the Stage 1 child provide symbolic representations that both express and provide models for their constructions of self and others in relation to an ultimate environment, but the preoperational child does not yet generate stories. He or she does not yet narratize experience. Concrete operational thinking brings new capacities. The convergence of the reversibility of thought with taking the perspective of another combined with an improved grasp of cause-effect relations means that the elements are in place for appropriating and retelling the rich stories one is told. More than this, the elements are in place for youngsters to begin to tell self-generated stories that make it possible to conserve, communicate and compare their experiences and meanings.

This capacity for and interest in narrative makes the school-age child particularly attentive to the stories that conserve the origins and formative experience of the familial and communal groups to which he or she belongs. Stories of lives and of great adventures—true or realistically fictional—appeal because of their inherent interest, but they also appeal because they become media for the extension of the child's experience and understanding of life. Of course, we never lose this fascination with stories, just as we never lose Stage 1's capacity for composing and responding to the symbolic and the fantastic. Any speaker recognizes the relaxation of facial expressions and the grateful shifts in body posture that occur when the talk calls for a change from conceptual prose to the telling of a story. But with further development we will later construct the ability to step back from our stories, reflect upon them, and to communicate their meanings by way of more abstract and general statements. Stage 2 does not yet do this. If we picture the flow of our lives as being like a river, Stage 2 tells stories that describe the flow from the midst of the stream. The Stage 2 person—child or adult—does not yet step out on the bank beside the river and reflect on the stories of the flow and their composite meanings. For Stage 2 meanings are conserved and expressed in stories. There is also a sense in which the meanings are *trapped* in the narrative, there not being yet the readiness to draw from them conclusions about a general order of meaning in life.

Let's listen to some sections of a lively interview with a *real* ten year old. Millie, a fourth grader from a Protestant family, plays the viola and loves singing and acting. Math, she says, is her hardest school subject: "It's so hard and so confusing—put this over there and everything!" (She's just been introduced to large multiplication problems and to long division). A short way into the talk Millie is asked the question about why there are people in the world.

> *Millie:* People in the world? Let's see. If there weren't any people, there wouldn't really be a world. And if there wasn't a world then the world would be blank. I mean everything—that's a tough question. Let's see. Why would there be people?

The concreteness of Millie's thinking and the unreadiness yet to formulate conceptual meanings of a more general order mark her responses to this and the next several questions. A short time later she is asked if she can imagine a world without her and what it would be like.

> *Millie:* It would be the same only there'd be a different person without me in it . . . Well there wouldn't be a Millie T. Well, there might be somewhere. And Sue T. [her sister] wouldn't have a person to share a room with. And there wouldn't be a little girl in the Willingham School who plays the viola. And there wouldn't be Millie T., Jacqueline M.'s best friend. There wouldn't be Millie T., who plays viola in the all-city orchestra. And it would be different, I think, it probably would be.

To her, Millie's identity is the story of Millie's relationships and roles. The concreteness of her thought leads her to depict a world without her in terms of the gaps in relationships and roles her absence would mean. Interestingly, her depiction of a world without people conceives it in terms of the gaps in roles and relationships *God* would experience:

Interviewer: Okay, now let's go back to the first question and see if you can tell me now why you think there are people here in the world. Are they here for any purpose?

Millie: There—well, if there wasn't any people in the world, who would keep God company?

Interviewer: Is that why people are here?

Millie: I don't know, but that question just popped into my mind. How—how would God keep busy?

Interviewer: And what does God do with people?

Millie: He—he makes the people. He tries to give them good families. And he, he, um, made the world. He made trees and everything. If you didn't have trees you wouldn't have books. And if you didn't—like he made the whole world, which has a lot of beauty and that makes up things. Like rocks make metals and some kinds of rocks make metal.

Interviewer: Well, since God made all of these things for us, does he expect anything from us?

Millie: He just expects us, probably, to believe in him. To love each other and forgive and try to follow the Ten Commandments.

Interviewer: Is that all?

Millie: I—let's see, to love and to forgive and to try—to try to be happy in the world.

Interviewer: And how can you be happy?

Millie: To not—to not do things that you don't want to and to try to keep ourselves, you know, used. Not just sit around and mope.

In the next several passages Millie shares some of her images and thoughts of God. Here we see the concrete operational mind working creatively, within its limits, to grasp and express paradoxical insights. We see a typical example of the literal quality of Stage 2's use of symbols. The interviewer has just asked her what God looks like.

Millie: Well, I don't know. But do you want me to tell you what I imagine that he looks like? I imagine that he's an old man with a white beard and white hair wearing a long robe and that the clouds are his floor and he has a throne. And he has all these people and there's angels around him. And there's all the good people, angles and—and um, cupids and that he has like—I guess I—he has a nice face, nice blue eyes. He can't be all white, you know, he has to—he has blue eyes and he's forgiving. And I guess that's the way I think he is.

Interviewer: How do you get to be a good person?

Millie: To believe in God and try your hardest to do what is good.

Interviewer: When we do something wrong, does God know?

Millie: Yeah. God's with you all the time.

Interviewer: He is? How is that?

Millie: Well, God's inside of you in a way. In a way God's inside of you but in a way God isn't. He's inside of you because you believe—if you believe in him then he's inside of you, but he's also all around.

Interviewer: How can he be all around?

Millie: Well, that's a good question. Um, well he's—he lives on top of the world, so in a way he's all around.

The anthropomorphic elements in Millie's image of God (the old man with the white beard who lives on top of the world), as in many of our Stage 2 interviews, are far more developed than the nascent anthropomorphic images in Freddy's depiction of God quoted in our discussion of Stage 1. And as the next passage will show, Millie's God has the capacity to take her perspective and the perspectives of his other people. He takes account of intentions and the struggles of people; he is inclined to be compassionate. Before we began this research I had assumed that full-fledged anthropomorphic images of God like Millie's would primarily be found among preschool children. What we have found, in fact, is that Stage 1 youngsters are far more likely to answer questions about God in terms of his being "like the air—everywhere," or as Freddy put it, "He spreads all around the world in one day," or "He can split or he can be like a God." As I suggested in a previous writing,[16] this unexpected delay in the emergence of fully anthropomorphic God-images until Stage 2, where it is very common, makes sense if we take account of the revolution in perspective taking that concrete operational thinking makes possible. The egocentrism of Stage 1 limits the child's ability to differentiate God's perspective from his or her own, just as it limits the ability to take the perspective of other persons. Stage 2's capacity to construct the perspectives of others ("Sue T. wouldn't have a person to share a room with. . . . And there wouldn't be Millie T., Jacqueline M.'s best friend.") means that the youngster now can also construct God's perspective, giving it as much richness—and some of the same limits—as the perspectives now consistently attributed to friends and family members. Let's listen to Millie again:

Interviewer: Does God care when you do something wrong?

Millie: Sure he—he cares. And he knows that you're—he knows that you are sorry about it. And he always tries—he always forgives you, usually.

Interviewer: What if you're not sorry about it?

Millie: Then he knows, probably. He probably will still forgive you probably because he knows that you're probably going through a rough time. And

I think that probably like some people who don't even believe in God, God still probably believes—uh, forgives them, because he knows that, you know, people have their own ideas and beliefs.

The concreteness and literalism that keep Stage 2 grounded come through plainly in this next passage, which sets forth the outlines of Millie's cosmology:

Interviewer: Well, what if somebody just came up to you and said, I've heard lots about this God. Can you tell me what God is? What would you say to them?

Millie: God is like a saint. He's good and he like—he like rules the world, but in a good way. And—

Interviewer: How does he rule the world?

Millie: Well, he—not really rule the world, but um—let's see, he like—he lives on top of the world and he's always watching over everybody. At least he tries to. And he does what he thinks is right. He does what he thinks is right and tries to do the best and—he lives up in heaven and—

Interviewer: Well can anyone go to heaven?

Millie: If people want to and believe in God then they can go to heaven.

Interviewer: What if people don't want to or don't believe in God? Then what happens to them?

Millie: They go just the opposite way.

Interviewer: And where's that?

Millie: Down under the ground where the devil lives.

Interviewer: Oh, I see, okay. Can you tell what the devil is?

Millie: Devil is a saint too, but he believes in evil and doing things wrong. Just the opposite of God. And he's always doing things that God doesn't want people to be doing.

Interviewer: Does he have power over the world?

Millie: The devil? Well like, no. God—no. I don't think . . . That's a hard question. God doesn't really have power over the world. He just kind of watches it. And the devil's just like a little mouse trying to get cheese. Like he's trying to get into it, but I guess he just doesn't.

In the next several passages we see Millie bringing to word some of what she feels and knows about death and the justice of God. It seems likely that here we are getting thoughts that grasp and repeat some things her parent or parents have recently offered her. Yet one judges that Millie is not merely parroting, but that she has passed the meanings they shared with her through the filters of her own structures of knowing and valuing and that we are getting her first foumulations on these matters. The interviewer has just asked why people die.

Millie: Well, if everybody stayed alive then, I mean, the world would just be so overcrowded. And, and things—it would make it harder for a family like to lead, to get money, to work, to find jobs and to find food and it would just be hard for the world. So God has to let some people die.

Interviewer: Is it up to God?

Millie: Well, well yeah. But like you know, he has to—let's see. Well, in a way, yes. Because he kind of controls. And I think that probably that— well actually he can't help it if somebody's going to die. Like he can't say that person's good, he can't die. He'd just say well I'm sorry but he's going to have to die. I mean like he can't really help. Like my friend, she had a puppy and he got ran [sic] over. And she was so mad. And she says, "I hate God, I hate God!" And I go, you know, that you shouldn't say that, 'cause God does work in mysterious ways. And you know you never know what's going to happen next. And neither does he.

Interviewer: But is it always the best thing?

Millie: It's always the best thing. Because if that puppy didn't die, then you know, you never know what would have happened next. And usually what God does is the best thing.

Interviewer: Usually?

Millie: Most of the time. All the time.

Interviewer: Which one?

Millie: All the time he does the best thing and the thing he thinks is best for us.

Interviewer: How does he know what's best?

Millie: Well, it's like your parents. They think they know what's best for you and so they try to do what they think is right. So that's what God does. And usually it turns out that he—what he does is the right thing.

With Millie's mentioning that God's doing what he thinks best is like parents doing what they think best for their children we are in position to grasp a useful insight. Millie's God-image takes forms offered by her culture, both the larger Western culture and the more particular Protestant culture of her family. But the forms are filled with the contents of Millie's perspective taking with her parents as decision makers. A little further in the interview, after she has likened God's actions to those of parents (God, too, is doing what he thinks is best for his people), she is asked if parents always do the right thing.

Millie: No, they don't always do the right thing, but they think what they do is best. Sometimes they make mistakes and I guess God probably makes mistakes too. See I keep changing my mind. You know, after I think, parents make mistakes because they think what they think is try to do the best. Sometimes it doesn't turn out to be the best and—well, God still I guess probably does what he thinks is right and it usually turns out—it turns out to be the right thing. But parents I guess don't always do the right thing.

Interviewer: How do parents find out what's right?

Millie: They have to think it over. Get all the things that happened and put them together and decide which would be the best thing to them.

This perspective taking with her parents and their apparent willingness to make their own processes of decision making accessible to their children enable her to construct an understanding of God that allows for divine mistakes and limitations of power. These factors help account for the fact that, in contrast to that of many of our Stage 2 respondents, Millie's God is not seen in excessively simple terms of strict reciprocity, invariably sending bad fortune to bad people and sending good fortune to the virtuous. Though still confined to the concreteness of the Mythic-Literal stage in this area of theodicy (explaining God's ways with humanity), Millie shows evidences of an emerging structuring in which seeming inequalities and differences in human fortune actually work for good. She is asked why some people seem to be luckier than other people.

Millie: Um, if God—if God evened up the whole world exactly even, then there wouldn't be good because there wouldn't be people who you could buy things from because I guess—to own like a company, you have to be very wealthy. You couldn't buy things from those people because there wouldn't be any companies and also you couldn't have jobs from other people because they wouldn't have enough money to give you because they have to use it, and things wouldn't work out . . . and usually—and usually its the person who's wealthy is the lucky—I mean, it's he—you can't really call him lucky because he worked really hard for that money and so like you can call him lucky for the money, but he still has to work very hard to get the money.

At the end of this passage, an eloquent ten-year-old formulation of a rationale for capitalism, we see Millie drawn back toward Stage 2's typical commitments to reciprocity and fairness in God's dealing with humans, but in a more subtle and sophisticated form than it is usually stated. ("You can't really call him lucky because he worked really hard for that money.")

Eleven-year-old Alan, for example, was also asked why some persons seem to be luckier than others.

Alan: I can't really say that there's any such thing as luck because, um, this, it's just that it's like coincidences most of the time.

He goes on to give a somewhat unclear explanation that suggests that what people get has to do with their intentions. His meaning comes clearer when the interviewer asks him whether God has anything to do with whether people get what they want or not.

Alan: No, because, um, after the first sin, then the Lord, he punishes the people who do wrong, but he can't make them do wrong.

Interviewer: Can't make them do wrong?

Alan: So, it's like he's seeing what they're going to do. . . . So, um, he really has no, no charge of whether they're lucky or unlucky.

Interviewer: Are you saying that people who do wrong things get punished and are therefore unlucky?

Alan: No, they aren't unlucky. It's, um, it's punishment if you, if you did something wrong then you would deserve it.

Interviewer: So, that people who don't get the things they want or who get disappointed in life are somehow being punished?

Alan: Yeah, yes. Not if they don't get the things that they want, but if they do something wrong and then they don't get things that they want, then they're sort of being punished . . . Oh, could I say that answer over again? See, it's like, not if they're doing wrong. Some, like in the first story you told me [the "Heinz dilemma"], he did wrong for good, so they don't always punish wrong, but if you do wrong deliberately for yourself, then you would most likely get punished.

Interviewer: I see. And God does that?

Alan: Mm-hm.

Alan's construction, while less sophisticated than Millie's, implies a similar understanding of reciprocal justice as an immanent structure in our lives. Presumably God created this ordering of things and even God is bound to the lawfulness he has created. This comes out even more plainly in our last excerpts from Millie's interview. Toward the end of the interview Millie too, was given the "Heinz dilemma" developed by Kohlberg for his research. A sparse story, it tells of a man in Europe whose wife is dying of cancer. He learns about a druggist nearby who has developed a new drug, derived from radium, which may help his wife get better. The druggist pays $200 for the radium and charges $2000 for the finished drug. Heinz does all that he can to raise the needed money, but is only able to get $1000. The druggist refuses to sell the drug for that price. Heinz grows desperate and he breaks in and steals the drug.

Interviewer: Should Heinz have stolen the drug?

Millie: Um—that's—I knew you were going to ask that, and that's a hard question. Well in a way yes, but in a way no. Because—his, because his wife really needed it and if God forgave him, then probably everybody says, oh, that's okay, and everybody would steal. And the world wouldn't be right.

Interviewer: The world wouldn't be right?

Millie: No, because it wouldn't be the way that God would want it to be, if everybody stole and did what was wrong.

This is fascinating. Here we see Millie, like Alan, working with the same structuring of fairness that typifies Kohlberg's stage two. This is the fairness of instrumental exchange, where whatever one person is entitled to each other person is also entitled to. But she has extended that to the construction of a kind of rudimentary social system in which ("even if God forgave him" and "probably everybody else says, oh, that's okay") it would still be wrong for Heinz to steal. Why? Because, in fairness, everyone else would also be entitled to steal. And more, the structure of rightness in the world would be violated: "And the world wouldn't be right . . . because it wouldn't be the way that God would want it." I think that here we see justice as fairness, based on a prelegal understanding, extended into what amounts, for Millie, to an ontological structure of rightness—a functional, preconceptual system of natural law. Even God, who might personally make allowances for Heinz, cannot change the fact that stealing, which could become generalized if Heinz "gets by" with it, goes against "the way that God would want it to be." So powerful is this sense that stealing is wrong in some ontological sense that Millie shows very limited readiness to take the perspective of Heinz's wife. She is asked, "Is it worse to steal than to save someone's life?

Millie: Um, I guess, but—I guess in a way it's better to save somebody's life.

Interviewer: In what way?

Millie: In a way that the person's dying. But in a way no, because in a while that person's going to die anyways.

Interviewer: So you're just kind of putting it off.

Millie: Yeah, Yeah.

Interviewer: So what do you think Heinz should do?

Millie: Heinz should have gone to try his best. He should have like tried to make a lot of money, like work really fast. He could have gone to some place like a high authority like the mayor.

Interviewer: And why would he go to the mayor?

Millie: To ask them if, um, if that there was anything that he could do to get the money for the medicine. And if anybody could help him with his wife, help take care of the wife if she was sick right now.

Interviewer: So he shouldn't have stolen the drug?

Millie: He should have tried his hardest. 'Cause when he—when his wife died he would have known—Say his wife died anyways. He would have known that he did something wrong and he was going to have to pay for it. He would have known he did something wrong.

Interviewer: How would he know?

Millie: He, he would know, 'cause he a feel—he would have a feeling inside him, now I did all this wrong just to save my wife's life.

The connection between God and the necessity of accepting punishment, even for well intentioned infractions against the "natural law" comes clear in the next eloquently concrete passage. Millie has just said, "He would have a feeling inside him, now I did all this wrong just to save my wife's life."

Interviewer: And where would that feeling come from?

Millie: From his conscience—conscience.

Interviewer: And what is your conscience?

Millie: It's like a person in you who always like talks inside of you, it talks like in your brain.

Interviewer: Um-hum. And where does it come from?

Millie: What?

Interviewer: Your conscience.

Millie: God. God gives everybody a conscience.

As the next passages indicate everyone's conscience is not the same (indicating again that Millie recognizes differences of perspective and judgment). Yet, still it is clear that, at least regarding stealing, everyone's conscience is likely to oppose it:

Interviewer: And everybody has the same conscience?

Millie: Uh-uh [no]. It depends on who you are. Like if you're an adult you have an adult conscience inside of you.

Interviewer: Um-hum. Well how is my conscience different from yours?

Millie: Because you—if you're older and you have different personalities than I do. And you probably have different thoughts than I do.

Interviewer: So—what kind—so Heinz had a different conscience than you?

Millie: Yeah. He probably thought what he was doing was right.

Interviewer: Why would he think that?

Millie: Because he was saving his wife's life. But then when his wife died, he would have said, why did I steal that?

Interviewer: What if his wife didn't die? What if she got well?

Millie: Then he would still know that he did something wrong, and he'd probably, probably, probably, he'd probably have to be put in jail and probably pay—have to work very hard to pay for the money for the thing.

In both Millie's and Alan's responses we see a structuring of the ultimate environment based on the strong intuition of a built-in, divinely constituted, natural lawfulness. Though there is some allowance for motives and intentions and the experiences that affect them in Millie's answers, she, like Alan, believes that even God is bound by the structures of reciprocity built into the order of things.

Though Stage 2 typically takes form in the elementary school years, some of the adolescents and a few of the adults we have interviewed exhibit the structural characteristics of Stage 2 as they speak of their faith. A few passages from one such respondent, a woman in her fifties, will provide an example. Please recognize that I could have chosen a man for this and that other examples one might have used could have included atheists or persons of religious orientations other than Catholicism.

Mrs. W., a mother of several grown or near-grown children, is in her fifties. Before her children began to leave home she devoted her full time to being a mother and to directing the affairs of their home. As the children have gone off to college or other pursuits she has returned to teaching school and seems to be kept very busy with her work. This seems to have cut her off from frequent conversations with friends. There is an undercurrent of loneliness and depression in her interview. As we look in on her conversation with our interviewer Mrs. W. is describing a talk given by one of the parish priests, a man whom she admires and whose approach to religion she appreciates.

Mrs. W.:   Well I tell you now, last week he was saying that it was Advent and that, you know, just do one good thing, he said, for someone—just one this week. Some kind of thing—hold a door for someone that doesn't expect it. Just one little thing, and offer it up. [Pause] Y'know, 'n this is what, this is what I find I need, you know. Sometimes you keep doing big things; you think, oh I have to say a whole rosary or any—to say a whole thing. Now I have a little picture of the Pope—oh, I have great faith in him, that Pope—Pope John—and over my sink I have a picture of him, and everyday I say a Our Father, a Hail Mary, and a Glory Be to God. And then when I need it, it's in the bank. And now I have my children doing it, when they're walking to class and all, I say, "Build up your bank account." And when you sit in that dentist's chair, and it goes, Oooh! You just say, "open the bank" and out it pours, and it works. . . . Well, it, you just know that if you get in a mess, you have that bank and it will open up and it will help you through the mess.

At another point in the interview Mrs. W. is asked about her faith.

Interviewer: Let me ask you in general to describe what your faith is. What sort of descriptions would you use to, to try to tell somebody what your faith means to you?

Mrs. W.:   Well, I don't know if other people feel this way, but I sort of sometimes feel you're plodding along, you know, all by yourself. But . . . because I have this great . . . because I have faith and believe in God, it seems to make the bumps a little easier, or the good times, you know, you have someone to share it with, really. Now I don't know why I say— I say this, because I was brought up with a sister. And we chatted and chatted, and chatted. And that's all we had, you know, each other. Then I got married, and Ben is not a gossipy type person. So that, I mean, you know, if . . . well, I can just sort of share my feelings with God more easily than I can with a person, I guess.

Interviewer: Do you find yourself during the day just kind of casually . . . . . . chatting . . . chatting with God?

Mrs. W.:   Yeah. Yeah, and I'd say, you know, "I don't mean to complain —I know I have my help, and I know I have feet, and I know I have food, but what do you say, you know, uh, let's have . . ." And I think we've tried to bring the children up this way to make it more human, so you don't feel that . . . Now I thought that one of the greatest things was Tom [one of her sons]. He decided, you know, that this going to mass was too much and all. And then, oh the draft came along for Mack [another of her sons], and then it came along for himself. And he said, "You know, Mother, I go to church every Sunday now because I felt I can't be asking for a big favor and then not showing up. And then when something else happens," he said, "so it's easier for me to make a little effort each week." So . . . , so I just feel that . . . , uh . . . Well, it, it just, I mean I can only talk about my children and myself's feeling because . . . other people just don't discuss it. But everyone seems to enjoy having this thing to share.

From these few passages the concreteness and narrative character of Mrs. W.'s outlook become evident. Her meanings are contained in her stories. And like Millie and Allan, our ten and eleven year old respondents, Mrs. W. constructs her understanding of God and the world in terms of reciprocity. Daily, or even hourly prayers and acts of praise enable her to "put money in the bank"—to store up God's good favor against times when special help or forgiveness may be needed. She has tried to teach this way of structuring the world to her children and is pleased when she sees evidence that they understand that if they want God's help and protection they have to do their part.

Later in the interview we get indications that Mrs. W.'s God is somewhat remote and impersonal. She says that her husband, in praying, "goes straight to the top," meaning that he prays directly to the God-head. She, however, finds a meaningful and personal mediation in her relation to God through a group of saints, who are for her also protectors and companions:

> *Mrs. W.*   Oh, down in that church I have it all there. I have both—Tom was born the day after Christmas, and there's a painting of the Blessed Virgin holding the Christ Child. Well, I pray to the Christ Child—the Christ Child takes care of Tom, and the Blessed Virgin Mary. And there's a lady with Christ, and she's Saint Anne—she takes care of Joan [a daughter]. And then there's a St. Anthony's over in the corner that takes care of Mack. So every time I walk into church I thank all of them for what they've done for them. [Pause] But it's these pictures, I think . . . that . . . that's who they all pray to . . . And Mim [another daughter] has a little Indian girl—Tekawitha, is that her name? . . . [Pause] I love that little chapel . . . But I, now, as I say, I, now when I pray to St. Anne—I used to pray to St. Anne for myself—and I'd think of her there in a rocker rocking there praying for me to God, you know . . . to help me along. But maybe I'm too friendly with them, you know?
>
> *Interviewer:*   With the saints?
>
> *Mrs. W:*   Yeah, I mean, you know, . . . St. Anne sitting there and she's telling her beads, and she'll say, "Throw one in for S.W.", you know. And that Christ Child; I mean, I say to him, you know, Tom's really working awful hard, and, and he'll, I mean he certainly—has come through, and I'll say St. Anthony worked for Mack like there's no tomorrow. . . . We're doing pretty well, and I say to him, "I don't mean to keep asking, but. . . . As I say, I'm kind of friendly with them. But this gives me a feeling of satisfaction. I mean I don't feel so alone. . . . They're like friends.

Mrs. W.'s account of her faith shows some elements of Stage 1's magical thinking. It also has hints of the interpersonal constructions that we will encounter as a key structuring characteristic of Stage 3. On the whole, however, the modes of her faith are best described as Stage 2, given the almost exclusive reliance on narrative as the means of organiz-

ing her meanings, and the central importance of re[
principle governing divine-human relations. Other Sta[
clude the overall anthropological character of her me[
and the literalism involved in her reliance upon those symbols. [...]
looked further at the interview you might have begun to see more clearly
that Mrs. W.'s forms of faith and her isolation from actual friends and
family are probably interrelated. At one point she begins to characterize
herself as a child. The interviewer failed to pick up on this self-descrip-
tion, but it appears that Mrs. W. is pretty painfully aware that her form
of faith does not serve her very well as an orientation in a complex and
dangerous world. One wonders if her college-aged children really find
her faith formulas helpful or viable or whether they collude with her
childishness by telling her only what she seems to want to hear.

As we conclude our look at the patterns and dynamics of Stage 2 let
us examine a summary of its main features.

*Stage 2 Mythic-Literal faith is the stage in which the person begins to
take on for him- or herself the stories, beliefs and observances that
symbolize belonging to his or her community. Beliefs are appropriated
with literal interpretations, as are moral rules and attitudes. Symbols are
taken as one-dimensional and literal in meaning. In this stage the rise
of concrete operations leads to the curbing and ordering of the previous
stage's imaginative composing of the world. The episodic quality of
Intuitive-Projective faith gives way to a more linear, narrative construction of coherence and meaning. Story becomes the major way of giving
unity and value to experience. This is the faith stage of the school child
(though we sometimes find the structures dominant in adolescents and
in adults). Marked by increased accuracy in taking the perspective of
other persons, those in Stage 2 compose a world based on reciprocal
fairness and an immanent justice based on reciprocity. The actors in
their cosmic stories are anthropomorphic. They can be affected deeply
and powerfully by symbolic and dramatic materials and can describe in
endlessly detailed narrative what has occurred. They do not, however,
step back from the flow of stories to formulate reflective, conceptual
meanings. For this stage the meaning is both carried and "trapped" in
the narrative.*

*The new capacity or strength in this stage is the rise of narrative and
the emergence of story, drama and myth as ways of finding and giving
coherence to experience.*

The limitations of literalness and an excessive reliance upon reciprocity as a principle for constructing an ultimate environment can result either in an overcontrolling, stilted perfectionism or "works righteousness" or in their opposite, an abasing sense of badness embraced because of mistreatment, neglect or the apparent disfavor of significant others.

A factor initiating transition to Stage 3 is the implicit clash or contradictions in stories that leads to reflection on meanings. The transition to formal operational thought makes such reflection possible and necessary. Previous literalism breaks down; new "cognitive conceit" (Elkind) leads to disillusionment with previous teachers and teachings. Conflicts between authoritative stories (Genesis on creation versus evolutionary theory) must be faced. The emergence of mutual interpersonal perspective taking ("I see you seeing me; I see me as you see me; I see you seeing me seeing you.") creates the need for a more personal relationship with the unifying power of the ultimate environment.

18. Stage 3. Synthetic-Conventional Faith

Puberty brings with it a revolution in physical and emotional life. The adolescent needs mirrors—mirrors to keep tabs on this week's growth, to become accustomed to the new angularity of a face and to the new curves or reach of a body. But in a qualitatively new way the young person also looks for mirrors of another sort. He or she needs the eyes and ears of a few trusted others in which to see the image of *personality* emerging and to get a hearing for the new feelings, insights, anxieties and commitments that are forming and seeking expression. Harry Stack Sullivan speaks of the "chum" relationship—a first experience of adolescent intimacy outside the family. In the chum—of either the same or opposite sex—a youth finds another person with time and with parallel gifts and needs. In their endless talking, scheming, fantasizing and worrying, each gives the other the gift of being known and accepted. And more, each gives the other a mirror with which to help focus the new explosiveness and many-ness of his or her inner life. Puppy love, as Erik Erikson tells us, is by no means merely a matter of glandular changes and sexual interests. In the assured regard and idealizing affections of the new love, one gathers and falls in love with a forming personal myth of the self.[17]

Formal operational thinking may first make its appearance in an algebra class or in an advanced biology lab. As it emerges it brings with it the ability to reflect upon one's thinking. It appraises a situation or a problem and forms a variety of hypothetical solutions or explanations. It generates methods of testing and verifying the hypotheses. In problem solving formal operational thinking can work with propositions and symbols, manipulating them to find solutions prior to any contact with the actual physical objects or contexts they represent. And just as it can generate hypothetical propositions of explanation, so it can envision a universe of possible realities and futures. Formal operational thought can conceive ideal features of persons, communities or other states of affairs. It can be idealistically or harshly judgmental of actual people or institutions in light of these ideal conceptions.

In social and interpersonal life the advent of formal operations has several significant consequences. In Stage 2, you remember, persons' meaning tend to find expression in their stories, the network of narratives that recall and represent their significant experiences. At Stage 2 the story teller speaks from within the flow of experience and does not typically reflect upon it in such ways as to formulate more general, propositional insights that could convey a synthesis of meanings. Formal operational thinking, with its new capacity for reflection on one's own thought and ways of experiencing, invites one mentally to step outside the flow of life's stream. From a vantage point on the river bank, as it were, one can take a look at the flow of the stream as a whole. One can see and name certain patterns of meaning arising out of her or his collection of stories. A myth or myths of the personal past can be composed; this represents a new level of story, a level we might call the *story of our stories.* And with this comes the possibility and burden of composing myths of possible futures. The youth begins to project the forming myth of self into future roles and relationships. On the one hand this projection represents faith in the self one is becoming and trust that that self will be received and ratified by the future. On the other it brings dread that the self may fail to focus, may find no place with others and may be ignored, undiscovered or shunted off into insignificance by the future.

A key to both the forming of a personal myth and to the dynamics of chumship or first love is the emergence of interpersonal perspective taking. With the formal operational ability to construct the hypothetical, there can emerge the complex ability to compose hypothetical images of myself as others see me. This, of course, is the mechanism by which the friend or first love becomes a mirror for us. I can summarize Kohlberg's discussion of this mechanism in Part II by offering a little couplet.

I see you seeing me:
I see the me I think you see.

The new burden of "self-consciousness" that the realization of this capacity brings is part of an adolescent version of egocentrism. The youth believes everyone is looking at him or her and may feel either a narcissistic inflation or a self-questioning deflation regarding "the me I think you see." Part of what helps to moderate this self-consciousness —and to overcome the usually temporary excesses of egocentrism—is the functional realization of the reciprocal of our earlier couplet. For soon one begins to recognize that,

You see you according to me:
You see the you you think I see.

The relational situation described by these two couplets is what we call mutual interpersonal perspective taking.

Stage 2 constructs a world in which the perspectives of others on the self are relatively impersonal. Lawfulness and reciprocity, as we have seen, are the principal characteristics of such a world. In its constructions of God or an ultimate environment, Stage 2 typically employs anthropomorphic images. These anthropomorphisms, however, are largely prepersonal, lacking the kind of nuanced personality in relation to which one could know oneself as being known deeply. With the emergence of mutual interpersonal perspective taking God undergoes a recomposition. Both the self and the chum or young love come to be experienced as having a rich, mysterious and finally inaccessible depth of personality. God—when God remains or becomes salient in a person's faith at this stage—must also be re-imaged as having inexhaustible depths and as being capable of knowing personally those mysterious depths of self and others we know that we ourselves will never know. Much of the extensive literature about adolescent conversion can be illumined, I believe, by the recognition that the adolescent's religious hunger is for a God who knows, accepts and confirms the self deeply, and who serves as an infinite guarantor of the self with its forming myth of personal identity and faith. It is not surprising that so many of the images for transcendence that appeal to persons in Stage 3 have the characteristics of a divinely personal significant other.

By the time of the teen years a young person has begun to relate to a widened set of environments. In addition to the sphere of the family now there are spheres of influence represented by peers, by school or work, by media and popular culture, and perhaps by a religious community. In each of these spheres of influence there are peers and adults who are potentially significant others. With this term I refer to those persons whose "mirroring" of the young person has the power to contribute positively or negatively to the set of images of self and of accompanying meanings that must be drawn together in a forming identity and faith.[18] The "identity crisis" of adolescence, as Erikson has taught us to call it, derives in signal ways from the discrepancies and dissonances between the images of self and value reflected by our significant others. Who of us can fail to remember the tightness we felt as adolescents when the significant others from our various spheres of influence were occasionally assembled in one place, focusing on us all at once the vectors of our sense of their different expectations?

Their expectations: in the interpersonal world of Stage 3 faith *their* expectations help us focus ourselves and assemble our commitments to values, but there is always the danger of becoming permanently dependent upon and subject to what Sharon Parks calls the "tyranny of the they."[19] For Stage 3, with its beginnings in adolescence, authority is located externally to the self. It resides in the interpersonally available "they" or in the certified incumbents of leadership roles in institutions. This is not to deny that adolescents make choices or that they develop strong feelings and commitments regarding their values and behavioral norms. It is to say, however, that despite their genuine feelings of having made choices and commitments, a truer reading is that their values and self-images, mediated by the significant others in their lives, have largely chosen them. And in *their* (the youths') choosing they have, in the main, clarified and ratified those images and values which have chosen them.

When God is a significant other in this mix—and the divine is always potentially what James Cone has called the "Decisive Other"[20]—the commitment to God and the correlated self-image can exert a powerful ordering on a youth's identity and values outlook.

Let us consider now some passages from interviews with two of our adolescent respondents which will give flesh to our discussion so far of the dynamics of the forming of Stage 3 faith and identity.

Linda is a petite and startlingly blonde fifteen-year-old of Finnish descent. Though born in this country, her first language was Finnish. The family continues to speak only Finnish at home. Her father works in construction. In his ongoing search for work the family has moved fourteen times in the last fifteen years. Her mother, a blonde woman even tinier than her daughter, works as a housecleaner and her services are in great demand in the area of the Florida city where they now live. The family, including Linda's baby brother Matt, live in a newly built tract house decorated elegantly, if sparsely, with modern Finnish furniture. Her family's move to Florida has been a happy one for Linda. She is popular and a good student. Very much in tune with her age group, she thinks a lot about fashion, boy friends and popularity. She sees herself as standing somewhat apart from her peers, however, because of her strong religious and moral beliefs. Linda is a Lutheran, active in teaching church school and playing the organ on occasions at church.

Earlier in their talk, Linda told our interviewer a lot about the experiences of her life. In that part of their conversation she spontaneously talked about the importance of her religion to her. Acknowledging that Linda seems to know how she feels about things, the interviewer asks her to talk about those feelings:

> *Linda:* Well, I feel like I'm not afraid of anything now because I know what I believe in and I know what I want to do in life, and nothing could really set me off course. We're not going to move any place now. Before, if we moved (like I told you we did) I got into people, different people, and I sort of changed as the people went. But I have learned that just the best thing is to be yourself.
>
> *Interviewer:* Linda, when you say you *know* what you believe in . . . can you try to trace *how* you came to know what you believe in?
>
> *Linda:* I guess religion. I've always gone to church and everything. And my parents, they always guided me. . . . They've always taught me that God's always there and, you know, he's the only way that you can really make it. . . . You depend upon him and I really believe in him and, you know how they say God talks in many mysterious ways? Well, in a sense he's told me lots of times . . . I really think that he's led me to where I am today. 'Cause lots of times I've just thought the world is just, you know, I just don't feel anything. But then that morning I'll just have a feeling that . . . I guess there is Somebody, you know?
>
> *Interviewer:* What do you think God is?
>
> *Linda:* God is different to a lot of people. . . . I don't go exactly by the Bible. I

think you should try to make the world . . . you should try to make people happy and at the same time enjoy yourself, you know? In a good kind way . . .

Asked further about her conception of God, Linda answers, "I just feel, I just feel he's there. There might not be any material proof but I *know*. I can bet my life on it. Really. I know because he *has* talked to me." Linda explains that God's talking to her comes in the form of feelings she gets when she has really struggled with a problem, feeling that God cares and that there is something she can do. Once when one of her friends had turned against her she went into her bedroom, thought about her situation and cried. She said, "Then I remembered that, you know, there was God and I just asked him to tell me something, tell me what I could do, because why do I have to be glued to one person? Why can't I be good friends with everybody? Go places with her one time and then with her and him, and you know, with everybody? And that's really true."

Notice the concerns with identity and interpersonal relations in Linda's conversation about her religion and God. Note also her reflection on her past and her future and on the effort to pull the diffusion of her life of fourteen moves into a dependable and stable unity. God for her is personal. Although some concrete imagery from a previous Stage 2 lingers in the next passages, Linda's dominant images of God have the Stage 3 qualities of companionship, guidance, support and of knowing and loving her. Her warranty for her beliefs comes from what she has been taught and what she *feels*.

In her talks with friends Linda often speaks about religion. She recognizes that frequently they are turned off by her talk. Our interviewer asked why that was so.

Linda: They get *scared* or something. . . . I guess they are just afraid of dying. . . . But I'm not afraid to die at all.

Interviewer: What do you think happens to you when you die?

Linda: Well, I *know*. I have this feeling, like, when *I* die I'm going to go to heaven because I've tried on earth to be good to people and I believe in God and I'm a *follower*.

Linda shows us further characteristics of Stage 3 when she speaks of the limits of knowing and acknowledges the penumbra of mystery she chooses to live with around her central convictions and beliefs.

Interviewer: What does it mean when you say you are going to go to heaven?

Linda: Well, nobody really knows. It's supposed to be paradise. And, I guess I'll find out sometime. But, see, I don't want to ask too many questions like that. I always want to . . . well, lots of people have really done research on religion and they've gone insane, you know? I've never wanted to go *that much* into it. I just want to do what the Bible says. Lots of people think how the earth started and everything. I, only, . . . there's a limit to me. I know that it started from God. God made it and I don't ask any more questions, you know? I'll find out later on.

Linda was asked if she ever had doubts about God.

Linda: Yeah. I have felt times when I have doubted God. But then I realize that it's just *me*. I'm walking *away* from God. I should have, like, at times like this people need to be so close to someone like God. You need to be so close and you need to have something to wake up to every morning. I mean, . . . and have a feeling inside you that, that it's worth living. I think people who live, go to work, come home, go to sleep, go to work, you know, I mean it's a regular *routine,* so that I think people should just believe in God and just follow him.

Authority for Linda's beliefs, religious and moral, resides principally with her parents. She has strongly identified with their teachings and standards and feels that they are her own. An instance is her firmly held belief that sexual intercourse prior to marriage is wrong. Our interviewer asked her where she thought she got that feeling.

Linda: I don't know. It's just . . . my mom. She's against it, but I haven't gotten it from her. I've thought about it lots of times, believe me, there *have* been chances and everything. But I've never done anything.
Interviewer: How important do you think your parents' influence has been?
Linda: My parents have guided me in the right direction. . . . I'm glad that they've done what they've done. They've taught me to do the right from wrong and everything, and I've taken it from there. From what I know. . . . They brought me to church and taught me about God and love and everything, and now I know what it is and . . . and I'll be telling *my* daughter or my son, or whatever, the same thing.

Linda's fervent religiousness gives us one example of the forming of a Synthetic-Conventional faith in adolescence. Brian, whose interview we next listen in on, provides an instance of a similar Stage 3 *structuring* of faith. The *contents* of Brian's faith, however, are quite different from Linda's. Where her faith community has encouraged a limit to questions about belief, Brian's has encouraged just the opposite.

Tall for his sixteen years, Brian has lived in his upper middle-class New England suburb since he was six. His father, an engineer, grew up in this town. The family continues their involvement in the local Unitarian church. Brian loves hiking and canoeing. He has traveled some and spends a part of each summer in rural Maine. He is bright; his marks are above average. He confesses, however, that he daydreams a good bit in class. He reads a lot on his own and seems more interested in learning than he feels free to admit among the friends with whom he hangs around. He sees his parents as strict and seems to feel considerable tension between their expectations of him and those of his peers.

Initially Brian's conversation strikes one as indicating that he is far more individuated than Linda. His outlook involves more questioning, less reverence, more cynicism than hers. Further reflection on his interview, however, helps us see how "conventional" the perspective Brian offers is in the context of the community and Unitarian church that have formed him. While it is likely that this rich, stimulating and critical environment will ensure that Brian constructs a Stage 4 perspective much sooner than Linda, it is important to see how conformist, how concerned with the "tyranny of the they" Brian still is and to recognize the degree to which the positions he takes are really his own versions of what his community stands for rather than being self-composed perspectives.

Brian was asked what his own approach to life involves, what rules or guidelines he finds important.

> *Brian:* Just, not to pick on other guys. I don't think you ought to interfere with a person's way of life. For example, a lot of kids now who are going out with someone, they try to change to become more suitable for the kid they're going out with, and I don't think you ought to change. I think a person is going to grow up and should grow up the way his life is going to lead him and anyone who tries to change that person's character . . . is really . . . infringing on his rights."

Brian's way of continuing this thought indicates his concern with identity and continuity in his life.

> *Brian:* And, you know, it is hard to change, it really is. . . . I couldn't just all of a sudden become a really goody-goody and really study in school and love mother and American flag and apple pie and be Jack Armstrong or whatever.

A bit later the interviewer asked Brian if he has a group of people or a community of peers who share his basic outlook on values.

Brian: "Well, people who I'm really close to . . . like a few of my friends who are really good friends of mine and who I really talk to a lot about this sort of stuff. We just sit around and talk about girls or whatever, past experiences and stuff like that. My really close friends that I really talk to, most of them are girls, because they talk about this stuff a lot, and I feel that I can talk about it more freely with a girl than with a boy, because the boys try to impress each other and impress the girls. But you can have a lot better talk with a girl on stuff like this than you could with a boy.

With girls Brian finds he can talk about "screwed up relations with your parents and stuff," and with a few "about deeper things like what we appreciate and what we don't, etc." The interviewer then asked him what types of things *he* appreciated.

Brian: Just life. It fascinates me. I don't know what goes on before or after birth and death. And some things scare me. The unknown is really a factor in my life because I like to think about it a lot and the reason why everything got here. It really bothers me a lot because I don't know the answers and no one knows the answers, and I can't turn to anyone to get the answers—except to God, if there is a God. Maybe someday I'll get a vision from the Almighty!

Brian had recently been looking for "answers" by reading some philosophical or religious books. He had just finished *The Prophet* by Kahlil Gibran. He was asked to characterize what it and some Buddhist thought he had heard about meant to him.

Brian: What they are trying to do, I think, is understand each other. They appreciate that everyone has faults and things of that nature, and they try to accept that and accept the world in general, which I think should be done. Certain people go around knocking the world, like I have been, but it's all we got, so why not make the best of it? . . . I'm sort of mixed up on what I'm trying to prove by anything that I do. It is sort of hard to explain what the meaning is to life and what the meaning is to your conscience; but it's just something . . . I guess the reason everyone knocks [the world] is because someone started knocking it, and other people started knocking it, and more people started knocking it, and pretty soon everyone was doing it. . . . But if everyone would stop procrastinating, then we wouldn't have the problems that everyone knocks.

Brian returns to one of his key themes as he explains why people don't overcome their negativity and apathy and really work together to transform the world. He also exposes where the authorities he appeals to clash in his life.

Brian: I would like to see them get involved; but then again there is the peer pressure where, you know, a person should like to get involved, but if his friends found out he was doing something like that they'd call stand around and laugh at him and he'd be sort of an outcast. So everyone doesn't want to get involved for the sake of keeping their friends or saving face—which I have done many times.

Interviewer: So there is a cost to being committed, if you really were, to changing things in the world in that your peers would look down on you?

Brian: Right. Like everyone is always trying to impress everyone in this world; it's a matter of social status and all this trying to be better than the Joneses or whatever. And if we stop doing that—which is impossible, but —well, just to say if we could stop that, the world would be a lot better because people wouldn't mind getting involved. They'd just go out and get involved for the sake of what they wanted to do.

Toward the end of Brian's interview the questioner seeks to get him to return to some earlier reflections about his questions regarding life's meaning.

Interviewer: Are there any specific things about meaning or value in life that you are uncertain about. Earlier you said you were concerned about the unknown. Right?

Brian: All right, well, I think actually that it bothers everyone, because if you have doubts about what is going to go on afterwards . . . like the idea —everyone talks about reincarnation and stuff like that and if it really is real—but I can't think of myself as being anything else. I do experience things like *dejà vu,* which is the feeling that you've seen something that you've just seen before; I think that's the right definition for it. I get quite a few *dejà vu's* a day. And just not knowing what's going to happen after you're gone. Let's just say life is: you're born, you gain knowledge, you die, and that's the end of your life, and there is nothing else, and you'll know nothing else of what happened after you die. That really bothers me because like gaining knowledge I like, and I'd like to know what's going to happen after I'm gone, whether someone appreciates what I've done or tried to do—if I've done anything, if I'm not apathetic about life after I grow up and I'm an old man. I'd like to leave at least some kind of mark in this world, and I'd like to see what my mark has proven or what it's done. And if you die and that's just the end of everything—which I cannot see —I don't know what the feeling would be. It's just a weird feeling.

Interviewer: It bothers you, this sense of the unknown about what happens at death?

Brian: Right, because it's unexplainable. We only make up what we feel is the answer. Just take that. Maybe the answer is something that no one can grasp because no one is really smart enough or it's something completely beyond our conceptions of being able to grasp what life is about and something like that. It makes me think quite a bit; I don't know about anyone else, but not being able to grasp an idea—it's physically impossible to grasp that idea—really bothers me and makes me think about it.

In these last passages we get some clear indications that Brian is thinking for himself and will soon be ready to challenge the conventions of his peers and of his liberal church. Though this observation is too simple, I think it is helpful to point out that Linda's Synthetic-Conventional faith has been formed in what seems to be a dominantly Stage 3 faith community. Brian's Synthetic-Conventional faith, on the other hand, is taking form in a faith community that is more likely to be modally Stage 4. That is to say, the *average expectable stage of faith development* for adults in the families and churches of Linda and Brian are probably Stage 3 and Stage 4, respectively. This will have a bearing on the rapidity and difficulty of their respective experiences of transition to Stage 4.

We have now to come to terms with the fact that a considerable number of the adults we have interviewed—both men and women—can be best described by the patterns of Stage 3 Synthetic-Conventional faith. For some adolescents, such as Brian, the forming of identity and faith in Stage 3 is open-ended and clearly anticipates a transition, in the late teens or early twenties, to Stage 4. But for others (and Linda may be one of these) it becomes a longlasting or permanently equilibrated style of identity and faith. To see how this can happen we need to look at several other structural characteristics of Stage 3.

For both adolescents in the forming phases and adults who find equilibrium in Stage 3 the system of informing images and values through which they are committed remains principally a *tacit* system. Tacit means unexamined; my tacit knowing, as Michael Polanyi calls it,[21] is that part of my knowing that plays a role in guiding and shaping my choices, but of which I can give no account. I cannot tell you *how* I know with my tacit knowing. To say that Stage 3's system of images and values is tacitly held reminds me of a statement attributed to the philosopher George Santayana. "We cannot know," he said, "who first discovered water. But we can be sure," he continued, "that it was not the fish." To live with a tacit system of meaning and value is analogous to the situation of the fish. Supported and sustained by the water, it has no means of leaping out of the aquarium so as to reflect on the tank and its contents. A person in Stage 3 is aware of having values and normative images. He or she articulates them, defends them and feels deep emotional investments in them, but typically has not made the value system, *as a system,* the object of reflection.

It is significant when persons at Stage 3 encounter and respond to situations or contexts that lead to critical reflection on their tacit value systems. Under such circumstances they begin the transition to Stage 4's *explicit* system. A new quality of choice and personal responsibility for their values and for their membership in the communities that bear them becomes possible. For many reasons, however, people resist or avoid these invitations to awareness of and a more conscious responsibility for their beliefs and values. They reaffirm their reliance on external authority and their commitments to their particular values and images of which they are aware.

The awareness or unawareness of *system* is a factor in another aspect of Stage 3's structuring of the world. Caught up in its sensitive orientation to the interpersonal, Stage 3 typically orients to other groups or classes than its own as though they were merely aggregates of individuals. It constructs social relations as extensions of interpersonal relationships. It does not think of society in terms of a network of laws, rules, roles and systemically determined patterns. This means that other persons are known and evaluated in terms of their supposed personal qualities and interpersonal ways of relating. In a real sense, in this way of knowing persons are separated from the social system factors shaping and limiting their lives. When anyone says "Some of my best friends are *X,*" and *X* refers to some racial, ethnic, religious or national "outgroup," this kind of structuring toward the interpersonal is likely going on. What happens is that the speaker assimilates her or his friends from the out-group into her or his notions of personal worthiness, while effectively excising them from the social contexts and political realities —and the group histories—which actually determine their lives in powerful ways.

Finally, our account of the structural characteristics of Stage 3 needs to indicate how persons best described by this stage employ symbols and relate to the transcendent through them. Previously we have seen that faith forms powerful and longlasting images of an order of meaning and value—an ultimate environment. For persons in Stage 3, with its largely tacit system of meaning and value, the symbols and ritual representations expressive of their faith are organically and irreplaceably tied to the

full realities of their meaning systems. Said another way, the symbols
expressive of their deepest meanings and loyalties are not separable from
the what they symbolize.

At Stage 4, as we will see, as part of the reflection on one's system
of meanings taken as a system, a kind of demythologization can occur.
Meanings can be separated from the symbols that bear them. This gives
the symbols a status as media for meanings that can be expressed in
other ways. For Stage 3, however, demythologization feels like a fundamental threat to meaning, because meaning and symbol are bound up
together. Consider an example. In the 1960s confrontations over the
American flag occurred between construction workers and harsh young
critics of the Vietnam war. For both groups, I suspect, the flag and its
meaning were inextricably and nonnegotiably intertwined. For the construction workers it represented a concatenation of dreams and loyalties
that participated in their deepest levels of meaning and identity. Any
attack on the flag—and protesters carrying it constituted an attack for
them—amounted to an attack on a sacred set of images and myths that
grounded identity and worth: "My country, right or wrong." For the
protesters the flag similarly stood for a powerful coagulation of images
of and feelings toward "America." But for the latter group it symbolized
a history and present reality that had to be changed, purged or cleansed.
These sometimes bloody struggles, often representing conflicts between
two generations of Americans whose experiences of the nation seemed
deeply different, cannot be explained without recognizing how the flag,
for both groups, was inseparable from their powerfully felt meanings.

Religiously, at Stage 3, meaning and symbol impinge on each other
in similar ways. It is not so much that persons at Stage 3 are locked into
their particular symbols in a kind of fundamentalism of symbolic forms.
Rather, symbols of the sacred—their own and others—are related to in
ways which honor them as inseparably connected to the sacred. Therefore, worthy symbols are themselves sacred. They *are* depths of meaning. Any strategy of demythologization, therefore, threatens the participation of symbol and symbolized and is taken, consequently, as an
assault on the sacred itself.

The other side of this coin, as regards Stage 3's way of relating
through symbols, is that when persons' symbols have undergone trivialization, or when a person has absented him- or herself from the ritual
celebrations of shared central symbols, the sacred itself is emptied.
When this kind of emptying of the sacred is widespread in a society—

as it is in ours today—the vacuum of meaning and of meaningful symbolic representations results in rampant anxiety and neuroses and in a resurgence of interest in all kinds of occult and spiritualistic phenomena.

Now let's review for a moment. We have pointed to the *tacit* character of Stage 3's system of values and meanings. We noted the way interpersonal relationships provide the paradigm for constructing social and political relations. Finally, we described Stage 3's way of relating to the transcendent through symbol and ritual, seeing these as inseparable, related to the realities they symbolize. Perhaps this discussion helps make more clear why persons and groups can and do find equilibrium in Stage 3. In many ways religious institutions "work best" if they are people with a majority of committed folk best described by Stage 3.

Many critics of religion and religious institutions assume, mistakenly, that to be religious in an institution necessarily means to be Synthetic-Conventional. This mistake by critics is understandable. Much of church and synagogue life in this country can be accurately described as dominantly Synthetic-Conventional. Moreover, television evangelists and the highly profitable media religious clubs have mastered the art of addressing the secularizing religious hungers of Synthetic-Conventional folk. They constitute a new set of charismatic external authorities, appealing to the residual resonance of central Christian symbols and offering a tacit version of Christian theology that centers in vicarious interpersonal warmth and meaning. In the so-called electronic churches all of this is ambiguously joined under the sacred mana of powerful electronic media, attractive personalities and sentimental "God talk." They constitute a parody of authentic Christianity and an abomination against biblical faith.

Let me introduce several adults we have interviewed. These persons, best described by Stage 3, will help illustrate the characteristics we have described and some of the variety of contents of Synthetic-Conventional faith.

Our first respondent is Mr. J. D.* He was sixty-three at the time of

---

*This interview was conducted and written up in the summary form presented here by Dr. Richard Shulik. It will appear in Lawrence Kohlberg's *Collected Works*, Vol. II in an article by Kohlberg and Shulik entitled, "The Aging Person as Philosopher; Moral Development in the Adult Years." I have altered Dr. Shulik's writing style at certain points to make the narrative more consistent with my own writing. The quotes from Mr. J. D., of course, have been left untouched.

his interview (1976). He described himself as a retired teamster who had driven a truck for a living for almost twenty-five years. He grew up in a poor white section of Gary, Indiana, where he attended Catholic and public schools. He dropped out of high school in his sophomore year to enlist in the United States Army. He served through the last two years of the World War II and spent some time in Japan after the war. A serious health problem forced him to give up driving at the age of fifty-eight. He regarded himself as a man who had worked very hard in life. He seemed to feel that his life had been rewarding and intrinsically satisfying. He was asked about his work:

> *Mr. D.:* I am familiar with the Detroit-to-New England route, and I often drove Chicago to Detroit. When I was working for another firm for a short time, I also had a Minneapolis–Seattle run, and on another occasion a Maine-to-Florida run. I know of nothing more satisfying than getting together with some of the other drivers at a truck stop or a tavern after a long day's haul.

Despite his illness and semi-retirement, Mr. D. still viewed himself as a teamster. When the interviewer asked him to describe his basic values and beliefs he tended to doubt that his views could really be of very much importance.

> *Mr. D.:* There is really very little that I could tell you. I am really not much of a thinker; my views are quite the same as those of any teamster, or any working man.

This was his way of saying that his philosophical system held nothing remarkable or very interesting. To him it was like that of "many other people."

When the interviewer pressed him to talk further, Mr. D.'s responses showed the global and nonanalytical features of many adults best described as at the Synthetic-Conventional level. He acknowledged, for example, that present-day society faces a great many problems. But he persisted in the belief that society generally has not changed.

> *Mr. D.:* Hell, there are problems today, and there were the same problems when I was a boy. And I expect that there will be the same problems forty years from now, long after we are gone.

He believed that there is the *appearance* of social change, but that underneath this appearance everything really remains quite the same. In discussing specific social issues Mr. D. tended to attribute controversies and concerns to corrupt politicians:

> *Mr. D.:* Since moving here from the greater Chicago area to New England I have learned that absolutely all politicians are corrupt. And so they create these issues for themselves and for their own benefit. . . . All of this hubbub about President Nixon, hell! Nixon was no different from Kennedy or Johnson or Eisenhower or any of the rest. And the fellas over here in our city all are all the same ilk. And you watch and see that Jimmy Carter will show himself in the end to be exactly like all the rest of them, or I'll be very much surprised.

He was asked if there truly is an energy crisis going on.

> *Mr. D.:* Of course there isn't! It's just that some politician somewhere is making a great deal of money convincing everyone that there is!

Recently Mr. D. suffered a serious illness that threatened and altered his life. He had an extremely rare malignant tumor, described by his physician as a "floating tumor"—not fixed in its position—and therefore difficult to remove. In all previous cases of this condition surgery had been unsuccessful, leading to the death of the patient. Mr. D., so weakened by the tumor that he had to give up working, agreed to surgery despite its risks. Having survived the operation his case became well known in medical journals.

> *Mr. D.:* I am somewhat famous in the medical journals, you know, and I'm still living on borrowed time, thanks to the very intelligent doctors at my hospital.

The discussion of these issues led to a consideration of life's basic meaning and to his thoughts about death and dying.

> *Mr. D.:* . . . I'm not now a religious man, never was, and never will be. Religion is just a lot of nonsense as I see it. As I see it, we are born, we live here, we die, and that's it. Religion gives people something to believe in, that there's something more, because they want there to be something more, but there isn't. So . . . you see, I'd rather put some money down on the bar and buy myself a drink, rather than put that same money into a collection plate! Wish others would do the same, too. They'd spare themselves a lot of needless bother.

Mr. D. indicated that these had always been his basic convictions, and that even his close brush with death, due to his unusual illness, had not changed anything.

> *Mr. D.:* No reason to see why an experience like that *should* change what
> I believe. That's just the way the cards fall. But I am grateful that this old
> body still has some life in it, if that's what you mean.

Mr. D. tended to dismiss the interviewer's question about the basic
purpose or meaning behind human life as being an essentially meaningless or incomprehensible question. It was, in his opinion, a question that
really could not be comprehended well, let alone answered, and so it
wasn't worthy of much serious reflection. Hence he answered with some
humor.

> *Mr. D.:* You go and ask a seventeen-year-old boy this question, and he may
> give you an answer or he may not, but the real answer to this question for
> him is some pretty young woman that he wants to take into his arms. And
> the pretty young woman, her answer to this question is that handsome
> young man. And that is how nature has made us, and that is it. . . . And
> [moreover], I am proud to be able to tell you that, even at the age of
> sixty-three, I still have an eye for pretty young women! And so! What do
> you think of that! I think it's great.

In brief, Mr. D. can present the interviewer with the outlines of a
faith system, but it is, in reality, a loosely aggregated collection of
opinions or convictions that he identifies as being essentially "just the
views of one common man." And, in a sense, he is right: he is not
particularly reflective, but he makes no pretense of reflection. Some of
his views appear to be almost platitudes (e.g., all politicians are corrupt,
without exception; all political crises are merely the fabricated contriv-
ances of corrupt politicians). As his statement of a personal philosophy
his view is not genuinely the result of an introspective process. Rather,
it makes him one with the community—or his perceived community of
hard-working men. This is the central meaning behind the terms *synthetic* and *conventional*. The Stage 3 individual's faith system is conventional, in that it is seen as being everybody's faith system or the faith
system of the entire community. And it is synthetic in that it is
nonanalytical; it comes as a sort of unified, global wholeness. In truth,
for Mr. D., the discussion of values and convictions is a means of
asserting his solidarity with the community he calls his own. He does
not discuss values to distinguish himself, or to examine the values, or to
be sure that his views are correct. Rather, in such discussion he seeks
to establish a sense of commonality or relatedness with the other person
present.

Now let's consider another example. At forty Anthony R. owns his own modest home in a predominantly Italian section of a New England city. Describing himself as a "working man," he takes pride in being the provider for his wife and two children. Anthony feels that his values and outlook are different from those of his immigrant parents and his brothers and sisters. This sense of being different from his family of origin is more a feeling he has than something he can put into words. Anthony speaks rapidly and talks a lot. Yet, as he himself says, he has a hard time really communicating what he feels and knows. Anthony believes, deep down, that the world is going to be much tougher for his two children than it has been for him. He is at a loss for anything he can do, either to help alter the world or to better prepare his children to cope with it. He trusts that values are transmitted in the family by parental example and that his children can pick up on those that he and his wife hold. She may be primarily responsible for the fact that they send the children to parochial school. Anthony shows no interest in religion and is not a practicing Catholic. He says he worries a good bit about the possibility of losing his job. His worst fear, in that connection, is that he might even lose his "manliness"—understood, I believe, both in the sense of being a good economic provider and of being a sexually potent male. His major center of value seems to be his family. He uses the image of a car with four wheels to symbolize the family. As head of the household he is driver and chief mechanic. He has responsibility to see that the wheels are going in more or less the same direction and that the engine is running efficiently and harmoniously. He knows, also, that family members—including the father—are mutually accountable.

> *Anthony:*   There's like four wheels turning here, right? And we've got to keep them all in the same line. And no matter which one gets out of line, you bring it back in. So, hopefully, no matter who the individual is, even though the—say the man, the big wheel—he's moving along on the straight path, you know, and he's supposed to keep order. Well, he can run off too and so, you know, it's a family relationship where somebody's got to take over and say, "Hey, wait a minute . . . you're running out of line and you better get back in." So you've got to be open too for suggestions and what-not and criticism.

At the midpoint of his life, Anthony R. shares his evaluation of how his life is going. It is just as much oriented to the judgment and the level of success of his peers as anything our two teenagers, earlier considered, would have said.

Anthony: My personal life? Well, I'm happy. . . . I'm adjusted. . . . The only
thing I believe in is that, you know, just playing the game right, going by
the rules, and and life is going to continue, and then, you know, poof! all
at once, you know, it's just like a guillotine falling down. It comes to a
complete halt. Now, my personal life, I feel is going along the normal
. . . you know . . . an even keel with the normal working man. I'm, you
know, no different. I don't feel I'm any better off or any worse off. I get
up and go to work, you know. It's the routine, it's the general routine. I
think it's a rat-race, but like I say, I'm adjusted to accept it. See, if I didn't
think it was right, I wouldn't be here. Or if . . . I didn't think working was
right, I wouldn't work. But I feel these are all the right things to do. Now
whether it was the way I was brought up or what, I don't know. I mean,
you know, it's me. I feel that, you know, everything's all right. It must be
all right if I get, you know, I've got my wife that seems to think it's all right,
or we wouldn't be here together, you know? . . .

In the world of Anthony R. it appears that coherence comes from
fitting into a network of expectations and duties that spread out from
his central commitment to the maintenance and welfare of his family.
We have already heard him speak about "going along on an even keel
with the norm for a working man." We have seen his image of the family
as an auto, each member being a potentially unruly wheel. At one point
he speaks about his sense of what gives order or rightness to his life.

Anthony: When everything you're doing—let's face it—when you're abiding the laws that were made—uh, not only the laws—it depends on your
—uh, we won't get into the religious thing—say, laws. If you're going by
—uh, what can I say? If you have, you know, a set of rules to live by—
whether they write them down openly, you know—and let everybody know
what they are actually—are—the rules and laws are or what they think their
rights and wrongs are—if you're going by that, then what you're doing is
right. . . .

Interviewer: Well, what are some—what are some of the rules you really
think—you've got inside your head in terms of your family?

Anthony: Being truthful with my family. Not trying to cheat them out of
anything—not breaking promises. . . . I feel like all of them are the right
things to do. I'm not saying that God or anybody set my rules. I really don't
know. It's what I feel is right. . . . I still feel like what I've been doing is
right.

With both Mr. J. D. and Anthony R. we recognize several related
factors that may help account for their having remained in the Synthetic-Conventional stage. Both come from backgrounds of limited education. Both exhibit difficulty in using language to communicate inner

states or their attitudes, values and feelings for others. Both show a need to feel that their life stances are right. They are limited in their self-reflection, however, to either comparisons with or the approval of others perceived to be like them. Both men, for reasons that may have to do with traditions of male withdrawal from religious involvement in working-class urban Catholicism, have had no sustained and meaningful relationship with the church.

Now for a final instance of adult Synthetic-Conventional faith we turn to Mrs. H.M., a Southern woman who grew up on tenant farms in poverty, and who, at age 61, recently "rededicated her life to Christ" and is back in the Southern Baptist Church.

Mrs. M. grew up in various parts of the South on farms where her father shared one-fourth of what he produced with the landowners as rent for the land he used. She was the third child in a large family. Her father she characterized as a very stern man who would allow his children to do little for fun besides go to school, attend Sunday school, or visit their grandparents. Their mother, a woman with some education and from a more privileged background than their father, never seemed able to stand up to him or to protect the children from his anger and excessive restrictions. At seventeen H. ran away from home to get married. She married a man a lot like her father. She had three children with him. He worked in construction and they moved frequently. He eventually began to run around with other women and became a borderline alcoholic. When he drank, he was abusive. When H. was thirty years old, her father and mother talked her into getting a job and divorcing her husband. Her mother kept the children while she worked. She enjoyed her work. Soon she began to form a relationship with a man at work. When they decided to get married, both families objected so strongly (because he was much younger than she) that they gave up their jobs and went to another state to the home of a relative of hers. They took her three children with them. In a few days they were married and found a place of their own. They both got jobs with the same company.

H. and her second husband had two children together. Socially, she says, their friends tended to be his friends. Their leisure activities focused principally on his interests in auto and motorcycle racing, and on football. Eventually she tired of going with him to these events. They did not find new ways to celebrate and enjoy their relationship. After a serious illness in his late forties he divorced her in order to marry his secretary. They had been married twenty-four years. Five years after her divorce at age fifty-seven, Mrs. H.M. tells us of the central theme in her life review and self-assessment.

> *Mrs. M.:*   I have never done with my life what I could have done after I was old enough to realize that you have to do something to get anything out of life. . . . I could have taken courses at [name] College, . . . but I didn't do anything but work. And I've always been unhappy. I think it was because I didn't do what other people did. Although I was saved during World War II, I did not go to church very long, because I was always moving. Then when I married the last time we tried to go, but the difference in our ages always separated us in Sunday school so we quit. All we ever did was go to the drive-in, out to nice restaurants for dinner, and to drag races and baseball games. He played golf and went to the Masters at Augusta several years. He used not to want to go anywhere without me and I'd finally just say, "I want to stay with the kids, find somebody else to go with you."
> . . . But I've always been frustrated. I've always wanted to write and I've always wanted to paint. And I've never tried either one. I have never made any effort to really do anything that I wanted to do. I think the reason that I've felt unhappy so much of my life is because I don't like *me*. I don't like what I've done to other people. I hurt my parents and took my three older children away from family and friends because of what I wanted. My last husband is a good person and was very good to me and my children—all of them. As I look back I see that so much was my fault. But now that I have rededicated my life to the Lord, and am back in church, I feel much better.

Mrs. H.M.'s despair comes from the sense that she has not done what everyone else has done. This deep-going sense of failure is the other side of Mr. J.D.'s and Anthony R.'s sense that their lives are "normal" or going along all right. The norm lies in the conventional pattern of life of those who constitute "everybody." Part of this social conscience tells her that she did well, waiting on and spoiling her children. But in a time when assertiveness and liberation in women have become a new consensual set of norms, Mrs. H.M. looks at her life choices with sadness.

Living now with a married daughter, Mrs. H.M. has to travel nearly fifty miles round trip to attend her church. She drives this sometimes twice on Sundays as well as on other evenings in the week. She is finding challenges there to be part of the church's outreach to new people.

We close our look into the world of Mrs. H.M. with her sharing some of her religious outlook. Here the Synthetic-Conventional reliance on external authority and its construction of meaning in interpersonal images and terms can be seen.

Do you think that life on this earth will continue for some time
ture, or do you think we're coming near the end of the world?

Mrs. M.: The Scripture tells of many things that will happen in the last days
and these very things are happening now. I think that we are very near the
end of time. A very learned Bible teacher that I hear each week tells us that
according to Scripture, the end will come before the year 2000.

Interviewer: Would you agree with her?

Mrs. M.: The more I listen to her, the more convinced I am that she is right.

Interviewer: You mentioned God. When you hear that word what do you
feel?

Mrs. M.: I feel very sad and ashamed for the way I have wasted my life. I
do know that God has forgiven me for every wrong that I've done, and that
He loves me. I feel very close to God most of the time, now that I am active
in the work of the church again. Of course there are times that I don't feel
as close to Him as I'd like to, but I know that I am the one who moves
away, not He. I've learned that we all have so much to be thankful for, if
we only stop and count our blessings.*

Now a review and summary of the features of the Synthetic-Conventional stage of faith.

*In Stage 3 Synthetic-Conventional faith, a person's experience of the
world now extends beyond the family. A number of spheres demand
attention: family, school or work, peers, street society and media, and
perhaps religion. Faith must provide a coherent orientation in the midst
of that more complex and diverse range of involvements. Faith must
synthesize values and information; it must provide a basis for identity
and outlook.*

*Stage 3 typically has its rise and ascendancy in adolescence, but for many
adults it becomes a permanent place of equilibrium. It structures the
ultimate environment in interpersonal terms. Its images of unifying
value and power derive from the extension of qualities experienced in
personal relationships. It is a "conformist" stage in the sense that it is
acutely tuned to the expectations and judgments of significant others*

---

*In reviewing this synopsis of her interview Mrs. M. asked me to insert the following
description she wrote of herself; I agreed to do so (JWF). "More than a year has passed
since this interview with Mrs. M. She now has her own apartment (she lived with a
daughter at the time of the interview) and is feeling much better about her life. She still
has many regrets, but leads a very active life and tries to help others when the opportunity
arises. She is active in her church and has many Christian friends with whom she enjoys
life."

and as yet does not have a sure enough grasp on its own identity and autonomous judgment to construct and maintain an independent perspective. While beliefs and values are deeply felt, they typically are tacitly held—the person "dwells" in them and in the meaning world they mediate. But there has not been occasion to step outside them to reflect on or examine them explicitly or systematically. At Stage 3 a person has an "ideology," a more or less consistent clustering of values and beliefs, but he or she has not objectified it for examination and in a sense is unaware of having it. Differences of outlook with others are experienced as differences in "kind" of person. Authority is located in the incumbents of traditional authority roles (if perceived as personally worthy) or in the consensus of a valued, face-to-face group.

The emergent capacity of this stage is the forming of a personal myth —the myth of one's own becoming in identity and faith, incorporating one's past and anticipated future in an image of the ultimate environment unified by characteristics of personality.

The dangers or deficiencies in this stage are twofold. The expectations and evaluations of others can be so compellingly internalized (and sacralized) that later autonomy of judgment and action can be jeopardized; or interpersonal betrayals can give rise either to nihilistic despair about a personal principle of ultimate being or to a compensatory intimacy with God unrelated to mundane relations.

Factors contributing to the breakdown of Stage 3 and to readiness for transition may include: serious clashes or contradictions between valued authority sources; marked changes, by officially sanctioned leaders, or policies or practices previously deemed sacred and unbreachable (for example, in the Catholic church changing the mass from Latin to the vernacular, or no longer requiring abstinence from meat on Friday); the encounter with experiences or perspectives that lead to critical reflection on how one's beliefs and values have formed and changed, and on how "relative" they are to one's particular group or background. Frequently the experience of "leaving home"—emotionally or physically, or both —precipitates the kind of examination of self, background, and life-guiding values that gives rise to stage transition at this point.

19. Stage 4. Individuative-Reflective Faith

At the time we interviewed him Jack was twenty-eight. He grew up in a large family in a lower-class ethnic enclave of a northeastern city. His Irish father and Italian mother had a stormy marriage. Jack, the fourth of their ten children, seems to have been particularly sensitive to their marital fights. He felt anger and sadness for his alcoholic father and genuine fear for his mother. People in his neighborhood, he said, never troubled to learn his and his brothers' first names. They just called them all "Donovan" (not their real name). Jack says that sometimes when he heard one of his brothers speak it was as though he himself was speaking, they sounded so much alike.

For the first six years of his education Jack went to public school. In the seventh grade he transferred to a Catholic parochial school, at considerable cost to the family. Parochial school was harder. He had been on the honor roll in public school. He suspected that he attained that status simply because he attended regularly, came clean and seemed interested. Then—and now—Jack has never allowed himself to think of himself as particularly bright or gifted.

In the parochial school, he said, teaching about religion pervaded everything. In his seventh-grade year Jack experienced a kind of religious conversion. In the spring, building up to Easter, he went to mass every day. He made two special observances called Novenas. He said, "I began to think of myself as one of Jesus' special children. I kind of made a bargain with him," he continued. "I promised that I would be his special boy if he would help my father sober up a bit."

Toward the end of that seventh-grade year his teacher, a nun, made a fateful error. She called Jack up before the class and said, "Jack is the only member of the class I have seen attending mass faithfully every day this spring. I'm really proud of him." "That did it," Jack said. "They got me then. The bullies." For the next two years his peers made him pay painfully for that moment of religious recognition. "I quit going to church," he said. "It was just as well, I guess, because my old man didn't quit drinking. In fact he began going out on Thursday nights to drink, in addition to Friday, Saturday and Sunday."

At age nineteen Jack joined the army. His travel to Maryland for basic training and his first base assignment marked the first time he had ever been out of his city. "It opened me up a bit," he said. "I seemed to get along well with people from other parts of the country, especially those from cities like me." He learned a lot in the service, he said, because, "just like in jail, there's nothing much else to do but talk. You talk a lot in the army."

Jack came to spend a lot of time in several bars that specialized in playing music by black artists. He came to love that music and his conversations with black soldiers opened up a whole new world to him. In those years *Ramparts* magazine ran a series of articles on the Black Panthers. This series included writings by Huey Newton, Eldridge Cleaver and, posthumously, Malcolm X. As he talked about these articles and about black power, Jack discovered a whole new world of politics.

"When I grew up," he said, "politics meant speeches, hoopla, voting and payoffs. I thought I knew about politics, but now I began to see politics differently. I began to see that the prejudice against blacks that I had been taught and that everybody in the projects where I grew up believed in was wrong. I began to see that us poor whites being pitted against poor blacks worked only to the advantage of the wealthy and powerful. For the first time I began to think politically. I began to have a kind of philosophy."

During this period Jack had a brother who had also been drawn into radical political thinking. When Jack got "busted" and put in the stockade for fighting, this brother sent him some money and wrote him about the political ideas that excited him. This encouraged Jack in his new perspectives.

When he came home from the service his old neighborhood bristled with tension over the threat of court-ordered busing to achieve racial desegregation in education. Jack tried out some of his new political philosophy on his old friends and acquaintances. "When anyone began making prejudiced statements about blacks," he said, "I found myself starting to preach. I explained how blacks had done nothing to make our neighborhood like it was. It was always bad. I told them that the rich people benefited from our being set against the blacks."

Jack soon found himself an alien in his old neighborhood. He began to seek the company of other groups in the city who shared something of his new political outlook. He felt marginal. His new political acquaintances were mostly college educated. They made him feel quaint and their articulate use of words made him feel uncomfortable. He missed the rhythms and style of his neighborhood. Yet, he didn't fit in there any more either. His new awareness seemed strange and threatening to his old friends. They had little capacity for or interest in the kind of political analysis in which he engaged. *His* new ways of using language intimidated them.

During this period Jack married a bright young woman from a middle-class family. She shared his new interests and commitments. He soon took a low-level bureaucratic job in state government. As their two children came along she eventually gave up her medical technician's job. At the time of our interview she worked in the evenings as a waitress to supplement his $12,000 a year income. Jack and his wife, when we talked with them, had emerged as leaders of a tenants' rights movement in their part of the city. Due to their success as organizers, they were each involved in lawsuits totaling a million dollars brought by landlord associations. Jack, explaining their commitments, said, "I don't know too much philosophy; I don't know Hegel and Marx too good. But I do know my class. I know we're getting stepped on. And I know that there are others worse off than us, who are fighting for their chance at life, too. If we're fighting in the alleys, then they're fighting in the cellars, you might say. We have to be careful not to step on those fighting below us. As long as there are people like these suffering and struggling for their rights, I'll still be in the fight."

Among other things, Jack's story shows us rather vividly one of the crucial steps in the transfer from a Synthetic-Conventional position to a Stage 4 Individuative-Reflective faith stance. In going to the army Jack left home, both emotionally and geographically. As he encountered the ideologically potent and threatening teachings of the Panthers, it drove him, for the first time, to look with critical awareness at the assumptive system of values he and his family had shared with most of their neighbors as he grew up. Here we see Santayana's fish leaping outside the fish tank and finding a place to stand in order to look at his own value ethos seriously. The analysis of "the system" provided by the Panthers awakened him to the insight that ideologies have particular histories and that persons and groups have world views that grow out of their particular experiences and the conditions with which they have had to deal. He began to see other people not just as individual persons with their particular quirks and qualities of temperament. Now he recognized that people get shaped by their social class, by the group histories they inherit and by the economic conditions and opportunities with which they and their groups struggle. Jack, we may say, became disembedded from his Synthetic-Conventional, assumptive world view. His first move beyond it, in a kind of counter-dependent step of opposition to it, was to embrace the explicit ideology of the Panthers, with its combination of black empowerment strategies and Marxist economic and semipolitical analysis. The tacit values and meaning system of his Stage 3 began to be replaced by the explicit system of Stage 4.

Some other factors in Jack's experience of stage transition help to illumine the character of the Stage 4 faith position. Previously, Jack's identity had derived from his belonging to a family, to a peer and a neighborhood world. The religious world, so important to him for a brief time in his early teens, seems to have diminished markedly in what may be seen as a Stage 2 to Stage 3 transition. Although Jack kept his promise faithfully at thirteen, God did not make his father cut back on his drinking. This collided with the structure of reciprocity in Jack's Stage 2 faith. Then the bullies and his peers hammered him into conformity with their conventional male aloofness from religion.

In the "hanging out" period of his mid- to late teens, Jack said, he had no special badge of distinction to make him stand out from—or in—the crowd he ran with. "I was not the lover, or the fighter, the leader or anything special," he said. His identity derived from his memberships; he was who he was able to be in those face-to-face groups in which fate placed him—family, school, peer group and neighborhood.

This is not to say that Jack's personhood was either exhausted or fully expressed in his derivative teen years' identity. He tells us that as a teen he spent long hours alone listening to his older brother's record player. He tells us how uncomfortable it made him feel when his gang would single out a guy in a bar, provoke a fight with him and then beat him up. He tells us how especially uncomfortable it made him when his gang baited black people and blamed all the problems in the projects on "the niggers." But these aspects of his personhood could find little expression in the identity his groups were willing to allow him. And with no good clothes and little money, Jack said, the thought of trying to get a girl's attention seemed hopeless as well.

For Jack, going into the service meant being extracted from the interpersonal groups that had largely formed, maintained and limited his identity. For many other youths going to college represents a similar extraction. In addition to encountering an ideology that enabled (and forced) him to examine his own conventional values, Jack now had the freedom (and burden) to explore who he could be away from home.

This represents a moment of crucial importance in the transition from Stage 3 to Stage 4. It can be a frightening and somewhat disorienting time of being apart from one's conventional moorings. Whether a person will *really* make the move to an Individuative-Reflective stance depends to a critical degree on the character and quality of the ideologically composed groups bidding for one's joining. Social fraternities or sororities in colleges often represent conventional ideological communities that in effect substitute one family group for another, making any genuinely individuative move as regards identity and outlook difficult. Many religious groups similarly reinforce a conventionally held and maintained faith system, sanctifying one's remaining in the dependence on external authority and derivative group identity of Stage 3. Marriage, for many young men and women, can serve to create a new Synthetic-Conventional ethos and because the couple are playing adult roles they are able, at least for a time, to evade the challenges of the individuative transition.

But when Jack identified himself with that group of black soldiers, held together by their commitment to soul music and the Panther ideology, he burned his bridges. Without full assurance of where it would lead, he began to shape a new identity and faith. His identity had previously derived from and been a function of the groups he grew up with in fated membership. Now, as is the case in any genuine Stage 4, his choice of groups, with the ideological perspectives they bear, became a function of the identity he was forming. He shaped his new identity in relation to the groups and outlooks whose invitation to life-redefining membership he accepted.

For a genuine move to Stage 4 to occur there must be an interruption of reliance on external sources of authority. The "tyranny of the they" —or the potential for it—must be undermined. In addition to the kind of critical reflection on one's previous assumptive or tacit system of values we saw Jack undertake, there must be, for Stage 4, a relocation of authority within the self. While others and their judgments will remain important to the Individuative-Reflective person, their expectations, advice and counsel will be submitted to an internal panel of experts who reserve the right to choose and who are prepared to take responsibility for their choices. I sometimes call this the emergence of an *executive ego*.

The two essential features of the emergence of Stage 4, then, are the critical distancing from one's previous assumptive value system and the emergence of an executive ego. When and as these occur a person is forming a new identity, which he or she expresses and actualizes by the choice of personal and group affiliations and the shaping of a "lifestyle."

We find that sometimes many persons complete half of this double movement, but do not complete the other. By virtue of college experience, travel or of being moved from one community to another, many persons undergo the relativization of their inherited world views and value systems. They come face to face with the relativity of their perspectives and those of others to their life experience. But they fail to interrupt their reliance on external sources of authority—and may even strengthen their reliance upon them—in order to cope with this relativity. On the other hand there is a significant group who shape their own variant way of living from a shared value ethos, break their reliance on consensual or conventional authorities and show the emergence of a strong executive ego. Yet they have not carried through a critical distancing from their shared assumptive values system. In either of these two cases we see an interesting and potentially longlasting equilibrium in a transitional position between Stages 3 and 4.

To complete our discussion of this stage let us look at several other correlated structural features of Individuative-Reflective faith. In social perspective-taking, for example, Stage 4 constructs a perspective genuinely aware of social systems and institutions. It retains Stage 3's orientation to persons and its richness of mutual interpersonal perspective taking, but it adds to it two related features. First, Stage 4, aware that the self has an ideology that it has formed and re-formed over time, works at apprehending other persons in terms of their personal qualities as well as taking into account the determinative shape of their ideologies and the group experiences that fund them. Second, it achieves an understanding of social relations in systems terms. No longer constructing social relations as merely the extension of interpersonal relations, Stage 4 thinks in terms of the impersonal imperatives of law, rules and the standards that govern social roles.

In keeping with Stage 4's critical reflection upon its system of meanings, its relation to and use of symbols differs qualitatively from that of Stage 3. Symbols and rituals, previously taken as mediating the sacred in direct ways and therefore as sacred themselves, are interrogated by Stage 4's critical questioning. In its critical reflection Stage 4 regards meanings as separable from the symbolic media that express them. In face of a liturgical ritual or a religious symbol the Individuative-Reflective person asks, "But what does it *mean?*" If the symbol or symbolic act is truly meaningful, Stage 4 believes, its meanings can be translated into propositions, definitions and/or conceptual foundations.

This demythologizing strategy, which seems natural to Stage 4, brings both gains and losses. Paul Tillich, writing about religious symbols and their powers, says that when a symbol is recognized to be a symbol by those who relate to the transcendent through it, it becomes a "broken symbol."[22] A certain naive reliance upon and trust in the sacred power, efficacy and inherent truth of the symbol as representation is interrupted. Instead of the symbol or symbolic act having the initiative and exerting its power on the participant, now the participant-questioner has the initiative over against the symbol. For those who have previously enjoyed an unquestioning relation to the transcendent and to their fellow worshipers through a set of religious symbols, Stage 4's translations of their meanings into conceptual prose can bring a sense of loss, dislocation, grief and even guilt.

I once heard theologian and cultural analyst Harvey Cox share with a class a memory of his experience of the loss of the primal naïveté regarding a central symbolic act for Christians. Though himself a Baptist, Cox said that as a high-school lad he often attended services with his friends at the Catholic church next to his home. In one period he had been dating a Catholic girl a year or so older than he. She went off to college while he stayed at home to finish high school. When she came back for Christmas vacation Harvey went with her to a beautiful midnight Christmas Eve mass. As the mass climaxed and the people were receiving the Eucharist, Harvey said his college-aged girl friend, who had just completed Anthropology 101, turned to him and whispered, "That's just a primitive totemic ritual, you know." Harvey said, "A what?" She replied with great self-assurance, "A primitive totemic ritual. Almost all premodern religious and tribal groups have them. They are ceremonies where worshipers bind themselves together and to the power of the sacred by a cannibalistic act of ingesting the mana of a dead god." Communion, Cox said, was never the same again. A symbol recognized as a symbol is a broken symbol.

But there are gains as well. Meanings previously tacitly held become explicit. Dimensions of depth in symbolic or ritual expression previously felt and responded to without reflection can now be identified and clarified. The "mystification" of symbols, the tendency to experience them as organically linked with the realities they represent, is broken open. Their meanings, now detachable from the symbolic media, can be communicated in concepts or propositions that may have little direct resonance with the symbolic form or action. Comparisons of meanings become more easily possible, though a certain tendency to reductionism and the "flattening" of meanings is difficult to avoid.

Jack's time of transition from Stage 3 to Stage 4 occurred at the most ideal time for this movement—his early to mid-twenties. Levinson calls this "novice adulthood" and sees it as the time when persons form their first adult life structures. Erikson identifies the crisis of Intimacy vs. Isolation with this period. Intimacy requires the ability to stand alone as well as to risk one's forming self and sense of identity in close engagement with other persons and with ideological commitments that channel one's actions and shape one's vision of life goals (Levinson's "dream").

For some adults, however, the transition to Stage 4, if it comes at all, occurs in the thirties or forties. It can be precipitated by changes in primary relationships, such as a divorce, the death of a parent or parents or children growing up and leaving home. Or it can result from challenges of moving, changing jobs or the experience of the breakdown or inadequacy of one's Synthetic-Conventional faith.

This transition represents an upheaval in one's life at any point and can be protracted in its process for five to seven years or longer. It

typically is less severe for young adults, however, coming in that era as
a natural accompaniment of leaving home and of the construction of a
first, provisional adult life structure. When the transition occurs in the
late thirties or early forties it often brings greater struggles. This is
because of its impact upon the more established and elaborated system
of relationships and roles that constitute an adult life structure.

*The movement from Stage 3 to Stage 4 Individuative-Reflective faith
is particularly critical for it is in this transition that the late adolescent
or adult must begin to take seriously the burden of responsibility for his
or her own commitments, lifestyle, beliefs and attitudes. Where genuine
movement toward stage 4 is underway the person must face certain
unavoidable tensions: individuality versus being defined by a group or
group membership; subjectivity and the power of one's strongly felt but
unexamined feelings versus objectivity and the requirement of critical
reflection; self-fulfillment or self-actualization as a primary concern versus service to and being for others; the question of being committed to
the relative versus struggle with the possibility of an absolute.*

*Stage 4 most appropriately takes form in young adulthood (but let us
remember that many adults do not construct it and that for a significant
group it emerges only in the mid-thirties or forties). This stage is marked
by a double development. The self, previously sustained in its identity
and faith compositions by an interpersonal circle of significant others,
now claims an identity no longer defined by the composite of one's roles
or meanings to others. To sustain that new identity it composes a
meaning frame conscious of its own boundaries and inner connections
and aware of itself as a "world view." Self (identity) and outlook (world
view) are differentiated from those of others and become acknowledged
factors in the reactions, interpretations and judgments one makes on the
actions of the self and others. It expresses its intuitions of coherence in
an ultimate environment in terms of an explicit system of meanings.
Stage 4 typically translates symbols into conceptual meanings. This is a
"demythologizing" stage. It is likely to attend minimally to unconscious
factors influencing its judgments and behavior.*

*Stage 4's ascendant strength has to do with its capacity for critical
reflection on identity (self) and outlook (ideology). Its dangers inhere in
its strengths: an excessive confidence in the conscious mind and in
critical thought and a kind of second narcissism in which the now clearly*

bounded, reflective self overassimilates "reality" and the perspectives of others into its own world view.

Restless with the self-images and outlook maintained by Stage 4, the person ready for transition finds him- or herself attending to what may feel like anarchic and disturbing inner voices. Elements from a childish past, images and energies from a deeper self, a gnawing sense of the sterility and flatness of the meanings one serves—any or all of these may signal readiness for something new. Stories, symbols, myths and paradoxes from one's own or other traditions may insist on breaking in upon the neatness of the previous faith. Disillusionment with one's compromises and recognition that life is more complex than Stage 4's logic of clear distinctions and abstract concepts can comprehend, press one toward a more dialectical and multileveled approach to life truth.

20. Stage 5.
Conjunctive Faith

I have not found or fabricated a simple way to describe Conjunctive faith. This frustrates me. I somehow feel that if I cannot communicate the features of this stage clearly, it means that I don't understand them. Or worse, I fear that what I call "Stage 5" really does not exist. I cannot accept either of these explanations. The truth, I believe, is that Stage 5, as a style of faith-knowing, *does* exist and it *is* complex. Moreover, while it has been—and is—exemplified in the lives of persons, in their writings and in writings about them, its structural features have not been adequately described, either in my own previous writings or in the writings of others.

As a way of opening our consideration of Conjunctive faith let me offer a few analogies, which may tease out an image of the character of the transition from Stage 4 to Stage 5. The emergence of Stage 5 is something like:

> Realizing that the behavior of light requires that it be understood both as a wave phenomenon *and* as particles of energy.

> Discovering that the rational solution or "explanation" of a problem that seemed so elegant is but a painted canvas covering an intricate, endlessly intriguing cavern of surprising depth.

> Looking at a field of flowers simultaneously through a microscope and a wide-angle lens.

Discovering that a guest, if invited to do so, will generously reveal the treasured wisdom of a lifetime of experience.

Discovering that someone who shares your identity also writes checks, makes deposits and stops payments on your checking account.

Discovering that one's parents are remarkable people not just because they are one's parents.

Stage 5, as a way of seeing, of knowing, of committing, moves beyond the dichotomizing logic of Stage 4's "either/or." It sees both (or the many) sides of an issue simultaneously. Conjunctive faith suspects that things are organically related to each other; it attends to the pattern of interrelatedness in things, trying to avoid force-fitting to its own prior mind set.

The phrase "dialectical knowing" comes close to describing Stage 5's style, yet the term is too methodologically controlling. Better, I think, to speak of *dialogical* knowing. In dialogical knowing the known is invited to speak its own word in its own language. In dialogical knowing the multiplex structure of the world is invited to disclose itself. In a mutual "speaking" and "hearing," knower and known converse in an I-Thou relationship. The knower seeks to accommodate her or his knowing to the structure of that which is being known before imposing her or his own categories upon it.

Stage 5's dialogical knowing requires a knower capable of dialogue. Epistemologically, there must be sufficient self-certainty to grant the known the initiative. What the mystics call "detachment" characterizes Stage 5's willingness to let reality speak its word, regardless of the impact of that word on the security or self-esteem of the knower. I speak here of an intimacy in knowing that celebrates, reverences and attends to the "wisdom" evolved in things as they are, before seeking to modify, control or order them to fit prior categories.

Stage 5's willingness to give reality the initiative in the act of knowing, however, is not merely a function of the knower's self-certainty. It also has to do with the trustworthiness of the known. In this sense Stage 5 represents a kind of complementarity or mutuality in relation.

In theological seminary I learned methods of studying scripture that employed language study, source criticism, form criticism and text criticism. All of these methods involved things I could learn to do to texts in order, as Martin Luther once said, to "crack them open like a nut." Not until I was in my thirties, undergoing my first experience of spiritual

direction in the tradition of St. Ignatius's *Spiritual Exercises,* did I begin
to learn a method of working with scripture that breathed more of the
spirit of Stage 5. The Ignatian approach did not require me to give up
or negate my critical skills, but it did teach me to supplement them with
a method in which I learned to relinquish initiative to the text. Instead
of *my reading,* analyzing and extracting the meaning of a Biblical text,
in Ignatian contemplative prayer I began to learn how to let the text
read me and to let it bring my needs and the Spirit's movements within
me to consciousness.

Put straightforwardly, Stage 5 Conjunctive faith involves going beyond the explicit ideological system and clear boundaries of identity that
Stage 4 worked so hard to construct and to adhere to. Whereas Stage
4 could afford to equate self pretty much with its own conscious awareness of self, Stage 5 must come to terms with its own unconscious—the
unconscious personal, social and species or archetypal elements that are
partly determinative of our actions and responses. Stage 5 comes to
terms with the fact that the conscious ego is not master in its own house.
As in the analogy of the mysterious *Doppelgänger* who also funds and
draws on our bank account, Stage 5 recognizes the task of integrating
or reconciling conscious and unconscious.

Stage 5 accepts as axiomatic that truth is more multidimensional and
organically interdependent than most theories or accounts of truth can
grasp. Religiously, it knows that the symbols, stories, doctrines and
liturgies offered by its own or other traditions are inevitably partial,
limited to a particular people's experience of God and incomplete. Stage
5 also sees, however, that the relativity of religious traditions that matters is not their relativity to each other, but their relativity—their *relate-*
ivity—to the reality to which they mediate relation. Conjunctive faith,
therefore, is ready for significant encounters with other traditions than
its own, expecting that truth has disclosed and will disclose itself in those
traditions in ways that may complement or correct its own. Krister
Stendahl is fond of saying that no interfaith conversation is genuinely
ecumenical unless the quality of mutual sharing and receptivity is such
that each party makes him- or herself vulnerable to conversion to the
other's truth. This would be Stage 5 ecumenism.

This position implies no lack of commitment to one's own truth
tradition. Nor does it mean a wishy-washy neutrality or mere fascination
with the exotic features of alien cultures. Rather, Conjunctive faith's
radical openness to the truth of the other stems precisely from its

confidence in the reality mediated by its own tradition and in the awareness that that reality overspills its mediation. The person of Stage 5 makes her or his own experience of truth the principle by which other claims to truth are tested. But he or she assumes that each genuine perspective will augment and correct aspects of the other, in a mutual movement toward the real and the true.

Conjunctive faith cannot live with the demythologizing strategy of Stage 4 as regards the interpretation of story or myth or the understanding of symbol and liturgy. Stage 4 is concerned to question symbolic representations and enactments and to force them to yield their meanings for translation into conceptual or propositional statements. As such, Individuative-Reflective faith wants to bring the symbolic representation into its (Stage 4's) circle of light and to operate on it, extracting its meanings. This leaves the person or group in Stage 4 clearly in control. The meaning so grasped may be illuminating, confronting, harshly judgmental or gently reassuring. But whatever its potential impact, its authentication and weight will be assigned in accordance with the assumptions and commitments that already shape the circle of light in which it is being questioned. It will not be granted the initiative. Nor will its self-authenticating character be fully translated into the conceptual or propositional communication.

Conjunctive faith, on the other hand, is not innocent of the critical impulse or critical capability. In Paul Ricoeur's powerful language, Conjunctive faith is not to be equated with a "first naïveté," a precritical relationship of unbroken participation in symbolically mediated reality.[23] That style more aptly describes Stage 3 Synthetic-Conventional faith. Conjunctive faith has experienced the breaking of its symbols and the "vertigo of relativity." It is a veteran of critical reflection and of the effort to "reduce" the symbolic, the liturgical and the mythical to conceptual meanings. But it cannot rest content with that strategy. It acknowledges the powerlessness of anything *it* can control to transform and redeem its myopia. It discerns the powerful residues of meaning that escape our strategies of reductive interpretation. With its attention to the organic and interconnected character of things Stage 5 distrusts the separation of symbol and symbolized, sensing that when we neutralize the initiative of the symbolic, we make a pale idol of any meaning we honor.

Ricoeur's term "second naïveté" or "willed naïveté" begins to describe Conjunctive faith's postcritical desire to resubmit to the initiative of the symbolic.[24] It decides to do this, but it has to relearn how to do this. It carries forward the critical capacities and methods of the previous stage, but it no longer trusts them except as tools to avoid self-deception and to order truths encountered in other ways.

Now, lest my descriptions make you believe that only professors, theologians, or adepts in hermeneutics become Stage 5, let me tell you about J. T. (not her real initials). At the time we interviewed her Miss T. was seventy-eight years old. She lived in a university city where she rented rooms to four graduate students, something she has done for the past twenty years. She has arthritic hips, walks with great difficulty and is expecting soon a third operation to improve her mobility and reduce her pain. She spends her time reading, conversing with "her students" and with other friends by phone. She currently devotes time most days to revising for publication a small book on life truths which she wrote during a period of recovery from a nervous breakdown in her early fifties. She has already published another, more popular book, about how to approach life problems. Reading the interview with Miss T. (I did not do the interview) one forms the image of an exceedingly lively, highly intelligent woman who looks squarely into life. She preserves few illusions and is not easy on those of others. But she seems to have found a ground of hope, of courage and of love for her life that is beyond illusion.

Across the years of her life Miss T. has done many things. She founded and operated a puppet theater on the West Coast. She taught art, having begun her own small art school in New York. She studied acting and worked for a number of years in the theater and movie industry in varying capacities from actress to make-up artist to script writer. She had an unusually productive voluntary career in mental health work. Except for the sudden onset of arthritis in her late fifties one suspects this would have become a late professional career of great significance. Miss T. devoted twenty years of voluntary work effectively aimed at the racial integration of summer camps for children and of the recruitment of black children to attend them. She traveled a good bit, lived on both coasts of the United States and has apparently been a seeker after moral and religious truth for most of her life.

Miss T. was born in New England in 1898. The daughter of a lawyer with inherited wealth and literary aspirations and a mother whom she characterized as "really wanting to have been a minister herself," she grew up privileged in many ways. About 1910, the quarreling between a headstrong father and an outspoken mother led to the latter's taking her two young daughters to Europe for the winter. Miss T., the older, was then twelve. She had just been confirmed in the Unitarian church, an event that she would always remember.

> *Miss T.:* I joined the Unitarian church and my uncle, who was a darling, saintly person . . . was minister of that little church. I remember that service. I had a little white dress and my pink hair ribbons, I remember, all fresh and new and lovely. And the service that he gave at that time I think was a religious experience for me. It went very deep; I felt as if I were going to be pure and holy for the rest of my life.

Years later at a time when she sought psychiatric help for recurring illnesses she suspected were psychosomatic, she recalled the pain of her parents' deep conflict over their children. She describes her first sessions with the psychiatrist.

> *Miss T.:* And it came, it came piling out in that first session, first few sessions, of what it had meant to me as a child to have our parents pulling in opposite directions over us. There was the scene in the railroad station when mother brought us home from camp and my father wanted to take us and my mother wouldn't let us go. People gathering around believe it or not. See parents fighting over their children. Well, these stories all came piling out and I was so tired when I got out of that office that I had to hold onto the railings to get down to the subway.

In her early teens the parents divorced. Her father remarried and had two sons with his new wife. The younger of those sons, who developed a lifelong mental illness in his teens, was to play an important role in Miss T.'s life. She was asked about her father.

> *Miss T.:* We adored him when we were little children and he adored his two little girls that came first, and I think I developed a father complex. I, when it came to picking a mate for myself, I wanted somebody as gifted as my father but who didn't have all his hazards, which was a very difficult proposition. This I never found. So I really lost those first dear fellows that loved me. And, well, I feel that my father gave me by inheritance a great deal that was splendid, and I've gotten way past the place where I hold him any grudges.

Miss T. recalls her mother as a "devout Unitarian, almost Episcopalian in her feelings." She had attended some of the first courses in religious education at Radcliffe College in her student years. Miss T. remembers her as a woman who always continued to study and grow.

Miss T.:   I think that mother, mother's integrity was superb. And I saw her grow, I saw her right under my eyes as a growing up young woman, developing from a spoiled child, which she certainly had been, although she wasn't an only child. She worked away every morning. I would find her with the little books that she was studying and I think before she died she was a very simple, wonderful person. I saw her develop; it was an inspiration for me to see it.

Miss T. also attended Radcliffe. While she was a student there the United States entered World War I. She read a book by a famous Unitarian minister of that era, John Haynes Holmes. It made her a lifelong pacifist. She left the church at about age twenty when, at someone's urging, the local Unitarian minister came to see her and to try to "correct" her pacifism. She speaks about the minister.

Miss T.:   I really felt sorry for him because he was a marvelous man. And he knew I was right; he knew that what I said about love and peace and understanding were true, and he was in a false position for him to try to tell me what attitude to take toward World War I. Any rate, I got in that war disillusioned in the church.

Disappointed that the church failed to take a stance critical of U. S. entry into the war, Miss T. turned in other directions.

Miss T.:   That's when I came to know the Quakers, God love 'em. I would say that I went with my whole heart instead into the labor movement which was then gathering strength. And A. J. Muste was leaving his parish and going in as a labor leader, and Roger Barwin was organizing the American Civil Liberties Union.

Her religion, she said, became a search for beauty.

Miss T.:   I think I've always been a religious person, but I had to stop calling myself a church-goer. I didn't go to church for years and years and years, except to please my mother at Christmas and Easter.

Details of Miss T.'s life from her early twenties to her mother's death about 1940 are sketchy in the interview. In its main lines it looks like this. Immediately upon graduating from college she travelled to the West Coast. There, with another young woman she met, she started a puppet theater and they began to tour in California. They planned to do a tour to the Far East, but ran out of money. She then returned to New York where she began a small art school for children. After a time she moved, apparently to her mother's home in upstate New York, where she taught art history and studio art in a girls' boarding school. After a few years she left home again, going to New York to work in theater. For what must have been ten to twelve years she worked as an actress and as a professional make-up artist for stage and screen. It was during those years that she sought a psychiatrist's help for her psychosomatic illnesses. It seems likely, also, that in these years she had some of the "unfortunate relationships" she mentions in talking about why she never married. She said, "I had unfortunate relationships, several important relationships. In lonely periods I made some mistakes."

Apparently in these years her mother wanted to bind Miss T. closer to herself than Miss T. could stand. She speaks of when she was working in theater and films.

Miss T.:   I used to go home for weekends to be with mother. . . . She was wrapped up in humane education for children—that was her old-age career when she found that I wouldn't let her make me into an old-age career for her. I had to be independent and she learned that the hard way, I think. But she did learn it and she went ahead with her own career.

The period from Miss T.'s early twenties to her early forties seems to have been a time when she dealt with issues of separation from her mother, with finding a career and with unresolved emotional binds with her father. We have seen how she earlier set herself critically over against her Unitarian background and left organized religion. She made her faith a search for beauty. Taken together, all this suggests that by around age thirty Miss T. had developed a pretty well equilibrated Stage 4 Individuative-Reflective faith stance.

The death of her mother in 1940 represented for Miss T. the end of an era. She was in her early forties. It appears that she had remained in the East, at some detriment to her career chances, in order to fulfill what she took to be her responsibilities to an aging mother. About a year after her mother's death Miss T. left for California. She took with her a book manuscript she had begun after her mother's death, one apparently dealing with a person's responsibility for how one meets, deals with and transcends adversities. For four or five years she worked in and around Hollywood. She used her make-up artist's skills to make a living, while taking screen tests to see if she could get going a career as a character actor. She also did some screen writing. Her breakthrough never came.

At about age forty-eight Miss T. had what she called "an acute nervous breakdown" in Hollywood. I suspect that today's name for what she suffered would be an acute, delayed mid-life crisis. In the midst of that crisis she was helped by a doctor who was a student and adherent of Rudolph Steiner. She also discovered the writings of Carl Jung and of other depth psychologists. Through friends she found a small cottage where she could live apart until she got herself together. In a kind of religious and artistic community near a river she began to write again and to find a new basis for her life. Through the friends who helped her find this place to live and write she had earlier come into contact with the Vedanta Society of Hollywood and, though it, with the Indian sage Krishnamurti. His teachings, available to her for two weeks in each of the three or four preceding summers, had given her powerful religious images with which to work.

> *Miss T.:* He [Krishnamurti] gave me so much of wisdom, I think, deeper than any other help I have ever received. He gave me a foundation for Christianity. I think Christians can get into trouble.

> *Interviewer:* What kind of trouble?

> *Miss T.:* The Christians who believe in hell and damnation for instance. That's a wicked philosophy and it's Christians who put it forth. And many people have been injured, have been damaged psychologically with that fearful philosophy.

> *Interviewer:* And what kind of foundation did Krishnamurti give you?

> *Miss T.:* That it doesn't matter what you call it. Whether you call it God or Jesus or Cosmic Flow or Reality or Love, it doesn't matter what you call it. It is there. And what you learn directly from that source will not tie you up in creeds . . . that separate you from your fellow man.

If Krishnamurti gave her the kind of help that brought her into a new and more inclusive religious community, it was a man from a group called the Camp Farthest Out who precipitated her return to Christianity. Hearing her speak of her religion as a quest for beauty, he responded, "But J., beauty can be pagan. . . . Where in that way of life is righteousness?" Miss T. remembers that question.

> *Miss T.:* That word righteousness sent shivers right down my back. It gave me the whole thing in one word. . . . I got the perspective on all that was lacking in my life. It was that one word, righteousness, opened up the whole thing of what's lacking without a religious foundation. A wonderful swami

in California, in Hollywood, Swami Prabhabananda said religion meant: *re* "back, again," *ligio* "to bind,"—"to bind again." The word religion means to bind again. And I felt that that one word *righteousness* bound me back again to those things I had been brought up to understand.

Shortly after that experience Miss T. returned to her native New England. Her half brother—her father's second son from his second marriage—had been rehospitalized with severe mental illness. She does not speculate on why she went back to try to care for him and help him recover, but she did. Her involvement with him led to a remarkable period in which she pioneered in teaching art, dance and folk music to patients in mental hospitals. Her stories of carrying a hand-crank Victrola into the wards and leading patients in singing and dancing are fascinating. She would take them out on the lawns for dancing and gymnastics. Nurses and psychiatrists apparently were impressed with the effectiveness of what she did. After several years it appeared that there might be state funding to support and broaden her program. At that time, however, late in her fifties, Miss T. began to develop serious arthritis and had to decline this opportunity.

In what she calls her "old-age career" Miss T. devoted a lot of time and energy with the Quakers, whom she joined in 1952, to integrating their summer camps for children. This meant establishing contacts in the black communities of her city and spending considerable time there each year recruiting children and their families for the camps. This she did with characteristic energy, verve and effectiveness for nearly twenty years.

As Miss T. talks today about her life and her outlook, her words and phrases disclose an almost textbook Stage 5 structuring underlying her faith. Before turning to some quotes that show this, perhaps it is worthwhile to reflect on the transition from the Individuative-Reflective stage of her thirties and forties to the Conjunctive stage that emerged after her breakdown. The factors leading to her mid-life breakdown—or at least some of them—seem to be obvious. With the death of her mother a few years before, she was now alone in the world. She suffered several years of career disappointment and probably began to face the conclusion that she would never be a success as an actress. Though we have few details, she had watched chances at marriage pass her by. Near fifty and childless, the state she vowed she would never accept—that of being an "old maid"—loomed more certainly as her future. For all these reasons, and more perhaps that we do not know, her faith, centering in the search for beauty, wore thin. The meanings sustaining her life collapsed.

As she had done after the death of her mother, she wrote herself back toward wholeness. The teachings of Krishnamurti, the psychology of Jung and the witness of her friends from the Camp Farthest Out sponsored her toward a new beginning in faith. As is characteristic of Stage 5, it was a new beginning that had to reclaim and reintegrate elements of strength from her childhood faith. It is revealing that in the interview her telling about the powerful impact of the question about righteousness upon her is followed immediately by the account of *religio* as a "binding back." Then she tells of her confirmation at twelve in the Unitarian church and of the power of that religious experience. With her return to New England, her joining the Quakers and her continuing and deepening relation with the Camp Farthest Out, she began to build a new faith stance, one that could sustain her in the second half of *her* life and ground her in finding fulfillment in service to others. What is the shape of that faith? What are its animating themes and anchoring convictions?

Miss T. was asked if there are beliefs and values everyone should hold.

> *Miss T.:*   If somebody asked me that and gave me just two minutes to answer it, I know what I'd say. It's a line from George Fox, the founder of Quakerism. It's old-fashioned English and it seems to me to have the entire program of anybody's life. Its a revolution, it's an enormous comfort, it's a peace maker. The line is: "There is that of God in every man." Now, you can start thinking about it. You can see that if you really did believe that, how it would change your relationships with people. . . . It's far-reaching. It applies nationally and individually and class-wise; it reaches the whole. To anyone that I loved dearly I would say, "Put that in your little invisible locket and keep it forever."

Mindful of her own suffering and of her devotion to other sufferers, our interviewer asked Miss T. how, if at all, she makes sense of the inequality and maldistribution of suffering in the world. Her answer began with her sharing her feelings about her younger half-brother, with whom she has worked for nearly thirty years in the state hospital.

> *Miss T.:*   Well, I can go back to my own experience with the problem of suffering. Take my brother R. If there ever was a pure, sinless, human soul, it's my brother R. Why did he have to have a life like this? I said to myself,

I've got to solve it if I am going to believe in a good God, a kind God. And I came out of it more or less this way: human life is a moment in eternity. I think there were two courses at college that meant more to me, philosophically, than any other two. One was astronomy. . . . You get a vista if you study astronomy. Your perspective opens out to an absolutely incredible degree. The other course was anthropology, where you get some idea of the development of the human being on this planet earth. They were both exercises in perspective. So I decided that a human being's life was his moment in eternity. It may be that R.'s—to use a figure of speech about the caterpillar—in the cocoon stage and the butterfly stage—it's a very telling figure because if you put that together with man as but a moment in eternity, maybe this is R.'s moment in the cocoon. I have had a sense that I should somewhere someday, along the pathways of God, meet R. when he is come into his own, and he comes with rushing wings. . . . I can't help but feel that all the suffering of all these people, all the people that are starving to death, that their time will come.

Miss T. continues with references to the vastness of eternity and the limited capacities for understanding of even the most enlightened human beings. She talks about suffering with finality,

Miss T.:   I know it has nothing whatsoever to do with guilt or sin or purity. That the pure in heart, Christ's line was, that they shall see God. And I believe that. At the same time there are a lot of human beings who have not had a chance to see God. So, as Christ told us, if we can believe without seeing, those are the real faithful. And I guess the trick is to be able to give your all to the people that are suffering, without losing your faith that there is some meaning to it.

When asked how she would speak about God to someone who knew nothing of what the term referred to, Miss T. took on the challenge. She began with an appeal that we acknowledge that there is a power beyond ourselves. Then she speaks of her convictions regarding the power beyond us.

Miss T.:   The Quakers call it The Light Within. I don't think it matters a bit what you call it. I think some people are so fed up with the word God that you can't talk to them about God. Call it Reality—all these would be spelled with a capital—let us say Reality, or Cosmic Flow or Love. And nobody can tell another about it. It has to come from within the individual, because, of course, everyone has the same inheritance. Religious structures in the mind. That interested me very much: that Carl Jung says if the analyst explores deeply enough he comes across the religious symbols that are in every human mind. It doesn't matter whether they call themselves agnostics or atheists.

Toward the end of her long interview Miss T. is asked about her understanding of sin.

Miss T.:   Sin!? I don't use the word sin, *ever.*
Interviewer: Why?
Miss T.:   I think, on the whole, people are doing the best they can with what light they have. And I think more in terms of mistakes than I do of deliberate sin. Everybody's made plenty of mistakes. In my own life I would perhaps describe it more as blundering because I didn't have the experience to handle things right. You blunder your way along. And you keep open to getting more light and to . . . well, sin surely. A good definition of sin would be thoughts and actions that bear no relation to the light within, call it what you will. They're severed, like a branch, severed. As Jesus said, the branches that are not functioning should be cut off and burned up. But I am absolutely convinced that there will have to be sin, have to be. Gigantic blunderings and mistakes and stupidities. It's past belief the stupidity of the world today. The American people that are shipping arms to the whole world because their industry has to make money. I think that's such a colossal stupidity. I call it stupidity rather than sin. . . . You go through life thinking that humanity . . . or you start as a young one thinking that people in general have sense. How is it that a concept of that sort can be a fact of today's experience? . . . You really have to have a deep faith in Almighty God and the power of good not to just go down under that gigantic stupidity and say it's hopeless. So I think sin, in one sentence, is the result of being cut off from God.

A few paragraphs later Miss T. speaks about how she struggles with that powerful temptation "to just go down under that gigantic stupidity and say it's hopeless." In the sense that Erikson means it, I think this statement breathes the integrity, hard won, that Miss T.'s struggle has yielded and the power on which her faith has depended.

Interviewer: When do you feel you are changing or growing now in your life as a religious person?
Miss T.:   Have to give me a moment to think about that one! [Pause.] I wrote this little second book of mine in California before 1950. Basically I had a hideout in the woods; I lived in a canyon as a little community there. And I found this place in the woods that was ideal for working out of doors and the people who owned the place let me take out an old kitchen table and a chair and we hid the typewriter in an abandoned beehive in the brush.

And this was written under the most ideal circumstances. Complete peace, complete sharing of nature, fragrance of the flowers from those slopes above, the Santa Barbara mountain range there. And the animals in the woods that visited me and the horses in the meadow out there that I made friends with. So I wrote something that I probably couldn't have written anywhere else. This place where I live now, that I love very dearly, is just full of interruptions. But I have succeeded; what I have been doing here in this last few years as my hobby is editing this material. And I find that this material helps me enormously. My own high moments help me. I would say that one of the things that has come to me in the immediate last few days is that this Cosmic Flow, which is God, call it what you will, is the life back of every cell in the body. It's a nice metaphor, the river is the flow, because it has come to me more deeply that I am just sort of porous. That this refreshing, healing love of God is flowing through me, and that's a very marvelous thing to believe, if you are seventy-eight and you've got arthritis, and you're burdened with the racial concept of old age that everybody gets sick and peters out and gets carried away. But it doesn't matter where you are physically, if you're sick or if you're well. That this Reality, of this actual life, all spelled with capital letters, Life flows through you at every moment of your waking-sleeping experience. Consequently you can be creative to your last breath.

There's even an illustration that was made by a man who produced the illustrations for the brochure of the place I was living. He made a drawing of the river flowing along over the rocks. There are some people who will think perhaps this is superstitious, but I think it's alright to use your imagination. I could almost feel that if I touch that illustration that it strengthens me to know that that river's flowing. You see an advantage to putting down your thoughts when you're inspired, you can go back to them when you're not inspired, when you're a little bit depressed physically, or if someone you do not vibrate to well has jarred on your nerves. Just let this thing flow through and know it flows through the other person. And peace comes.

Let's sum up some of the central structural features of Conjunctive faith.

Stage 5 Conjunctive faith involves the integration into self and outlook of much that was suppressed or unrecognized in the interest of Stage 4's self-certainty and conscious cognitive and affective adaptation to reality. This stage develops a "second naïveté" (Ricoeur) in which symbolic power is reunited with conceptual meanings. Here there must also be a new reclaiming and reworking of one's past. There must be an opening to the voices of one's "deeper self." Importantly, this involves a critical recognition of one's social unconscious—the myths, ideal images and prejudices built deeply into the self-system by virtue of one's nurture within a particular social class, religious tradition, ethnic group or the like.

Unusual before mid-life, Stage 5 knows the sacrament of defeat and the reality of irrevocable commitments and acts. What the previous stage struggled to clarify, in terms of the boundaries of self and outlook, this stage now makes porous and permeable. Alive to paradox and the truth in apparent contradictions, this stage strives to unify opposites in mind and experience. It generates and maintains vulnerability to the strange truths of those who are "other." Ready for closeness to that which is different and threatening to self and outlook (including new depths of experience in spirituality and religious revelation), this stage's commitment to justice is freed from the confines of tribe, class, religious community or nation. And with the seriousness that can arise when life is more than half over, this stage is ready to spend and be spent for the cause of conserving and cultivating the possibility of others' generating identity and meaning.

The new strength of this stage comes in the rise of the ironic imagination[25]—a capacity to see and be in one's or one's group's most powerful meanings, while simultaneously recognizing that they are relative, partial and inevitably distorting apprehensions of transcendent reality. Its danger lies in the direction of a paralyzing passivity or inaction, giving rise to complacency or cynical withdrawal, due to its paradoxical understanding of truth.

Stage 5 can appreciate symbols, myths and rituals (its own and others') because it has been grasped, in some measure, by the depth of reality to which they refer. It also sees the divisions of the human family vividly because it has been apprehended by the possibility (and imperative) of an inclusive community of being. But this stage remains divided. It lives and acts between an untransformed world and a transforming vision and loyalties. In some few cases this division yields to the call of the radical actualization that we call Stage 6.

21. Stage 6. Universalizing Faith

As our structural-developmental theory of faith stages has emerged and undergone refinements, it has become clear that we are trying to do both descriptive and normative work. Our empirical studies have aimed at testing whether there is a predictable sequence of formally describable stages in the life of faith. The hypothesized stages with which we began, however, and the versions of them that have withstood empirical scrutiny exhibit an indisputably normative tendency. From the beginning of our work there has been a complex image of mature faith in relation to which we have sought for developmentally related prior or preparatory stages. It is this normative endpoint, the culminating image of mature faith in this theory, with which I want to work now. What *is* the normative shape of Stage 6 Universalizing Faith?

In the little book *Life-Maps* I described Stage 6 in the following way:

In order to characterize Stage 6 we need to focus more sharply on the dialectical or paradoxical features of Stage 5 faith. Stage 5 can see injustice in sharply etched terms because it has been apprehended by an enlarged awareness of the demands of justice and their implications. It can recognize partial truths and their limitations because it has been apprehended by a more comprehensive vision of truth. It can appreciate and cherish symbols, myths and rituals in new depth because it has been apprehended in some measure by the depth of reality to which the symbols refer and which they mediate. It sees the fractures and divisions of the human family with vivid pain because it has been apprehended by the possibility of an inclusive commonwealth of being. Stage 5 remains paradoxical or divided, however, because the self is caught between these universalizing apprehensions and the need to preserve its own being and well-being. Or because it is deeply invested in maintaining the ambiguous order of a socioeconomic system, the alternatives to which seem more unjust or destructive than it is. In this situation of paradox Stage 5 must act and not be paralyzed. But Stage 5 acts out of conflicting loyalties. Its readiness to spend and be spent finds limits in its loyalty to the present order, to its institutions, groups and compromise procedures. Stage 5's perceptions of justice outreach its readiness to sacrifice the self and to risk the partial justice of the present order for the sake of a more inclusive justice and the realization of love.

The transition to Stage 6 involves an overcoming of this paradox through a moral and ascetic actualization of the universalizing apprehensions. Heedless of the threats to self, to primary groups, and to the institutional arrangements of the present order that are involved, Stage 6 becomes a disciplined, activist *incarnation*—a making real and tangible—of the imperatives of absolute love and justice of which Stage 5 has partial apprehensions. The self at Stage 6 engages in spending and being spent for the transformation of present reality in the direction of a transcendent actuality.

Persons best described by Stage 6 typically exhibit qualities that shake our usual criteria of normalcy. Their heedlessness to self-preservation and the vividness of their taste and feel for transcendent moral and religious actuality give their actions and words an extraordinary and often unpredictable quality. In their devotion to universalizing compassion they may offend our parochial perceptions of justice. In their penetration through the obsession with survival, security, and significance they threaten our measured standards of righteousness and goodness and prudence. Their enlarged visions of universal community disclose the partialness of our tribes and pseudo-species. And their leadership initiatives, often involving strategies of nonviolent suffering and ultimate respect for being, constitute affronts to our usual notions of relevance. It is little wonder that persons best described by Stage 6 so frequently become martyrs for the visions they incarnate.[26]

Before commenting on the passages I have just offered from *Life-Maps* let me share another effort to describe the shape of Stage 6, this time from a more recent writing. This will serve as our summary in advance:

Stage 6 is exceedingly rare. The persons best described by it have generated faith compositions in which their felt sense of an ultimate environment is inclusive of all being. They have become incarnators and actualizers of the spirit of an inclusive and fulfilled human community.

They are "contagious" in the sense that they create zones of liberation from the social, political, economic and ideological shackles we place and endure on human futurity. Living with felt participation in a power that unifies and transforms the world, Universalizers are often experienced as subversive of the structures (including religious structures) by which we sustain our individual and corporate survival, security and significance. Many persons in this stage die at the hands of those whom they hope to change. Universalizers are often more honored and revered after death than during their lives. The rare persons who may be described by this stage have a special grace that makes them seem more lucid, more simple, and yet somehow more fully human than the rest of us. Their community is universal in extent. Particularities are cherished because they are vessels of the universal, and thereby valuable apart from any utilitarian considerations. Life is both loved and held to loosely. Such persons are ready for fellowship with persons at any of the other stages and from any other faith tradition.[27]

Even as I read these descriptions I am haunted—as I am sure you are —by memories of Jonestown, Guyana and the Reverend Jim Jones. Also in my mind, images of the deeply angry, mystical eyes of the aged Ayatollah Khomeini look out across the frenzied, impassioned mobs he inspires with his mixture of chauvinistic nationalism and religious absolutism. The followers of both these men—and those of many other persons like them—would likely hear my descriptions of Stage 6 as depictions of their revered, and feared, leaders. To hear the qualities of Stage 6 in these ways, however, is to miss some extremely important qualifications and dimensions of Stage 6 faith. Fascinated with the charisma, the authority and frequently the ruthlessness of such leaders, we must not fail to attend in the descriptions of Stage 6 to the criteria of inclusiveness of community, of radical commitment to justice and love and of selfless passion for a transformed world, a world made over not in *their* images, but in accordance with an intentionality both divine and transcendent.

When asked whom I consider to be representatives of this Stage 6 outlook I refer to Gandhi, to Martin Luther King, Jr., in the last years of his life and to Mother Teresa of Calcutta. I am also inclined to point to Dag Hammarskjöld, Dietrich Bonhoeffer, Abraham Heschel and Thomas Merton. There must be many others, not so well known to us, whose lives exhibit these qualities of Stage 6. To say that a person embodies the qualities of Stage 6 is not to say that he or she is perfect. Nor is it to imply that he or she is a "self-actualized person" or a "fully functioning human being"—though it seems that most of them are or

were, if in somewhat different senses than Abraham Maslow or Carl
Rogers intended their terms. Greatness of commitment and vision often
coexists with great blind spots and limitations. Erik Erikson, writing his
book on Gandhi, set out to illumine the religious and ethical power of
Gandhi's doctrine of *satyagraha*, the reliance on nonviolent strategies in
the aggressive pursuit of the social truth that is justice. In the middle
of the book Erikson had to stop. He found it necessary to write a stern
and sad letter of reprimand to the Mahatma—dead those twenty-five
years—pointing out the unfairness and the muted violence of Gandhi's
treatment of his wife, Kasturba, and of his sons.[28] (Gandhi, in forming
his ashram, had insisted on bringing Untouchables into the household.
Kasturba had accepted this without complaint. She found it too much,
however, when Gandhi insisted that she take on the job of removing
their toilet wastes from the house—something he himself was patently
unwilling to do.) To be Stage 6 does not mean to be perfect, whether
perfection be understood in a moral, psychological or a leadership sense.

I do not believe that people set out to be Stage 6. That is not to say
that some, who later come to fit that description, did not set out to be
"saints." Thomas Merton, while still a student at Columbia University
came to be clear in his own mind that he wanted to become a saint.
Students of his career, however, recognize that his growth toward what
we are here calling Stage 6, took paths and required difficulties that were
unforeseen in Merton's early visions of sainthood.[29] It is my conviction
that persons who come to embody Universalizing faith are drawn into
those patterns of commitment and leadership by the providence of God
and the exigencies of history. It is as though they are selected by the
great Blacksmith of history, heated in the fires of turmoil and trouble
and then hammered into usable shape on the hard anvil of conflict and
struggle.

The descriptions I have read to you of Stage 6 suggest another note
of realism in our efforts to understand the normative endpoint of faith
development in the Universalizing stage. Here I refer to what has been
called the "subversive" impact of their visions and leadership. Even as
they oppose the more blatantly unjust or unredeemed structures of the
social, political or religious world, these figures also call into question the
compromise arrangements in our common life that have acquired the
sanction of conventionalized understandings of justice. King's "Letter
from Birmingham Jail" was written not to "Bull" Connor or the Ku Klux
Klan, but to a group of moderate and liberal religious leaders who had

pled with King to meliorate the pressure his followers were exerting through nonviolent demonstrations on the city. King's assault on the more blatant features of a segregated city proved subversive to the genteel compromises by which persons of good will of both races had accommodated themselves in a racist society.

This subversive character of the impact of Stage 6 leadership often strikes us as arising from a kind of relevant irrelevance. Mother Teresa of Calcutta's ministry illustrates this powerfully.[30] Mother Teresa, a foreign-born nun in her late thirties, head of a girls' boarding school, was going on retreat. As she traveled through the city she became overwhelmed by the sight of abandoned persons, lying in the streets, left to die. Some of these forgotten people were already having their not yet lifeless limbs gnawed by rodents. Under the impact of those grim sights she felt a call to a new form of vocation—a ministry of presence, service and care to the abandoned, the forgotten, the hopeless. In a nation and a world where scarcity is a fact of life, where writers and policy makers urge strategies of "triage" to ensure that resources are not "wasted" on those who have no chance of recovery and useful contribution, what could be less relevant than carrying these dying persons into places of care, washing them, caring for their needs, feeding them when they are able to take nourishment and affirming by word and deed that they are loved and valued people of God? But in a world that says people only have worth if they pull their own weight and contribute something of value, what could be *more* relevant?

In these persons of Universalizing faith these qualities of redemptive subversiveness and relevant irrelevance derive from visions they see and to which they have committed their total beings. These are not abstract visions, generated like utopias out of some capacity for transcendent imagination. Rather, they are visions born out of radical acts of identification with persons and circumstances where the futurity of being is being crushed, blocked or exploited. A Martin Luther King, Jr., prepared by familial and church nurture, by college, seminary and doctoral studies, influenced theologically and philosophically by Gandhi's teachings on nonviolent resistance, gets drawn into acts of radical identification with the oppressed when Rosa Parks refuses any longer to let her personhood be ground underfoot. Gandhi, steeped by a Jain mother with the doctrine of *ahimsa* (the doctrine of noninjury to being), influenced by a tradition of public service in his father's family, prepared by legal study in Britain, is physically abused and removed from the first-class section of a South African train. Through this shock of recognition of his identification with the oppressed and despised minority of a colonized people he is drawn eventually into the leadership of a nonviolent struggle for Indian independence. We have already spoken of the identification with the hopeless and abandoned dying street people that launched Mother Teresa's vision of a ministry where one meets Christ in the person of the forgotten ones.

In such situations of concrete oppression, difficulty or evil, persons see clearly the forces that destroy life as it should be. In the direct experience of the negation of one's personhood or in one's identification with the negations experienced by others, visions are born of what life is *meant* to be. In such circumstances the promise of fulfillment, which is the birthright of each mother's child and the hope of each human community, cries out in affront at the persons and conditions that negate it. The visions that form and inform Universalizing faith arise out of and speak to such situations as these.

Stage 6 and the Jewish-Christian Image of the Kingdom of God

Since I began systematically to work on a theory of faith development it has been clear to me that my normative images of Stage 6 have been strongly influenced by H. Richard Niebuhr's descriptions of radical monotheistic faith.[31] As we saw in Part I of this book, in speaking of "radical monotheism" Niebuhr chose a category from anthropology and comparative religion. Originally it was intended to characterize the religions of the West, Judaism, Christianity and Islam, which lay stress on the oneness and the sovereignty of God. Niebuhr's use of the term in no way compromises the conviction of God's oneness or sovereignty. He does not, however, want to identify the term simply as a generic category by which to designate traditionally monotheistic religious groupings. Radical monotheism, for Niebuhr, means a faith relationship characterized by total trust in and loyalty to the principle of being. Radical monotheism, in Niebuhr's usage, describes a form of faith in which the reality of God—transcendent and ever exceeding our grasp —exerts transforming and redeeming tension on the structures of our common life and faith. In radical monotheistic faith the particular forms of religious and ethical life to which a people hold are seen as partial apprehensions of and responses to the true state of affairs, namely

God-ruling, or the Kingdom of God. In radical monotheistic faith all our beliefs, practices and images of the divine-human relationship are seen as relative to the reality they try to apprehend. This is not to fall into an assertion of relativ*ism*—the assertion that all religious outlooks are relative to each other and to the circumstances, experiences and interests of the communities who form around them. Rather, it is to call for a theory of relativ*ity* in faith in which forms of religious life are considered as relative representations or modes of response to that determinative center of power and value that is the sovereign reality with which we humans have to deal in life, whether we know it or acknowledge it or not.[32]

Radical monotheistic faith has powerful ethical correlates. With roots deep in the Jewish tradition, yet in a manner resonant with Eastern ideals of nonattachment, radical monotheism interrupts all attachments to centers of value and power that might be prized for ego or group-ego reasons. The sovereign God of radical monotheistic faith is an enemy to all idolatrous gods. This includes the gods of nation, self, tribe, family, institutions, success, money, sexuality and so on. These partial gods are not *negated* in the judgment of a sovereign God, but they are relativized to the status of proximal goods. Any claims of ultimacy for them or by them must be avoided or relinquished. In radical monotheistic faith the commonwealth of being, unified in the reign of God as creator, ruler and redeemer, is universal. This means that principles by which human beings divide themselves from each other—and from other species in the orders of creation—are not divisions that finally determine their relative worth and value. The sovereign God of radical monotheistic faith intends the fulfillment of creation and the unity of being. This is not a homogenous unity in which differences and particularities are molded into a monolithic oneness. Rather, the unity envisioned in the Kingdom of God, as expected in radical monotheistic faith, is richly plural and highly variegated, a celebration of the diversity and complexity of creation. The hallmark of the Kingdom of God is a quality of righteousness in which being is properly related to being, a righteousness in which each person or being is augmented by the realization of the futurity of all the others.

In developing the concept of radical montheistic faith, Niebuhr understood himself to be bringing to expression the dominant thrust of biblical faith. He understood it as the central element in the covenant relationship between a liberated Israel and the God of the Exodus. He understood that the Torah was given and elaborated in order to give form to a righteous community, a community fit to be priests to other nations. He saw Jesus as steeped in the Jewish vision of a covenant relationship with God and in the Jewish hope of a coming reign of God that will redeem, restore and fulfill God's creation in a kingdom of right-relatedness between God and humanity, between peoples and between people and nature. Niebuhr saw Jesus as the pioneering embodiment of radical monotheistic faith, the "pioneer and perfector" of the faith to which we are called. He saw the resurrection of Jesus, in power and glory, as God's ratification of the truth for all people, of the proclaimed coming Kingdom of God.

I suspect that by now many of you find yourselves forming objecting questions to what I have said. I suspect you are asking yourselves, "Does he think he can take a Jewish-Christian image of faith in the Kingdom of God and generalize it to serve as the normative and descriptive endpoint of a supposedly formal and inclusive theory of faith development?" For some of you—Jews and Christians alike—there is undoubtedly some offense in my designating "radical monotheism," as developed here, as "Jewish-Christian." I am sure that the position, as I offer it here, sounds more Christian than Jewish. I hear you asking, "What kind of religious and cultural imperialism are we being asked to buy?"

These are legitimate objections. They point to serious issues we must face and deal with. In my previous published works on the faith development theory I have chosen to avoid them. In writing the present book, however, a book I hope will give adequate expression the full range of findings and insights that this work has yielded, I find I cannot and do not wish to avoid the issues raised in this instance of trying to move from the particular to the universal.

The case I am trying to make is this: the fact that the image of the most developed faith that informs the normative and descriptive endpoint of the faith development theory derived initially from a theological formulation of the central thrust of *biblical* faith need not disqualify it as more generally or universally valid. Put another way, the fact that descriptions of Stage 6 seek to express in a formal and inclusive way the contours of radical monotheistic faith does not negate the possibility of its universal truth and usefulness.

To keep this from becoming something other than a solipsistic confession of my convictions or the arrogant assertion of a biblical apologist, I need to deal with three critically important kinds of claims. First, in a way that I believe potentially applies to the central thrusts of *any* of the lasting great religious traditions, I think we must learn again to take seriously what I will call the "absoluteness of the particular." Second, with regard to Jewish and Christian understandings of the Kingdom of God, I will want to explore with you the significance of the claim that the Kingdom of God is an *eschatological reality*—a reality that is coming to us from the future and that comes to us as the unifying power of the future.[38] And third, I want to test with you how seriously we are prepared to take the category *revelation*—revelation when it is connected with the truth claims of our own religious traditions and revelation when it is claimed for truths of others' traditions.

The Absoluteness of the Particular

We all know something about "the scandal of the particular." The particular is the time-bound, the concrete, the local. The particular means *this* relatively undistinguished group, and not another. The particular has warts, and dust from the road; it has body odors and holes in its sandals. The scandal of particularity arises from the fact that over and over again disclosures of ultimate moment find expression to and among very finite, undistinguished, local and particular peoples. Cryptic phrases and questions express our sense of the scandal of the particular: "How odd of God to choose the Jews." "Can any good thing come out of Nazareth?" Or more straightforwardly we ask, "Why Abraham, why Moses? Why Mary and Jesus? Why Gautama, why Confucius, why Muhammad?" These particulars are scandalous precisely because something of transcendent and universal moment comes to expression in them or through them.

Concern about particularity arises out of the collision of communities of faith, each of which—directly or indirectly—makes claims of universal truth and validity for their faith. With these implicit or explicit claims of universality there are usually clear assertions that the alleged universal truth is an exclusive possession of the community that has been formed around it. Religious wars, inquisitions, heresy trials, persecutions, pogroms, holocausts and histories of prejudice and suspicion have been the results. Out of the blood and ashes of such struggles have come efforts by philosophers of religion to generate criteria, independent of any one tradition, by which the truth claims of each and all can be tested, evaluated and generalized in relation to presumably more universal standards. The responses of many others go in the direction of the adoption—often in considerable disillusionment—of forms of secularist relativism, marked by varying degrees of tolerance, indifference and cynicism toward religious faith. From this latter perspective the truth claims of religions are evaluated, if at all, on the basis of utilitarian criteria. Whatever truth a faith may have is seen, from this angle, as a matter of its pragmatic usefulness for particular individuals or groups.

Sometime ago Orbis Press published a fine collection of papers called *Christian Faith in a Religiously Plural World,* [34] edited by Donald G. Dawe and John B. Carman. In it the topic indicated by the title was addressed by Christians, a Buddhist, a Hindu, a Jew and a Muslim. Dawe, in the keynote address, pointed out, with proper irony, that secularist solutions to the clash of religious truths neither overcome the divisions in the human family that prove so destructive, nor do they address the pervasive hunger for truth that characterizes our age. Let me quote Dawe:

> Modern secularity has offered another way of dealing with religious pluralism. As religious traditions lose their importance as means of self-understanding and community identification, their differences and mutual exclusiveness diminish in importance. Alienation from any particular religious faith tends to move the question of religious particularity into the realm of indifference, as life is determined by nonreligious values and institutions. Yet secularity has been no more successful in establishing human community than has the religious vision. The competing claims of nationalism, economic imperialism, and ideological triumphalism are also demonic forms of particularity that have not been able to establish a new universality in human community. . . . So the fact remains that the religious question has to be dealt with in the religious perspective. The problem of Christian faith in a religiously plural world cannot be solved by ex-Christians learning to relate to ex-Jews, ex-Buddhists, ex-Muslims, or ex-anything else, in the name of conceptions that do not take these traditions seriously.[35]

For persons committed to and through religious faith to work together on questions of religious truth means to take with radical seriousness *the absoluteness of the particular.* Now let me say what I mean when I use this intentionally provocative term. Absoluteness means here "bearing the quality of ultimacy." Absoluteness in a tradition of religious faith is constituted by those moments in it in which the structure and character of the ultimate conditions of existence are disclosed. Absoluteness in a tradition of religious faith is a function of the faithful shape it gives to human life as a correlate of the revelation of divine character and intention that it has been given. Absoluteness is that quality of a tradition of religious faith given to it by the instances in which the Unconditioned has come to expression in it.[36]

Now let me make some crucial clarifications. The absoluteness that comes to expression in some moments of a religious tradition is not to be identified with the absolutes that adherents of that tradition may fashion about it. Put another way, absoluteness is a quality of the transcendent that comes to expression in revelation, but not necessarily of the symbols, myths, propositions or doctrines formulated to represent or communicate it. Further—and this is the most important point—absoluteness, as a quality of the transcendent that comes to expression, *is not exclusivistic.* [37] Presumably, the absoluteness of the divine character can come to expression in different forms and in different contexts, with each of these instances bearing the full weight of ultimacy. All of this means—if it is correct—that the most precious thing we have to offer each other in interfaith encounters is our honest, unexaggerated and nonpossessive sharing of what we take to be the moments of absoluteness in the particular faith traditions in which we live as committed participants.

The descriptions of Stage 6 Universalizing faith are offered for that kind of testing and refinement. I take those descriptions to be formal and generalized expressions of that radical monotheistic faith with which Jews and Christians respond, in trust and loyalty, to the present and coming reign of a God of sovereign universality. This I take to be a worthy offering in the faithful effort to which we all are called, to discern and respond to the absoluteness in the particular.

The Eschatological Character of the Kingdom of God

Radical monotheistic faith is faith oriented toward the coming Kingdom of God. One of the reasons why the reality referred to by Christians and Jews with the political metaphor "Kingdom of God" may claim absoluteness has to do with its being an *eschatological* reality. To take eschatology seriously is to see that present and past come to us out of the future. Out of the freedom of God came creation and possibility. Freedom and responsibility in our present come to us out of the freedom of God's future for us and for all being. Receiving the present from God's future, we are freed over against the past. As the power of the future, God is the promise of a unified and unifying future for all being.[38] In ways that surely transcend the specificity of Jewish and Christian images of the coming Kingdom, God has disclosed the divine intention to redeem, restore and fulfill all being.

Seen in the light of this vision the human vocation—and it must be understood as a universal human vocation—is to live in anticipation of the coming reign of God. The human vocation is to lean into God's promised future for us and for all being. It is to be part of the reconciling, redeeming and restoring work that goes on wherever the Kingdom of God is breaking in. It is to be part of the suffering rule of God, to oppose those structures of life that block and deny the future of persons and being in God. The human vocation in response to the coming Kingdom of God is to live so as to honor—in others and in oneself—the futurity grounded in the promises of the faithful, sovereign God.

In light of their particular vision of the reality they call the coming Kingdom of God and of the understanding of the human vocation that flows from it Christians and Jews have a witness to offer. First, we are called to live as pioneers of the coming Kingdom of God, to give flesh and communal form to the anticipatory righteousness that is an advance colony of the Kingdom. Second, without expecting or requiring that others become Christians or Jews, we are called to point to the futurity of God and to the coming Kingdom as the universal, shared future of all being. Intrinsic to that witness is the assurance that the reality and character of the coming reign of God exceeds and spills over all our images, symbols and beliefs about it. Equally intrinsic to that witness, however is the conviction that through the symbols, metaphors and beliefs with which we have tried to apprehend the disclosure of God's promised and powerful future, there comes to expression a calling to divine-human partnership that bears the weight of ultimate truth. Third, we bear *special* responsibility for testifying to the depths of the human capacity for distorting our apprehensions of and our efforts to respond to the coming Kingdom. The reality of *sin* as personal, corporate and cosmic in character comes clear to us from moments of disclosure in our histories of revelation. The reality of sin comes clear to us as well, when we reflect upon the intractability of our own and of our companions' capacities for self-righteousness and destructive hatred in dealing with each other.

The bearers of Stage 6 faith, whether they stand in the Jewish,

Christian or other traditions, embody in radical ways this leaning into the future of God for all being. I have noticed that whenever I speak on stages of faith and try to describe the structural features and style of each stage, it is always Stage 6 that people are most interested in. The more "secular" the audience, the greater the interest. I ask myself, What is it about those people best described by Stage 6 that enlivens our excitement and draws us out of our embeddedness in the present and the past? What is it about these persons that both condemns our obsessions with our own security and awakens our taste and sense for the promise of human futurity? I believe that these persons kindle our imaginations in these ways because, in their generosity and authority, in their freedom and their costly love, they embody the promise and lure of our shared futurity. These persons embody costly openness to the power of the future. They actualize its promise, creating zones of liberation and sending shock waves to rattle the cages that we allow to constrict human futurity. Their trust in the power of that future and their trans-narcissistic love of human futurity account for their readiness to spend and be spent in making the Kingdom actual.

NOTES

1. Paraphrased and shortened from Erik H. Erikson, *Toys and Reasons* (New York: Norton, 1977), pp. 85–90.
2. For a fine survey of recent literature on these topics see Selma Fraiberg, *Every Child's Birthright: In Defense of Mothering* (New York: Basic Books, 1977).
3. See Walter J. Lowe, "Evil and the Unconscious," *Soundings,* vol. 63, no. 1 (Spring, 1980).
4. See Erik Erikson, *Childhood and Society* (New York: Norton, 1963), p. 249.
5. See Ana-Maria Rizzuto, *The Birth of the Living God* (Chicago: University of Chicago Press, 1979).
6. See Lev Semenovich Vygotsky, *Thought and Language,* ed. and trans. Eugenia Haufmann and Gertrude Vahar (Cambridge, Mass.: M.I.T. Press, 1962), pp. 33–49.
7. See Rizzuto, *The Birth of the Living God.*
8. Bruno Bettelheim, *The Uses of Enchantment: The Meaning and Importance of Fairy Tales* (New York: Random House, Vintage Books, 1977).
9. Bettelheim, *Enchantment,* p. 27.
10. See William F. Lynch, S.J., *Images of Faith* (Notre Dame, Ind.: University of Notre Dame Press, 1973).

11. Bettelheim, *Enchantment,* p. 61. Remarks in brackets are mine.

12. Philip M. Helfaer, *The Psychology of Religious Doubt* (Boston: Beacon Press, 1972).

13. Jerome Berryman, "Being in Parables with Children," *Religious Education,* vol. 74, no. 3 (May–June, 1979), pp. 271–285.

14. See John Dominic Crossan, *In Parables: The Challenge of the Historical Jesus* (New York: Harper & Row, 1973).

15. See Edmund V. Sullivan, "The Scandalized Child: Children, Media and Commodity Culture" in *Toward Moral and Religious Maturity* (Morristown, N.J.: Silver Burdett, 1980), pp. 549–573.

16. Jim Fowler and Sam Keen, *Life-Maps: Conversations on the Journey of Faith* (Waco, Tex.: Word Books, 1978), p. 46.

17. Erik H. Erikson, *Childhood and Society* (New York: Norton 1963), p. 262.

18. In the past I have, mistakenly, attributed this phrase to George Herbert Mead. See *Mind, Self and Society* (Chicago: University of Chicago Press, 1934). His phrase is the "generalized other," a kind of composite representation of the recognition, expectations and evaluation of the self accorded by one's experience of social relations. I am unable to trace the origin of the phrase "significant other," though it clearly resembles the I-Thou relation described by Martin Buber.

19. See Sharon Parks, "Faith Development and Imagination in the Context of Higher Education" (Th.D. diss., Harvard Divinity School, 1980).

20. James M. Cone, *The God of the Oppressed* (New York: Seabury Press, 1975).

21. Michael Polanyi, *The Tacit Dimension* (Garden City, N.Y.: Doubleday, 1966).

22. Paul Tillich, *Dynamics of Faith* (New York: Harper & Row, 1957), chap. 2.

23. Paul Ricoeur, *The Symbolism of Evil,* trans. Emerson Buchanan (Boston: Beacon Press, 1967), pp. 351–352.

24. Ibid. See also Paul Ricoeur, "The Hermeneutics of Symbols and Philosophical Reflection" in *The Philosophy of Paul Ricoeur,* ed. Charles E. Reagan and David Stewart (Boston: Beacon Press, 1978), pp. 36–58.

25. See Lynch, *Images of Faith.*

26. Fowler and Keen, *Life-Maps: Conversations on the Journey of Faith* (Waco, Tex.: Word Books, 1978), pp. 87–89.

27. Fowler, "Perspectives on the Family from the Standpoint of Faith Development Theory," *The Perkins Journal,* vol. 33, no. 1 (Fall, 1979), pp. 13–14.

28. Erik H. Erikson, *Gandhi's Truth* (New York: Norton, 1969), pp. 229–254.

29. See Thomas Merton, *The Seven Storey Mountain* (New York: Harcourt, Brace 1948), esp. pp. 233–234.

30. See Malcolm Muggeridge, *Something Beautiful for God* (New York: Ballantine Books, 1971).

31. H. Richard Niebuhr, *Radical Monotheism and Western Culture* (New York: Harper & Row, 1960).

32. For a similar call for a theory of relativity in faith see Wilfred Cantwell Smith, *Faith and Belief* (Princeton, N.J.: Princeton University Press, 1979), pp. 155–156, and esp. note #41, p. 208.

33. See Wolfhart Pannenberg, *Theology and the Kingdom of God* (Philadelphia: Westminster Press, 1969), pp. 72ff.

34. (Maryknoll, N.Y.: Orbis Press, 1978).

35. Ibid., pp. 16–17.

36. This language is indebted, of course, to Paul Tillich. See especially *The Protestant Era*, 2d. ed. (abridged), trans. James Luther Adams (Chicago: University of Chicago Press, 1957), p. 32, note #1, and p. 78.

37. In this crucial respect my position differs markedly from that of Ernst Troeltsch in his *The Absoluteness of Christianity and the History of Religions*, trans. David Reid (Richmond, Va.: John Knox Press, 1971). See especially his chapter 4, "Christianity: Focal Point and Culmination of All Religious Developments." It is precisely the claim embodied in this title (which Troeltsch subsequently gave up) that I, in principle, do *not* want to make.

38. See Pannenberg, *Theology and the Kingdom of God*.

Part V

*Formation and
Transformation in Faith*

22. Mary's Pilgrimage: The Theory at Work

||||||||||||||||||||||||||||||||||||||||||||||||||||||||||||||||||||||||||||||||||||||||||||||||||||||||

Experience has taught me that the best way to help people gain a working understanding of the stage theory of faith development is to put them to work with it. I have done this many times in classes and seminars. Until now, however, I have not tried this method in a book. Therefore I must rely upon the reader to join me in this experiment. In the following pages I invite you to overhear major portions of an actual interview with a remarkable young woman. Once we have shared those segments of the interview that I want to include here, I will ask you to reflect with me upon them. I will ask some questions, taking care to clarify and define what I mean in asking them. After you have answered the questions for yourself, you can read my answers to them, comparing and contrasting your perceptions and judgments with mine. Then I will ask you to take another step with me. Based upon the answers to the earlier questions about the interview I will proceed to offer an analysis of the interview. My hope is that you will find this procedure—and your participation in it—interesting and illuminating and that by the end of this part you will have a better grasp of the meaning of a faith stage.

Before we turn to the interview, let me offer a couple of observations that come from my efforts to teach this theory. There is a developmental history involved in learning a developmental theory. Most people find that the effort to identify the structural features of a person's faith involves them in a new kind of thinking and attending. This does not mean that the task is particularly difficult. It simply means that it takes time, it takes some practice and it involves the construction of some new ways of thinking. My goal in offering you greater familiarity with this theory in this inductive way is to allow you to gradually construct these new patterns of thought and analysis for yourself. Therefore, do not be impatient with yourself or with me if you find you need to reread parts of the interview, or the answers I give to the questions. Normally the analysis of a faith development interview requires a minimum of three careful readings. I invite you to read and reread and to spend some time formulating and testing your own answers. As you do so you will be building up a working understanding of the stages of faith.

Meeting Mary

Mary is a neatly dressed young woman who seems a bit younger than her twenty-eight years. I have never met her before. We spend thirty minutes or so getting acquainted. I explain to her that for some years I have been conducting interviews of this kind. My interest is to invite people to share with us—in their own words and from their own points of view—something about their ways of seeing life, their values, what's important to them and so on. I explain that our work is part of the field of lifespan developmental psychology and that we are interested in knowing something about the life experiences and the important relationships that have helped to shape people's perspectives, their values, and their lifestyles. I make it clear that in this interview there are no right or wrong answers, only her answers. She is free to decline to answer any question with which she does not feel comfortable. I promise to keep the information she shares with me confidential and assure her that in the event of its use in any publication, her anonymity and that of any persons she mentions in the interview will be carefully protected.* The interview begins:

> *Interviewer:* Mary, I would like to begin by asking you what may seem a strange question; I hope it will be a useful one to begin our conversation. If you were to divide your life into chapters—like the chapters in a book —what would the chapter divisions look like? What are the chapter periods in your life?
>
> *Mary:* I don't really think in terms of chapters of my life before the age of seventeen. At that time I left for college a year early, after my junior year of high school. The five years between seventeen and twenty-two, before I became a Christian, were really what I call my lost years or seeking years,

---

*"Mary" has read this chapter and given her permission to publish it in this form. All of the names of persons and places mentioned in the interview have been changed, as have the religious movements or ministries to which she was related. The numbers in parentheses at the end of each passage are to aid in referring back to particular statements when they are discussed in the commentary.

because I didn't accomplish anything during those years. And yet, I was
really seeking after truth and purpose in life, and I think I found that truth
and purpose when I became a Christian. But I was involved in all sorts of
things; you know, Eastern religions, pop psychology, the occult, illicit drugs
and sex, and all that kind of stuff. You know, I was leading a real immoral,
irresponsible sort of life . . . disobedient to my parents. Dropped out of
school several times, and I just really made a mess out of my life. But I know
that in my heart I was really looking for the truth, too.   (1)

Interviewer: This was seventeen to twenty-two?

Mary: Yes. And I couldn't find anything that really satisfied me in life, that
really seemed worth committing myself to.   (2)

In the next few exchanges I ask about what college or colleges she
attended. She explains that she spent one year at a private college in the
northern Midwest. Then she left and went to California, where she was
enrolled for a short time in a big state university.

Mary: I dropped out of there too. . . . I kind of gravitated to college
campuses, and lived around the periphery. But I didn't get back in school.
I guess I really didn't know what I wanted to do with my life. I knew I really
wanted to love somebody and to be loved by somebody, and I really wanted
to find truth and meaning, and that's about it.   (3)

Interviewer: You were born in 1951?

Mary: 1950.   (4)

Interviewer: 1950. So this was going on about 1967–1968, the time of the
Vietnam War . . .

Mary: Yeah, it was the time of all the student riots and the hippie movement
was just passing its zenith, so . . .   (5)

Interviewer: It was a very confusing time in terms of the society and the
culture; college campuses were in a lot of ferment and struggle. I gather
it was around age twenty-two that you became a Christian?

Mary: Yeah, it was in December of 1972 when I was twenty-two. (6)

Interviewer: I'd like to hear about that in some detail in a little bit. Let's just
say that a whole new chapter started with that.

Mary: Right, but at the same time I can see that the Lord was really working
in my life to draw me to himself before that happened. About a year before
that happened I was living with a guy up in Indiana. I got . . . well, this
probably was the major turning point in my life, this whole crisis. The
upshot of that relationship was that I attempted to take my own life. And
also I got into all kinds of other trouble: I wrecked my car; I got busted
for shoplifting. You know, just all kinds of things that I never dreamed I'd
get involved in. When I was recuperating from this attempt on my life, the
Lord began to show me that there was a divine law and that I had violated

it; and that as why I was having all these unhappy effects in my life. But I was only seeing it in a very vague way to start with. And then, about three weeks after I tried to kill myself, I had a really exceptional experience on LSD. I can't deny that it was really a spiritual experience. It was just revealed to me in such a real way during this experience that our only purpose on earth is to worship and glorify the Lord—that our whole purpose is to be filled with his spirit and to worship him. And yet, I had no concept of Jesus Christ as Lord, but this experience revealed to me the reality of God, that there is a spiritual other.   (7)

Eight months after that experience I set out to really find God, and I sought through Eastern religions. I even read the Bible a little bit. A friend of my father's, who is a Christian, witnessed to me. But I couldn't accept Christianity at that point because it seemed very anti-intellectual to me; it seemed foolish to me—which is exactly what the Bible says, "The preaching of the cross is foolishness." So I was seeking through Eastern religions and through the occult. I was very involved with the occult: astrology, Tarot cards, that sort of thing. I was really trying to find a way to God. And about December, after this had been going on for about eight months, I guess it really began to dawn on me that if this was the only way to God, then God was really only for the elite, for the few. . . . Because very few could reach him through yoga and meditation and all this sort of thing; I mean, very few people have the discipline.   (8)

I guess you could say I was a gnostic during those eight months: I was always trying to find the perfect knowledge that would bring me to God.   (9)

About a month before I became a Christian, Ron, my brother, became a Christian. He wrote a letter to the family in which he included a long list of scriptures. Just out of idleness one day, I sat down with his letter and started looking up these scriptures, many of which were end-time prophecies. And I read this passage in 2 Timothy 3:1–7; it's a description of the character of people in the end times. At the end it says something about "for such are they who creep into houses and leave captive silly women laden with sins, burning with . . ." I can't remember all of it, but then it says, "ever learning but never able to come to the knowledge

---

*The passage from 2 Timothy 3:1–7 reads: "But realize this, that in the last days difficult times will come. For men will be lovers of self, lovers of money, boastful, arrogant, revilers, disobedient to parents, ungrateful, unholy, unloving, irreconcilable, malicious gossips, without self-control, brutal, haters of good, treacherous, reckless, conceited, lovers of pleasure rather than lovers of God; holding to a form of godliness, although they have denied its power; and avoid such men as these. For among them are those who enter into households and captivate weak women weighed down with sins, led on by various impulses, always learning and never able to come to the knowledge of the truth." (From the New American Standard Translation, which seems to correspond most closely to the fragments Mary remembered.)

of the truth."* And when I read these verses I saw as if in a mirror an exact picture of myself and the men that I had been associating with, and that I was truly one of those who was ever learning and never able to come to the knowledge of the truth because I wasn't any closer to God then than I was when I started, although I had a lot of vain knowledge. So that really opened me up. This was the time I was really convicted of sin for the first time in my life; that was the first time I ever really realized that I was really a sinner through and through and through.   (10)

Interviewer: How did that come about? Was it just a culmination of all these rock-bottom experiences of being busted and other things?

Mary: Just reading those verses, the spirit really made them alive to me and convicted my heart that I was that person that Paul was talking about. Because even before that, all the terrible things that I did, I never saw myself as a sinner. My whole concept of ethics was, "anything goes as long as you don't hurt somebody else deliberately." I guess that's pretty characteristic of the world today that we live in. Anyway, I was convicted of sin and found that I couldn't enjoy sin the way I had been. A couple of days later, Ron came home unexpectedly. He wasn't going to come home at all that Christmas, but he did come home, and I think that the Lord really sent him for my sake because he really wasn't minded to come home at all. And he started to witness to me about the Lord and I really fought him tooth and nail; I really asked him a lot of questions because I had a lot of intellectual doubts. The Lord just gave him supernatural wisdom, and he was able to answer my questions and really pin me down. Through him the Lord made me aware that I had to make a decision then—that it was either then or not at all, I guess you could say. I really had that sense of, you know, that this is it; that I either decide now or the opportunity will pass. So I just put down my pride and made a decision that I was going to believe in Jesus Christ and follow him. That was the end of that chapter of my life . . . and the beginning of the next chapter.   (11)

Mary's Childhood and Family

At this point in the interview I ask Mary to go back with me and to tell me some things about her family of origin and her experiences and relationships in it. She explains that she is the oldest of four children. Her brother, Ron, who played—and will continue to play a crucially important role in her conversion and postconversion life—is three years younger than she. There are two other younger siblings who seem not to be very important factors in the shaping of her life. Her father and mother met while attending a state university. They married and moved to a village in the rural area where the father had grown up.

Interviewer: What was going on in your parents' lives when you came along?

Mary: I've been trying to figure that out myself. I know I've asked a lot of questions, but I haven't really . . . I can't tell you anything more specific than that they had been married about a year when I was born, a little over a year. And my mother was very homesick; she was from New York, and she was very isolated because my dad had a lot of friends that he could go out hunting and fishing with and stuff. She was pretty lonely and pretty frustrated with the situation. I know she really wanted me, but right from the first there was antagonism between us. I don't understand why, but it was.   (12)

Interviewer: Between you and your mother?

Mary: Yeah, just right from the day I was born, which I don't understand. (13)

Interviewer: Can you help me understand how that antagonism manifested itself? Was there just tension? Your rhythms didn't fit? How was it?

Mary: It's really hard to explain to someone who hasn't witnessed the family in operation. My mother is an extremely giving person. She's always faithfully served her family, far above what most women would do. And yet, I've always felt that her attitude toward me was very negative and critical. Like she didn't accept me the way God made me, you know, she always wanted to make me into her own image. She wanted to change me; it's really hard to explain. It seems like she's always vented her own frustrations on me; her unhappiness, her lack of fulfillment. It always comes out in the form of irritation or anger and disgust toward me and the way I do things. (14)

Interviewer: So nothing you could ever do was very pleasing?

Mary: Right. I could never please her. I guess I just gave up at a really early age and just became a really rebellious brat towards my parents.   (15)

Interviewer: Now is that really the way you see it, or is that the way they see it?

Mary: I could see that I was a very difficult child. I think by nature I'm very strong-willed and very sensitive, and I just . . . my relationship with my mother was just a constant source of grief for both of us. It was very painful. It still is.   (16)

Interviewer: You say your dad was on his home turf and had plenty of friends. What do you think was going on in his life at that period?

Mary: I really don't know. I know that my father has always been the type of person that really enjoys doing a lot of things by himself. He works very, very hard, like his own father had done. When he's not working hard he's engaged in some pastime he enjoys doing by himself, generally speaking. Like playing bridge or golf; back then it would be hunting or fishing. He and my mother have never done a lot together. I really don't feel like I know my father very well. He's been a very faithful father in the sense of a very faithful provider and really caring about his family, and yet, I'm not very close to him. I don't know him really.   (17)

Interviewer: Is he the kind of man who expresses his feelings easily, or is it hard for him?

Mary: No, he doesn't. He can express physical warmth towards us, but he's not able really to open up about what he's feeling. He's very closed in that way.   (18)

Interviewer: What about the family's religious orientation or background, at the time of your birth? Where were your parents in that regard?

Mary: When I was two years old they moved to New York, so I don't really know what they were doing back then. But from the time I can remember when we lived in New York, we always went to a United Church of Christ church. We were required to go to Sunday school. My parents went to church fairly regularly when I was little, but it seemed to taper off as I got older. When I was in about the fifth grade, we moved to a suburb of the city, and they just stopped going to church, and I stopped going to Sunday school. . . . They never had a real . . . I guess churchgoing to them was just the thing to do, you know, the thing that respectable people do. I think they really do have a belief in God of a sort. They believe in a personal God, I think, but they don't have any . . . they're not born again. They don't have any relationship with Jesus Christ that I know of. I wouldn't say that spiritual things are uppermost in their minds by any means. So I don't ever really remember having salvation preached when I was growing up. (19)

Interviewer: I get the picture of a little girl who had a pretty lively internal life even as a very small child. Can you remember events or experiences or visions or fantasies—things that happened by the time you were three or four that are still vivid and sharp?

Mary: I can remember quite a bit about my childhood after the age of two. I remember that I used to spend quite a bit of time by myself because we lived in a neighborhood of mostly elderly people. There were two little boys up on the corner who were very naughty, and I used to play with them. But other than that I really didn't have too many children to play with. So I used to sit in my room and play records and sing and dance and look at books. I was always an avid reader from the time I could read. I used to read my coloring books. I used to play outside a lot. I was very imaginative; I was very involved in whatever I did. I never lacked for things to do. (20)

Interviewer: Can you remember when you first encountered or thought about death or God, or things that were frightening, or things that were awesomely beautiful in this period? Anything of that sort?

Mary: Hmmm. Death is not something I can relate to too well, because no one in my family has ever died, other than my grandparents and a cousin. So I've never encountered it at close hand. I remember hearing the . . . minister preach a sermon about death, about how there was no place you could hide from it. I remember that pretty vividly. I remember that I was suicidal from a very early age, and it was always a reaction to my relationship with my mother.   (21)

Interviewer: Do you mean you felt like, "I'm going to kill myself and show her"? Or, "I'd like to kill myself and get out of this"?

Mary: Both. . . . I remember I used to get sent to my room a lot and then I'd think about it when I was brooding in my room.   (22)

Interviewer: What was kindergarten like for you?

Mary: On the whole it was good. I was always really sharp in school, and I got along well with the other kids. But I didn't get along too well with the teacher. I remember one time when she was reading a story about the Easter bunny. And there was this phrase in it about he came hippity-hoppity down the trail. And I remember laughing out loud and getting put out in the hall for it.   (23)

Interviewer: Were you demythologizing Easter or something?

Mary: I was just laughing about it. It was funny the way she did it. She didn't think that was funny. . . . I remember she reminded me of Captain Hook in Mary Martin's *Peter Pan*, Cyril Richard, or whoever. . . . I remember getting punished a couple of times for things like that, for being unruly, although I wasn't extremely so. I had various other run-ins with teachers: I was very strong-willed.   (24)

Interviewer: How do you think you felt about yourself at that time. Was there a way in which you labeled yourself a "bad girl" or "trouble-maker," or did you feel good about yourself?

Mary: I don't think I've ever felt good about myself. Let's see, well, it's gotten better. I still have a real problem with that. I don't think I felt especially good about myself then because the reflection I always got about myself from my mother was always negative. She doesn't realize that to this day, and she will never admit it, and it's not my place constantly to hammer away at it to her. But that's the way it was. And also, I had a . . . seems like I grew up a lot faster than the other kids. I was very mature physically at a very early age. I had a real acne problem in the third grade. I remember that, and that really hurt. I remember I had a really close friend in fifth and sixth grade, and she and I were just inseparable. She became the most popular girl in school and then the most popular girl in junior high, and I sort of fell by the wayside. And that really hurt a lot. But all these things are just sort of incidental to my relationship with my mom. That's really the main thing, I think . . . because I don't think that things that happen in school can really override a good situation at home. (25)

Interviewer: In your junior-high and high-school years, you obviously moved ahead with intellectual vigor, because you left high school a year early and went to college. What was going on then? Did you find some things that you did well, and did you . . .

Mary: What happened was we moved to Birmingham when I was in the middle of my ninth-grade year, and I was just starting to make friends in high school, you know—to find a group of people with whom I was compatible and had similar interests.

Interviewer: This was while you were still in New York?

Mary: Right, and then we moved to Birmingham in the middle of my ninth grade, and it was really a cultural shock because it was just so completely different from living in suburban New York. I just couldn't seem to find any friends who had similar interests to mine, became really withdrawn, and my mother really got onto me about that because she wanted me to be outgoing and have a lively social life and everything, for my own sake. I just couldn't be the way she wanted me to be. I got very withdrawn, and I read. I'd just close myself in my room and read or listen to classical music. Also I had several changes of high school. I started in a public high school. I was so unhappy there that they sent me to a private school for a year. Then I was very unhappy there because all the girls were from really wealthy families and they lived over on that side of town. I just couldn't seem to break into the social life over there either. Then I went to another public high school for a year, and I was starting to adjust pretty well there and felt at home. And then the opportunity of going to college a year early was presented to me and that sounded like a good idea, so off I went. . . . I was maybe intellectually ready, but not socially or emotionally ready for that change at all. It turned out to be a really devastating experience too. (26)

Mary explained the circumstances that opened up the opportunity for early college admission. A brother-in-law of one of her parents was an administrator of the private, north-midwestern college at which she spent a year. She had hoped and planned to go to another college—of somewhat higher caliber but in the same region.

Mary: I'd always dreamed of going to college, I mean I had been groomed for college ever since I could remember. That's what my parents always had in mind for me, was to go to college. So it sounded like a good idea at the time.

The Years from Twenty-Two to Twenty-Seven

Interviewer: Now, in terms of our chapters, we've gotten childhood and we've gotten some view of elementary school, high school, and we've gotten a kind of sense of what was going on between seventeen and twenty-two —in the years of the search. Now let's talk about the years from twenty-two to twenty-seven. What has your present movement been?

Mary: Okay. I became a Christian just after my twenty-second birthday, and I guess right from the moment I became a Christian, the only thing I wanted from the Lord, other than to know him and to do his will, was a husband. I became very obsessed with that idea. I guess that was really the one thing in life I really wanted, was to be happily married. So I really began to seek the Lord for that. But at the same time I really wanted his will in my life. You know? So there was a conflict because I wanted my will, but I wanted his will too. And also right after I got saved I got involved with the Followers of God. Ron had been involved with them briefly and had decided that that wasn't for him. But I was really turned on by their lifestyle, you know, I mean after having been in total rebellion for twenty-two years, I couldn't see the rebellion in what they were doing. It appeared to be a very good idea to live in colonies, to live communally, to live totally for the Lord; just being with other Christians twenty-four hours a day, and studying the word and witnessing and all that kind of stuff constantly. So I joined the Followers of God, and I was involved in that for three months. It was a very valuable time in the sense that all that I did was learn scripture a good part of the time the Lord also showed me the deception in that, so I got out of it.   (27)

Interviewer: What is the deception in that?

Mary: There's quite a bit of deception in it, and it has become more and more so. The Lord showed me at that time that something that starts out as a small deviation from the truth, if it continues, will get further and further away from the mainline of truth. I could see that they were deviating from the truth already because they were exalting this man—the founder of the Followers of God—as God's endtime prophet. They were almost making him equal with Jesus Christ. Everything he said contained divine revelation; and he wrote these letters to us, and we would have them read to us every night. They were putting those on a level with scripture. There were other things too, like they had a very arrogant attitude toward the body of Christ. You know, they felt "We're the chosen ones. We're the only ones who are right. Everyone else is wrong."   (28)

   The marvelous thing about it is that even though I was right in the thick of it, living amongst them and constantly being brainwashed with their way of thinking, the Lord was able to show me his truth just by his spirit out of his word. That was really a testimony to me that if we really want the truth, God is always going to see to it that we get it, even in the midst of deception.   (29)

Anyway, I got out of the Followers of God, and then I moved to Birmingham and lived with a Christian girlfriend for a while. I still wasn't completely out of the Followers of God. It took me about three months after actually leaving to get over the withdrawal pains because I felt such fear and condemnation that I was out of God's will by even leaving that I didn't know where to go from there.   (30)

Somehow the Lord arranged for me to meet these people who had a ministry over on Logan Road. This couple had trekked out from the West Coast, picking up people as they came along, and started this house. They found me and invited me to come live there, and I felt the Lord was leading me to do that, so I did move in there. A short time after I moved in there . . . well, this is something that I haven't quite gotten over yet. A short time after I moved in there, I felt that God showed me that I was going to marry a certain brother at that house. It was a very sudden thing. I hadn't even been thinking about it, and all of a sudden I was just absolutely sure that he was the one for me. I didn't say anything to him about it, but he sensed that something was going on and confronted me, so I made known my feelings for him. That resulted in a big uproar because he wasn't really interested in marriage, and he wasn't interested in me. And yet he was interested in me, you know, he was attracted to me, but not attracted enough to be interested in marriage. So that resulted in my having to leave the ministry because I was so emotionally involved that I just could not lay aside my feelings for him and just accept that he wasn't interested and so on. I really believe that it was of God, that God had showed me that he was the one. I'm still struggling with that after five years, because he's still not married, and he's still the only man I've ever loved.   (31)

So I left the ministry, and they advised me not to come back because they felt it would be best for me and best for him if I didn't. In other ways it was a very positive experience because I really had close relationships with the brothers and sisters there, and I really loved the people there.   (32)

Interviewer: And it was less of a deviation and distortion than you'd found with the Followers of God?

Mary: Right. I really felt that they were right on with the Lord, you know —the people who were running the ministry. All of the people who lived there really loved Jesus and wanted to serve him.   (33)

Anyway, that was a positive experience, except for that. That really hurt very deeply because I felt really rejected that they wouldn't let me come back on account of this guy. They were looking at me as being really in sin because of my attitude about him; and yet I didn't feel it was sinful because I really loved him.   (34)

Meanwhile, I went down to Daytona. Ron was down there, and he had gotten really involved with one of these little house churches. Since I was constantly looking to Ron for spiritual direction, I got involved with it too. I didn't see any alternatives to it at the time.   (35)

This was another really devastating experience because at the time they were really into this teaching about submission to eldership, submission of women, you know, everything was submission, submission, submission. And they were also really getting into the teaching about discipleship and that every person who really wanted to go on with the Lord should be discipled by another, older Christian. I can't explain everything that was going on, but because of my emotional make-up and the problems that I was having, I was interpreted as being really rebellious and unsubmissive to authority, which I was in part. But a lot of my behavior was a manifestation of the hurt that I felt about that guy in Birmingham and the rejection that I felt—the kind of helplessness I felt about my life and all. I couldn't see any fulfillment, anything I really wanted in life. That was an experience that I can't really talk about without getting emotional, I guess. The upshot of it was that I got kicked out of the church for being—for saying some angry words to this guy who was in charge of this house church. There was only one leader and he had absolute, total, unquestioned authority over everyone in the group. And if you didn't do exactly what he said, you were in rebellion, period. So I locked horns with him, and I got kicked out of the church. He said I couldn't come back unless I did all these things. (36)

Well, first of all, I had to really humble myself and ask his forgiveness. And the first time he wouldn't accept it because it wasn't in a spirit of real humility. So when I finally got to the point that I asked his forgiveness in real humility, he said, "I'm going to give you a thirty-day trial period. During that period you have to pull your hair back (I had real long, bushy hair at the time), you have to smile and talk to people at the meetings." I guess he was really trying to help me in a way, but it just had the effect of putting an unbearable yoke of the law on me, you know. The more I tried to do it, the more I failed. I was utterly incapable of doing what he wanted me to do.   (37)

The first time I went to a meeting after that, I cried, and it was reported back to him, so he set up a new thirty-day period in which I'd have to be out of the church. Being a young Christian and having had so much teaching about spiritual authority, I felt that if he rejected me, God rejected me. So I was really going through this terrible anguish at the time, and

when he decided that I had to have another thirty-day period, I just really
freaked out.   (38)

Mary explains at this point that she was distraught enough that for
a time hospitalization was being considered for her. To her, the rejection
by this house church group, coming after the experience of being sent
away from the Birmingham group, seemed too much to take.

Mary: I was just so upset because I felt like God was rejecting me if he [the
house church leader] rejected me. I just couldn't bear the rejection, you
know?"

She explained that her being forced to leave that group resulted in a
temporary, but painful breach with her brother, Ron, who remained a
member of the church. We resume her narrative with her feelings about
this:

Mary: That really hurt because Ron said some pretty harsh things to me at
the time. But a short time later Ron's eyes were opened to what was going
on, too, and he became very disenchanted with this group. He asked to be
released, which was a better way to do it, and that's something that I've
really learned since then: That if you're in the wrong thing, it's better to
appeal to your authority than to rebel and get all excited. So, anyway Ron
got out of it, too. Meanwhile, I kept trying to do what they wanted me to
do to get back in their good graces, and I couldn't do it. In the meantime
the Lord was really ministering to me alone. He was really showing me his
love and speaking to me out of his word, just really ministering to me in
a very private, personal way, making himself known to me. So that showed
me that they weren't my avenue to God, my means of grace, this elder. God
could have a relationship with me even apart from them, and he still loved
me and accepted me in Christ, no matter what they did. After all these
futile attempts to get back in their good graces, I prayed, "Lord, will you
please show me if this group is really for me or not?" So I went to a meeting
that night and I just felt such a heaviness over the whole meeting. It seemed
that everything they were talking about had to do with the law rather than
with grace. I decided right then and there that "This is it; I'm not coming
back."   (39)

That was in the middle of December, and then a couple of weeks later
(I was really just trusting in the Lord for fellowship) on New Year's Eve
Ron got invited to a party by a Christian friend, and he asked me if I
wanted to go. That turned out to be the means the Lord used to bring us
into contact with a new group of Christians. It was really for me because
Ron went to a northern Bible institute shortly after that. This turned out

to be a group of young people; there weren't any older people in the group, and they met in an apartment in the north part of Daytona. They were the means that the Lord used to bring me out of a lot of bondage, a lot of legalism. They really taught me a lot about the grace of God and the love of God. I was involved with them off and on from about January to about April, 1974. And during that time I also went up and stayed with Ron at the Bible institute for a month.   (40)

That was really a fantastic month that I spent up there. I met some really beautiful, older Christians who shared the Lord with me in a very significant way. That was a real help for me. The Lord used that, too, as a means because after I got back to Daytona one of the teachers at the institute had been out to Wisconsin just the weekend before and had been in contact with a ministry there that he thought would be really good for me. He called me in Daytona and told me about it. At this point I was really praying that the Lord would lead me to shepherds after his own heart, because I was so disgusted with this business that was going on in Daytona that I had experienced several months before.   (41)

Interviewer: Were you working during this time?

Mary: Yes, I was working doing temporary stints for a fast food corporation as a temporary office person, which gave me a lot of freedom to work or not work. I really couldn't get a good job because I didn't have any skills, not having stayed in school.   (42)

Interviewer: So a man from the Bible institute called and suggested this Wisconsin ministry?

Mary: Yes. His name was Brother Kelvin. He was one of the ones that really ministered to me while I was up there . . . So I started really praying for the Lord to show me what he really wanted me to do. All this time my heart was in Birmingham because that guy was there, and I was so sure that God had told me that I was going to marry him, and the waiting was really painful. Yet God seemed to be opening a different door in Wisconsin. My parents, well, my mother, was really urging me to go. During this time when I was really praying for the will of God, three different people, who had no relationship with one another, gave me a word about stepping out like Abraham. You know, it says in Hebrews 11 that he went to a place where he didn't know anybody, and he left everything familiar behind. That's paraphrasing; I can't remember the exact words.*   (43)

---

*Hebrews 11:8-10: By faith Abraham, when he was called, obeyed by going out to a place which he was to receive for an inheritance; and he went out, not knowing where he was going. By faith he lived as an alien in the land of promise, as in a foreign land, dwelling in tents with Isaac and Jacob, fellow-heirs of the same promise; for he was looking for the city which has foundations, whose architect and builder is God. (New American Standard Version)

So I really believed that that was the word of the Lord to me, to do as Abraham had done and just step out on faith, believing that God was leading me to a place. So I did, and it was rather frightening since I didn't know a soul in Wisconsin. I remember sitting on the plane and being absolutely astonished to see the number of my flight was 777, three 7's. It seemed a very auspicious sign.   (44)

The place where I went in Wisconsin was a ministry called Bethel House. There's a whole network of Bethel Houses around the country, but this is a completely independent ministry. It's not a drug rehabilitation house or anything like that. It was completely an independent ministry and it's under the leadership of a very special woman. It's just a place where young people can go and live with other Christians and just learn to live as Christians. It's constant Bible study and meetings every night. It's really a beautiful ministry. I went there, and I think that the first three weeks that I spent at Bethel were probably one of the high points of my life as a Christian. I just had such a vision of the Kingdom of God on earth those first few weeks I was living there, just being among my brothers and sisters and seeing the body of Christ being built up there, and the spirit of the Lord ministering through them. It was so real to me that I was part of the Kingdom of God, and that Kingdom was there.   (45)

Interviewer: It sounds like you could taste it, feel it . . .

Mary: Yeah, I could really taste the goodness of the Lord. Just a short time after I moved into Bethel my future husband came back there. He had been one of the original members of the house, and then he had back-slidden, fallen away from the Lord, and then he came back. I guess because he and I had had such a history of rejection, and both of us felt that we had such a need for a relationship. I guess that's what really drew us together, just our common need. So we started doing a lot of things together, and at first I was kind of stand-offish because I could see that his heart was still half in the world, that it wasn't completely committed to the Lord. I was somewhat wary of him. But the more time I spent with him, the more I got involved. So that really drew me away from being involved in the ministry there, and being involved with my brothers and sisters, and I became more and more involved just with him. Which was kind of tragic, I can see now, because the ministry there could have been such a valuable experience. We got married the following October, having only known each other for four months.   (46)

Interviewer: Did you marry in the community?

Mary: Yes, we did. We got married in the church to which this house was submitted. Everybody supported us, but I knew that they didn't really approve.   (47)

Interviewer: They questioned?

Mary: Yes. I can see now that my marrying him, that I convinced myself that my marrying him was of God, and I can see now where I really . . . I can see a lot of holes in my thinking now, looking back on it. It was really a mess, the whole thing. I mean, our relationship was all wrong right from the beginning.   (48)

Interviewer: Let's not look at it from hindsight for a moment. I would imagine that given the kind of promise that seemed to be in the Wisconsin trip, and given the power of what you found there for the first three or four weeks, that it would have been very hard for you not to have felt that his coming and the need you realized was there was part of the plan for this period. And that perhaps your relationship with him was one in which he could give the rest of his life to Christ.

Mary: Yeah.   (49)

Interviewer: I don't imagine that you should be too hard on yourself for what you were feeling or being drawn toward in that . . .

Mary: I do appreciate your looking at it that way because that does show a great deal of insight on your part, because that's the way it was in fact. One of the elders of the church to which Bethel was submitted was really pushing the relationship. In fact, even before I started to get involved with Harry, he gave me a prophetic word that I was going to meet my future husband within the next few weeks. Which was a pretty dangerous thing for him to do. He was really encouraging it because he had a real concern for Harry, and he felt that I could really be a stabilizing influence in his life. I guess I really believed that I could help Harry, and I got other prophetic words that seemed to buttress this feeling at the time. As you said, I could see this was the answer to my need even though he wasn't the one I really loved or really wanted, you know? I felt that "Maybe this is the one the Lord really wants me to have." Also, at this time, one of the brothers from Birmingham came up to visit me, and he told me just to forget about the guy in Birmingham, in essence. So that was like the death blow to my hope about him. Although it wasn't really, because it's never been completely done away with.   (50)

I married Harry in October, and right from the beginning our marriage was just so troubled. I mean we entered into sexual relations before we were married which was a tragedy, you know, that was really wrong. I didn't want that to happen, but once it did happen, we should have repented, but we didn't. We rushed into the marriage to relieve the guilt. We weren't planning to get married in October, but we did. Right after we got married Harry started using marijuana again and lusting after other women. He decided he was no longer interested in being a Christian, which really took me by surprise, because I knew that his heart wasn't totally given to the Lord, but I didn't expect that at all. I had no intimation at all that that would happen. I guess I was very naive, and I really wasn't a very good judge of character at the time. Right after we got married he started doing all that, and I got pregnant as soon as we got married. So I was sick all the time. We were living in a tiny basement apartment, very dark and damp. We were really isolated, we didn't have much fellowship. The people from the ministry that we had been involved with just didn't seem to really reach out to us. They couldn't really relate to the situation. I guess they felt "You made your bed, you can lie in it." They still loved us, but they didn't really reach out to us. I didn't really reach out either; I became very withdrawn in that situation. I was desperately unhappy. I felt that I had made a really serious mistake, but that I had to live with it; I had to make the best of it. The January following our marriage, the Lord brought it about that . . . well, Harry knew this older couple who were involved with another fantastic ministry in Green Bay called Pilgrim's Way. It's a great big charismatic church, started out as a Lutheran house church and it's grown to about a thousand people, I guess. But it's a very strong ministry where there's a great deal of body ministry.   (51)

Interviewer: When you say body ministry, do you mean that the body itself is in ministry?

Mary: Everybody is involved in ministry, and ministering to one another especially, and to outsiders as well. So Harry knew this older couple who went to this church, and they invited us over for dinner one night. And it just turned out that that night they were having a shepherding meeting in their house. The whole church was divided into shepherding groups, you know, small groups that meet in people's homes once a week. So they were having this shepherding meeting in their house, and I'm sure that Judy had that in mind when she invited us over for dinner. And it just sort of turned out that Harry was going out to look for his own apartment that night. He was already thinking in terms of separation, so he went out to look for his own place right after dinner, and I elected to stay and go to the shepherding meeting. And the Lord just met me in a marvelous way through those people; the love that they showed me was so real. It's something that God has done again and again in my life, is really meet me when I was at the end of my rope, you know, when I was really up against the wall, and that's what he did.   (52)

These people just really took me under their wing, took a real interest in my life, so I started going to shepherding meetings every week and going to this church, Pilgrim's Way, because that's where I felt the Lord wanted me because that's where my needs were being met.   (53)

Mary explained that during this time the patterns of drug use and unfaithfulness by her husband increased. She felt supported by the shepherding group at Pilgrim's Way, and tried to follow their advice that she should not try to play God in Harry's life, but give him up "to the Lord and repent of trying to control the situation." Yet, their marriage grew more and more intolerable. She recognized that, to Harry, she was a reminder of his failings. They had bitter arguments and he physically abused her on a number of occasions. When he finally left her again she told him he could not come back unless he repented and returned to Christ. Harry went to the West Coast; she moved in with a family in the shepherding group. Mary thought she would never see him again. She was six months pregnant when she went to live with the family. She stayed with them until after the birth of her child, a daughter. Her stay there did not seem to be a very pleasant time. While her host family were away on vacation her husband, Harry, returned. We pick up her narrative as she tells about accepting him back:

Mary: Harry came back, and when I saw that he had really made a new commitment to the Lord, I decided to take him back, but I didn't consult anyone about it. So when the people I was living with came back from their vacation, they were aghast at what I'd done, and the whole church was aghast, and I was really . . . I kind of got in trouble with the leadership of the church for doing . . . for having done that without asking their advice. So we did go and counsel with them, and they gave us their blessing, just really ministered to us and wished us well. And then we got our own apartment . . .   (54)

I won't go into everything that happened in our marriage, but it was just one constant series of moves, job changes—Harry could not stick to one job for very long. He had a lot of real . . . a lot of other blows, like we rented a house, and then we found out that the house had been foreclosed on. The guy had skipped the state with all our money. Harry went into business for himself and failed. It was just awful. We were care-taking some apartments, and Harry and I had a disagreement, and he started getting back into drugs. He sent me to Daytona so he could get rid of me so he could do what he wanted to do. He got involved with a girl who lived in the next apartment, you know, stuff like this that was just a constant mess.   (55)

And yet the Lord was really so good to me, because all this time I really had the support of this church, and I was very close to those people. The Lord never once forsook me; he was really faithful to me. After Harry sent me to Daytona I came back a couple of weeks later because I just couldn't stand to sit down there and wonder what he was doing, and I was so hurt that he didn't call me or anything, that he didn't seem to care about our marriage. So I came back of my own accord and tried to patch things up.

I'd read *The Total Woman*, and I decided I was going to put that into practice, and I was going to do everything I could to have the right attitudes as a wife and everything. But that didn't last too long, and it wasn't long until he moved out again because we just couldn't get along.   (56)

With Harry gone, this time Mary—with the support of the shepherding group of which she was a part—took an apartment near a junior college and enrolled. Members of her church provided child care while she attended classes. Her life seems to have taken on structure and purpose. Harry began to return to see their daughter. Mary was advised by the couple from the church closest to her not to admit him. They told her that they had prayed about this matter and, as she put it, "they felt that the Lord had showed them that I should just give them complete authority over the situation and tell Harry that he couldn't visit me at all without their say so." Mary explains why she resisted that advice:

Mary: I wasn't willing to do that. For one thing, I really wanted my family back together again. Another thing, having been through that experience in Daytona, I was really afraid of that kind of authority over my life, that kind of absolute authority. Also, I felt that the scriptures enjoined me to do anything I could to make my marriage work, that I had to forgive him and just really try to help him if I could and try to be faithful to my marriage. So I did take him back, and that—I can see now that I was wrong —but I allowed that to result in a breach in my relationship with the church and with those people. I stopped going to that church, and Harry wanted to go to another church. So we went to another charismatic church called Agape, which is also a very strong ministry in Green Bay. It just so happened that the man who had really pushed our relationship was now a teacher at Agape, so he was there. And another one of the elders from that original church that we had been involved with was now an elder there. We went there for about five months, and I thought things were really going to work out. I was really determined that my marriage was going to work out, and I was not going to let go, I was going to make it work, no matter what.   (57)

From February to July of that year (1977) it worked—or at least it partly worked. Gradually, however, Harry became disaffected with the church. Soon they no longer read the Bible together. Harry seemed always to be griping about his job; Mary suspected that he was getting back into drugs and, as she put it, "lusting after other women." On a hot July evening, shortly after their daughter's second birthday, things blew up.

Mary: No warning at all. We had a disagreement about something, and Harry took that as an occasion to go out and get stoned. He could see how disappointed I was, how upset I was about what he was doing, and he reacted to that tension in me by . . . one night he stood out in front of the apartment building, you know everybody had their windows open, and he just cursed me at the top of his voice and called me names that you'd only read in pornographic literature. He just couldn't stand the tension in the situation, and I couldn't stand it either. That moment when he stood outside and cursed me at the top of his voice was the moment when I knew the Lord was saying, "This is it. That's enough." (58)

Mary spent the next few days with a friend. During that interval Harry left. Mary saw clearly that the marriage was over. Moving toward divorce, however, involved a difficult decision for her. In her words, "I was really seeking the Lord about whether to get a divorce." In her struggle her brother proved to be a decisive help again:

Mary: The Lord spoke to me in a very powerful way through Ron and showed me that . . . he gave me that verse "Neither do I condemn thee, go and sin no more."* And he showed me that I didn't have to get a divorce on the basis of loopholes in the scripture because there is no loophole for divorce. Marriage is absolute; it's supposed to be a lifelong commitment, there's no getting around that. But he showed me that he himself was absolving me of that commitment and forgiving me and giving me a second chance. [It is not clear in the tape whether the "he" here refers to Mary's brother or to God. In any case, it is clear that Ron played a very effective priestly role in this difficult situation.] So I went ahead with the divorce proceedings and I felt a real peace about it. (59)

During the month that the divorce became final Mary gave birth to the couple's second child, another daughter. In anticipation of the baby's birth Mary's parents, who had moved into a large home in a Georgia city, gave her a strong and clear invitation to bring her two children and come to live with them. Her shepherding group in Green Bay at first urged her not to return to her family. "They didn't think that I should move home with a non-Christian family." Mary was proud of the fact that she neither immediately complied with the shepherding group's advice, nor did she rebelliously act against it. "For once in my life I just trusted in the Lord to change their minds if they were wrong, instead of arguing and rebelling. . . . So I just waited, and the Lord did change

---

*John 8:11. Jesus' words of forgiveness to the woman caught in the act of adultery.

their minds in a very powerful way, and they were all of one accord that
I should go home." Her mother came up and stayed with her at the birth
of her daughter. When she was able to travel her mother helped her load
everything into a U-Haul trailer and they moved her to Georgia.

> *Mary:*   It was very hard for me to leave [Green Bay]. I loved the people there,
> I loved the brothers and sisters. I felt I really had a place there. . . . In spite
> of the hardship that I went through, I was very happy there. But I knew
> what the Lord was saying, and I had to do that. . . . That was the end of
> that chapter in my life, when I moved to Georgia, got the divorce and
> moved."

Mary's Present and Future

My interview with Mary took place about four months after she had
reestablished her home with her parents. The parents' welcome of her
had been genuine; their affirmations of love for her and for her children
had been clear. Still, there were tensions as she sought for a community
of support and for a sense of direction. She spoke about her present in
these terms:

> *Mary:*   I feel now again that I'm in a new place, and that the Lord wants
> to do something new in my life, but I'm not sure exactly what. Another
> thing is that I've never completely lost that hope about that guy in Birming-
> ham; and now here I am living 150 miles away. Marvel of marvels, I was
> praying for a church, and the Lord led me to a group that is associated with
> a group in Birmingham where he is. The pastor of my church is good
> friends with his pastor, you know, it's just really strange. And yet I feel that
> it could all be a big deception, too. It really bothers me because I want it
> settled, I want to just forget about it if it's not of God, and put it out of
> my life completely. I guess I'm really seeking the Lord, you know, I feel
> that if I can't have a happy marriage, if I can't have a husband, that I need
> instead to fill up my life with God's work. I really need a purpose that I
> can feel is worthy of committing myself to, and I don't feel that computer
> programming is it. I feel that my children are really valuable: that's an
> important ministry, and I do have to take care of my children. I'm looking
> beyond that and thinking that I might like to get into Christian education,
> you know, teaching at a Christian school or something like that. Thinking
> about going back to college and completing my B.A. And I feel that I'm
> in a new place with the Lord because I feel that he is really calling me to
> trust Him absolutely and really enter into more of a relationship with him
> than I've ever had with him before. So that's where I'm at now.   (60)
> *Interviewer:*   How do you listen to the movement of the spirit in your life

now? I gather that it's been a kind of progressive thing, that it began in some ways and then it's evolved. How are you doing it now?   (61)

Mary: Well, for one thing, I do not look for visions and prophecies like I used to. I feel like God does speak to me on occasion through a living word. He'll quicken a certain scripture to me that is just for me in that particular time. But I think that on the whole, God just leads me by giving me a sense in my heart of what I ought to do, giving me a piece of what he would like me to do. I don't feel like I'm walking in the spirit like I should, not anywhere near . . .   (62)

For reasons I will say more about subsequently in the analysis of Mary's interview, at this point in our conversation I departed from the neutral role of researcher and made some responses to what she was saying. I suggested that while her story was full of pain and difficulty, I thought one also could see some signs of strength in what she had told. I suggested that it sounded to me as though she might be ready to undertake a new quality of direct responsibility for her own life now— one in which she recognized her co-responsibility with God for making her life choices and decisions. She responded by affirming that everything she had done had failed. She then addressed the issue of self-worth:

Mary: I have such a hard time feeling that I'm worth anything when no man wants me. I don't have a ministry, a vocation that I'm really, you know, that I feel good about.   (63)

Interviewer: What if the word of the Lord is "I'm holding those things back until you no longer *have* to marry for that sense of worth, but marry *out of* that sense of worth . . . or minister *out of* that sense of worth, instead of ministering to find it?"

Mary: Hmmm. That's a good point, a very good point. And I feel that it's right in line with what God has shown me. In fact, I went to counsel with my pastor a few months ago, and I was telling him about the conflict I have with my mother, which is ongoing, even in spite of all the Lord's done to heal the relationship. I had been to the Bill Gothard seminar* and he emphasizes very strongly asking forgiveness of those you've offended, especially parents, and I was wondering if I should make a big production of going and asking my parents' forgiveness. I feel a need for it sometime down the line. And [my pastor] said that he didn't think I should do that right now, that he thought instead I needed to work on self-acceptance. Because the way that I react to my parents, which offends them, is a result

---

*In this single instance the name given is not fictional.

of my lack of self-worth. So asking their forgiveness really wouldn't accomplish too much right now, I guess. So what you're saying is really the same thing that he said to me. A lot of people have said that to me, but I don't exactly know how to go about gaining a sense of self-worth. . . .   (64)

The Structuring of Meaning in Mary's Faith

Choosing Mary's interview as the material with which to introduce the analytic categories of the faith development theory involves taking a calculated risk. Mary's interview is atypical in many ways. First, it is an incomplete interview. Comparison with the schedule of questions in the interview guide in the Appendix A will show that my formal questions to her were largely limited to part one of the guide. In what was supposed to have been a brief overview of "chapters" of her life Mary began to share her past and present experiences in such depth that I chose to let her go ahead at greater length, trusting that most of what I needed to begin to understand the flow of her way of seeing and being would emerge. Second, Mary's interview is atypical because of the pain and the patterns of repetition we find in it. Mary came of age in very troubled and troubling times. For reasons we will go into in greater detail as we proceed, her experiences in childhood and adolescence—and of course in infancy—gave rise to patterns of need, expectation and ways of relating that give her struggle with faith some distinctive features. Third, Mary's interview is different from most of our others because it was conducted for purposes of possible counseling rather than primarily for research. A member of Mary's family, knowing of the research I had been pursuing, asked if I would spend some time talking with Mary. Since she didn't know me and had good reason to question the usefulness of talking to a stranger, the most straightforward way to begin our conversation seemed to be to share with her the fact that we had interviewed a number of people and that the interview procedure seemed to provide a comfortable way of getting acquainted. As indicated in the preface to the interview Mary consented to the procedure and it took off from there.

If Mary's interview deviates from the rest of our sample in these ways, why have I chosen it as an example with which to share with you our methods of interpretation and analysis? One reason is I have found it a troublingly compelling interview. My impressions of Mary were and are that she is a highly intelligent person. In the course of the interview

I found her to be courageous and ready to look fairly at her experiences and relationships and to deal compassionately with those to whom she has been and is related primally. Yet her life exhibited repetitive patterns that were destructive to her and brought heartache to those who love and care about her. Further, hers is a story of religious conversion. It poses important questions of what changes and what does not in the kind of conversion experience she recounted. Related to this is the fact that Mary's story leads us into the world of cult religions. In this case the cultic communities are a variety of neo-Christian groups. I believe, however, that Mary's experiences with these groups is representative of what many persons encounter in those of other religious traditions as well. Moreover, the turbulent experiences of Mary's late adolescence and young adulthood are inexplicable apart from the background of political and social struggle over civil rights, Vietnam and the counter-cultural revolution. Mary is not atypical among the many other young men and women who came of age in that era. In reflecting on Mary's story we are drawn into the interplay of psychosocial factors in human development, with ways of giving shape and meaning to experience that are studied by structural-developmental theories. This means that her life story is theoretically very, very rich. For all these reasons I decided that to work with Mary's story would be productive for us all.

It makes most sense for us to begin with a series of questions which will pave the way for an analysis of the structural features of Mary's faith.* As we do so, let me ask you to keep in mind the issue of time perspective. In the interview we are told a lot about various phases of Mary's past. At points, she is telling us how she thought and felt at various of those moments. We must keep in mind, however, that the thoughts and feelings she attributes to herself at those times in the past represent her construction or remembering of them at the time of the interview and do not necessarily describe the events as they were seen or stated when they occurred. In our interpretation and analysis we need to remain critically aware that the accounts of the past that we have been given represent the past *as it was presently being constructed.* Therefore, as we examine her remembrances we want to look both at

---

*In conducting this structural analysis I will focus first on the years from twenty-two to twenty-seven, the postconversion years. Mary's faith, at the time of the interview showed signs of transition. In considering what has happened to her in the three years since the interview, which we will do later, it makes most sense to try to identify the dominant stage of the period leading up to the present turning.

what was being remembered—its substance and significance—but also at *how* it was being remembered—what operations of thought and valuing underlay the reconstructive memory.

In the course of our research into structural aspects of faith development we have identified seven categories in relation to which the dominant features of the stage of a person's faith may be identified. I want to introduce these here, expanding on them by suggesting the kinds of questions you might ask yourself in order to understand them. Then I will ask you to reflect with me on Mary's interview to see how she carried out those operations. The first category we should consider is what we call the *Locus of Authority*. In relation to Mary's interview, ask yourself, to whom or to what did she look for decisive guidance as regards her decisions about actions or beliefs? To whom or what did she look for approval and sanction of her beliefs and values? What criteria—explicit or implicit—operated in her choice of which authorities to trust and depend upon? What constituted worthy authority for her, and where was it located? We may also ask, what indications of the locus of authority do we get in her accounts of earlier phases of her life? How has the locus of authority changed for her?

Now think back over Mary's interview. How shall we characterize the locus of authority as it appeared in her account? (I will use the numbers that appear at the end of each paragraph of Mary's narrative as a way of referring to specific passages in her statement.) Mary's first references to authority in her near adult life come in relation to the failure of the values and practices she pursued in what she called her "lost period"— the years from age seventeen to twenty-two (1, 3, 7, 8). These values seem to have been conventionally held, part of the shared ethos of the anti-establishment counterculture of the late sixties and early seventies. With their failure in her life, Mary seems to have held, for a time, to a kind of stubborn intellectuality (9, 11). Though we have insufficient data to be sure of this, I suspect that this constituted in fact a kind of counter-dependent, anti-establishment posture, not truly characterized by very much critical, reflective depth or any systematic ideological perspective. Her brother Ron says that during her high-school years in Birmingham Mary did feel a strong identification with blacks in the human rights struggle. She read the writings of Martin Luther King, Jr., and other leaders and followed the movement in the news.

Her first positive characterization of authority in the beginnings of her conversion experience refers to scripture—to 2 Timothy 3:1–7 (10).

In the description this pastoral letter gives of the corruption that will be found among sinful people in "the last days" Mary found a resonant reflection of herself and of the men she had been associating with (10). In a way that marks her use of scripture as authority at later points in the interview, Mary was drawn to subjectively meaningful passages which she appropriated without attention to the context of the passage, to its meanings in the larger framework of New Testament thought or in relation to any theology of Christian faith. Also, the power of the scripture was linked—as will often be the case in other references—to her relationship with her brother, Ron. I believe that in every reference except one that Mary makes to a significant scripture as authoritative for her, we see that the passage was pointed out to her by Ron.

In paragraph 11 it is Ron, who comes home for Christmas unexpectedly, and who is given "supernatural wisdom" by the Lord which enabled him to answer her questions and "really pin her down." By virtue of the crucial role he played in bringing her to Christ and by virtue of the fidelity of his love and care for her Ron was established as the most consistent guide in seeking the divine will that she had during most of the time covered by the interview. She placed some trust and reliance in the authority of the various "elders" and "shepherding groups" of which she was a part in the various phases of her Christian odyssey. But these could be defied or countermanded if her sense of God's will and Ron's support were clear. One of the most painfully dislocating times for her came when she was expelled on the basis of her "rebelliousness" from the house church in Daytona and Ron continued to be part of the group (38, 39). While Ron exerted the most important and lasting influence on her ways of relying on scripture and of interpreting God's will for her, the voices of others provided crucial guidance and confirmation at particular points. Brother Kelvin of the Bible institute gave her an important clue by phone that she might find the right faith community in Wisconsin (41, 43). Her mother also urged her to go (43), and three different people—not related to each other—pointed to the example of Abraham who stepped out on faith and went into a distant and unknown land. Another elder associated with the ministry to which she went in Wisconsin gave her "prophetic words" to the effect that she would be meeting the man she was to marry in the next few weeks (50). In many of the instances in which Mary interpreted and acted on the will of God on her own it proved disastrous: the feeling that she was to marry the man in the Birmingham ministry, which led to her having to leave it (31, 32); falling into the relationship with Harry, which had the effect of isolating them both from the Bethel community (46–48); accepting Harry back without "counseling" with the shepherding group in Green Bay, after they had helped her set up a livable pattern of study and care for her child (54, 55).

Without going further we can say that authority for Mary during most of the twenty-two to twenty-seven age period was located externally to herself. First, and most powerfully, it was located in God's will. Regarding the interpretation of God's will, however, it was located in persons on whom she depended for love, emotional support and guidance. Authority was located in scripture (in highly selective passages, which were usually brought to her attention by valued others and made salient by their resonance with her immediate existential situation). For reasons we can say more about as we consider the path of Mary's psychosocial development, she evolved a certain pattern of passivity in relation to initiatives and decisions. In those years, when she acted on her own intuitions she often found that she had made unwise choices and decisions. These experiences added to her reliance upon external authority, located in trusted others or in the consensus of groups by which she felt accepted and loved.

Let me ask you now to look at the chart labeled Table 5.1. This is a summary overview of the descriptions of the seven categories we use in the analysis of faith stages. Each of the vertical columns delineates the transformations in that structural feature of faith that heads the column as one moves from stage to stage. If we look at the column headed "Locus of Authority" we can ask, which of the brief descriptions best fits with what we have said about the locus of authority as it appeared in the postconversion years in Mary's interview? Clearly the description of Stage 3 most aptly characterizes the way Mary then constituted and relied upon authority. The Stage 2 description of incumbents of authority roles does not fit. Mary's conventional counterculture posture had emerged to negate that locus of authority. On the other hand, in those years she clearly lacked the internalized locus of authority described in Stage 4, "one's own judgment, as informed by a self-ratified (self-chosen) ideological perspective."

As a second point of vantage on the structuring of Mary's faith in her postconversion years, we may consider what we call the *Form of World Coherence*. As you reflect over Mary's interview again let me ask you to consider the following questions. Insofar as Mary's faith brought a

Table 5.1 Faith Stages by Aspects

ASPECT:	A. Form Of Logic (Piaget)	B. Perspective Taking (Selman)	C. Form of Moral Judgment (Kohlberg)	D. Bounds of Social Awareness	E. Locus of Authority	F. Form of World Coherence	G. Symbolic Function
STAGE:							
I	Preoperational	Rudimentary empathy (egocentric)	Punishment –reward	Family, primal others	Attachment/ dependence relationships. Size, power, visible symbols of authority	Episodic	Magical -Numinous
II	Concrete Operational	Simple perspective taking	Instrumental hedonism (Reciprocal fairness)	"Those like us" (in familial, ethnic, racial, class and religious terms)	Incumbents of authority roles, salience increased by personal relatedness	Narrative- Dramatic	One- dimensional; literal
III	Early Formal Operations	Mutual interpersonal	Interpersonal expectations and concordance	Composite of groups in which one has interpersonal relationships	Consensus of valued groups and in personally worthy representatives of belief-value traditions	Tacit system, felt meanings symbolically mediated, globally held	Symbols multi- dimensional; evocative power inheres in symbol
IV	Formal Opera- tions (Dichotomizing)	Mutual, with self-selected group or class— (societal)	Societal perspective, Reflective relativism or class-biased universalism	Ideologically compatible communities with congruence to self-chosen norms and insights	One's own judgment as informed by a self-ratified ideological perspective. Authorities and norms must be congruent with this.	Explicit system, conceptually mediated, clarity about boundaries and inner connections of system	Symbols separated from symbolized. Translated (reduced) to ideations. Evocative power inheres in *meaning* conveyed by symbols

V	Formal Operations (Dialectical)	Mutual with groups, classes and traditions "other" than one's own	Prior to society, Principled higher law (universal and critical)	Extends beyond class norms and interests. Disciplined ideological vulnerability to "truths" and "claims" of outgroups and other traditions	• Dialectical joining of judgment-experience processes with reflective claims of others and of various expressions of cumulative human wisdom.	Multisystemic symbolic and conceptual mediation	• Postcritical rejoining of irreducible symbolic power and ideational meaning. Evocative power inherent in the reality in and beyond symbol *and* in the power of unconscious processes in the self
VI	Formal Operations (Synthetic)	Mutual, with the commonwealth of being	Loyalty to being	Identification with the species. Transnarcissistic love of being	In a personal judgment informed by the experiences and truths of previous stages, purified of egoic striving, and linked by disciplined intuition to the principle of being	Unitive actuality felt and participated unity of "One beyond the many"	Evocative power of symbols actualized through unification of reality mediated by symbols and the self

unity and overall meaning to her experience, what *form* or *focus* did that unifying grasp of things take? To what degree was Mary reflective about her meanings and their integration? To what degree was Mary critically self-conscious about the meanings that sustained her and about how they differed from those of other persons or groups? How concerned was she about internal consistency between elements of her system of meanings and values?

Our answers to these questions depend less on quoting specific passages from the interview and more on reflecting on the quality or characteristics of Mary's way of seeing things taken as a whole. Mary's life, as recounted in the interview, had been full of moves, changes of community and several major crises and disappointments. In the years after her conversion, however, one central theme, one dominant motif or image, tended to provide assurance and sustaining meaning in the good times and the bad. The first time we see this is in paragraph 7, where Mary told about the events leading up to the rock-bottom time just before her conversion. She says: ". . . At the same time I can see that the Lord was really working in my life to draw me to himself before that happened." When she left the Followers of God and moved back to Birmingham (30) she tells us, "Somehow the Lord arranged for me to meet these people who had a ministry over on Logan Road. . . . They found me and invited me to come live there, and I felt the Lord was leading me to do that, so I did move in there" (31). While in that community she says, "I felt that God showed me that I was going to marry a certain brother at that house" (31). What is striking about each of these latter instances is that while "God" or the "Lord" was credited with providing guidance and sanction for the decisions or actions she took, when the consequences of those choices turned out to be painful or disastrous for her, God was never questioned or held accountable. Similarly, after she went to Wisconsin, following the advice of elders, a parent and other advisors, and after she entered into an unfortunate marriage on the encouragement of other elders and on the supposition that, "Maybe this is the one the Lord really wants me to have" (50), she says of the time when Harry first left her, "And the Lord just met me in a marvelous way through those people; the love that they showed me was so real. It's something that God has done again and again in my life, is really meet me when I was at the end of my rope, you know, when I was really up against the wall, and that's what he did" (52). And referring to another time, near the end of their marriage, when Harry sent her away to Daytona, she says, "And yet the Lord was so good to me, because all this time I really had the support of this church, and I was very close to those people. The Lord never once forsook me, he was really faithful to me" (56).

Coherence in Mary's tumultuous postconversion world inhered in her images of God. I say *images* for two reasons. First, her uses of "God," "the Lord" and even of "Jesus Christ" involved a largely unreflective use of these symbols. She had not reflected upon her images or symbols so as to form concepts. Second, I speak of images in the plural because the coherence of Mary's faith world at that time involved at least two major images of God. On the one hand, there was the God who gives guidance and sanctions initiatives. When these initiatives turned out to have been mistakes or to have had extremely painful consequences, the goodness, fidelity or authenticity of this God were never questioned. On the other hand, there was God the rescuer—the one whom she saw as meeting her when she was at the end of her rope, the one who never forsook her. We will need to look at these two images of God in light of aspects of Mary's psychosocial development at a later point, but for now it is enough to point to their coexistence in her postconversion faith.

If we examine the column in Table 5.1 headed "Form of World Coherence," which stage description best fits the patterns we see in Mary's young adult faith? Hers was clearly not the "explicit system, conceptually mediated . . ." of Stage 4. Nor was it the "Episodic" or "Narrative-Dramatic" forms of Stages 1 and 2. Again the structuring pattern of Stage 3 best describes this aspect of Mary's faith. During most of the years from twenty-two to twenty-seven her form of world coherence was a *tacit* system. She had strongly felt meanings mediated by symbols and images. These she had not examined or questioned. She did not require that her "system" exhibit internal consistency.

Now we can consider the structuring of Mary's postconversion faith with reference to another of the categories in Table 5.1—the *Bounds of Social Awareness*. Here we ask ourselves regarding Mary's faith, who (what persons, what groups or classes) got included as she shaped and formed her meanings? Similarly, who got excluded? How diverse was the range of experiences and outlooks of others that Mary coordinated with her own as she composed images of self, others and ultimate environment? Who were the significant others in relation to whom Mary maintained her sense of identity and the vitality of her faith? Whose questions and criticisms—intellectual and/or social and existential—did her faith have to "stand"?

As we reflect on Mary's narrative with these questions in mind, I find striking the virtual absence of references to any persons or groups other than those with which Mary had face-to-face, interpersonal relationships. There is a real sense in which the only actors who counted at all in the world's drama, for Mary, were herself, "the Lord," and the people on whom she depended for fellowship, for support in her faith and for family loyalty. With the exception of passing references to colleges and the church of her childhood, there were no social institutions in her story. The large churches to which she referred—the parent institutions for the various house churches and shepherding groups to which she belonged—had significance only as umbrellas for these small, intimate, face-to-face groups. Social class, ethnic, racial and ideological differences seemed not to play any role in her faith constructions. In the interpersonally constructed and interpersonally maintained world of her faith, theological or ideological conflict would have presented grave problems. The bonds of community were constituted by friendship, love and emotional solidarity in faith. Theological precision was not important in those communities; there were "elders" whose responsibility it was to "know" for the membership. Ethical issues, when they arose, concerned the relations of persons within the community to each other. There was little need for ethical reflection dealing with relations to the other world of social structures, political processes and cultural meanings.

While I have extrapolated a bit beyond what Mary actually told us in her interview, I have done so with the judgment that omissions of concern about matters beyond the life of these small communities are significant. If we look again to Table 5.1 and examine the column dealing with bounds of social awareness it should be rather clear which stage best describes this aspect of her postconversion faith outlook. If "ideology" involves self-reflective adherence to a rather explicit body of norms and values, as it does in Stage 4, and if the inclusiveness of communities is based on ideological agreement, then plainly Mary's bounds of social awareness are not to be characterized by that stage. On the other hand, Mary long ago had broken away from biological family ties as a principal reference for community. (Remember the concern of the Green Bay shepherding group, which Mary took seriously, that she not go home to live with a "non-Christian group" (59).) Again it is Stage 3, with its "composite of groups in which one has interpersonal relationships," which most accurately describes Mary's young adult way of taking—and of not taking—account of others in her faith constructions. Later I will suggest some of the implications of this characteristic of Mary's faith and of the communities to which she has been drawn for the possibility of her further development in faith.

Perhaps by now the reader is beginning to get a feel for what we mean by *structural* stages. We are looking at the "how" of Mary's faith—at the *ways* she went about the business of shaping her outlook on life and her initiatives and responses to it. There is a distinction to be made between *structure* and *content* in faith. The *contents* of her faith are critically important—her notions of God, her understanding of the church, her images of sin and salvation. What I hope is becoming clearer, however, is that Mary's way of being Christian was profoundly shaped by the structuring operations with which she appropriated and responded to God in Christ after her conversion. The structural "style" with which Mary—and the communities she found supportive—went at being Christian shaped the character of their common and individual lives as much as did their allegiance to scripture and to Christ. Let me remind you, however, *that persons and groups can exhibit Synthetic-Conventional structuring in relation to quite other theological or faith contents and orientations* than those of Mary's communities. There are Stage 3 Christians in many different denominations whose tacitly held and conventionally committed faith orientations differ markedly in content from Mary's. When teaching college sophomores and freshmen, I encountered a number of Stage 3 atheists and agnostics. At present our society seems to be populated by a substantial number of Synthetic-Conventional adherents of what might be called a "low" civil religion that involves mainly tacit trust in and loyalty to a composite of values such as material success, staying young, and getting the children out successfully on their own. Such persons may or may not be members of churches or synagogues. But, on the other hand, there are also a great many devout and committed members and subgroups in each of our religious traditions and denominations, the integrity of whose faith is best described by the Synthetic-Conventional position.

Now let's return to Mary's interview and the analytic categories of the stage theory. In previous sections of this book I have pointed out that faith employs images and symbols as it orients us to the ultimate conditions of existence. In this regard, one of the important categories of faith stage analysis focuses on a person or group's way of relating to and through symbolic representations. We call this the *Symbolic Function.* My use of Mary's interview to introduce these categories finds its greatest limitation with regard to the symbolic function. There is no place in the interview as printed here (or indeed, as conducted) in which I asked Mary to interpret and clarify her references to such central symbols as "God," "Jesus Christ," "the Lord," "the Spirit," "Kingdom of God," or "body of Christ." While the lack of this data requires that we keep tentative any judgments we make concerning this aspect of her faith structuring, still, to examine her interview in this respect will repay our attention. First, what questions do we ask as we inquire into the role of symbols? We ask, With what terms, images, or metaphors does the respondent refer to the transcendent? Are such references intended as literal or metaphorical in quality? Are symbols, myths or metaphors taken as one-dimensional and literal (that is, as having only one reference) or are they taken as multileveled and multivalent in character? Has the respondent distanced him- or herself from the symbol or metaphor and recognized it *as* a symbol or metaphor? Has the symbol, myth or metaphor been questioned for conceptually statable meanings?

I have already given in the previous paragraph the principal symbols Mary employs in expressing her faith in this interview. We also anticipated some of the discussion in dealing with the Form of World Coherence. By far the *symbol for transcendence* most frequently used by Mary is "the Lord." If we review her uses of this term and of the related symbols "Jesus Christ" and "God," we find that in a few instances she differentiated between them. In paragraph 7, after saying that ". . . the Lord was really working in my life to draw me to himself . . ." she tells about the impact of the experience she had while on LSD. ". . . It was just revealed to me in such a real way during this experience that our only purpose is to be filled with his Spirit and to worship him. And yet, I had no concept of Jesus Christ as Lord, you know. I had . . . but this experience really revealed to me the reality of God, that there is a spiritual other." In paragraph 11 she says that the words of the scripture text from 2 Timothy convicted her because "The Spirit really made them alive to me . . ." In describing the religious orientation of her parents she said, "I think they really do have a belief in God of a sort. They believe in a personal God, I think, but they don't have any . . . they're not born again. They don't have any relationship with Jesus Christ that I know of" (19).

In contrast to the instances in the last paragraph where distinctions

are made between the persons of the trinity, in most of the other
instances when Mary uses the phrase "the Lord" it seems to include all
the persons of the trinity in an undifferentiated manner. We must
remind ourselves at this point of the two dominant *personae* or masks
of the Lord we identified in Mary's usage. We recognized the Lord in
one guise as the God who sanctions initiatives and gives guidance. We
pointed out that Mary apparently never held this God accountable for
the consequences of the initiatives she has taken and directions she has
chosen under his "direction." The other face of the Lord, for Mary, is
God the rescuer, the one who never forsakes her and who seems to be
most real and powerful precisely in her times of greatest anguish and
degradation. In ways that we will want to examine more closely in
relation to Mary's psychosocial development, it may be that some of the
motivation leading her into disastrous choices had to do with testing the
reality and fidelity of a God who is most unambiguous in his love when
he meets her as rescuer at the end of her rope (52). In any event, it is
clear that in Mary's account of her faith "the Lord" is a powerful,
multidimensional symbol, filled with highly personal and subjective
emotive content. I think it is equally clear that Mary, properly speaking,
has sharply delineated no *concept* of God. That is to say, she has not
questioned the powerful symbol "the Lord," either in its meanings for
her or for others, so as to clarify, reflect upon and draw together explicitly its many dimensions of meaning.

A similar vagueness coupled with emotional power inheres in Mary's
use—each in a single instance—or two other symbols. In referring to the
joy of her first several weeks at the Bethel community in Wisconsin, she
says, "I just had a vision of the Kingdom of God on earth those first few
weeks . . . , just being among my brothers and sisters and seeing the body
of Christ being built up there, and the Spirit of the Lord ministering
through them. It was so real to me that I was part of the Kingdom of
God, and that the Kingdom was there" (45). This is a very meaningful
use of the Jewish-Christian political metaphor for the rule of God or
God-reigning. It suggests some of the power that metaphor is regaining
in the renewed understanding of the eschatological character of the
Kingdom in the theologies of hope and of liberation. It is impossible to
tell without further comment from Mary, however, whether she is
simply using phrases with which that community talked about the richness and warmth of the fellowship they were experiencing, or whether
she—and perhaps they—also meant by it something of the critical,

prophetic character of a transcendent but in-breaking reality. Her use of the other major symbol—the body of Christ—presents a similar ambiguity.

When we turn to the column "Role of Symbols" in Table 5.1, I think it is clear that in this respect also Mary's faith structuring in her postconversion period also fits best the descriptions given of Stage 3. Had I pursued, as we usually do in interviews, the clarification of the central symbols we have identified in Mary's narrative, then we could have confirmed this stage assignment with less tentativity than we must maintain here. Regardless of the lack of adequate data for determining the level of the symbolic function, however, I think it is easy to see that Mary's way of using her central symbols and images in those years went beyond either the magical-numinous quality of Stage 1, or the one-dimensional and literal quality of Stage 2. And I would be surprised indeed if further probing of her use of symbols at the time of the interview would have disclosed the kind of critical distance from and conceptual translation of symbolic meanings that characterize Stage 4.

It remains now for us to give some consideration to the three other columns found in Table 5.1. The first of these, the *Form of Logic*, requires us to recall our reporting of Piaget's structural stages of cognitive development in the imaginary conference of Part II. Similarly, the columns on *Perspective Taking* and the *Form of Moral Judgment* depend on the structural-developmental research and theories of Selman and Kohlberg, as presented in Part II.

Obviously in this interview with Mary I did not test for formal operational thinking by administering the problem of the metal bars of varying lengths, shapes and materials, described in Part II. Nor did I administer any of the verbal problems sometimes used to assess cognitive development. To assess the stage of her form of logic in this instance, as in the majority of our interviews, we will rely on Piaget's clues regarding the varying qualities of self-reflection characteristic of the different cognitive developmental stages. We do make some refinements of the Piagetian stages, however. You will note that I have extended the Piagetian stages of formal operational thinking to include three substages or "styles" of formal operations we find useful to distinguish in dealing with the faith interviews. We see a *dichotomizing* style at Stage 4: this is a logic which, in dealing with symbols, beliefs and propositions, is particularly attuned to making distinctions and establishing boundaries. Dichotomizing logic tends towards "either/or" distinctions. At

Stage 5 we see a *dialectical* style of logic. In dialectic, truth requires maintaining and honoring the tensions between the various perspectives on a complex problem or issue. Dialectical logic is alive to and appreciative of paradox, that the truth appears in the "coincidence of opposites." The logic associated with Stage 6—the *synthetic* form—carries forward the strengths of the previous stages, but it overcomes the paradoxical by discerning and responding to a "oneness in and beyond the many."

Returning to Mary's interview, let us reflect on those elements of her narrative that give indications of the stage of her cognitive operations in her postconversion years. Particularly we are interested in the kind and quality of her reflections on the directions—and their causes—of her own life. You may remember that in Parts II and IV we were alerted to a significant difference in the respective ways in which concrete operational and formal operational persons reflect on their lives. Concrete operational persons (whether children, adolescents or adults) tend to reflect on the flow of their lives, as it were, from within the flow. Relying on narratives and stories of their experiences, they speak out of the flow and share it. By and large, they lack the cognitive operations required for stepping out of the flow—for constructing a "place" beside the stream of their lives from which it can be observed as a whole, assessed and generalized about. Formal operations, on the other hand, allow for the sort of transcending of the life-stream that enables one to compose a myth of one's past, present and future. Formal operations make it possible to reflect on particular events and their meanings in relation to the more encompassing grasp of the total movement and its direction. In light of these considerations, how did Mary relate to the data of her own life and experience? From what kind of vantage point was she constructing and reflecting on her memories, her hopes, her present?

One clue is her readiness to pick up on the device of dividing her life into chapters (1). As much as this is taken for granted in the responses of formal operational persons, I find it striking in adolescents and adults who have not developed formal operational thinking that they have difficulty doing this—or even in understanding what is being requested. They simply share stories from their past—or about others—but never "rise to the level of general statement" about meanings. In the interview we have read Mary does make such general statements. She speaks of herself in the eight-month period of searching for God as a "gnostic" —one who sought for an intellectually reliable path toward knowledge of God (9). She generalizes about the impact of the early and persisting experience of alienation from her mother on her feelings about herself (12–15, 25). She speaks out of a myth of herself as "a very difficult child" (16), and as one who "became a really rebellious brat towards her parents" (15). She characterizes the main issue in her life at that time as one of gaining a sense of self-worth (64). All of these instances suggest that as regards self-reflection Mary exhibited at least the early formal operations we find correlated with faith Stage 3. While noting this, we may point out, however, that Mary seems to have exhibited *less* capacity for reflective transcendence in relation to her life after seventeen than she showed in dealing with her childhood and adolescence before leaving her family of origin. As we have pointed out in discussing the Form of World Coherence, the Locus of Authority and the Symbolic Function, at the time of the interview Mary showed somewhat limited abilities to reflect critically on the contents and operations of her faith. These limitations may have been part of what Mary had in mind when she said of herself, remembering the time of her marriage to Harry, "I guess I was very naive, and I really wasn't a very good judge of character at the time" (51). But we must remember that this interview put much more emphasis on lifestory and narrative than on asking for critical reflections, so no firm conclusions about Mary's capacities in these regards may be drawn.

Indications that Mary could best be described as Stage 4 in cognitive development would have been the capacity to differentiate herself and her world view—to be conscious that she *has* a perspective on the world and that it, as well as the world, can be an object of her reflection. Further, the cognitive operations that characterize Stage 4 make it possible to distinguish between one's identity or one's "self" and the roles one plays and the relations one has. The lack of these kinds of differentiations shows up in Mary's poignant words near the end of the interview: "I have such a hard time feeling that I'm worth anything [that I have any valued identity or selfhood] when no man wants me. I don't have a ministry, a vocation that I'm really, you know, that I feel good about" (63).

The role of cognitive structuring in social relations comes into sharper focus as we examine Mary's exercise of *Perspective Taking* and her *Form of Moral Judgment* in her young adult years. In Parts II and IV we presented a rather detailed account of the revolution in perspective taking made possible by the emergence of formal operational thinking.

We distinguished the steps from "interpersonal" perspective taking ("I see you seeing me") to the "mutual interpersonal" style ("I see you seeing me; I see you seeing me seeing you"), and on to the transcendence of third-person perspective taking. In relation to Kohlberg's moral Stage 4 we also examined the addition of societal perspective taking—seeing the self in relation to others from the standpoint of society, understood as a cooperative network of rules and roles that shape, preserve and enhance the common good.

As we bring these categories to Mary's interview we are again hampered by lack of specific questions or tests designed especially to assess her structuring of relationships. There are, however, a fair number of instances in which we see Mary constructing the point of view of others. We also get some indications of how she perceived and made moral judgments. Beginning with perspective taking, we encounter first Mary's constructions of her mother's point of view. Initially in the interview, and afterwards as I have read and reread it, I have been impressed by a kind of gentleness with which Mary attempted to see things as her mother saw them. A quality of fairness—and the ability to differentiate her mother's perspective from her own—marked her way of saying, "My mother is an extremely giving person. She's always faithfully served her family, far above what most women would do" (14). In that same set of comments she appealed to the need for a third-person perspective on the family system: "It's really hard to explain to someone who hasn't witnessed the family in operation." Mary demonstrated the use of interpersonal perspective taking in her next comments, reporting her *own* sense of how her mother sees her. She did not, however, take the standpoint of her mother, and attempt to sense how her mother sees herself in their relationship: "I've always felt that her attitude toward me was very negative and critical. Like she didn't accept me the way God made me, you know, she always wanted to make me into her own image. She wanted to change me; it's really hard to explain. It seems like she's always vented her own frustrations on me; her unhappiness, her lack of fulfillment. It always comes out in the form of irritation or anger and disgust toward me and the way I do things. . . . I could never please her. I guess I just gave up at a really early age and just became a really rebellious brat towards my parents" (14–15). I asked her, ". . . is that really the way you see it, or is that the way they see it?" She replied, again appealing slightly to a third-person perspective, "I could see that I was a very difficult child. I think by nature I'm very strong-willed and very sensitive, and I just . . . my relationship with my mother was just a constant source of grief for both of us. It was very painful. It still is" (16).

In talking about her father Mary gave us very little in terms of penetration into his personality or into his perspective—on her or on anything. We cannot tell from the interview whether this arose from a lack of emotional salience in her life by the father, or whether, on the contrary, the taking and reporting of the father's perspective on her would have been too painful for her. There is no indication anywhere in the interview that the latter possibility is the case. But since I did not probe these factors in the interview, we cannot be certain. What is clear is that Mary gave us virtually nothing that would indicate any invest-ment in constructing the experiences and point of view of her father. Indeed, her lack of imaginative reconstruction of her parents' first years of marriage (12, 17) and the virtually "empty" characterizations she gives of them as persons, point to a quality of self-absorption (of egocen-trism in the cognitive sense) at that time which was undoubtedly a factor of considerable importance affecting her possible further growth in faith, as well as in the patterns of her autobiography. On the basis of the data we have it is impossible to say whether this self-absorption was dominantly a cause or an effect of Mary's life experiences. Plainly, it was both. But it leads me to say, that in regard to perspective taking, Mary employed consistently only the interpersonal form. She did not dependa-bly construct the points of view of others upon themselves; she did not as a matter of course construct others' experiences of her point of view.* This gave her social interactions a quality very like one we see in early adolescents. This pattern of perspective taking structurally fits with the overall Stage 3 character of Mary's faith development at that time. It would have been an important place to begin work in sponsoring her growth in faith and as a person.

The limits of Mary's dominant ways of constructing the perspectives of others at this time in her life exerted a powerful impact on her *Form of Moral Judgment.* The absence of mutuality in her interpersonal perspective taking meant that her perceptions of the judgments or evaluations significant others made about her had a kind of absolute

---

*These observations are borne out if we look at the several other instances of perspective taking in the interview: Her perceptions of the "absolutist" elder in Daytona, "I guess he was really trying to help me in a way . . ." (37); her representations of Harry—and of her part in Harry's difficulties (53, 54, 55, 58).

quality. Having limited ability to interpret what "psychological bag-gage" the significant others brought to their relationship or to construct the other's interpretation of her own attitudes toward him or her, the evaluative response of the other had to either be accepted or rejected —largely without qualification. To understand this means to understand why Mary so desperately needed to live in the context of a supportive, loving group. It also clarifies why, apart from roles and relationships in an intense group or in a marriage relationship, Mary felt that she could have no self or self-worth. She had no third-person perspective from which she could coordinate and evaluate her interactions with others. There was no transcendent "cognitive ego" that could hold Mary's reflective sense of herself constant, while comparing it with the assess-ments or evaluations of others in such a way that the assessor and assessment could be evaluated as well as Mary. In this situation we see Kohlberg's stage three, "interpersonal expectations and concordance" operating, but operating in a way, also characteristic of earliest adoles-cence, where there is as yet only a very fragile and provisional sense of the self as the unification of the images reflected by one's significant others. To see this is to see that intrinsic to any effort to assist Mary in moral development as part of overall faith development there would have to have been relationships of quality and consistency in which she could build and strengthen a moral self. In my judgment, providing her with some theoretical and practical images of her situation and of what she needed to grow toward would also have been an important part of helping her grow through relationship and reflection.

Faith and Identity: Some Psychosocial Reflections

I hope that the structural analysis of Mary's interview has succeeded in the twofold goal I intended. On the one hand, I hope it made possible the beginnings of an operational grasp of the structural perspective on faith and of the categories with which we conduct an analysis of the structures of a person's faith. Second, I hope it has given the reader a "feel" for the integrity of a stage—for the way the structuring operations "hang together" and overlap in an integrated set of operations. Specifi-cally, I hope it has enabled the reader to put him- or herself inside the Synthetic-Conventional stage and to understand in a felt way the range and limits inherent in that style of faith structuring. To the degree that we reached these goals, you were able to begin to see how the structuring of self, others and ultimate environment mutually interpenetrate in the structuring activity that is faith. Perhaps you also begin to see how, in this perspective, faith and action—one's ways of *seeing* and one's ways of *being*—interpenetrate. Particularly in the final paragraphs, where we looked at Mary's perspective taking and her form of moral judgment, we began to understand that her troubled identity and faith could be described—and perhaps prescribed for—in terms of the patterns of her structures of faith.

Now we take on the challenge of bringing the structural-developmental analysis of Mary's story into interplay with some psychosocial reflections. I tried to lay the groundwork for this interplay in Part II where I related the structural-developmental perspectives of Piaget and Kohlberg to the psychosocial framework of Erikson. We have also anticipated it in Part III in the section, "Structural-Developmental Theories and Faith."

If we reflect on Mary's narrative in light of Erikson's eight ages some rather illuminating hypotheses suggest themselves. Mary told us that from the beginning it seemed there had been tension between her and her mother. Her account of the mother's isolation during the first two years of Mary's life and the depression and despondency the mother seems to have felt before they moved back to New York suggest that despite Mary's assertion that "I know she really wanted me" (12), the dynamics of their relationship during that earliest period gave her strong grounds for doubt. Other than Mary's testimony that "right from the first there was antagonism between us," we do not have access to the quality of the mother-daughter relationship in the era in which Erikson tells us the foundations are laid for some ratio of basic trust—in others, world and self—to basic mistrust. It seems likely that Mary emerged from infancy with considerable mistrust.

Mary told us that, "I guess I gave up [on trying to please her mother] at a really early age and just became a really rebellious brat towards my parents" (14). This pattern of rebelliousness, which she picks up on again in several places, suggests that in the psychosocial unwinding of the formation of her personality we might well spend considerable time on her struggle with the crisis Erikson calls autonomy vs. shame and doubt. In talking about her attraction to and joining of the Followers of God Mary said, "I was really turned on by their lifestyle, you know, I mean after having been in total rebellion for twenty-two years, I couldn't see the rebellion in what they were doing" (27). Erikson tells us that the child who is made to feel that he or she is identical with that which others find shameful in his or her behavior or way of being may preserve the integrity of the nascent self by asserting a kind of shameless willfulness. Given Mary's struggle in later years with alternating willfulness and passivity—with autonomy and conformity—it makes good sense to hypothesize some relational disturbance in the second or third years of her life that made autonomy problematic and that gave rise to a style of willful assertiveness and stubborn secretiveness in Mary's way of relating to the primal others in her life.

Our data is too limited to do more than hypothesize about the period in which, Mary tells us, she spent a lot of time alone in her room "reading" and dancing. In this period, from ages three to six, she tells us, "There were two little boys up on the corner who were very naughty, and I used to play with them" (20). She remembers in that era "hearing the minister preach a sermon about death, [and] about how there was no place you could hide from it." And she adds, "I remember that I was suicidal from a very early age, and it was always a reaction to my relationship with my mother" (21). Those scant windows into the world of a bright and active but lonely preschooler do not give us a very comprehensive picture of her way of dealing with the crisis of initiative vs. guilt. There is enough, however, to suggest that the fantasies of suicide and the probable accompanying childhood depressions had a good deal to do with the contemplation of angry initiatives toward the mother. Playing with the "naughty" boys may have involved sex-play or other activities that led to feelings of guilt. Expressed in ways that were unacceptable and punished or kept within in a stubborn secretiveness, it seems likely that these gave rise to guilt, depression and the ambivalent aggression of the suicide fantasies. One would like to know more about the relational pattern between Mary and the kindergarten teacher that led to her being put out in the hall when she laughed at the teacher's rendition of "Here Comes Peter Cotton Tail" (23–24). She says, "I didn't get along too well with the teacher."

Apparently Mary brought with her to her elementary school years a mixed emotional legacy. She was bright, had plenty of ability and seems to have exhibited competencies that were recognized by parents, teachers and her schoolmates. Yet, one gets the picture of a continually lonely little girl and one who carried considerable private burdens of anxiety, guilt and shame. She felt set apart by what she called "a real acne problem in the third grade." She began to mature physically well ahead of most of her peers. After moving between ages ten and eleven she formed a very meaningful friendship with another girl, but this ended after two years with Mary feeling surpassed and abandoned: "I had a really close friend in fifth and sixth grade, and she and I were just inseparable. She became the most popular girl in junior high, and I sort of fell by the wayside. And that really_hurt a lot" (25). Mary concludes the assessment of her early school years by returning to the relationship with her mother: "But all these things are just sort of incidental to my relationship with my mom. That's really the main thing, I think . . . because I don't think that things that happen in school can really override a good situation at home" (25).

As Mary sees it in her ninth-grade year she was beginning to find a group of friends with whom she felt compatible. At age fourteen, we may surmise, she was well into interpersonal perspective taking. She would also have begun to be "at home" in her body—many of her friends having caught up with her in physical maturity. Apparently she was beginning to feel some distance from the family as the major context for intimacy and found that she could draw emotional support and encouragement for a more positive self-image from her friends. At this point the family moved from the New York area to Birmingham. Relationally, Mary never seems to have recovered from that move. "It was really a cultural shock, because . . . it was just so completely different from living in suburban New York. I just couldn't seem to find any friends who had similar interests to mine, and I became really withdrawn, and my mother really got onto me about that because she wanted me to be outgoing and have a lively social life and everything, for my own sake. I just couldn't be the way she wanted me to be. I got very withdrawn, and I read. I'd just close myself in my room and read or listen to classical music" (26). The family, obviously trying to support Mary in this difficult time— and ready to go to considerable expense to help her find a good school context—sent her for the tenth grade to an outstanding local private high school. When that did not work out she returned to yet another public high school, one where, she said, "I was starting to adjust pretty well . . . and felt at home" (26).

The proposal by a visiting uncle that Mary leave high school after her junior year and start college at the institution where he was an administrator seems to have been a relief to Mary and her family alike. Clearly the years in high school had been miserable for them all. Beginning college must have seemed, for parents and daughter, to hold the possibility of fresh, new beginnings. It provided a respectable, even prestigious way for her to leave the South and the tense home situation. For the parents it provided a way to turn the frustration of dealing with Mary over to the faculty and administrators of a college twelve hundred miles away.

Mary mentions no close friendships after the move south from New York. While she must have done outstanding academic work in the several schools she attended from ages fourteen to seventeen, no teachers, friends or absorbing extracurricular activities seem to be part of the story. How did these circumstances affect her dealing with the psychosocial crisis of adolescence, identity vs. role confusion? While our data is sketchy, it seems clear that Mary's experiences during her high-school years provided little that would have helped her construct a clear, integrated and positive image of herself. The strong undercurrent of negative self-worth, which was the legacy of her infancy and childhood, must have only found confirmation in her inability to adapt through all the moves she made. Her anger, apparently present in muted form throughout her childhood, likely deepened due to the uprootings with which she had to deal. If the parents, who obviously at conscious levels intended and sought to provide the best for her, unconsciously responded to her anger and withdrawing moodiness with their own anger and despair, then the elements of negative identity in her were undoubtedly reinforced. Then we must remember the larger social context of the times. In the years from 1964 to 1967 the country had suffered the assassination of revered president. His successor had escalated our very controversial involvement in the war in Vietnam. Civil rights confrontations and tensions were running very strong. Mary had a special sense of identification with and interest in the black struggle for equal rights. At the same time, also, media were heavily engaged in creating divisions between the establishment and various counterculture movements. A lot of angry talk and hardened feelings gathered around the notion of the "generation gap." Adolescents and young adults romanticized revolutionaries, called law enforcement officers "pigs," and began to take seriously their own rhetoric about not being able to trust anyone over thirty. The struggle in which Mary and her parents found themselves was—for that period —very representative. One might even say it was "normal." In the midst of all this Mary's assessment of herself at seventeen, as she went off to begin college, seems accurate: "I was maybe intellectually ready, but not socially or emotionally ready for that change at all. It turned out to be a really devastating experience too" (26).

In the interview Mary talks about the years from seventeen to twenty-two in the general, almost formulaic terms often used in the testimonial witnesses of new religious converts. Her experiences with sex, drugs, the occult, Eastern religions and pop psychology are made to sound as lurid and sinful as one can make them without going into any specifics or details. I did not ask for details; she did not volunteer them. From a psychosocial standpoint, however, the other themes from this period that she identifies are quite significant. She says, "You know, I was leading a real immoral, irresponsible sort of life—disobedient to my parents. Dropped out of school several times, and I just really made a mess out of my life. *But I know that in my heart I was really looking for the truth, too. . . . And I couldn't find anything that really satisfied me in life, that really seemed worth committing myself to*" (1, 2). In the willfulness of Mary's "disobedience to her parents" and in the counter-dependent rebelliousness of this period we can imagine that she again, as in the bratty time of early childhood, attempted to form the negative identity fragments in her personality into a positive identity. The ideological mood on and around campuses provided resonant images and support for this. Drugs, to the degree they were in the picture, cemented the pseudo-intimacy of a conspiratorial community and facilitated the overcoming of the parentlike voices in Mary's superego conscience. But alongside that "acting out" of the negative identity, she remembers— and I think the memories are accurate—that she was also in search of truth, in search of something "that really seemed worth committing herself to." Erikson speaks of this hunger as the adolescent's readiness for *fidelity*, a readiness to test what one is becoming by pledging it to a movement, cause or group that will ratify one's identity and give one "place" and purpose. We do not have to have the details to sense the many ways in which Mary's combination of angry negative identity and naive hunger for fidelity set her up for betrayals, exploitation and deep disillusionment.

At twenty-one Mary hit rock-bottom: a crisis in her relation with a man she was living with; a serious automobile accident; getting in trouble with the law for shoplifting; a suicide attempt. She began to face her situation and its causes: "When I was recuperating from this at-tempt on my life, the Lord began to show me that there was a divine law and that I had violated it; and that was why I was having all these unhappy effects in my life" (7). We do not know who else was present to her at this time as a participant in her coming to these insights. Certainly one of the decisive points in her facing the fact that her crisis was centrally spiritual was her experience on LSD. This occurred about three weeks after the suicide attempt. "I can't deny that it was really a spiritual experience because it just revealed to me in such a real way during this experience that our only purpose on earth is to worship and glorify the Lord. That our whole purpose is to be filled with his Spirit and to worship him. . . . This experience really revealed to me the reality of God, that there is a spiritual other" (7). This experience initiated an eight-month time of search, through a variety of means, for "a way to God."

At home for Christmas, the way came to Mary. The witness of scripture, called to her attention in a compelling way by a letter from her newly Christian brother, gave her a conviction of her sinfulness. Ron's unexpected visit home, his witness and "supernatural wisdom" broke through her defenses. "Through him the Lord made me aware that I had to make a decision then—that it was either then or not at all, I guess you could say. I really had that sense of, you know, that this is it; that I either decide now or the opportunity will pass. So I just put down my pride and made a decision that I was going to believe in Jesus Christ and follow him" (11).

Here we are dealing with a genuine conversion experience. Her previously scattered and ambiguous vectors of fidelity found a focus in Jesus Christ. Her negative identity and the life patterns through which she had acted it out could be left behind—indeed, she was promised that it could be obliterated, negated. She embarked upon the promise of a new way of life, one in which she could submit her will to the will of the Lord. But Mary was a new Christian without a church. There was no immediately available community in which the shape of her new identity in Christ could begin to take form. Her discovery of or by the Followers of God opens the first of that very mixed series of short-lived involvements she had in the next five years with various house churches and shepherding groups. Though these groups were undoubtedly well intentioned, it is painful to see the spiritual and psychological violence Mary continued to experience in their midsts. From the standpoint of faith development, it is painful to observe that Mary seems not to have grown either in the structuring of her faith or in the strength of her identity while she was part of these various ministries. In order to understand this we must see that the neo-Christian strategy of requiring Mary to relinquish her willfulness amounted to asking her to deny or negate the seat of the most promising strengths she had. To ask her to submit the willful self to negation meant that she was left with a mainly passive fragment of self which became dangerously dependent upon external authority—or upon strong internal subjective impulses or needs understood as the working of "the Lord"—for impetus, guidance and sanction in her actions. What I am trying to say is this: Mary's conversion, genuine and powerful though it was, was seriously affected by the failure of the communities in which she found fellowship to sponsor her in the *transformation*, rather than the *negation*, of the willful self. There is a terrible kind of cruelty, no matter how well intended, in demanding the denial of self when there is no selfhood to deny. It is sad that Mary was not found by a community of faith that could have shown Christ's promise that he came to bring life and to bring it abundantly. It is sad that she did not find a community in which, with Christ as the "decisive other," Mary could have been supported in the development of an individuated identity, calling forth and integrating her potential strengths in a maturing faith.

Following Mary's conversion the groups with which she found fellowship interpreted her new being in Christ as arising out of the cancellation of her old being. This meant the cancellation of what I have called the "willful self"; it also meant the obliteration of her past. To honor the new being required that there be a separation from all that was before. It meant seeing the people in one's past and the person one was in one's past as hopelessly fallen and sinful. Because of the pain and chaos in the past—particularly in the recent past—the new convert welcomes this obliteration. If there has been strong imagery of satanic forces contending for or possessing the soul in the past, there will be considerable fear in the new convert and in those working with him or her about remembering or reworking the past. To acknowledge that the past, in its pain and grief as well as its times of grace and gladness, still is present in the psyche and is part of the person's ways of seeing and responding to life is threatening. The submitting of one's will to Christ, it is supposed, puts those powers of the past into bondage and knocks them off the throne of the convert's life.

The problem of this strategy of obliterating the convert's past life is that it short-circuits the conversion process. The rock-bottom phase of Mary's conversion, with its radical facing of the mess she had made of her life, had to occur. The eight-month time of searching, punctuated by the revelatory experience on LSD, played a necessary role in her conversion. The volitional struggle and submission to the Lordship of Jesus Christ with her brother at Christmas was a crucial and decisive step. These were all necessary and powerful movements in Mary's conversion. But the conversion needed to continue. After a time of radical discontinuity with her past, supported in the disciplines of group life of prayer, of scripture reading, of worship, of service, there should have begun a time when, in addition to these things, Mary could be led, through experiences of contemplative prayer and active imagination, combined with a correlated psychotherapy, into a healing recapitulation of the earlier stages of her life. In ways that I will say more about in the next chapter of this book, I am beginning to see that conversion, to be complete, involves a revisiting, a revalencing and recomposing of the stages of one's past faith in light of the new relationship to God brought about in the redirecting phases of the conversion. Ego psychologists speak of "regression in the service of ego development." I prefer the concept of recapitulation, but I refer to a similar phenomenon.

As we have seen, Mary's particular combination of strengths and vulnerabilities, which became visible in the interview, have a history that goes back at least to earliest infancy and possibly to prenatal life. Conversion, for Mary, will not be completed until, through recapitulative return to the places where that past lives in her, she can be met by a spirit that can re-ground the foundations of basic trust in her life. There needs to be a similar re-dwelling in the time of early childhood, where the primal images and intuitions of self-world and God took form. With contemplative prayer and active imagination—under the guidance and protection of the divine spirit—perhaps there could be a re-formation of the primal images of her faith. A similar revisiting of later childhood would enable Mary to let the stories and liturgical drama of her faith community become stories of her life. Re-founded in these ways, Mary's "new being in Christ" could go on to become the genuine reintegration of her identity and outlook she sought for in her first decisive step toward discipleship. Through such a process Mary could have become ready for the kind of intimacy and ministry for which she longs. But intimacy and ministry would then be ways of expressing and sharing the personhood Mary is, rather than being the means by which she tried to find and confirm identity.

Mary's interview took place nearly three years ago. Some important developments have occurred in her life since her move to the city where her parents live. In the process of asking for Mary's agreement to share her interview her brother Ron and I talked. I asked Ron if he would be willing, from his perspective and having read the interview and my commentary, to describe the recent changes in Mary's life. Here is Ron's statement as he wrote it describing what has happened to Mary to date.

I think that Mary has made real progress in the past three years since she came to Georgia—progress toward gaining a greater sense of that self-worth that she felt she lacked at the time of the interview. She's had to overcome many obstacles during that time and it would seem that in doing so she's gained confidence in herself and a sense of inner strength.

Although, as she stated during the interview, Mary did not have a great deal of enthusiasm about learning computer programming, she did attend classes at a nearby technical school for over a year in order to obtain a degree in that field. She did outstanding work there, impressing several of her teachers, which of course made me very proud—and thankful—for I knew how much this success would mean to Mary, computer programming or not. Soon after her graduation she landed a terrific job with a new company in the area, much to her own amazement. Apparently the man who hired her saw her potential, for she said there were one or two others interviewing for the job whom she was sure were more qualified. This gave her a tremendous boost because the man was looking for someone to train for a key position in his new and growing company. Mary had to be trained for this position for a full year and the knowledge she has since acquired has made her a practically indispensable employee.

In spite of her success at school and the new job, Mary still struggled with a sense of failure at home. She and Mom just couldn't seem to live together under the same roof in harmony. At first Mary felt extremely guilty about this, often blaming herself and thinking that she had failed the Lord by being a poor witness. She felt that it was her duty to stay at my parents' house until she could learn to "overcome" and "walk in victory." Finally, though, she decided that it would be best for everyone if she and the kids found a place of their own. Again a door opened, and I think what happened was especially important for Mary. I had been advising her for some time to get an apartment, but she felt that the Lord had spoken to her about a trailer that belonged to some friends who were thinking about moving. She kept waiting for that trailer, while things on the home front only seemed to be getting worse, and finally I lost my patience with her for not taking my advice. But Mary stuck to her guns and, lo and behold, she got the trailer! She got a fantastic deal on it, too. When I saw it for the first time I couldn't believe it—a few miles out in the country on a beautiful lot with a swing set for the kids, a separate storage shed, a washer and dryer that were practically brand new, and so on—all for practically nothing. Of course, what was important about all this was not just that Mary and the kids now had a place of their own, but that Mary had the strength to trust her own judgment more than mine or anyone else's, and it had paid off.

Other things seem to have fallen in place for Mary. Having to work full-time she was forced to look for someone who could look after her children during the day. Mary's very conscientious about the quality of care that her children receive, and therefore it seemed providential when she happened to hear about Mrs. Thomas, a very special Christian lady who runs a unique daycare center at her home.

Mary also has found a church fellowship with which she has been very happy for the past couple years. Following her interview with Jim, Mary continued for a while to maintain some contact with charismatic groups in her area, but gradually began to move away from them. She began to attend a nondenominational church in the Reformed tradition and has since become very fond of the fellowship there. She especially likes the preaching and teaching. To my surprise, my mother has gone to one or two of the services with Mary and even she has been impressed. That leads me to another thought . . .

In the past few months Mom and Dad have gotten involved in the church again after many years of inactivity. In fact, last month they both became charter members of a new Presbyterian congregation in their city. Mom has gotten involved in the choir and two weeks ago Dad was elected as one of the church elders. Now, Mary will say that this change in Mom and Dad has happened in spite of her, but I know that is not so. The fact is that the transformation that has been taking place in her life—especially in the past few years—has made a real impression on my parents. I've heard them both say so. There is still friction at times—I don't know if Mom and Mary will ever be real close—but things are looking up.

Finally, Mary is engaged to be married in a few months. She met her fiancé at work. In fact, he was the one responsible for training her, so they worked together very closely for a number of months and that's how they got to know one another. (Incidentally, Mary seems to have forgotten about "that guy in Birmingham." She finally did see him again and realized, I guess, that there was really nothing between them. I would imagine, also, that her movement away from the charismatics points to the fact that this bridge has finally been burned behind her.) Mary confesses that she wasn't attracted to Dillan at first, other than as a friend. Her love for him has grown gradually, as has his for her. They waited a considerable length of time before they finalized their decision to marry. What I'm trying to say is that their relationship seems to be really solid, for they've taken time and care to lay a good foundation. And speaking of foundations—that's another thing. As Mary and Dillan began to spend more time together, Dillan began to attend church with her. This led to a renewed Christian commitment in his life and an intense involvement with Mary in the church. Thus, it seems that they both are building together on the only ultimately firm foundation.

Dillan gets along very well with Mary's children. He enjoys them, likes to spend time with them, and knows how to be firm but very patient and understanding. And they are quite attached to him.

All in all, I would say that Mary has never been happier in her life. Not that everything is wonderful, but there is a stability, a peace, no real turmoil, nor has there been for some time now. I do not mean to imply that there has been an absence of struggle. By turmoil I mean the destructive, debilitating, paralyzing conflicts that Mary used to face. And I would not characterize her current stability completely in terms of the construction of defenses. It seems obvious to me that Mary is also becoming a more integrated person and I expect this process of integration to continue. In short, I do not see Mary as leveling off at some plateau, rather I see her for the first time in her life prepared for and moving toward the greatest progress in her personal growth and faith development.

23. Form and Content: Stages of Faith and Conversion

||||||||||||||||||||||||||||||||||||||||||||||||||||||||||||||||||||||||||||||||||||||||||||||||||||||||||||||||||||||||||||||||

In 1975 I accepted an invitation to share the faith development perspective with a select group of college and university campus ministers. Being veterans of encounters with many professorial types bearing freshly baked scholastic wares, they were a discerning and critical audience. For two days we wrestled over the strengths and limits of the structural-developmental approach to faith. After the sessions formally ended, a distinguished rabbi in his fifties, serving at a first-rank eastern university, sat with me at lunch. In the course of our conversation we had the following exchange:

Rabbi: Mr. Fowler, when did you begin this work on faith development, and how old are you now?

Fowler: The first writings I did on these topics came in 1972, when I was thirty-two. Presently I am thirty-five.

Rabbi: This is a right impressive body of work for a young man to have undertaken.

Fowler: [Grateful after the grilling I had endured.] Thanks. I think it has some important contributions to make.

Rabbi: Mr. Fowler, may I ask you, do you *believe* your theory of faith development? Do you *have faith* in your own theory?

Fowler: Well, . . . yes. Yes. On certain days, at least, I do. I take it very seriously. It's not the whole story, of course; it obscures some things while illuminating others. But, yes, I believe it.

Rabbi: Do you think you will still believe it when you are forty?

A developmentalist hoist on his own petard! The completion of this book, which virtually coincided with my fortieth birthday, has provided the opportunity to answer my friend's shrewd question. In this section

I want to indicate some of the changes in focus, emphasis and conceptual features this body of work has undergone since that conversation in 1975. In doing so readers will be brought close to the growing edge of our present research and reflection. In order to do this I must share a bit of background perspective.

In 1972 when I first became seriously aware of Lawrence Kohlberg's structural-developmental research on moral development, his work had only recently burst onto the screen of popular awareness. This sudden recognition resulted from several factors. Kohlberg, having been brought to Harvard with a mandate to develop a center for research on moral development and education, had published in the late sixties and early seventies a series of groundbreaking statements of his research and theory.[1] Passionate about the need for an approach to moral education in public schools that would not abridge the constitutional separation of church and state, Kohlberg aggressively undertook to provide the psychological, philosophical and educational foundations for such an approach.[2] His seminal articles showed uncommon energy and intellectual breadth. The range of his claims and the virtuosity of his arguments for them outflanked the writings and claims of other theorists in what, at the time, was a relatively moribund field. In 1969 *Psychology Today*, still in its first flush of impact and influence, published a crisp, short article by Kohlberg which set forth his theory and research.[3] Impressed by his contention that there is a sequence of formally describable stages of moral reasoning, that the sequence is universal and that secular educational methods going beyond values clarification were emerging to stimulate moral development, educators everywhere began to look toward Cambridge.

Though I couldn't know it then, in 1972 two major trends were beginning to emerge in the structural-developmental camp based at Harvard, both of which were to have significant consequences for the growth and gradual transformation of the structural-developmental paradigm as inherited from Piaget and decisively reshaped by Kohlberg. The first of these was the impact of trying to put the "moral discussion" method of moral education to work in schools, prisons and religious education settings. These early efforts began to raise questions about the influence of existing institutional patterns of moral decision making and behavior on the levels of moral reasoning of those being "educated." Questions of community and the sociology of morality began to emerge, pressing the early strategies of intervention to become more complex and comprehensive.[4] The second kind of emergence, while related to the first, is of more immediate concern to us. Kohlberg had opted in the late sixties not to follow in the direction of the great social psychologist, George Herbert Mead, who had written about moral development as an aspect of the forming of a "social self." For purposes of keeping his own focus of inquiry epistemological and to achieve a formal description of stages of moral reasoning that met the criteria for structural stages set by Piaget, Kohlberg decided against trying to generate a psychology of the moral self.[5] This meant that strictly speaking, he elected to follow Piaget in separating moral cognition from the affections and from the broader questions of the relation of moral reasoning to ego or personality development.

In 1973 Kohlberg took up concern again with the relation of moral judgment stage development to psychosocial development as presented in Erik Erikson's writings.[6] Earlier he and Carol Gilligan had jointly published an article on moral development in adolescence that had also related moral and psychosocial stages.[7] Though Kohlberg himself was reluctant to relinquish the epistemological focus of his theory and turned to efforts to refine techniques for the scoring and structural analysis of moral judgment interviews, a number of his younger colleagues began to pursue research and theory building that extended structural-developmentalism in the direction of personality theory and ego development. Carol Gilligan, Bob Selman, Harry Lasker and later Bob Kegan emerged as leaders of research and theory enterprises indebted to Kohlberg, but they sought in various ways to broaden the structural-developmental paradigm in the direction of accounting for the constitution and transformation of "selves." As an outsider from theology, though also deeply indebted to Erikson, I entered these discussions with a strange portfolio labeled "Faith Development." It is beyond the scope of our present interest to sketch the subsequent directions of these various persons and their work, though individually and collectively they are making significant impacts.[8] My purpose, rather, is to trace briefly how the faith development enterprise has evolved out of those beginnings.

If we allow ourselves the playfulness of using stage categories to talk about stage theories and their patterns of evolution, I think it makes sense to say that Kohlberg's theory of stages of moral judgment, at the time I encountered it in 1972, was in a Stage 4 (faith stage) position. Lawrence Kohlberg had worked hard to clarify the distinctive aims and theoretical rigor of Piaget's structural-developmentalism as applied to moral reasoning. He had drawn sharp boundary lines between his own approach to the understanding of moral development and those of behaviorists, social learning theorists, psychoanalytical thinkers and maturationists. He had made powerful claims not only for the descriptive accuracy of his sequence of stages, but had also defended the contention that each successive stage represented a qualitative advance in the ethical adequacy of moral judgments. He had made serious sorties into the world of philosophical and theological ethics in order to argue for the ethical normativity of his stage sequence. The "identity" of the paradigm was clear; the boundaries between it and others were distinct. The values and world view undergirding Kohlberg's approach were explicit. The theory, in the eyes of its proponents, had the "power" to assimilate other positions to its own, while offering more adequate explanations. Kohlberg's 1973 article and the virtually simultaneous emergence of the projects of Selman, Gilligan, Lasker—and then Fowler—marked, I believe, the beginning of a serious and consequential "Stage 4 to 5 transition" in the Cambridge family of structural-developmental theories. By this I mean that each of these efforts represented an expansion of the Piaget-Kohlberg paradigm. Each extended the structural-developmental metaphor in a direction more holistic and inclusive of broader patterns of personality or ego functioning. Each, though in different ways, found itself restive with the narrow formalism of Piaget and Kohlberg's strictly cognitive focus. Engaging variously with other psychological approaches and research traditions, these theorists sacrificed some of the precision of Piagetian structuralism for the more comprehensive inclusiveness of models that dealt with the formation and transformation of selfhood.

My earliest preliminary sketch of stages of faith owed a great deal to Erik Erikson's theory. Shortly, however, under Kohlberg's influence I and my students began to try to become more rigorous in the structural description of stages. This meant taking seriously the distinction between the *structures* and the *content* of faith. From the beginning I knew that I could not follow Piaget and Kohlberg in identifying the structural features of faith with the formal, logical structures of reason Piaget had identified. Nor could I afford to accept the Piaget-Kohlberg assertion that cognition and the affections, though intertwining in behavior and choice, must be analytically separated in cognitive-structural research. Faith, I knew, involves rationality and passionality; it involves knowing, valuing and committing. In the structuring activity that is faith, I saw, we had to have a wider understanding of cognition than that with which Piaget worked. So, while insisting that the formally describable structuring patterns we sought for in faith development research had to hold together cognition and affection, I did commit myself to the project of searching for a developmental sequence of structural "styles" of faith which might be shown to underlie persons' ways of appropriating the great variety of different "contents" of faith.

As a theologian I never lost sight of the crucial importance of the "contents" of faith—the realities, values, powers and communities on and in which persons "rest their hearts." I never tried to argue that the structural "style" of a person's or community's faith is more determinative for their lives and action than their centering values, their images of power or the master stories they take as descriptive of reality. It is true, however, that in trying to construct these empirically founded descriptions of structural stages in faith I and my associates neglected, until very recently, any effort at a theoretical account of the interplay of structure and content in the life of faith. And we have not taken adequate account of the various patterns of relationship of structure and content in either of two significant kinds of change in faith: *stage change* and *conversion*.

Reflection on a life story like Mary's in the previous section helps us see how the structuring activity that is faith involves *both* the formally describable operations of her knowing and valuing and the structuring power of the symbols, beliefs and practices of the faith community of which she is a part. In faith both the "forms" and the "contents" exert power in shaping a person's life-sustaining, life-guiding meanings. Changes or blocks in either one or the other can have transforming (or deforming) effects on a person's faith. Readers of this book who are familiar with my previous writings will have noted, I suspect, that my use of interview materials here has been much more inclusive of life histories and of the impact of changes in faith on their subjects' sense of selfhood than before. To try to account for the interplay of structure and content in faith means to look more radically and inclusively at faith as a *particular* person's way of constituting self, others and world in relation to the particular values, powers and stories of reality he or she takes as ultimate. This has been our goal throughout this book. If we now can clinch an account of the dynamic interplay of formal structures and the structuring power of particular contents in faith, perhaps it will serve to remind us of the main lines of argument and demonstration in the book and to draw them into a dynamic, if provisional, unity.

Structural Stages and the Contents of Faith

At various points earlier in this book I have hinted at a conception of the sequence of faith stages and their interrelations in terms of a rising spiral movement. Although models can be misleading and each has decisive limits, I have found it helpful in communicating my understanding of faith stages and of the processes of transition, regression and conversion, to introduce the following graphic presentation (Figure 5.1). Try to imagine the whole process as dynamically connected, each successive spiral stage linked to and adding to the previous ones. Each stage, as explained in Part IV of the book, marks the rise of a new set of capacities or strengths in faith. These add to and recontextualize previous patterns of strength without negating or supplanting them. Certain life issues with which faith must deal recur at each stage; hence the spiral movements in part overlap each other, though each successive stage addresses these issues at a new level of complexity. Overall, there is a movement outward toward individuation, culminating in Stage 4. Then the movement doubles back, in Stages 5 and 6, toward the participation and oneness of earlier stages, though at quite different levels of complexity, differentiation and inclusiveness. Each stage represents a widening of vision and valuing, correlated with a parallel increase in the certainty and depth of selfhood, making for qualitative increases in intimacy with self-others-world. Please do not forget that transitions from one spiral stage level to another are often protracted, painful, dislocating and/or abortive. Arrests can and do occur at any of the stages. Also I ask you to keep in mind that each stage has its proper time of ascendancy. For persons in a given stage at the right time *for their lives,* the task is the full realization and integration of the strengths and graces of that stage rather than rushing on to the next stage. Each stage has the potential for wholeness, grace and integrity and for strengths sufficient for either life's blows or blessings.

The model needs to be imagined as at least four-dimensional. Looked at from above or below the "spiral" of your stage or mine will not appear perfectly rounded or smooth. We all exhibit warps and indentations, skews and broken places. The broken line passing through the centers of the stages indicates thematic and convictional continuities across stage transitions. These may be centering and supportive, funding the readiness for the relinquishment of one's way of making meaning that

Figure 5.1   Stages of Faith

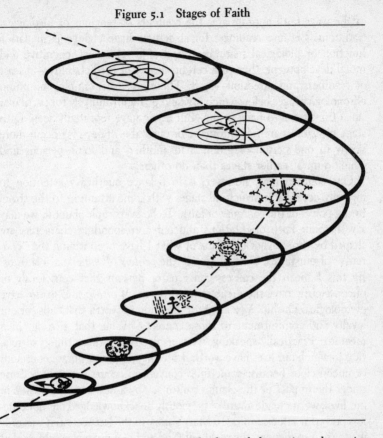

begins the process of stage change. The line of thematic and convictional continuities may, on the other hand, symbolize a deficit of assured meanings, salient in our lives as crippling images of faith and as convictions of an untrustworthy ultimate environment. The new structural features of each successive stage mean a reworking of the contents of one's previous faith stage. Radical changes in the contents of one's faith —as in conversion which we shall discuss shortly—may either lead to or result from structural stage change.

To this point our focus has primarily been on structural stage change and its dynamics. By now it should be clear that his means changes in the *ways* or *operations* of faith knowing, judging, valuing and committing. A structural stage change represents a qualitative transformation in the ways faith appropriates the contents of religious or ideological traditions. Because readiness for structural stage change is in part a function of biological maturation and of psychosocial, cognitive and moral development, there is a certain degree of predictability—at least of readiness and direction—to it. There are, for example, minimum chronological ages below which it would be highly unlikely for particular stage transitions to have begun. But as we have repeatedly seen, faith stage transitions are not automatic or inevitable. They may occur more slowly in one person or group than another, and some persons find equilibrium at earlier stages than do others.

Our concern now, however, is to balance our heavy attention to formally describable structural stages with some attention to the structuring power of the *contents* of faith. To be oversimple about it, we may say that our faith orientations and our corresponding characters are shaped by three major elements of what I have been calling the "contents" of our faiths. First, there are the *centers of value* that claim us. By this I mean the causes, concerns or persons that consciously or unconsciously have the greatest worth to us. *Worship* and *worth* have etymological kinship. We attribute the kind of worth that calls for our loyalty and commitment to those centers of value that give our lives meaning. Practically speaking, we worship that or those things in relation to which our lives have worth. I use the qualifying phrase conscious or unconscious because sometimes conversion occurs precisely because under the impact of the claim of ultimacy by a new center of value in our lives, we are made aware of previously unacknowledged but nonetheless powerful value centers. In Mary's story in the last section it was only when she experienced the reality of God and of a divine lawfulness that she began to bring to consciousness the centers of value around which her life had recently been spinning and to face how chaotic it had been. Whether our valuing in faith exhibits the *polytheistic, henotheistic,* or *radical monotheistic* pattern, the actual center or centers of value in our lives that have god value for us exert a powerful structuring on our ways of seeing and being in the world.

Equally important in affecting our orientations in life are the *images of power* we hold and the *powers* with which we align ourselves to sustain us in the midst of life's contingencies. We live in a dangerous world of power; we are finite beings. Of course not all of the powers that have an impact on our lives are destructive or dangerous. We are supported by institutional power, constrained by physical limits and affected by the power of others' presences. Governments attempt to protect their citizens even as they impose on them taxes, call them to military service and control their travel abroad. Other persons exert power on us in the ways they respond, individually or corporately, to our presence and potentials, recognizing them and calling them forth, or failing to acknowledge or recognize them. In such a world—a world of wars, of natural catastrophes, of senseless random or intentional assaults, of sudden accidental death for us or loved ones, of opportunity and denial, of good health or bad—in such a world we seek for the images and reality of powers that can be relied upon in life or death. Through the quest for wealth, for office or recognition, through bonds of love and marriage, through institutional affiliation or attachment to groups, through insurance policies and investment portfolios, we look for safety, security or significance in the face of such contingencies. We try to align ourselves with power sufficient to sustain us and these persons and things we love.

In the third place, our characters and faith orientations are shaped by the *master stories* that we tell ourselves and by which we interpret and respond to the events that impinge upon our lives. Our master stories are the characterizations of the patterns of power-in-action that disclose the ultimate meanings of our lives. When a playwright-lawyer tells me that the fundamental truth about us and the universe is that "everything runs down," he is sharing with me in highly condensed form, his master story. When Miss T. tells us in her interview that "there is that of God in every man" and that this has come to be the central premise of her sense of life's meaning, she is letting us in on her master story. When the 1980 Nobel peace prize winner, Adolfo Perez Esquival, gives up the security of his teaching and architectural practice to found and lead the "Service for Peace and Justice in Latin America," he lives out a story that tells us something like "the universal vocation of persons is the humanization of humankind."

Let me share with you a more extended example of how our characters and faith are shaped by our centers of value, our images of power and our master stories—the *contents* of our faiths. Not long ago I found an article in *Fortune* magazine with the arresting title "On a Fast Track to the Good Life."[9] The article caught my eye because it grew out of interviews with eighty 25-year-old men and women who are beginning careers in business. In 1955 *Fortune* had interviewed a similar group about their hopes and plans for their careers and about their perceptions of the future. In the earlier group only men had been interviewed. A

generation later *Fortune*'s editors sent their reporters to talk to eighty
of the country's most promising young businessmen and women. What
did they learn?

The *values* that seem central to the 1980 group of 25-year-olds have
primarily to do with the achievement of success. Success means for them
the eventual achievement of financial independence and, on the way to
that, achieving top-rank leadership in one or more of the major institutions of our corporate society. The *images of power* on which they rely
begin with their own abilities, their luck and their capacities for hard
work. They believe their own myths; they believe they are among the
most promising and able young people of any generation. Beyond faith
in their own abilities and luck, they trust the power of the international
corporations they hope to lead. Far more than government, they believe,
today's and tomorrow's corporate giants are the entities that will determine our global future.

Perhaps most interesting of all are the *stories* they are telling themselves—stories that add up to a composite master story correlated very
well, not surprisingly, with their images of value and power. First, they
tell themselves that this is an increasingly crowded, competitive world.
They recognize that there are more 25-year-olds alive right now than
there ever have been before. In a world of growing scarcity they feel a
deep urgency about getting what they feel are their shares of power and
its rewards. They tell themselves that in their urgency they cannot afford
relationships that place any "drag" on their progress. Marriage is possible if it does not hamper career. Children, for most of them, must wait
until both members of the marriage have claimed lucrative posts. For
many of them the decision to remain childless feels final. Even their
leisure activities, they tell themselves, can be defended only if they
contribute to career enhancement. Further, these young respondents
tell themselves that the most rapid paths toward advancement and salary
lie in making frequent moves from one corporation to another. They ask
themselves regularly whether they are staying too long at their present
posts. Excessive loyalty to any one employer, they say, can be detrimen-
tal. They live with the "ever-ready resume." Another set of substories
they tell themselves say that most of the men and women presently at
the top are probably less imaginative and less competent than they are
(or will be). They do not believe, therefore, that they have too much to
learn on the way up. The major obstacles to their rising that they see
are the inertia and self-protecting power of the present incumbents.

Finally, they believe that in order to make it to the top in their chosen fields they must be within striking distance of a chief executive's post by the time they are thirty-five.

How shall we sum up their master story? At the risk of sounding judgmental it might be capsulized as "the human vocation is to take care of number one; those number ones who have the most talent, drive and luck will—and should—inherit the earth."

Undoubtedly these young men and women have other stories, values and images of power that are meaningful to them. Interviewers—including of course faith development interviewers—often get only what they look for. Nonetheless, it seems likely that in their sharing this gifted group did disclose some of the central generative themes of their lives at present. Their statements give us access to what would appear to be some of the central elements of their faiths, understood in the sense of this book.

How will their futures deal with these young men and women? How will their centers of value, their images of power and their cluster of stories serve them in the world of their next forty years? Will their value centers hold? Will they confer a sturdy enough sense of worth on their lives to offset their stress and struggle, their loneliness and pain? Will the powers they attach to prove sufficient? Will having, doing and directing sustain them in face of death, betrayals, aging and the eroding banality of evil? Will their collection of stories prove rich enough to open depths of meaning in the midst of failure and loss? Will their stories have enough ethical substance to help them avoid moral self-deception? Will their faith orientations, taken in their totality, enable and impel them in any way to contribute to the enhancement of species life on this globe for now and in the future? And how will their centers of value, images of power and master stories change? These are all questions about the structuring power of the *contents* of their faiths.

As we reflect on the structuring power of the contents of persons' faiths, it may pay to consider the story of Albert Speer. During the rise of the Nazi Third Reich a brilliant young architect and family man, Albert Speer, came to the attention of Adolf Hitler. Speer came from a moderately well-to-do German family. He had the advantages of education, culture and social graces. Eager to make a name for himself by building magnificent public edifices, Speer was attracted to Hitler's vision for a Third Reich whose architecture would be worthy of the imperial aspirations of the soon-to-be master race. Hitler, himself a frustrated amateur architect from childhood, embraced Speer and soon placed him in charge of all the Reich's building and renovation programs. He also put him in charge of designing the environments for the great rallies of hundreds of thousands of people at which Hitler's speeches captured the imaginations of large segments of the German population.

After his conviction at the Nuremberg war crime trials Speer wrote his memoirs in Spandau Prison.[10] His writings show us a sensitive and intelligent man trying to come to terms with and take responsibility for the crimes against humanity to which he had been party. As Hitler's Minister of Armaments in the latter part of the war, Speer has been credited with extending the fighting by at least two years, so effective was his administration. For a period he was "the second most powerful man in Germany as he organized Germany's industry to provide the military hardware for Hitler's armies. In that capacity he also approved of and willingly accepted the use of slave labor in Germany's factories and mines. It was this policy that earned him twenty years in prison at Nuremberg."[11]

Ethicist Stanley Hauerwas, whose analysis of Speer's moral self-deception I am drawing on here,[12] states that Speer "not only knew slave labor was being used; he saw the inhumane conditions under which these men lived and worked. He did try to assure them at least minimal living conditions, but he was forced to admit that he really did not see these men at all."[13] And then from Speer himself we read:

> What preys on my mind nowadays has little to do with the standards of Nuremberg nor the figures on lives I saved or might have saved. For in either case I was moving within the system. What disturbs me more is that I failed to read the physiognomy of the regime mirrored in the faces of those prisoners —the regime whose existence I was so obsessively trying to prolong during those weeks and months. I did not see any moral ground outside the prison system where I should have taken my stand. And sometimes I ask myself who this young man really was, this young man who has now become so alien to me, who walked through the workshops of the Linz steelworks or descended into the caverns of the Central Works twenty-five years ago.[14]

Hauerwas's account helps us to see how Speer's obsession with being Hitler's architect so absorbed him that he "chose not to know" about the death camps and ignored many other objectionable features of this regime. Speer said, ". . . before 1944 I so rarely—in fact almost never —found the time to reflect about myself or my own activities, that I never gave my own existence a thought. Today in retrospect, I often have the feeling that something swept me up off the ground at the time, wrenched me from all roots, and beamed a host of alien forces upon me."[15] Hauerwas sums up the dilemma that entrapped Speer:

> Towards the end of the war Speer was able to distance himself from Hitler's will to realize that the future of Germany overreached that of Hitler, yet, that very patriotism had drawn him to Hitler originally. He had no effective way to step back from himself, no place to stand. His self-deception began when he assumed that "being above all an architect" was a story sufficient to constitute his self. He had to experience the solitude of prison to realize that becoming a human being requires stories and images a good deal richer than [merely] professional ones, if we are to be equipped to deal with the powers of this world.[16]

There is good reason to follow the account of the *Fortune* interviews with these reflections on Speer. With Speer we look retrospectively at his young adult values, images of power and master stories. Though more dramatic than most lifespans turn out to be, Speer's subsequent forced reflections upon the faith and moral outlook that shaped his life in the Nazi years may be instructive for both 25-year-olds and 40-year-olds in our day—and for those younger, older and in-between. The operative contents of our faiths—whether explicitly religious or not—shape our perceptions, interpretations, priorities and passions. They constitute our life wagers. Our loves and trusts, our values and visions, constitute our characters as persons and communities of faith. Few things could be more important than serious reflection on how we form and commit ourselves to (and through) the *contents* of our faiths. Few things could be more important than serious reflection on what constitute *worthy*, life-giving and life-enhancing master stories and centers of value and power.

Conversion and Stages of Faith

Conversion has to do with changes in the *contents* of faith. Lewis Rambo, in a brief article published in advance of his forthcoming major book on conversion, offers a useful brief definition. Conversion, he proposes, is ". . . a significant sudden transformation of a person's loyalties, patterns of life, and focus of energy."[17] Building on Rambo, but drawing on language and approaches we have used in this book, let me offer a supplementary characterization: Conversion is *a significant recentering of one's previous conscious or unconscious images of value*

*and power, and the conscious adoption of a new set of master stories in
the commitment to reshape one's life in a new community of interpretation and action.*

Conversion, understood in this way, can occur in any of the faith
stages or in any of the transitions between them. Let us consider an
example. In a remarkable book entitled *All God's Dangers* Theodore
Rosengarten published the memoirs of an illiterate black Alabama tenant farmer named Nate Shaw.[18] Eighty-four at the time of the interviews (1969), Shaw had joined the Alabama Sharecroppers' Union in
1932, an organization started by the American Communist Party to try
to secure a better living and the chance for education for black sharecroppers and their children. The boll weevil and foreign competition
had about destroyed the possibility of making a living farming cotton.
Many blacks were forced to leave farming and go to the cities at that
time.

Nate Shaw had been the most successful sharecropper in his county.
He owned four cows, nine hogs and an outstanding pair of mules in
1932. He was among the first blacks to buy an automobile, which he paid
for in cash. He did not own his own land, however. He had achieved
his relative success by using his mules to haul lumber while his teenage
boys, under his supervision, did a lot of the farming.

Shaw was a proud man and an angry man. When the organizers came
with their economic and political analysis of racism and with their
promises of the empowerment organization could bring, Shaw joined
the union. Almost immediately he began to receive warnings from white
landowners and merchants not to join. He persisted and worked at
recruiting others to the movement.

The word came that one of Nate's fellow members was going to be
arrested and his property taken away as an example. Nate and half a
dozen other members gathered at the friend's house to protect him. A
white deputy sheriff came to make the arrest. Nate confronted him and
sent him away. While the blacks waited in the sharecropper's house the
deputy returned with a number of armed reinforcements. When they
drove up and got out of the cars, all of the men in the house, except
Nate, jumped out the back windows and doors and fled into the fields
and woods. Alone, Nate went out to face the deputies. One of them put
a shotgun on him immediately and held it there while the others
searched around the house. Nate stood still for a long time; the deputy
holding the gun on him said nothing. Then Nate decided he would walk

into the house. At the doorstep another officer took hold of Nate's arm as if to stop him. Nate, who had had his hand on a .32 Smith and Wesson revolver in his overall pocket all of the time, turned loose of the pistol and grabbed the deputy's shirt, pulling him up to him; then he threw him back. He turned to continue into the house. At this point the deputy with the shotgun fired, hitting Shaw in the buttocks. Then he fired twice more, shredding the skin of Nate's backside from his knees to his waist. Shaw continued walking till he reached the door. As he went in he whirled, drawing his pistol. He shot at the deputy, forcing him to take cover behind a large tree. He filled the tree with bullets. Then he reloaded, even as his boots were filling with his own blood. The other deputies, thinking the house to be full of armed men because of the number of shots Nate fired, fled.

This incident led to the deaths of several other members of the Sharecroppers' Union. Nate Shaw was arrested and charged with assault. He served twelve years of his life in Alabama prisons as the result of his refusal to capitulate to intimidation that December day in 1932.

In a study of Nate Shaw's faith development Rita Dixon contends that by age forty-seven, when this incident occurred, Nate had constructed a Stage 4 Individuative-Reflective style of faith.[19] Clearly he had rejected the conventional position and roles of black persons in his society. Also, he had kept his distance from the church. He was critical of the fact that when white people came to black churches they were given the seats of honor, yet blacks would never be admitted to their churches. He saw religion as a means of social control and had no love for it. I tell his story here, however, because Nate Shaw underwent a striking conversion experience during his first few months of imprisonment. Let's hear about it in his words:

> Any person that have never received the love of Jesus in his soul, he can't imagine it until it hits him. When it hits you, you'll know it. There's a great undiscussable change takes place with you, somethin' that never had before. And on the twenty-eighth day of April, 1933—I was placed and bound down in Beaufort jail, couldn't help myself, couldn't do nothing but laugh and cry and talk and study over my troubles. O, I tell you, it was bluesy times. Right there I was converted; right there I received the love of Jesus.[20]

Shaw had been having a bad time of it in jail. Other inmates, all blacks, picked at him about what he had done. They knew he had been in the union movement. Now that it had been crushed they taunted him about having gotten into it. He said of them: "They knowed I was in that riot and they had no respect for it. Really they had no respect for theirselves so they picked at *me*. I done something they wouldn't a done—stood up for myself. . . . That was a great disconsolation to me. Talk about what I was in there for—and all the time it was somethin' for the benefit of them."[21]

Then he tells of his experience:

> The morning I was converted, I was walkin' around there in the jailhouse fixin' to shave. And I couldn't satisfy myself to save my life—walkin' around, leapin' everywhere, in a trance. I couldn't rest nowhere—they looking at me. And all of a sudden, God stepped in my soul. Talk about hollerin' and rejoicin', I just caught fire. My mind cleared up. I got so happy—I didn't realize where I was at. I lost sight on this world to a great extent. And the Master commenced a-talkin' to me just like a natural man. I heard these words plain— I dote on it, dote on my friends too—the Lord spoke to me that mornin' and said, "Follow me and trust me for my holy righteous word." I just gone wild then, feelin' a change. "Follow me and trust me for my holy righteous word. . . ." Good God Almighty, I just felt like I could have flown out the top of that jail. I commenced a shoutin' bout the Lord, how good and kind and merciful he was. Freed my soul from sin. I was a raw piece of plunder that mornin' in jail. God heard me and answered my prayers.[22]

Shaw had a friend write a letter to his wife, telling her of his experience and of his new relation to God: "I had him tell her that God had answered my lonely calls. I had seeked my soul's salvation and found it. And she came bustin' in there when she got the letter just as quick as she could come." Shaw quotes his cellmate's report to his wife on the power of his conversion: " 'Mrs. Shaw, if there's ever been a man converted, Nate's one of 'em.' She felt so good about that—she was cryin', she was so happy. She was a woman—she was a Christian girl when I married her and I was a sinner boy."[23]

Rita Dixon's careful study suggests that Shaw's conversion, while dramatic and authentic, did not represent or lead to a change of faith stage. His was a change in the *contents* of his faith. Blocked from continuing his effective, if difficult, struggle for financial security, closed off from the family he loved and for whom he sought to leave a legacy of enhanced opportunity, forced to live with the taunts of fellow prisoners and the hatred of his guards, Shaw's basic self-reliance had reached its limits. His experience of God's assurance of love and protection for him and his people freed him to relax his striving. Centering now on the value of God's love for him, trusting in the power of God to preserve him and his loved ones in life and death, Shaw was given the nerve and calmness to stand his twelve years of incarceration.

Romney M. Moseley has studied conversion from the faith development perspective.[24] He coined the term *lateral conversion* for the sort of recentering experience arising from new commitment that Shaw seems to have undergone. Moseley calls it *lateral* because it does not involve or lead to a change in the formal structuring operations of his faith. Rather it represents a powerful change in its content. Moseley, seeking to highlight the contributions that structural analysis can offer, reserves the term *conversion* for the kind of transformation in faith that involves both a change of content and a change of structural stage. For religious experiences that have the impact of renewing or revivifying a person's faith outlook, but with neither a structural stage nor a content change, Moseley coined the term *intensification experiences*.

After several years' reflection I am finding it most useful to reserve the term *conversion* for those sudden or gradual processes that lead to significant changes in the *contents* of faith. Structural stage change separate from or as a part of a conversion process should be identified in terms of stage change. Moseley's terms *lateral conversion* and *intensification experiences* seem to me very useful in precisely the ways he has defined them. Theoretically—and I expect in empirical reality, though we cannot demonstrate this yet—we expect to find the following possible relations between formal structural stage change and conversional change in faith. I believe there can be:

1. *Stage change without conversional change*—as when a person born into an Orthodox Jewish family grows up in the rich tradition of ritual and story, and in successive stages elaborates and reappropriates his or her patterns of commitment, observance and valuing.

2. *Conversional change without faith stage change*—as in both Nate Shaw's story and in that of Mary's conversion.

3. *Conversional change that precipitates a faith stage change*—as when a Synthetic-Conventional youth with a bland, humanistic background becomes passionately committed—intellectually and emotionally—to the existentialism of Sartre or Camus, requiring the rethinking of his or her commitments and lifestyle.

4. *Faith stage change that precipitates conversional change*—as when a Synthetic-Conventional Hindu student, whom we interviewed, became restless with the religious tradition of his family,

critically questioning its intellectual, moral and religious adequacy, and then found in Christian theology the kind of content
that more adequately fit the structures of thought and criteria for
truth he had constructed for himself.

5. *Conversional change that is correlated with, and goes hand in
hand with, a structural stage change*—as when an agnostic, hu-
manist psychiatrist in her early forties begins the decisive structural shift from Stage 4 to Stage 5, and finds the right expressive
images, rituals, techniques of spirituality and community of support, through the making of her commitment to Christian faith
in the Episcopal church.

6. *Conversional change that blocks or helps one avoid the pain of
faith stage changes*—as when a boy or girl of seven to ten is led,
in a fundamentalist Christian environment, to a powerful conversion experience that brings assurance of forgiveness and salvation
when the child has been convinced of her or his sinfulness and
by images of the destructiveness of hell. Such a childhood conversion can lead to what Philip Helfaer has called "precocious identity formation"[25] in which the child takes on prematurely the
patterns of adult faith modeled in that church. In such cases the
growing boy or girl goes through no adolescent identity crisis.
And short of an extraordinarily disruptive young adult "breaking
out" of those cast-iron images of identity and faith formed in
childhood, the person remains in that stage for life.

This sketch of the variety of observed and predicted relations between
structural stage change and conversion is but an early formulation of
perspectives that will have to be much more thoroughly studied. These
suggestions may help, however, to grasp more clearly the interplay of
"contents" in faith with the formally describable operations of knowing
and valuing that constitute the "structures" of faith.

Conversion, Sponsorship and the Recapitulation of
Previous Stages

When a conversion experience such as those described in this and the
previous section occurs it matters a great deal how the new community
of faith provides for the ongoing sponsorship of the new convert. In
speaking of sponsorship, I take a term that Erik Erikson has reclaimed
in our time—a term that has had long antecedent use in the context of

preparation of children and adults for Christian baptism and church membership. By sponsorship in this context I mean the way a person or community provides affirmation, encouragement, guidance and models for a person's ongoing growth and development. The sponsor is one who walks with you; one who knows the path and can provide guidance. The sponsor is one who engenders trust and proves trustworthy in supporting you in difficult passages or turns. The sponsor may, as needed, confront you, insisting that difficult issues be faced and that self-deceptions or sloth be avoided. The sponsor or sponsoring community should be able to provide both models and experiences in education and spiritual direction that deepen and expand one's initial commitments and provide the nurture for strong and continuing growth.

In the case of Mary's conversion, it might have saved her untold grief and perhaps have accelerated her movement to a new and more individuated stage of faith had she had access to a community of faith prepared to provide the sponsorship she needed after her decision to follow Christ at age twenty-two. Mary would have been most helped, I believe, if she could have received a combination of consistent experiences of community worship and education supplemented by individual or small-group work in spiritual direction and psychotherapy. It is proper to ask where Mary might possibly have found such a community. At present they are few and far between. Part of the hope and vision that animates the faith development research, however, and that has led in this year of 1980 to the founding of the Center for Faith Development, results from the recognition of our need for models and methods for such communities. In the interest of considering what such communities might provide by way of sponsorship in faith, let's begin with considering how the spiral model of stages of faith that we introduced in this part contributes to our understanding of conversion and of the kind of community support that might have been helpful to Mary in the months and years after her conversion experience.

On the version of the image of the spiraling movement of stages of faith in Figure 5.2, I have introduced a new dynamic. I have placed an X inside the circle that represents Mary's Stage 3, conventional countercultural faith at the time of her conversion. This X symbolizes her experience of encounter with God and her subsequent decision to follow Christ. It marks the point of her decisive conversion experience. This event meant a life-changing shift in the "contents" of Mary's faith. It represents a time when she gave up her old centers of value, admitted the impoverishment of the images of power on which she had relied and made a self-conscious decision to undertake the reshaping of her life in accordance with a new master story. The communities to which Mary turned provided a kind of postconversion sponsorship that assumed that she could negate her past life and obliterate her previous personal history. In many contemporary cult groups, to be "born again" literally means to undertake the disciplines and invitations of the new group's life without reference to the persons, experiences and places of one's past. In certain charismatic groups one gives one's age by reference to the date of one's second birth. The communities to which Mary turned thought of new life in Christ in these terms.

Clearly, after the turbulence of Mary's late teen and early twenties years, any conversion that meant real change would have had to sponsor a decisive break with her old images and her old way of life. There had to be a surgical cutting away of her old habits and attachments. Based on our understanding of the five years that actually followed Mary's conversion, however, we can see that a preconversion past that is buried and not reworked operates as a dangerous fate and an "internal saboteur." The series of negations and separations in Mary's earlier life that left her with a strong substratum of mistrust and self-doubt, on the one hand, and gave rise to her willful, stubborn insistence upon autonomy on the other could not simply be obliterated and left behind. Moreover, Mary's intelligence and potential for critical reflection could not simply be subordinated to authoritarian external control if there was to be the possibility for constructive growth in her new faith. After a period of separation from her past Mary needed a context for and help in a process that would enable her to recapitulate earlier stages and phases of development. Through a skillful combination of therapy and the use of forms of prayer and spiritual direction involving guided meditations, Mary might have been helped to rework images of God, self and others formed in infancy and childhood in the light of her new relation to Christ. Prior to or concurrent with this recapitulative work the relationship with Christ—primarily moral and volitional for Mary at first—could have grown and deepened, strengthening and integrating her appropriation of and by Christ's healing, guiding and remaking power.

Here in Figure 5.2 I have added arrows flowing backward and downward on the spiraling movement of the faith stages. When those arrows reach to the first stage then we see a turning and a return forward and upward through the stages.

Certain ego psychologists speak of therapy and some of the dynamics

Figure 5.2   Conversion and Recapitulation of Previous Faith Stages in
Healing and New Growth

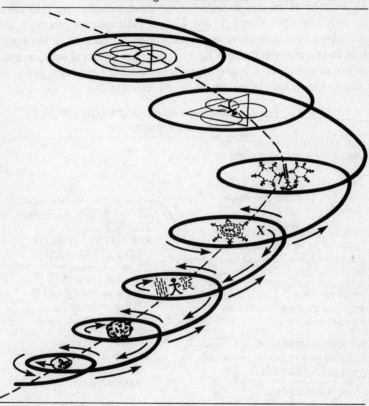

of natural stage transition as involving "regression in the service of the ego." By this they mean to describe a process of return from present levels of ego functioning to earlier and more primitive ones (from "secondary processes" to "primary processes" in the psyche) in order to rework or reconstitute certain aspects of ego formation. Such a movement can lead to release from and transformation of crippling patterns of earlier development, making ongoing growth possible. Psychoanalyst William Meissner has helpfully adapted this idea to the study of transformation in the process of faith development. I have been trying to suggest what such a "recapitulation in the service of faith development" might look like in structural developmental terms.

Now let us examine this recapitulative process in a more detailed way. In my account of the emergence of the successive stages of faith in Part IV I identified the new strengths or virtues of faith that first take form in their respective stages. In the kind of recapitulative process I am describing here conversion would result in a re-grounding of these virtues and their reorientation in light of faith's new center of value, images of power and decisive master story. Schematically (and vastly oversimplified) the recapitulative process might look like this:

Figure 5.3   Transformation and Redirection of Virtues of Faith in Post-Conversion Recapitulation

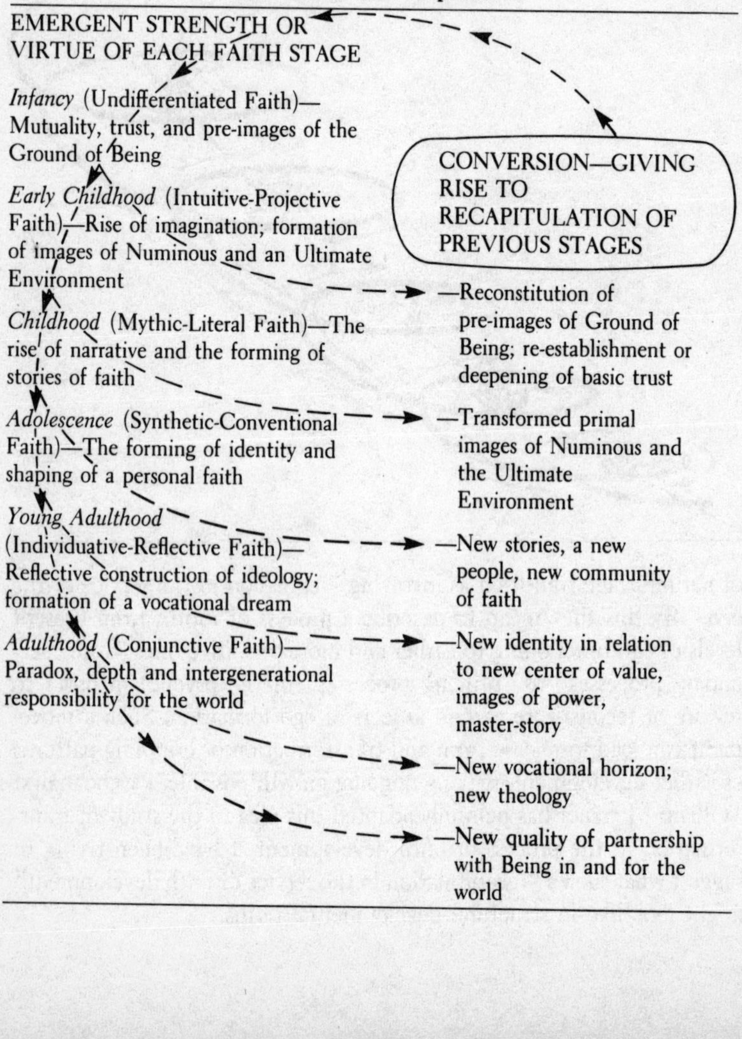

EMERGENT STRENGTH OR
VIRTUE OF EACH FAITH STAGE

Infancy (Undifferentiated Faith)—
Mutuality, trust, and pre-images of the
Ground of Being

Early Childhood (Intuitive-Projective
Faith)—Rise of imagination; formation
of images of Numinous and an Ultimate
Environment

Childhood (Mythic-Literal Faith)—The
rise of narrative and the forming of
stories of faith

Adolescence (Synthetic-Conventional
Faith)—The forming of identity and
shaping of a personal faith

Young Adulthood
(Individuative-Reflective Faith)—
Reflective construction of ideology;
formation of a vocational dream

Adulthood (Conjunctive Faith)—
Paradox, depth and intergenerational
responsibility for the world

CONVERSION—GIVING
RISE TO
RECAPITULATION OF
PREVIOUS STAGES

—Reconstitution of
pre-images of Ground of
Being; re-establishment or
deepening of basic trust

—Transformed primal
images of Numinous and
the Ultimate
Environment

—New stories, a new
people, new community
of faith

—New identity in relation
to new center of value,
images of power,
master-story

—New vocational horizon;
new theology

—New quality of partnership
with Being in and for the
world

Such a recapitulative process would not necessarily take place in the orderly fashion suggested by this model. In fact, as suggested by Figure 5.2, the recapitulative movement is most likely to begin by partially reworking the preceding stages in reverse order of their development, or "from the top down." When the recapitulative process has done its work, the person has a new foundation of inner integration from which to move decisively toward the next stage. In Mary's case the recapitulative experience, if truly Spirit empowered and thorough, should free her to make significant movement toward an Individuative-Reflective appropriation of her Christian faith.

24. Faith on Earth

IIIIIIIIIIIIIIIIIIIIIIIIIIIIIIIIIIIIIIIIIIIIIIIIIIIIIIIIIIIIIIIIIIIIIIIIIIIIIIIIIIIIIIIIIIIIIIIIIIIIIIIIIIIIIII

> But when the Son of Man comes, will he find faith on earth?
>
> LUKE 18:8

Central among the qualities that make and keep humans human is our capacity for trust and fidelity. As creatures who cannot live without meaning, our meaning making is intrinsically tied up with promises and fidelity. As we saw in Part I of this book our lives, our identities, our roles and meanings are sustained by covenants. Some of these covenants are tacit, informal, and taken-for-granted. Nonetheless they are vital and real. Other of our covenants are explicit. These we formalize, celebrate, renew and occasionally dissolve.

Throughout this book our task has been to clarify a developmental perspective on the human enterprise of committing trust and fidelity and of imaging and relating ourselves to others and to the universe. Rather steadfastly I have kept the focus on *human* faith. Except for a brief theological passage in Part IV's discussion of universalizing faith, I have avoided giving direct attention to normative perspectives on the being, character or will of God. I have hoped that readers form a variety of religious traditions and readers who have no religious affiliation would find this way of looking at so fundamental a feature of human life to be fruitful and informing.

Yet I am sure that my own faith commitments and the religious expressions of them have not gone unnoticed. Santayana is often quoted as saying that no person can be religious in general. As I pointed out in the discussion of Universalizing faith, the disclosure of absoluteness or of the genuinely transcendent or holy come to expression in *particular* historic moments and communities. The way toward religious truth—and toward Universalizing faith—leads through the *particular* memories, stories, images, ethical teachings and rituals of determinate religious traditions. I think it unlikely that persons will develop in faith beyond the Individuative-Reflective stage without committing themselves to some image or images of a faithful ultimate environment and shaping their lives in the human community so as to live in complementarity with it. Faith, at Stages 5 or 6, will take essentially religious forms. And while the Conjunctive or Universalizing stages appropriate their religious faith traditions in inclusive and nondichotomizing ways, they nonetheless require a representation of the ultimate environment as objectively real and as the final and primal source of all being and value.

The question from Luke's gospel with which I began this section points in the direction of what justifies both the writing and the reading of such a book as this. The issue is finally not whether we and our companions on this globe become Muslims, Jews, Buddhists, Taoists, Confucianists or Christians, as important as that issue is. The real question is, will there be *faith* on earth and will it be *good* faith—faith sufficiently inclusive so as to counter and transcend the destructive henotheistic idolatries of national, ethnic, racial and religious identifications and to bind us as a human community in convenantal trust and loyalty to each other and to the Ground of our Being?

The structural-developmental perspective, with its formal descriptions of stage-like positions and styles of being in faith, has a contribution to make in clarifying what might be meant by *good faith*. The stage theory is not a theology. In itself its highly formal stage descriptions have no religious richness or sufficiency to offer. Apart from the stories, the images of power and the centers of value that particular faith traditions can offer the faith stages are mere scaffolding. What these stages do offer, however, is this: they provide formally normative criteria for determining how adequate, responsible and free of idolatrous distortions our ways of appropriating and living from our particular traditions of faith actually are. The stage theory provides a formally descriptive and normative model in relation to which the adequacy of our particular ways of being in faith can be assessed and faced.

Religious faith traditions cannot be judged solely by utilitarian criteria. Traditions of religious faith, if life-giving and life-transforming, do much more than call us to live in covenant fidelity with our companions in being. Religious faith must enable us to face tragedy and finitude in the devastating and bewildering particular forms they come to us without giving in to despair or morbidity. Religious faith must name and face that deep-going tendency in us to make ourselves and the extensions of ourselves central in the world. From sin, self-absorption and all the life strategies and structures arising from them religious faith must provide liberation and redemption. Religious faith must link us to communities of shared memory and shared hope with which we join in symbolizing our human condition and in enacting the visions that can animate and give new life. Religious faith cannot be reduced to the ethical or to the merely utilitarian. But, as part of this larger and indispensable contribution that religious faith can provide to making and keeping life human, it needs also to be held accountable for the renewal and extension of a universal covenant with being. It needs to be held accountable for its broader contribution to *good* faith on earth.

Communities of Faith Sponsorship

The vision of particular faith traditions nurturing persons who are fit to be partners in a global covenant of good faith raises issues of faith sponsorship. How can particular communities of faith structure their internal lives in such ways as to provide intensive and extensive grounding in their faith vision, while at the same time calling their members to a vocation of global fidelity? The faith stage model enables us to see the readiness and capacities of persons at each stage to be part of the covenant intended by their communities. Attention to the capacities of each stage help us avoid expecting too much too soon. On the other hand, stage theory warns us against the coerciveness of what Kenneth Keniston has called the "modal developmental level" in communities.[26] The modal developmental level is the *average expectable level of development for adults* in a given community. In faith terms, it refers to the conscious or unconscious image of adult faith toward which the educational practices, religious celebrations and patterns of governance in a community all aim. The modal level operates as a kind of magnet in religious communities. Patterns of nurture prepare children and youth to grow up *to* the modal level—but not beyond it. Persons from outside the community are attracted to the community because of its modal developmental level. The operation of the modal level in a community sets an effective limit on the ongoing process of growth in faith. My observations lead me to judge that the modal developmental level in most middle-class American churches and synagogues is best described in terms of Synthetic-Conventional faith or perhaps just beyond it.

Careful theological work is required in a faith tradition to determine the normative images of adulthood which that tradition envisions. By normative images of adulthood I mean to ask, what developmental trajectory into mature faith is envisioned and called for by a particular faith tradition, at its best? While unable to speak for others, I am convinced that the normative image of adulthood envisioned in Christian faith leads out toward Universalizing faith. That is to say, discipleship to Christ, if radically followed to full maturity, would bring persons to a way of spending and being spent in their lives that would express loyalty to the rule of God and in covenant relations with a commonwealth of being. In light of this, we ask ourselves, how can faith communities avoid the coerciveness of the modal developmental level, and how can they sponsor appropriate and ongoing lifelong development in faith?

My vision for such a community as this begins with taking ongoing faith development in adulthood seriously. I believe that when a community expects and provides models for significant continuing faith development in adulthood its patterns of nurturing the faith of children and youth will change and become more open-ended. What might providing for ongoing adult development mean?

It would begin, I believe, with re-envisioning the nature of religious truth. As our reference to the work of Wilfred Cantwell Smith in Part I suggested, the dominant understanding of religious truth in our period centers in *belief.* Most often faith is understood as belief in certain propositional, doctrinal formulations that in some essential and static way are supposed to "contain" truth. But if faith is relational, a pledging of trust and fidelity to another, and a way of moving into the force field of life trusting in dynamic centers of value and power, then the "truth" of faith takes on a different quality. Truth is *lived;* it is a pattern of *being* in relation to others and to God. In this light, doctrines and creeds come to be seen as playing a different though still crucial role. Rather than being the *repositories* of truth, like treasure chests to be honored and assented to, they become guides for the construction of contemporary ways of *seeing* and *being.* Doctrines and creeds are formulations of the reflective faith of persons in the past. They are the stories they told themselves about the meaning of the ways of living with each other and God that they found truthful. These credal and doctrinal expressions tell the stories—the master stories—into which and by which they tried to shape their lives. As such, inherited creeds and doctrines become for present members of the faith community invitations and stimuli for *contemporary* experiments with truth. Adult living in faith becomes a matter of entering into the master stories that animated the faith of our

forebears and of shaping our lives of faith with all their present impinge-
ments and challenges in trust and loyalty to those stories.

Communities that call persons to ongoing adult development in faith
will not fear the intimacy of conflict nor the inevitable presence in
growing faith of doubt and struggle. Provision will be made for adults
to bring their struggles with faith to word. Before prescriptions are
offered, and without condemnation or accusation, they will be given the
help of active listening in order to tell their present stories and visions
of faith and to hear those of others. Such a community, by its regular
celebrations and sharing of the master stories of its faith, will provide
models by which adults can construct or reconstruct the faith-truth in
their lives for *this* period. In the meantime, they, with others in the
community, will be engaged in acts of responsibility and compassion on
behalf of the needs of persons in and beyond the community.[27]

A faith community that provides for the nurture of ongoing adult
development in faith will create a *climate of developmental expectation.*
I do not mean by this that such a community will become a hothouse
garden, seeking to rush persons from one stage of faith to the next.
Rather, in ways that take the full development of faith at each stage
seriously, it will provide rites of passage and opportunities for vocational
engagement that call forth the gifts and emergent strengths of each
stage of faith.[28] And it will provide help for people in naming and
clarifying the shape of their callings and challenges, in the community
and the wider world, at each stage of their faith growth.

Much, much more needs to be said about faith development theory
and its implications for sponsorship. Future writings I have projected
should provide these opportunities. In bringing the present book to a
close, however, there are a series of issues raised by our speaking of the
stage sequences as *formally descriptive* and *normative* which I judge it
important to address. In discussing these issues some of the future
directions of our empirical and theoretical inquiry in faith development
studies will become visible.

Stages of Faith: Their Descriptive Range

When people ask me whether these structural stages apply to persons
in Eastern religious traditions or in tribal societies the truthful answer
is, "I don't know." We have not yet done any serious cross-cultural

research on faith development. Preliminary work with Hindus, Muslims and Christians in India and with Malaysian and Liberian Christians[29] suggests that the stage sequence helpfully illumines differences in the ways persons make meaning in those different traditions and contexts. We presently are projecting more comprehensive research with indigenous religious groups in West Africa and with Tibetan Buddhists in northern India. But the gathering and analysis of convincing data on the issue of cross-cultural validity of the stage descriptions and sequence is still several years ahead of us.

In the meantime we are working on longitudinal follow-up interviews with a select sample of our respondents in this country. Based on our data to this point I am willing to make the following observations about the probable range of descriptivity of the theory of faith stages.

I believe that the sequence of stages as now described does reflect a developmental process in human beings that makes both *ontological* and *ontogenetic* sense. Here I introduce two terms, both built on the Greek word *ontos,* meaning "being." To say that the stage theory makes ontological and ontogenetic sense means that it brings to expression the structural characteristics of a sequence of developmentally related systems of *constitutive knowing* by which we construct (and therefore "know") self-others-world as related to transcendence. With the phrase *constitutive knowing* I mean to suggest that *being*—in others, in self, in world and in God—becomes real to us as we *construct* it in our knowing in response to the sense data and symbolic representations that impinge upon us. Put more simply, we constitute our own *subjective* experience of others, self and world as related to transcendence. The stages give us a model by which to represent and examine the evolution of the systems of operations by which we do this constitutive knowing.

Manifestly and demonstrably the systems of operations underlying most adults' constitutive knowing in faith are qualitatively different than the systems of operations underlying children's constitutive knowing in faith. If we take structural descriptions of the former and compare them with structural descriptions of the latter we can see some of the necessary qualitative developmental steps required to move from the one way of constitutive knowing to the other. The faith stage theory, at its present level of refinement and elaboration, provides a plausible model, empirically supported, for linking those two structural styles with intervening stages, consisting in themselves of integrated structural styles. Both in terms of their fit with the cross-sectional data we now have, and in terms of the logical requirements of a developmental sequence, the stages prove illuminative. If there is a "lawful" or ordered process of structural development in the construal of others-self-world-God, it makes sense to suppose that it will prove to be—in any culture—broadly analogous to the stages we have described.

"Broadly analogous" hardly means "demonstrated to have precisely the structural features we have described." My claim is that a developmental sequence of "faith epistemologies," correlated with what we know of physical, psychosocial and cognitive development in childhood and adulthood, will likely exhibit—in any culture—a series of equilibrated styles separated by transitional-constructive periods that parallel, in terms of elaboration of structural operations, the stage sequence we have described. In the conduct of cross-cultural research I fully expect that our present stage descriptions will undergo a significant process of elimination of Western and Christian biases and that the genuinely structural features will emerge with greater clarity. It may well be that the emerging structural descriptions of faith epistemologies will lead to the replacement or altering of some of the seven aspects we have generated to help us describe the respective integrities of the stages. Clearly the issue of the relation of formal structuring tendencies and the structuring power of the "contents" of faith will have to be further refined. Having said all this, however, I do believe that the stage sequence that will emerge from that work will bear a close relationship to the formal sequences with which we now work.

Before leaving this question of the descriptive range of the stage theory of faith, let me introduce one another set of considerations. Studies we and others have done suggest that the stage sequence identified here is not applicable just in the modern period.[30] It seems likely, for example, that St. Paul can be understood as being best described by Stage 4 Individuative-Reflective faith at the time of his life-changing encounter on the Damascus road. His early writings reflect the sharp dichotomies, the concern with inclusion and exclusion and the passion for authenticity and purity of commitment that are hallmarks of Stage 4. Paul's later writings, moreover, exhibit the more dialectical style of the Conjunctive stage. He struggles with the vocation of Jews *and* Gentiles, with how to be *in* but not *of* the world, with how to square weakness with power and death with life. Then, in certain passages of his mature writings, Paul clearly manifests the universalizing qualities of Stage 6 faith.[31]

But the issue is not just whether certain extraordinary persons in any of our ancient traditions can be said to have followed a developmental path approximating the faith stages. The real issue is whether the faith development of average people in other cultural eras can fruitfully be understood and characterized by the stage constructs we are working out. On this we have virtually no data. My observations, therefore, are necessarily in the domain of speculation and conjecture.

In my judgment the emergence of Individuative-Reflective faith as a relatively widespread structural style in a society could and would emerge only in a cultural setting marked by ideological pluralism, by some degree of individualism as an ideological ethos and by the spirit of critical methods of empirical inquiry. Synthetic-Conventional faith as a widespread cultural style could only emerge, I should think, in a social context where the uniqueness and value of each person is recognized and where the clash and competition of cultural myths has given rise to a speculative and synthetic literary tradition. In preliterate societies, untroubled by the issues raised by pluralism, faith development typically would consist in adult versions of Intuitive-Projective or Mythic-Literal faith. "Adult versions" is an important qualifier here. Undoubtedly in such societies adult persons construct dimensions and directions of richness within the structural frames of the Intuitive or Mythic styles that children in societies that sponsor movement to later stages never develop. Cross-cultural research in tribal or so-called primitive societies will need to be alert not only for the presence or absence of structural parallels to our early stages, but also for these dimensions of richness that may move in patterns this theory is poorly equipped to describe.

Faith Development Theory and Issues of Normativity

Our discussion in the previous section of the interplay of structure and content in faith helps clarify the complexity involved in trying to account for the normative tendency built into the structural faith stage sequence. In Kohlberg's work, claims are made that each new structural stage of moral reasoning is more adequate and yields more consistent and "truthful" moral decisions than the last. These claims are justified by appeal to the qualitatively new capacities for perspective taking (overcoming one's egocentrism), the new capacities for including a wider range of morally relevant actors or interests in one's reasoning and the new degree of flexibility, stability and transferability of one's modes of moral reasoning in the new stage. Kohlberg's case is, I judge, convincing. Its success depends, however, on the claim that in moral reasoning the structures of judgment can be separated from the "contents"— where the contents consist in the particular interests, actors and their context in a given situation. But Kohlberg's focus is exceedingly narrow. It really deals only with the operations of moral judgment, understood as cognitive operations. It avoids dealing with the structuring power of emotion or the affections. Equally seriously, it avoids dealing with what we called, in the last section the *contents* of faith—the centers of value, the images of power and the master stories constitutive of an actor's orientation to life and by reference to which his or her character has been formed.

The normativity inherent in the sequence of formal faith stages is similar to what Kohlberg claimed for moral judgment stages. Each new stage expands the capacities of the person or community of faith. Specifically, each new stage means:

- a new degree of reflective liberation with respect to the use of reason in faith (form of logic).
- an augmented capacity for accuracy in taking the perspective of others and in balancing their perspectives with a newly decentrated grasp of one's own outlook (role taking).
- as in Kohlberg's theory, a qualitatively new, more complex and comprehensive logic for moral reasoning (form of moral judgment).
- a widened, more inclusive accounting for the interests, stories and visions of others in the course of composing and maintaining one's own normative perspectives (bounds of social awareness).
- a more self-reliant and increasingly objective accounting for the warrants and justifications of one's faith outlook and for its consequences in life structure and patterns of commitment (locus of authority).
- a qualitatively new degree of self-responsibility for the forming system of images, values and stories that constitute the unity and coherence of one's meaning world (form of world coherence).
- a qualitative increase in choice, awareness and commitment regarding the symbols and representations which express, evoke and renew one's faith (symbolic functioning).

As John Chirban's doctoral dissertation has shown, the further one moves beyond a Synthetic-Conventional structuring of faith, the more likely one is to exhibit increased commitment in faith. Using the distinction between *intrinsic* and *extrinsic* forms of religious motivation, Chirban found that at Stage 4 and beyond, the incidence of extrinsic motivation (utilitarian commitments to religion which really serves other interests one has) virtually disappears. Intrinsic motivation (loyalty and commitment to one's world view as true, regardless of whether it brings benefits or blame) characterizes postconventional faith.[31]

The tricky thing, however, is that an intrinsically motivated Marxist, an intrinsically motivated individualist follower of Ayn Rand and an intrinsically motivated Orthodox Jew may all be best described by the structural features of Individuative-Reflective faith. Relative to other persons who share their *content* commitments, but who hold them in Synthetic-Conventional ways, the faith of each of these may be said to be more adequate structurally than that of their co-religionists (or ideologists) in the Synthetic stage. Evaluations based on the truth, ethical adequacy, or humanizing power of their faiths *relative to each other*, however, would have to be based on criteria that included both structural and content-structural dimensions. In short, they would have to be philosophical or theological evaluations.

Within a given faith tradition, say Christianity, appropriations of the Christian story and vision will be shaped in important ways by the structural stage of the theologian or community doing the appropriating. The apocalypticism of Hal Lindsay's *The Late, Great Planet Earth* organizes the content of Christian faith in a way designed to appeal most to Mythic-Literal or very early Synthetic-Conventional faith. Robert Schuller's television preaching and writings represent a presentation of culture-Christianity aimed dominantly at Synthetic-Conventional listeners. C. S. Lewis's apologetic writings aim, if I am an accurate judge, to bring sophisticated agnostics and conventional Christians to decide for commitment to Jesus Christ understood in the framework of an Individuative-Reflective faith. James Cone's early theology aimed at calling Synthetic-Conventional black Christians into self-aware and passionate solidarity for justice in terms of Individuative-Reflective commitments.

The point in all this is that criteria of adequacy for faith include, but are not limited to, the formal structures of the faith stages. As I said above, in the case of Christianity, I believe that a *full* appropriation of the normative structuring tendencies contained in its *content* (the centers of value, the images of power and the master stories that constitute its normativity) moves toward the development of Universalizing faith. The formal structural characteristics of faith stages can be employed, I contend, to test the normative structuring tendencies of a given content tradition. They can also be employed to evaluate a given faith community's *particular* appropriation of the content-structural vision of its tradition.

On Grace—Ordinary and Extraordinary

There is a limit to how much one can talk about faith and development in faith without acknowledging that the question of whether there will be faith on earth is finally God's business. Faith development theory, focusing resolutely on the human side of the faith relationship, comes up against the fact that the transcendent other with whom we have to do in faith is not confined by the models we build or to the patterns we discern. In the biblical tradition, at its best, the radical freedom of God is a central and indispensable testimony. God is recognized as sovereign reality—as creator, ruler, and as redeemer of *all* being. At the end of this long book, reporting the results of our research on faith to this point, I think it is well to end with a note of humility and wonder regarding this phenomenon on which we have spent so much time and so much ink.

When we speak of God's involvement in initiating the relationship we call faith, we normally do it—at least in the biblical tradition—in terms of the categories of *revelation* and *grace*. By revelation we mean those initiatives on God's part that result in God's self-disclosure and in God's clarifying the intent he has for his creation. In moments of revelation God breaks through and makes illuminative contact with his sensible creatures. These acts of self-disclosure, which may be experienced as intrusive and overwhelming, as judging and confronting or as liberating and exalting, are understood in the biblical tradition as the free expressions of God's grace. Grace implies both gift and gift freely given. It also implies a gift bestowed beyond the powers of the recipient to claim or to demand. Grace is a freely given gift of exceeding worth.

Faith development theory in its empirical descriptiveness aims to help us understand patterns of grace given in "nature." Aligned with that long tradition that affirms God as creator of the world, we affirm that in God's provision for the beings that issue from God's creativity, grace is built into the processes of birth, of maternal or parental care and into the orders our species has evolved for the sustenance and maintenance of life. We might call the kind of grace that comes as part of creation *ordinary grace.*

But in insisting upon the radical freedom of God, we must also take account of what might be called *extraordinary grace*—the unpredictable and unexpected manifestations of God's care and of God's claims upon our loves and our passions.

In the faith development theory, while we have tried to describe the expectable and predictable stages of growth in faith, we have also sought to acknowledge this more mysterious and unpredictable vector of extraordinary grace. We have honored the latter under the rubric of "conversion." When we put together the possibility—always present—of interventions of extraordinary grace with the fact that we are heirs to living traditions of faith that arise from revelatory acts of God in the past, which disclosed God's promises for the future, then it is difficult to speak simply or solely of faith as a developmental matter.

Perhaps the most important thing that can be said in concluding this book is that our study of faith development, so far, underscores the fact that we human beings seem to have a generic vocation—a universal calling—to be related to the Ground of Being in a relationship of trust and loyalty. That vocation calls us into covenantal relationship with the transcendent and with the neighbor—when the neighbor is understood radically to be all being. Faith development studies confirm the judgment that human beings are genetically potentiated—that is to say, are gifted at birth—with readiness to develop in faith. Perhaps our studies and the account of stages of faith this book has offered will enable us to see something of how we can become co-responsible with God for the quality and extensiveness of faith on earth. It is my hope that this book results, for those who read it, in an enlargement of that awareness and of gratitude for the gifts of God's grace—both ordinary and extraordinary. I hope that it leads to enlarged commitment to be part of God's work of righteousness and faithful liberation in our world.

NOTES

1. Lawrence Kohlberg, "Stage and Sequence: The Cognitive-Developmental Approach to Socialization" in David A. Goslin, ed., *Handbook of Socialization*

Theory and Research (Chicago: Rand McNally, 1969), pp. 347–480; Kohlberg, "From Is to Ought: How to Commit to the Naturalistic Fallacy and Get Away with It in the Study of Moral Development," in T. Mischel, ed., *Cognitive Development and Epistemology* (New York: Academic Press, 1971), pp. 151–284.

2. Soon Lawrence Kohlberg's *Collected Papers on Moral Development* will be published in three volumes on the philosophical, psychological and educational dimensions of his work. The first volume will appear in the spring of 1981, published by Harper & Row.

3. Lawrence Kohlberg, "The Child as Moral Philosopher," *Psychology Today*, (September, 1968).

4. See Lawrence Kohlberg, "The Moral Atmosphere of the School", in N. Overley, ed., *The Unstudied Curriculum and its Impact on Children* (Monograph of the Association for Supervision and Curriculum Development, Washington D.C., 1970.); Kohlberg, Scharf and Hickey, "The Just Community Approach to Corrections: The Niantic Experiment," in *Collected Papers on Moral Development and Moral Education*, vol. 2 (privately published, 1975), chap 28; Kohlberg, Wasserman and Richardson, "The Just Community School: The Theory and the Cambridge Cluster School Experiment," in *Collected Papers on Moral Development and Education*, vol. 2, chap. 29.

5. See Kohlberg, "Stage and Sequence," pp. 394ff.

6. Lawrence Kohlberg, "Continuities in Childhood and Adult Moral Reasoning Revisited," in Paul B. Baltes and K. Warner Schaie, eds., *Life-Span Developmental Psychology* (New York: Academic Press, 1977), pp. 179–204.

7. Lawrence Kohlberg and Carol Gilligan, "The Adolescent as Philosopher," *Daedalus*, 100 (Fall, 1971), p. 1063.

8. Kegan and Gilligan both have major forthcoming volumes.

9. Gwen Kinkead, "On a Fast Track to the Good Life," *Fortune*, vol. 101, no. 7 (April 7, 1980), pp. 74–84.

10. Albert Speer, *Inside the Third Reich* (New York: Avon Books, 1970).

11. Stanley Hauerwas, *Truthfulness and Tragedy* (Notre Dame, Ind.: University of Notre Dame Press, 1977), p. 90.

12. Ibid.

13. Ibid.

14. Speer, *Inside the Third Reich*, p. 480.

15. Ibid., p. 64.

16. Hauerwas, *Truthfulness and Tragedy*, p. 93.

17. Lewis Rambo, "Psychological Perspectives on Conversion," *Pacific Theological Review*, vol. 13, no. 2 (Spring, 1980), p. 22.

18. Theodore Rosengarten, *All God's Dangers* (New York: Knopf, 1974).

19. Rita Dixon, "Stories and Structures of Faith: A Black Perspective," (Paper presented at the Southeastern Region of the American Academy of Religion in Atlanta, March 15–17, 1979).

20. Rosengarten, *All God's Dangers*, p. 332.

21. Ibid., p. 333.

22. Ibid., pp. 333–334.

23. Ibid., p. 334.

24. Romney M. Moseley, "Religious Conversion: A Structural-Developmental Analysis" (Ph.D. diss., Harvard University, 1978).

25. Philip M. Helfaer, *The Psychology of Religious Doubt* (Boston: Beacon Press, 1972).

26. Kenneth Keniston, "Psychological Development and Historical Change," in Robert Jay Lifton, ed., *Explorations in Psychohistory* (New York: Simon & Schuster, 1974), pp. 160–164.

27. For the theological and educational foundations of such an approach see Thomas H. Groome, *Christian Religious Education* (San Francisco: Harper & Row, 1980).

28. See the writings of John H. Westerhoff, III, especially *Will Our Children Have Faith?* (New York: Seabury Press, 1976).

29. Fr. Thomas Kalam conducted Kohlberg moral dilemma interviews and brief religious faith interviews with Hindus, Muslims and Christians in one Indian state for his doctoral dissertation at University of London (not yet completed). Mrs. Marilyn Robertson and some colleagues are conducting full-length faith development interviews in Liberia and Nigeria.

30. James W. Fowler, Robin W. Lovin, *et. al.*, *Trajectories in Faith* (Nashville, Tenn.: Abingdon, 1980).

31. Prof. William Thompson, S.J., an able New Testament scholar, has informally shared these reflections on St. Paul with me. His unpublished paper employing faith development stages to study the Gospel of Mark is a very promising adaptation of this theory in the service of biblical interpretation and teaching.

32. John Chirban, "Intrinsic and Extrinsic Religious Motivation and Stages of Faith" (Th.D. diss., Harvard Divinity School, 1980).

Appendix A. The Research Interview

||||||||||||||||||||||||||||||||||||||||||||||||||||||||||||||||||||||||||||||||||||||||

Try an experiment with me: imagine that you have agreed to be interviewed as part of our faith development research. Before the actual interview begins, I explain the procedure. I tell you that our interview will be like a conversation, except that I may ask for more extensive clarification of some of your comments than I would in a casual talk. I explain that there are no right or wrong answers to the questions I pose, but only *your* answers. I invite you to feel free to decline answering any question you find unduly invasive. I assure you that your interview will be kept confidential; your anonymity will be protected.

In my orientation comments I do not call this a "faith development interview," because I expect that you would immediately associate *faith* with religion and belief, and that is not my intention. Rather I ask you to share some of your attitudes and values in life, and something of the life experiences that have helped to shape them. I tell you that you are one of nearly 400 persons, ranging in age from young children to the elderly, whom my associates and I have interviewed in this way over the last seven years. I ask your permission to record our conversation on audio tape, explaining that your tape will eventually be transcribed and that, if you wish, you can have a copy of the text. I assure you that if at the end of the interview you should decide you do not wish to let your interview become part of our study, I will gladly hand you the tape. Then we begin.

In Part I, *Life Review* (see the "Faith Development Interview Guide" on pp. 310–12), I ask you some straightforward questions about your place and family of origin. I want to know something about your family's makeup, your place in the sibling order, the occupation and characteristics of your parents, and your family's social class as you were growing up. Then I ask you a broad kind of question: "If you were to write a book about your life and its flow, what might the chapter titles be?" I restate the question in several ways, making it clear that I am interested in turning points, marker events, the different eras of your life to date. I amplify this by suggesting that you recall geographical moves, changes in primary relationships, illnesses, losses of significant others, and times of breakthrough or particular growth. As you respond to this question I note both what you say and how you say it. I identify places I want to return to in order to understand you more fully and at the same time "tune" my ear to your ways of speaking, conceptualizing and reflecting. I want to gear my questioning to your ways of thinking and feeling as much as I can. As much as possible I want my questions to frame a blank slate or screen onto which you can project your ways of seeing and making sense of life.

Piaget and Kohlberg gain access to the structuring operations of their respondents by posing problems and observing how respondents interpret the problems and work toward solutions. My goal is similar; I want respondents to let me overhear their ways of shaping and interpreting meanings from their lives. Instead of posing intellectual problems or moral dilemmas, however, I make the person's own life experiences, responses to challenges and constructions of meaning the subject of the interview.

When you have given me a kind of time line of "chapters" and I have an initial impression of the flow of your life, we turn to Part II, *Life-Shaping Experiences and Relationships,* for a more in-depth life review. Our principle of selectivity continues to be the effort to identify the persons, events, relations, special experiences, opportunities and crises that have most decisively affected the ways in which you shape your values priorities and interpret meaning and significance in your life. Although in this part of our conversation we may return to some of the marker events identified in Part I, new aspects of one's past often emerge as important here. In interviewing persons who have frequently had to write or share their autobiographical "sketches," it is important to communicate directly or indirectly that this telling of the story needs to deal with the way the past appears and feels to you *now.* As we live and change we *re-member* our past in different ways. Past, present and future are dynamically interrelated and all three are continually undergoing reimaging and reinterpretation. (For the full range of questions I use to try to help persons in this life review, refer again to the interview guide.)

As we complete Part II we have probably been talking for an hour or more. I have given you space to be silent, when needed, as you struggled to formulate aspects of your experience in the way that feels right to you. Both of us are glad by now that this is not an interview on the "Today" show. (We all stammer and speak haltingly when we talk about these kinds of matters.) If it has gone well, we both have a feeling of working together to illumine and bring to word some of your most vital memories and continuing sources of energy, and perhaps of pain. As an interviewer I am probably feeling again what a wonder of complexity and richness a human life is. As a respondent you may be feeling a kind of fullness and release, a product of the intense concentration you have given and of the sense that you are really being "heard."

In Part III of the interview, *Present Values and Commitments,* we come closer to the Piaget and Kohlberg strategy of research by problem-posing, as you can see in the schedule. In this section I ask you a series of questions that invite you to let me overhear your thoughts and feelings about a set of issues with which faith everywhere must deal. Here are included questions about death and its finality, and about life after death. I ask what gives life meaning for you. I ask about personal and group destinies—whether there is a "plan" for lives or history. I ask you to reflect on the future and its prospects. I ask what it means to be a man or a woman. I ask why good fortune and bad are distributed in the ways they are in this world, and whether you are accountable to anyone or anything beyond yourself for the way you lead your life.

You may find Part III of the interview less enjoyable than Parts I and II; the questions are hard and require you to talk of things other than yourself. You may wonder why anyone would be interested in hearing you talk about these kinds of matters.

Even though you may have answered earlier questions from the stand-point of an openly religious faith, Part IV, *Religion,* begins by asking if you consider yourself a religious person. Whether you answer yes or no, my interest lies in getting you to share what you mean by your answer, and why. Then, as the sample schedule shows, I pursue a line of questioning designed to clarify further what kind of religious or nonreligious person you are. For those who have answered previous sections in religious terms, this last segment provides an opportunity to check for congruence and to reach greater depth. For those who have not answered previous questions in reference to religion, these probes lead to insight regarding your experiences of and relation to religious symbols, communities and world views.

Throughout the interview I will ask you to share instances from your life in which the values and outlook you espouse have been tested or have affected your actual decisions and actions. In all four parts, particularly III and IV, I will ask you for examples that allow me to see how beliefs and values relate to action in your life.

After the two to two and one-half hours of interview we might sit and review your feelings about the experience. I will be interested to know where my questioning may have "missed" in trying to help you tell your story or share your position. I will want to know about areas you see as important that our conversation may not have gotten to. We might turn the recorder back on and talk further about one or another of these areas. Then, if you are typical of the vast majority of our adult interviewees, you might say something to the effect that, although you feel tired, you appreciate the experience of the interview. Many of our respondents follow words of appreciation with the remark, "I never get to talk about these kinds of things."

Our interviews with children are briefer and do not expect as much self-aware reflection as does the adult and adolescent approach I have just described. Samples of these can be seen in our discussions of Stages 1 and 2 in Sections 16 and 17.

FAITH DEVELOPMENT INTERVIEW GUIDE

Part I: Life Review

1. Factual Data: Date and place of birth? Number and ages of siblings? Occupation of providing parent or parents? Ethnic, racial and religious identifications? Characterization of social class—family of origin and now?

2. Divide life into chapters: (major) segments created by changes or experiences—"turning points" or general circumstances.

3. In order for me to understand the flow or movement of your life and your way of feeling and thinking about it, what other persons and experiences would be important for me to know about?

4. Thinking about yourself at present: What gives your life meaning? What makes life worth living for you?

Part II: Life-shaping Experiences and Relationships

1. At present, what relationships seem most important for your life? (E.g., intimate, familial or work relationships.)
2. You did/did not mention your father in your mentioning of significant relationships.

   When you think of your father as he was during the time you were a child, what stands out? What was his work? What were his special interests? Was he a religious person? Explain.

   When you think of your mother . . . [same questions as previous]?

   Have your perceptions of your parents changed since you were a child? How?

3. Are there other persons who at earlier times or in the present have been significant in the shaping of your outlook on life?
4. Have you experienced losses, crises or suffering that have changed or "colored" your life in special ways?
5. Have you had moments of joy, ecstasy, peak experience or breakthrough that have shaped or changed your life? (E.g., in nature, in sexual experience or in the presence of inspiring beauty or communication?)
6. What were the taboos in your early life? How have you lived with or out of those taboos? Can you indicate how the taboos in your life have changed? What are the taboos now?
7. What experiences have affirmed your sense of meaning in life? What experiences have shaken or disturbed your sense of meaning?

Part III: Present Values and Commitments

1. Can you describe the beliefs and values or attitudes that are most important in guiding your own life?
2. What is the purpose of human life?
3. Do you feel that some approaches to life are more "true" or right than others? Are there some beliefs or values that all or most people *ought* to hold and act on?
4. Are there symbols or images or rituals that are important to you?
5. What relationships or groups are most important as support for your values and beliefs?
6. You have described some beliefs and values that have become

important to you. How important are they? In what ways do these beliefs and values find expression in your life? Can you give some specific examples of how and when they have had effect? (E.g., times of crisis, decisions, groups affiliated with, causes invested in, risks and costs of commitment.)

7. When you have an important decision or choice to make regarding your life, how do you go about deciding? Example?

8. Is there a "plan" for human lives? Are we—individually or as a species—determined or affected in our lives by power beyond human control?

9. When life seems most discouraging and hopeless, what holds you up or renews your hope? Example?

10. When you think about the future, what makes you feel most anxious or uneasy (for yourself and those you love; for society or institutions; for the world)?

11. What does death mean to you? What becomes of us when we die?

12. Why do some persons and groups suffer more than others?

13. Some people believe that we will always have poor people among us, and that in general life rewards people according to their efforts. What are your feelings about this?

14. Do you feel that human life on this planet will go on indefinitely, or do you think it is about to end?

Part IV: Religion

1. Do you have or have you had important religious experiences?

2. What feelings do you have when you think about God?

3. Do you consider yourself a religious person?

4. If you pray, what do you feel is going on when you pray?

5. Do you feel that your religious outlook is "true"? In what sense? Are religious traditions other than your own "true"?

6. What is sin (or sins)? How have your feelings about this changed? How did you feel or think about sin as a child, an adolescent, and so on?

7. Some people believe that without religion morality breaks down. What do you feel about this?

8. Where do you feel that you are changing, growing, struggling or wrestling with doubt in your life at the present time? Where is your growing edge?

9. What is your image (or idea) of mature faith?

Appendix B. Interview Analysis and the Characteristics of Our Sample

||||||||||||||||||||||||||||||||||||||||||||||||||||||||||||||||||||||||||||||||||||||||

The empirical foundations of the theory of faith development rest upon 359 interviews that my associates and I have conducted in the years from 1972 to 1981. This appendix tells how we analyze interview data and make stage assignments, explains where and by whom our interviews were conducted, and describes the characteristics of our sample of respondents as a whole. At this point our sharing of the characteristics of the sample will be kept simple. Information about interviewees includes age-group, sex, race, religious orientation and stage of faith. These and other characteristics of the sample (such as social class of respondents) have not yet been coded into machine-readable form, and tests of statistical significance and other indices of the reliability of the sample have not yet been undertaken. Nonetheless, it should be of help to readers of this book to have an early look at the characteristics of this sample and at some of the patterns we see in the distribution of respondents.

Interview Analysis

The structural analysis of Mary's interview in section 22 provides an example of the process by which stage assignments of interviews are made. The aspects summarized in Figure 5.1, and spelled out more fully

This appendix was prepared jointly by the author and G. Melton Mobley, Ph.D., Director of Research, Rollins Center for Church Ministries, Candler School of Theology, Emory University.

in *Life Maps*, guide the analyst in discerning structure-indicating passages of the interview. These passages are sometimes assignable to more than one aspect column. In making a stage or stage-transitional assignment, a passage should only be weighted once, however. Discrete passages are assigned a structural stage under one of the aspects. Then all of the passages in that aspect area are brought together with the assigned stage of each designated. These assignments are averaged, yielding a stage for the interview under that aspect. This is done for each of the aspects. Then these aspect averages, are themselves averaged, yielding an overall stage assignment for the interview. I include here a simple display chart from one of our interview analyses, which shows a typical pattern of averages across the aspects:

Table B.1   Sample Aspect Averages

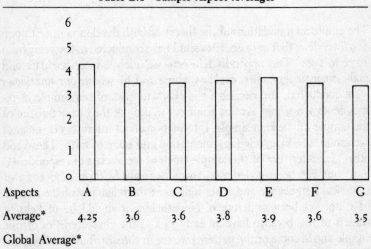

Aspects	A	B	C	D	E	F	G
Average*	4.25	3.6	3.6	3.8	3.9	3.6	3.5
Global Average*							

*3.25 is counted as 3; 3.40–3.60 is counted as Stage 3-4 transitional; 3.75 is counted as Stage 4.

We find that an analyst needs to conduct a minimum of three careful readings and stagings in order to overcome her or his biases and to correct for confusions of structure and content. Each interview is also separately analyzed by a second reader, working independently of the first. Trained analysts achieve inter-rater reliability in the range of 85 to 90% agreement.

The Sample

As stated previously, the interviews from which and against which we have developed and tested the stage constructs number 359. Of this total, 134 interviews were conducted primarily in the Boston area by the principal researcher and by paid members of his research staff. Another 30 interviews were conducted and analyzed by Dr. Eugene J. Mischey in the Toronto area as part of the research for his doctoral dissertation at the University of Toronto.[1] Dr. Richard Shulik contributed an additional 40 interviews from his doctoral study at the University of Chicago on faith development and aging.[2] His respondents, all 62 years of age or older, also came primarily from greater Boston. The remaining interviews were conducted by my graduate students at Harvard Divinity School, Boston College, and Emory University. The Emory interviews, which number 24, were conducted primarily in the Atlanta area.

All of these interviews, except those of Dr. Mischey, were both audio-taped and transcribed.* A typical adult interview of two and one-half hours duration yielded a 35 to 40 page single-spaced typed verbatim transcript. Analyses of the interviews are made on the basis of typed transcripts. Though we have begun longitudinal follow-up interviews on a selected number of our first respondents, the analysis given here is based solely upon cross-sectional data from persons distributed in age across the life cycle. We have not yet conducted significant cross-cultural interview research.

Characteristics of the Sample

The preceding discussion of the gathering of data makes it clear that the sample is not random; we make no attempt to suggest that this group of respondents is like any other. We can, however, examine certain characteristics of this group.

Table B.2 presents information on the age, sex, race and religious orientation of the respondents. The respondents ranged from 3.5 to 84 years of age, with the largest number in the 21-30 age group. The majority (54.1%) of the respondents ranged in age from 13 to 40 years old. Males and females shared almost equal representation in the sample, but whites (97.8%) dominated the sample. There were more Protestants

---

*Mischey, with the permission of his dissertation advisors, developed a careful method of analysis from aural study of his interviews.

Table B.2

Distribution by Age, Sex, Race and Religious Orientation

Age	Frequency	Percentage			
61+	62	17.3	Protestant	148	45.0
51–60	17	4.7	Catholic	120	36.5
41–50	32	8.9	Jew	37	11.2
31–40	48	13.4	Orthodox	12	3.6
21–30	90	25.1	Other	12	3.6
13–20	56	15.6		329†	100.0%*
7–12	29	8.1			
0–6	25	7.0			
	359	100.0%*			

Sex	Frequency	Percentage
Male	180	50.1
Female	179	49.9
	359	100.0%

Race	Frequency	Percentage
White	351	97.8
Black	8	2.2
	359	100.0%

*Total may not equal 100% due to rounding errors
†This information was missing for Mischey's 30 interviews.

(45%) than Catholics (36.5%) or Jews (11.2%) in the sample, and only a small representation of Orthodox (3.6%) and other orientations (3.6%).

In sum, the sample is overwhelmingly white, largely Christian, evenly divided by sex and distributed throughout the age categories.

Stages

Expected relations between chronological age and stages of faith were discussed at points throughout Part IV of the book. Here the evidence for those discussions is presented in graphic form. The age groupings used in the graphs are regular ten-year spans, except for the years from 0 to 20. There, in order to accommodate the typically more rapid developmental changes of childhood, we have used more compact groupings. Table B.3 charts the percentage of persons at each stage found in the various age groupings.

Among the children in the 0–6 age group we find 88% to be in Stage 1. Another 12% are Stage 1–2 transitionals. Of the boys and girls in the 7–12 age group the majority (72.4%) are Stage 2. Another 17.2% are Stage 2–3 transitionals, while 10.3% are still best described by Stage 1 or Stage 1–2 transitional. (Please notice, however, that persons best described by Stage 2 are lightly represented in the 13–20, 21–30 and 51–60 age groups.)

Among the youth in the 13–20 age group 50% are best described by Stage 3, 28.6% by Stage 3–4 transitional, 5.4% by Stage 4 and 12.5% by Stage 2–3 transitional.

In the 21–30 age group we find the largest number (40%) best described by Stage 4. A substantial group (33.3%) are Stage 3–4 transitionals, while much smaller percentages of Stage 2s, Stage 2–3 transitionals and Stage 3's are represented. A small number (3.3%) are Stage 4–5 transitionals.

The 31–40 age group, interestingly, has a larger number (37.5%) of Stage 3 respondents than the previous group. While this may be due to a sampling bias, it may also be a result of different generational cohort experiences. This intriguing fact, and the questions it suggests, cannot be explained without further research and more sophisticated analysis of our present data. We also note a substantial increase of Stage 4–5 transitionals and persons best described by Stage 5 in the 31–40 age group. It is significant that there are no Stage 5's in the 21–30 age group,

Table B.3

Distribution of Stages of Faith by Age

Stages of Faith	0-6 %	7-12 %	13-20 %	21-30 %	31-40 %	41-50 %	51-60 %	61+ %	Percentage of Total Sample in Each Stage %
					Age Groups				
6	—	—	—	—	—	—	—	1.6	0.3
5-6	—	—	—	—	—	—	—	—	0.0
5	—	—	—	—	14.6	12.5	23.5	16.1	7.0
4-5	—	—	—	3.3	18.8	21.9	5.9	14.5	8.1
4	—	—	5.4	40.0	20.8	56.2	29.4	27.4	24.8
3-4	—	—	28.6	33.3	8.3	—	—	14.5	16.4
3	—	—	50.0	17.8	37.5	9.4	35.3	24.2	24.0
2-3	—	17.2	12.5	4.4	—	—	—	1.6	4.7
2	—	72.4	3.6	1.1	—	—	5.9	—	7.0
1-2	12.0	6.9	—	—	—	—	—	—	1.4
1	88.0	3.4	—	—	—	—	—	—	6.4
	100.0%	100.0%	100.0%	100.0%	100.0%	100.0%	100.0%	100.0%	100.0%*
	(25)	(29)	(56)	(90)	(48)	(32)	(17)	(62)	(359)

*Totals may not equal 100.0% due to rounding errors.

and only a very small number of Stage 4–5 transitionals.

The 41–50 age group includes the largest percentage (56.2) of persons best described by Stage 4. A much reduced number of Stage 3 assignees (9.4%) appears, as do a substantial group of Stage 5's and Stage 4–5 transitionals (combined, 34.4%).

The 51–60 age group includes persons who range across Stages 2–5. These distributions confirm that faith stages are not perfectly correlated with chronological age and that adult persons of normal intelligence and emotional stability can and do reach long-lasting equilibration of faith stage at any of the stages from 2 on. In the 51–60 age group a plurality of persons best described by Stage 3 are found (35.3%). A slightly reduced percentage (29.4%) are Stage 4, while Stage 5 persons constitute 23.5%. (Notice, however, that the 51–60 age group constitutes the smallest number of any age segment in the sample [17 in all].)*

The 61 + age group again shows well-spaced representation, from Stage 2–3 transitionals (long equilibrated) to a lone Stage 6 respondent.

Table B.3 reveals the stairstep pattern of the relation between age and stage for this sample. The pattern is tighter in the younger years and in the earliest stages. For later ages and stages the pattern is more spread out.

Figure B.1 presents the percentages of persons at each stage found in the respective age groupings by way of a line graph. This illustrates the age-span of each of the stages, depicting points of separation and overlap. As expected, Stages 1 and 2 appear as relatively discrete stages, having the smallest areas of overlap with the other stages. Stages 3 and 4 correspond most extensively across the age groups, with Stage 5 occurring in the middle to late years. There is only one person at Stage 6, and that person is in the 61 + age group.

The remaining tables and figures add another variable to the relationship—sex. Although there is an almost equal number of males and females in the sample, they are unevenly distributed across the age categories. Females are somewhat overrepresented in the 21-30 age group and underrepresented in the 41-50 age group (see table B.4).

The distribution of sexes by age for the sample raises an important question about the findings in Table B.5. According to the table, more

---

*Even though the frequencies are smaller than desirable for percentage comparison in some categories of this table and Table B.6, we have chosen to present the percentages because they make the explanation more readable.

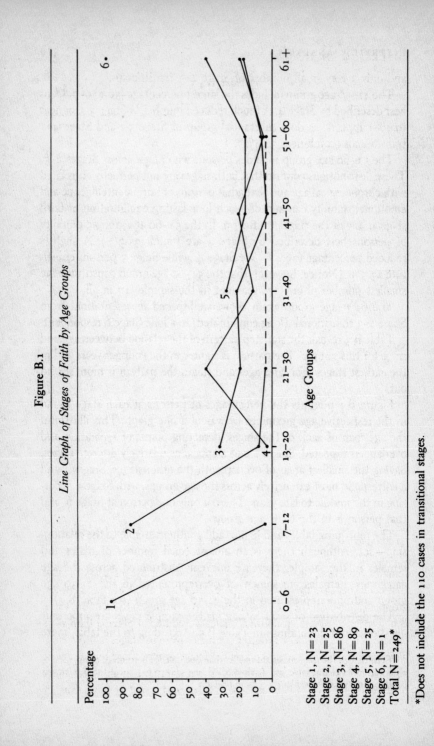

Figure B.1

Line Graph of Stages of Faith by Age Groups

Percentage

Age Groups

Stage 1, N=23
Stage 2, N=25
Stage 3, N=86
Stage 4, N=89
Stage 5, N=25
Stage 6, N=1
Total N=249*

*Does not include the 110 cases in transitional stages.

Table B.4

	Percentage Distribution of Age by Sex	
Age	Male	Female
61+	17.8	16.8
51–60	5.5	3.9
41–50	10.6	7.3
31–40	13.3	13.4
21–30	21.1	29.0
13–20	14.4	16.8
7–12	8.9	7.3
0–6	8.3	5.6
	100.0%*	100.0%*
	(180)	(179)

*Total may not equal 100.0% due to rounding errors

Table B.5

	Percentage Distribution of Stages of Faith by Sex	
Stages	Male	Female
6	0.5	0.0
5–6	0.0	0.0
5	7.2	6.7
4–5	10.0	6.1
4	25.0	24.6
3–4	15.6	17.3
3	21.1	26.8
2–3	2.8	6.7
2	8.3	5.6
1–2	1.7	1.1
1	7.8	5.0
	100.0%*	100.0%*
	(180)	(179)

*Total may not equal 100.0% due to rounding errors

females than males were at Stage 3, and fewer at Stages 4 and 5. Did that occur because there were more females than males in the 21-30 age group and fewer in the 41-50 age group? According to the data in Table B.6, in the 21–30 age group more males were rated at Stage 4 than were females; in the 31-40 age group more males were in Stages 4 and 5 than were females; but in the 41-50 and 51-60 age groups more females were at Stage 5 than were males. Although these variations suggest that there may be a relationship between age and sex and stages of faith, further

Table B.6

Percentage Distribution of the Stages of Faith Development by Age and Sex*

| | Age Groups | | | | | | | | | | | | | | | | |
Stages	0–6 M	0–6 F	7–12 M	7–12 F	13–20 M	13–20 F	21–30 M	21–30 F	31–40 M	31–40 F	41–50 M	41–50 F	51–60 M	51–60 F	61+ M	61+ F	
6	—	—	—	—	—	—	—	—	—	—	—	—	—	—	3.1	—	
5–6	—	—	—	—	—	—	—	—	—	—	—	—	—	—	—	—	
5	—	—	—	—	—	—	5.3	1.9	20.8	8.3	5.3	23.1	20.0	28.6	15.6	16.7	
4–5	—	—	—	—	3.8	6.7	44.7	36.5	20.8	16.7	26.3	15.4	—	14.3	18.8	10.0	
4	—	—	—	—	26.9	30.0	31.6	34.6	25.0	16.7	57.9	53.8	40.0	14.3	18.8	36.7	
3–4	—	—	—	—	53.8	46.7	15.8	19.2	—	16.7	10.5	7.7	40.0	28.6	28.1	—	
3	—	—	—	—	7.7	16.7	2.6	5.8	33.3	41.7	—	—	—	—	12.5	36.7	
2–3	—	—	6.2	30.8	7.7	—	—	1.9	—	—	—	—	—	—	3.1	—	
2	—	—	81.2	61.5	—	—	—	—	—	—	—	—	—	14.3	—	—	
1–2	7.0	20.0	12.5	—	—	—	—	—	—	—	—	—	—	—	—	—	
1	93.0	80.0	—	7.7	—	—	—	—	—	—	—	—	—	—	—	—	
	100%	100%	100%	100%	100%	100%	100%	100%	100%	100%	100%	100%	100%	100%	100%	100%*	
	(15)	(10)	(16)	(13)	(26)	(30)	(38)	(52)	(24)	(24)	(19)	(13)	(10)	(7)	(32)	(30)	(359)

*Totals may not equal 100.0% due to rounding errors

analysis on a larger, more scientifically drawn sample is needed to press the point any farther.

Summary

This description of the data collected to this point is provided not to confirm or refute the theory developed herein. The data are in rough form, and we hope that we have urged the necessary caution and exercised the necessary restraint in our examination. It has been encouraging to find that the preliminary evidence does reveal the predicted pattern for this sample. It is impossible to determine, at this point, the extent to which bias and error account for the observations. These findings are offered to provoke thought and comment from the readers and to provide a glimpse at the evidence that does now exist.

NOTES

1. Eugene J. Mischey, "Faith Development and Its Relationship to Moral Reasoning and Identity Status in Young Adults" (Ph.D. diss., Department of Educational Theory, University of Toronto, 1976).
2. Richard Norman Shulik, "Faith Development, Moral Development, and Old Age: An Assessment of Fowler's Faith Development Paradigm" (Ph.D. diss., Committee on Human Development, Department of Behavioral Science, University of Chicago, 1979).

Index